5-19

Genevieve S. McGee

DISCARD

D1454029

CLEARING NEW GROUND

THE LIFE OF JOHN G. TOWNSEND JR.

Clearing New Ground: *U.S. Senator John G. Townsend Jr. is seen test-driving a new Caterpillar tractor in his Indian Swan Orchard near Millsboro in the early 1930s. The term "new ground" was very familiar to farmers of Townsend's generation. It referred to the tracts of land which were laboriously timbered, then cleared of stumps and snags and converted to usable farmland. Few Delawareans of his or any era cleared more new ground both literally and figuratively than he did during his nearly 93 years (courtesy of Delmarva Poultry Industry, Inc.).*

CLEARING NEW GROUND

THE LIFE OF
JOHN G. TOWNSEND JR.

*For Genevieve Magee
with the best wishes of
the author*

RICHARD B. CARTER

Richard B. Carter

THE DELAWARE HERITAGE PRESS

2001

CLEARING NEW GROUND
The Life of John G. Townsend Jr.

By Richard B. Carter

Copyright © 2001
P. Coleman Townsend Jr.

A DELAWARE HERITAGE PRESS BOOK

Privately printed in limited edition, 1984

First Delaware Heritage Press printing of revised edition, November, 2001

ISBN: 0-924117-20-6

Library of Congress Control Number: 2001094772

The Delaware Heritage Commission
Carvel State Office Building
820 North French Street, 4th Floor
Wilmington, DE 19801

Delaware
•••••• ◆ ••••••
Freedom's First

For

Mrs. Lyla Townsend Savoy

and

Mr. Preston C. Townsend,

without whose invaluable assistance
this book could not have been written,

and for

Captain William E. Lowe, Jr.,

through whose encouragement
and unflagging support
this new, and, I hope,
much improved
edition came to be done.

CONTENTS

Introduction

The death of John G. Townsend Jr. in April 1964 was the sort of occurrence which heralds the passing of an era. The old Senator had been one of the four or five individuals most responsible for bringing Delaware into the modern age. He had been a familiar presence in Delaware for three generations. For many, particularly in Sussex where he made his home, he represented living proof that the rags-to-riches story, such a persistent theme in American popular culture, can indeed work in real life. The father of a large, close-knit family of children and grandchildren, and the employer of many men and women who had worked for the various Townsend companies in some cases for many years, he was for many of his fellow Sussex Countians a kind of patriarch.

Six years before the turn of the century he and his young wife, Jennie, had moved across the Maryland State Line into Delaware. They came in search of greater opportunities than those available in their native St. Martins District of Worcester County. They were drawn to the bustling, and still relatively new, southern Delaware community of Selbyville, bringing their two babies with a third on the way. They had little in the way of material possessions, but they had an abundance of ambition, energy, and imagination.

John quickly distinguished himself both in business and in politics. Eight years after moving to Delaware he was elected to the General Assembly. Fourteen years after his election to the legislature he was governor. His wife taken from him in a tragic accident while still relatively young, he raised his younger children with the help of the older ones, the family growing closer in response to their trouble. They worked together to run the family enterprises. Over the next half century, John G. Townsend Jr. and his family built a sprawling and diverse business empire.

He also forged one of the most noteworthy political careers in Delaware history. As governor he accomplished more in one term than most, if not all, other governors in the state's long history. He went to Washington as a United States senator on the eve of the Great Depression. He soon came to play a pivotal role in Congress as America struggled through the greatest economic calamity in its history. A consummate politician, his wise counsel was sought by many of the national leaders of his party long after his retirement from active politics. Gifted in the art of friendship, he developed close ties with many leaders in both major parties. One of these, Harry S Truman of Missouri, appointed him a member of the U. S. delegation to the first United Nations General Assembly in London. Though he was nearing his seventy-fifth birthday, to no one's surprise he handled himself on the international stage just as well as he had done at home in Sussex County.

More important even than his prominence was the affection in which he was held in his adopted state. He was "Delaware's Grand Old Man," probably the most beloved public figure of his time in the state. During the first quarter of the twentieth century, he helped the men and women of southern Delaware escape the hardscrabble existence of their parents and grandparents. His great contributions to Delaware life gave their children, members of the generation that came of age in the 1930s and 1940s, many new opportunities. For these young men and women of the World War II generation, he was as much a part of the background scenery of their lives as the Indian River or the vast Townsend orchards which then spread across thousands of acres of southern Delaware. Now, in the spring of 1964, he was gone.

Even as the state's editorialists tried to assess his significance in the days following his passing, many focused on his picturesque charm and missed some of his most significant achievements. He had long been known as the "strawberry king," as one of America's greatest orchardists, or as "the world's greatest chicken farmer." Yet by 1964 his battles for modern highways in southern Delaware, for woman's suffrage, for improved schools for blacks and whites, for better care for the mentally retarded, for safer working conditions for factory workers, and so many other accomplishments had receded from the public consciousness.

The purpose of this book is to present an accurate and balanced portrait of John G. Townsend Jr. and the times in which he lived to a new generation of Delawareans–to show the pivotal role he played in the early twentieth century history of Delaware and America. His accomplishments in business and government were considerable; his achievements as a man were more so. He had a positive gift for friendship and was a loyal friend to hundreds, if not thousands, of people around the world. Throughout his life he was more interested in others than in himself.

People loved to tell stories about him, about his love of buying land, of his phenomenal memory for names and faces, but beneath all that was the enormous respect in which he was held. Those who knew him could sense his bedrock integrity and commitment to the people of Delaware, even as they enjoyed his sense of fun and took pride in his accomplishments. What follows is a portrait of John G. Townsend Jr., and his world.

Acknowledgements

The Delaware Heritage Commission began several years ago issuing a series of books on the lives of 20th Century Delaware governors. To date it has published accounts of the lives and careers of Elbert N. Carvel, Sherman W. Tribbitt, Russell W. Peterson and Charles L. Terry Jr. This new and extensively revised edition of *Clearing New Ground–The Life of John G. Townsend Jr.*, will take its place as the fifth book in the series. The publication of this book, which is both considerably larger and much broader in scope than the earlier books in the governors series, is made possible through the good offices of the Heritage Commission and the generous financial support of the Townsend family.

Very rarely is one given an opportunity to do something over again, improving upon a first, flawed effort. Through the good offices of the Delaware Heritage Commission and the kindness and generosity of Mr. P. Coleman Townsend Jr. and other members of the family of John G. Townsend Jr., I have been given such a chance in bringing out this new edition of *Clearing New Ground– The Life of John G. Townsend Jr.*, the original version of which was printed privately in a very limited edition in 1984.

I began researching the life of John G. Townsend Jr. in the late 1970s at the request of Mr. Preston C. Townsend, the senator's youngest child. He told me that the Townsend family had long wanted to have a biography written of their father. Senator Townsend was a modest man and for much of his life he didn't feel that he had done anything especially unusual. In his later years, he finally came to accept what he had heard said often–that his career had been far from ordinary. As he prepared to leave the U.S. Senate at the end of 1940, he first expressed a desire to have his life story told. He asked his old friend and trusted Washington assistant, Mrs. Louise S. Johnson, to undertake the task. She agreed that such a book should be written, but she was not prepared to do it. However, she did set about preparing a foundation for a later biography by compiling a series of scrapbooks containing a wealth of newspaper clippings and other materials from every phase of the Senator's public life. Though she wrote a series of chapter outlines, in the end she told the Senator that she could not do the book. "I asked him to get someone else to do the job and I would contribute all I knew. He kept talking about it as long as he lived and I felt sad that I could not accept the challenge," she later wrote.

The services she did render were of great value to the present work. In addition to the scrapbooks, Mrs. Johnson also left an unpublished memoir in which she included many recollections of life during the Townsend administration in Delaware, when her husband, Everett had served as the governor's secretary of state and chief political advisor, and during Senator Townsend's later U.S. Senate career.

When I began work on the original book, Mrs. Johnson was still alive, as were three of Senator Townsend's children, his youngest son, Preston, and his two daughters, Mrs. Lyla Townsend Savoy and Mrs. Edith Townsend Tubbs. A number of others who had known and worked with Senator Townsend were also still active. I was therefore able to get firsthand recollections from many who have now departed. As I look back over the list of those who had contributed their memories to the first edition, I realize that an entire generation has passed from the scene since this work began.

The original edition of *Clearing New Ground* was flawed by a lack of editing and by being rushed into print, something which I have greatly regretted ever since. Even with its flaws, I believed the book's content was of considerable value as an account of the life and times of a man who by any standard must qualify as one of Delaware's greatest governors and finest statesmen. Moreover, the times in which John G. Townsend Jr. lived and worked were of the utmost importance in the shaping of our own age. I am grateful to be given this opportunity to bring out a thoroughly rewritten and revised second edition. It is my hope that it will serve to bring a remarkable figure in our history to the attention of a new generation of Delawareans.

This edition of *Clearing New Ground*, like its predecessor, is dedicated to the two members of the Townsend family who were most responsible for the original project. I have added a third person to the dedication in this second edition–my good friend, the late Captain William E. Lowe Jr. of Lewes with whom I had the honor and privilege of serving on the Delaware Heritage Commission during the last several years of his life. No single individual is more responsible for this project than Bill Lowe. As chairman of the commission before his untimely passing in the early summer of 2000, Bill made the republication of this book a high priority. In our last conversation he entreated me to see the revision and republication of the book through to completion. That it now exists, in a form which I consider to be greatly superior to the original version, is largely his doing.

Among the many other persons to whom I owe a considerable debt of gratitude for their support and assistance in this new project are the following:

Mr. P. Coleman Townsend, Jr. and the Townsend family;

Dr. James A. Soles, chairman, and the members of the Delaware Heritage Commission;

Dr. Deborah P. Haskell, Mr. Paul E. Bauernschmidt and Ms. Ann Dente of the Heritage Commission staff–their assistance was invaluable, particularly in that most onorous of tasks, indexing;

Dr. Constance J. Cooper of the Historical Society of Delaware for the superlative job she did of editing the manuscript;

Ms. Debbie Messina, Mr. Marvin Stayton and Mr. Donald Sellers at the Legislative Hall Print Shop, who were of great assistance with photographs;

Mrs. Judith M Pfeiffer and Mr. Robert C. Barnes for wonderful photographs and for new material concerning the lives of Mr. and Mrs. Everett C. Johnson;

My colleagues on the staff of the Delaware State Senate, Mr. Bernard J. Brady, Ms. Brigitte Conner, and Mr. Stephen P. Tanzer for running materials back and forth between Dover and Wilmington, and Mr. Chris Bradley for his able assistance;

My friend and colleague, Dr. William H. Williams, for a number of useful suggestions and insights; and

My friend and colleague, Mr. Lewis M. Purnell, for his able assistance.

I also wish to thank several members of my family for their help:

My sister, Melinda Carter Luedtke, for her many hours of editorial assistance and for her constructive criticism;

My daughter, Katy Carter, my son, Matt Carter, and my father, Dr. William A. Carter, for their invaluable help with the index.

In particular, my father, who is now 82, spent many hours proofreading the index, a terrible job because it is both boring and painstaking all at the same time. As we worked, he entertained me with his own recollections of Senator Townsend, whom he had gotten to know in the late 1940s and early 1950s. In those days Dad was the sales manager for Houston-White Company in Millsboro and shared an office with Senator Townsend's close friend (and my godfather), J. Reese White Sr. As their office was on the senator's route from his home in Selbyville to his Swan Creek orchard and poultry complex, he often stopped by for a chat. My father moved with his parents to Sussex County from Maryland in the late 1930s and was then absent from the area for five years during World War II, so he didn't have a built-in store of local lore. He said that he attributes much of his knowledge of Delaware politics to the wonderful stories told during these visits by Senator Townsend, a Republican, and Mr. White, a Democrat. The only problem was that as he delved here and there into the text, checking index entries, he said once or twice, "that's not exactly how the senator told that story."

To the foregoing list must be added those whose help was gratefully acknowledged in the first edition, many of whom have since passed on:

Mrs. Edith Townsend Tubbs;
Mrs. Dorothy Williams Pepper and her husband, Paul, wonderful friends who were unfailingly generous in sharing their wealth of knowledge and Mrs. Pepper's research into the history of Selbyville and environs, and the strawberry business, in which her family were pioneers;
Mrs. Louise S. Johnson;
Mr. Ronald F. Dodd;
Mr. William Hastings;
Mr. William Conn Scott;
The Hon. John J. Williams;
The Hon. J. Caleb Boggs;
Mrs. Mary Houston Robinson;
Mrs. Sarah White Mahler;
Mrs. Sharon Mitchell;
Mr. Edmund H. Harvey, for his wonderful stories about his uncle, T. Coleman du Pont and the building of the du Pont Boulevard;

Mr. and Mrs. John K. Jenney, Jr.;

Dr. E. D. Bryan for his insights into the early Delaware canning and preserving industry;

Mrs. Mary Williams, who worked for the Townsend family for somewhat more than 70 years and shared her wonderful recollections of Indian Swan Orchard in the old days;

Mr. Lee Derrickson and his aunts, Mrs. Nettie Cropper Rickards and Mrs. Mary Cropper Rayne, who provided wonderful tales of old Bishopville;

Dr. Harold Bell Hancock, to whom I owe a major debt of gratitude for his early, unpublished work on the Addicks era;

and the staffs of the Delaware Public Archives, Dover; Delaware Technical and Community College's Betze Library at Georgetown; the Georgetown Public Library; the Eleutherian Mills Historical Library, Wilmington; the Hugh M. Morris Library of the University of Delaware, Newark; the Library of the Historical Society of Delaware, Wilmington; and the Delaware State University Library, Dover.

Richard B. Carter
Millsboro, Delaware
August, 2001

PART I: ORIGINS

1. The Townsends of Worcester

The Eastern Shore of Maryland had few more isolated corners in 1871 than the St. Martin's District of northern Worcester County. St. Martin's was cut off from the rest of the county and the Eastern Shore by the great stretches of cypress swamp bordering the Pocomoke River to the west and by the St. Martin's River to the south. On the east were the shallow bays and the nearly uninhabited sandspit of the Atlantic Coast. Bishopville was the principal village of the district. It lay at the head of the St. Martin's River and of St. Martin's Neck, which separates the river from Assawoman and Isle of Wight Bays to the east and southeast.

Bishopville and St. Martin's could be reached easily only from neighboring Sussex County, Delaware, the southern boundary of which was only a mile or so to the north of the village. Until well into the 1880s Bishopville residents continued to receive their mail and freight from the Indian River and the public road running south from Delaware through Selbyville. The part of Sussex County adjacent to St. Martin's, known as Baltimore Hundred from the days when it, too, had been a part of Worcester County, was almost as isolated. This geographical isolation had served to keep the local agricultural economy depressed. It had slumbered away in the economic backwoods of Delmarva since colonial times.

By the 1870s, life in St. Martin's bore little resemblance to the great world of "the Gilded Age," of transcontinental railroads and robber barons, of New York's "melting pot" and Boss Tweed, of the burgeoning Chicago stockyards and the development of the West. Isolation had been at the heart of life on much of the peninsula lying between the Atlantic and the Chesapeake since its earliest European settlement. And that settlement had come very early indeed–some six years before the Mayflower settlers arrived at Plymouth. In 1614 an outpost of the Jamestown colony was established on the peninsula's southern tip.

In much of the rest of what was coming to be known in the 1870s as "Delmarva" the age-old isolation was giving way to relative progress. On the peninsula's western side, along the Chesapeake Bay and its many tributaries, and in the northeast along the Delaware River and Bay, the age of steam was well established. Farmers in those areas could use the railroad for their perishable produce and ship bulkier crops by steamboat to the great markets of Philadelphia and Baltimore. Business was flourishing as mechanization slowly influenced agriculture and as the economic slump that followed the Civil War was giving way to prosperity.

In those more advantageously situated parts of Delmarva the rivers led to major routes of commerce. Railroads ran from north to south near their headwaters and new lines were being built from east to west, connecting Chesapeake and Delaware ports. The St. Martin's District and neighboring Baltimore Hundred in Sussex County were not so fortunate. Though some limited commerce could be conducted through the shallow, sandy Indian River Inlet, it was an uncertain operation at best. The railroad had not yet arrived in these historically depressed sections.

The St. Martin's District and Baltimore Hundred had much in common. Having once been adjoining portions of the same county, they shared a common ancestry and culture. The same families had settled the two areas and they possessed many of the same customs,

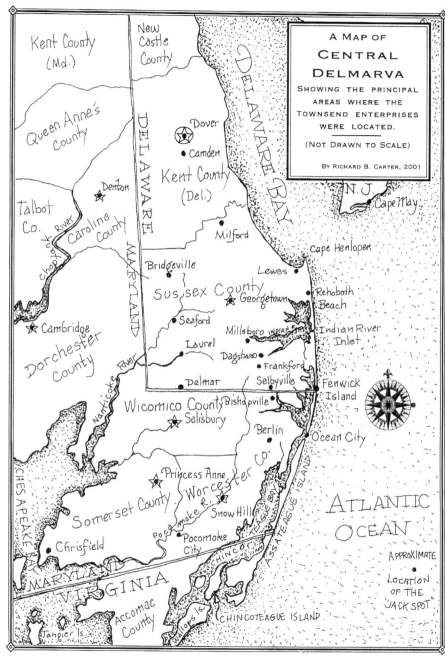

A map of the central Delmarva Peninsula, showing the heartland of John G. Townsend Jr.'s business and political activities.

traditions, and aspirations. Their agricultural economies were identical. Though low in many areas and swampy, their land was not unproductive. Great stands of pine, oak, bald cypress, and cedar were among the finest in the region. Fish and shellfish were abundant. A Selbyville lumberman and farmer began experimenting in 1871 with the cultivation of strawberries. He found that the new crop flourished in the well-drained, sandy soils that were to be found in much of the area.

The problem was transportation. Besides the hazards posed to navigation by the shallow, shoal-filled bays, the roads were generally atrocious. Even when the railroad reached Frankford, a village on the northern edge of Baltimore Hundred a few miles above Selbyville, in the mid-1870s, it was difficult to get agricultural products the seven miles from Bishopville to the railroad. At nearly the same time the railroad reached Frankford, another line was approaching St. Martin's District from the southwest. This new line was not much more convenient for Bishopville-area farmers, however. To the south and west it ran through Whaleysville, six miles distant, and Berlin, eight miles below Bishopville. While the new railroad lines were an improvement, they did not bring immediate prosperity locally.

Those looking back on life in northern Worcester County at or before the turn of the century generally say something like "you didn't have and you didn't want. You just had a happy time home with everybody." Northern Worcester County was still without banks in the 1870s. The local economy was still largely based on the barter system. People raised most of their own food at home and took their surplus to the village store to trade for sugar or salt or shotgun shells or whatever nonagricultural commodity they needed. If one took more eggs or milk to the store than one used up in purchasing power, the storekeeper issued a "due bill," indicating how much merchandise was due the customer. To a great extent such papers were the currency of the neighborhood. Some money was necessary; but a family that obtained several hundred dollars in cash in the course of a year was considered to be doing well. Storekeepers acted in effect as factors and merchants, even as bankers.

The water-powered gristmill, the steam sawmill, and a few other such enterprises were still about the extent of technological progress. The populace consisted overwhelmingly of farmers and small lumbermen, part-time fishermen, and small-scale craftsmen and artisans. It was not uncommon for a man to involve himself in all of these occupations at different times of the year. At the top of the social and economic scale were the few professional men–doctors, bankers and the like–and large landowners and merchants, some of whom owned their own coastal vessels and hauled cargo to Philadelphia from Indian River and St. Martin's River points. Ministers and school teachers were respected more for their erudition than their affluence.

Most of these "upper classes," such as they were, came from the same background as everyone else. Many farmed on the side when they were not practicing their professions, and, if they did not, they had fathers and brothers who did. Two of the principal families of St. Martin's District, the Showells and the Bishops, owned perhaps seven thousand acres of farmland and timber between them and considered themselves to be farmers. William Showell, who lived several miles south of Bishopville at the village named for his family, owned three thousand acres himself. Worcester, like many parts of the Delmarva Peninsula, had a typically Southern plantation economy for much of its history. But Worcester's plantations tended to be smaller and far more humble than those in more affluent Eastern

Shore counties like Talbot and Dorchester on the Chesapeake Bay with their vast holdings and grand old mansions.

The Worcester County seat at Snow Hill was twenty-five miles away. On the Delaware side, the Sussex County seat of Georgetown was twenty-four miles from Bishopville. Those residing in the region between the Indian and St. Martin's Rivers were as passionately addicted to politics as everyone else on the lower peninsula, but they had less-direct relations with the world of law and government than if they had been nearer to the center of things. In the aftermath of the Civil War both sides of the line were still strongly Democratic in politics. A few miles northeast of Bishopville in Sussex County's Baltimore Hundred, for instance, lay the hamlet of Bayard, named for the staunchly Democratic—and southern-leaning—U.S. Senator James A. Bayard of Civil War days.

Although more than six thousand of Worcester County's nearly nineteen thousand residents were black, most of them worked for wealthier landowners to the south, in the belt of prosperous farmland which ran southwestward from Berlin past Snow Hill. The white families who inhabited St. Martin's had generally lived in the area for at least a century. Many were descended from the earliest settlers who had come there in the late 1600s. Most were of English ancestry, although a few leading Worcester County families like the Prideauxes of Sinepuxent Neck had descended from French Huguenot refugees of the early eighteenth century. Among the old families of the area were the Bishops, the Croppers, the Purnells, the Fooks family, the Truitts, the Robbins, the Collins, the Taylors, the Timmons, the Whites, the Morrises, and others. One old Worcester County family was the Townsends, who, like most of the others, had arrived in the vicinity in the late 1600s from elsewhere on the peninsula.

By the last quarter of the seventeenth century, those families who had settled in Accomac and Northhampton Counties on Virginia's Eastern Shore and in the rich Maryland counties bordering the Chesapeake were seeking to expand their land holdings. Their families were growing with the passing generations. Original plantations in the Virginia and Maryland Eastern Shore counties had, by the 1670s, been divided among heirs at least once and in some cases several times. Eastern Shore families did not have the easy access of their mainland counterparts to the wilderness lands of Virginia's Piedmont. To seek new lands, the most logical direction was toward the relatively unsettled regions in central Delmarva. Prime areas included the seaside in the vicinity of the Indian River, Rehoboth and Assawoman Bays, and near the headwaters of bayside rivers like the Pocomoke, the Manokin, and the Wicomico.

As the eastern side of central Delmarva became more settled with the passing years land holdings were divided many times until, by the 1870s, most family farms were small. They tended to be anywhere from twenty or thirty acres to a few hundred acres in size. Despite the fact that some few prosperous families like the Showells and the Dennises had held onto extensive acreage, a kind of simple, classless, natural democracy prevailed among the residents of the area. This was largely because most people were descended from the same stock and were in roughly the same circumstances. With the exception of Worcester County's old plantation families, most of whom were well to the south of St. Martins, what "aristocracy" there was owed its status more to individual enterprise and merit than to inherited position. In that closely-knit and homogeneous society was perhaps the most favorable atmosphere on the old, established eastern seaboard for self-advancement. Hard work and initiative were required, certainly, but there were no true class or ethnic barriers to surmount. As the nineteenth century entered its closing decades the combination of the old agrarian economy and the rapidly-developing technology of turn-of-the-century America presented the perfect opportunity.

The Townsend family of lower Delmarva was of English origin. They had arrived in Worcester County in the late 1600s from Virginia (though at the time of their arrival what became Worcester after 1742 was still considered a part of Somerset County, the original lower Eastern Shore Maryland county from which Worcester and Wicomico as well as a significant portion of Sussex County, Delaware, were later divided). The ancestor of the Worcester County clan was John Townsend, who died in 1698. Different lines of Townsends had also settled in New England and in New York during the seventeenth century. Among the more prominent members of the latter branch of the family was another John Townsend, the master cabinetmaker of Newport, Rhode Island, in the eighteenth century. The residents of St. Martin's District of Worcester county in the 1860s had their own John Townsend, joiner and cabinetmaker. Though his skills were far from the high level of refined sophistication achieved by Townsend of Newport a century before, John Gillis Townsend Sr. was generally considered the leading carpenter in the district at a time when craftsmen were among the more respected members of the community.

The elder John Gillis Townsend was born in Worcester County in 1838. He was the third child and eldest son of a St. Martin's farmer, Arthur Williams Townsend, and his wife, Nancy B. Brasure Townsend. The couple had married in the spring of 1832 and went on to have a total of eight children, of whom all but the eldest girl, Mary, lived to adulthood. The family was related to most, if not all, the families in St. Martin's in one way or another. Among their connections were Williamses, Selbys, Brasures, Dickersons, and Eshams, to name a few of the closer relatives.

Arthur Townsend's father had also been named John. He and his wife had both died while Arthur was still in his teens, leaving him, an only child, an orphan. But in those days of vast and extended families there was always someone to take in a young relative. The Townsends were an especially large clan and a confusing one in the sense that the same names appear and reappear. In the late eighteenth century, for instance, there were several Luke Townsends, three John Townsends, two Barkley Townsends, and three William Townsends all living in the same county at the same time. The old John Townsend, grandfather of John Gillis Townsend Sr., was the son of one of the two Luke Townsends. It is interesting that Luke's grandfather, the son of the Worcester County founder of the clan, bore the unusual name of Brickhouse Townsend. Luke's uncle, the son of Brickhouse, was William Barclay Townsend, a prosperous local planter during the 1770s, who became Worcester County's staunchest Loyalist during the American Revolution.

This interesting chapter in the family's history was not at all unusual in the central Delmarva of Revolutionary War times. It has been estimated that well over half and possibly as much as four-fifths of the population of Sussex and Worcester, Somerset and Dorchester Counties were Loyalists during the early days of the conflict. The persistence of this sentiment was not surprising, considering the predominant English origins of the inhabitants (as opposed to Welsh or Scotch Irish). The residents were not as dependent on trade with England as the great planters of the upper Eastern Shore and had not been as adversely affected by the restrictive measures of the Crown.

The Townsends of Worcester were split between the two camps. Three members of the family served as officers in the Worcester County Battalions. William Barclay Townsend and his three sons, Levin, Elias, and Luke (the first cousin of John G. Townsend Sr.'s great-grandfather, Luke Townsend) were the county's most active Loyalists. A very interesting account of their activities appears in Reginald Truitt and Millard G. Les Callete's book, *Worcester County–Maryland's Arcadia*. Levin even served briefly as an officer in a Loyalist regiment formed by the British during their occupation of Philadelphia. After the war, all returned home to Worcester and resumed their lives once more, regardless of the side on which they had fought.

It is unlikely that the remote kinsmen of these Revolutionary War Tories, John G. Townsend Sr. and his son, ever knew that their ancestors had fought for the British during the war. Yet it is certain that the same staunch conservatism and respect for tradition which had characterized the forefathers was passed down to become a central facet of John G. Townsend Jr's political philosophy. This loyalist heritage was simply another factor in the "separateness" of the Delmarva culture of the nineteenth century.

After the Revolution, the Townsend clan of Worcester grew and continued to be deeply involved in the history of Worcester County. In 1800, the U.S. census listed thirty-two Townsends as heads of families. Among them were Elias and Levin Townsend. The census also listed three John Townsends. Seven of the heads of families were women. One of these was likely the widow of Luke Townsend and the mother of John, the grandfather of John G. Townsend Sr.

Of the two Stephen Townsends listed, one was the grandfather of the famed Delmarva author of the late 1800s, George Alfred or

"GATH" Townsend. The son of an itinerant Methodist minister, he was born in Georgetown, Delaware. During his childhood and youth, he moved frequently with his family, living in towns all over the peninsula.

Townsend became a journalist, adopting the name "GATH" as his nom de plume and evolving into one of the leading war correspondents of the Civil War era. Later he published *The Entailed Hat*, a best-seller of the 1880s. The novel is a tale of adventure centered in Somerset County, Maryland, and Kent and Sussex Counties in Delaware. While its accounts of the murderous Patty Cannon and other historical characters are the central part of the book, Townsend also presents perhaps the best picture available of life in central Delmarva as it was experienced by John G. Townsend Jr.'s parents.

It was sometimes the custom on Delmarva during the nineteenthth century and afterwards to name children after the doctor who had delivered them, especially if the birth had been difficult. This was apparently the case with John Gillis Townsend Sr. The leading "physician and surgeon" in the area of western St. Martin's and Whaleysville from the late 1830s onward was Dr. John P.R. Gillis, a scion of the prosperous Gillis family of the village of St. Martin's. Gillis was born in 1808, just a year before Arthur Townsend's own birth in the same neighborhood. One might reasonably conclude that the two had been boyhood friends. In later years Gillis served as one of the first presidents of the Worcester County Board of School Commissioners. While there is no absolute proof that the elder John G. Townsend was named for him, it is a reasonable conjecture.

John Gillis Townsend Sr. grew to manhood amidst a large family of brothers and sisters. He had a still larger connection of

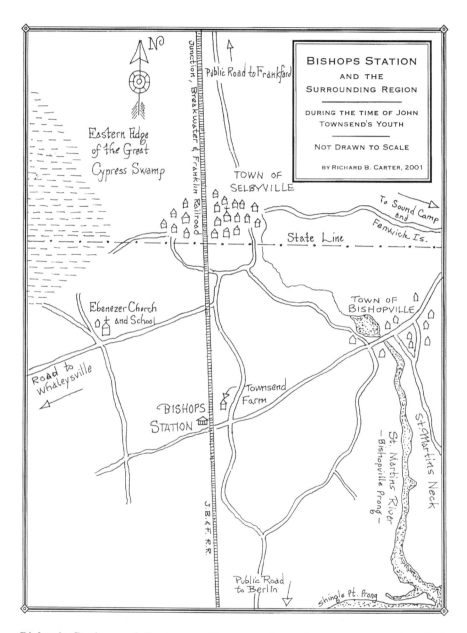

Bishop's Station and Environs: *This map shows the area surrounding Bishops Station with which John G. Townsend Jr. would have been familiar during his youth. Note that the present-day U.S. 113 does not appear since it had not yet been constructed.*

uncles and aunts, cousins, and neighbors. He attended a local school for a few years. It is likely that he was apprenticed to a master carpenter during his youth. Though he was in his twenties during the Civil War, he apparently did not take part in the conflict. The war once again split public sentiment in Eastern Shore Maryland's most remote county just as the Revolution had done eighty-five years before.

The young carpenter was reasonably successful even during his first years in that trade. As early as 1868, he was in a position to purchase a farm of ninety-two acres about one and a half miles west of Bishopville. He paid a total of $920, or $10.00 per acre, for the partly wooded farm, which he had bought from two of the more prominent men in the neighborhood–State Senator Israel Townsend and Col. Lemuel Showell. It is also quite obvious from his purchase of the land that Townsend was not without at least a touch of the instinct for real estate that later characterized his son. Some twenty years after he bought the property the railroad was extended south from Selbyville to Berlin. It ran right along the edge of the farm.

Less than a year after John G. Townsend Sr. bought his farm he married Mariedeth A. Dukes, the daughter of Lemuel and Amelia Dukes. The young woman was from Bishopville near the Delaware state line. The couple went home to John's ninety-two acres to live. On May 31, 1871, just over two years after her marriage, Mariedeth Townsend gave birth to her first child, a boy. He was named John Gillis Townsend Jr. When young John was three and a half, a second child was born, this one a daughter, Mary Elizabeth. Then, eighteen months later, on April 23, 1876, came the third child, James Covington Townsend, and the family was complete.

Not many specific facts are known about the family's life during the years the children were growing and becoming aware of the

*A sketch of the house at Bishop's Station, Maryland, built by John
G. Townsend Sr., in which his children grew up. (Sketch by the author)*

community around them in St. Martin's and beyond. But of the
community itself quite a bit can be said and of the family a fair amount
can be surmised. At some time in the early 1870s John Townsend
Sr. acquired a farm of nearly eighty-six acres, possibly by inheritance.
It was known variously as "Friend's Lot," "Friend's Assistance" or,
more ominously, as "Townsend's Trouble." The last must have
described John Townsend's views because on January 4, 1873, he
sold the land, which was located "on the south side of the state road
leading from Berlin to Frankford." The buyer was James H. Quillen
and Townsend took his mortgage for $370.75. It is uncertain whether
or not that amount represents the full purchase price. If so, the land
must have been troublesome indeed.

In 1877, an atlas was published containing maps of
Maryland's Eastern Shore counties together with each of their
subdistricts. To defray the cost of publication patrons were found in
each town and district to put up some of the expense. St. Martin's
was represented by nine patrons among whom was John G.
Townsend Sr. Others were L. W. H. Bunting, H. J. King, J. M.

Layton and Brother, all of whom were merchants; Thomas Holloway, William Showell, and John T. P. Moore, all farmers who owned 4,700 acres of land between them; G. T. B. Melson, a miller; and Dr. J. A. J. Holloway. One of the sponsors in the next district was none other than Dr. John P. R. Gillis, now a resident of Whaleysville.

In later years John G. Townsend Jr., like many another politician of the late nineteenth and early twentieth centuries, allowed it to be known that he was a poor boy who had made good. At any rate he did not work too strenuously to correct that impression. While he certainly was not rich, neither was his family hovering on the brink of poverty. They were a good, middle-class family and seem to have been among the solid citizens of the district in which John Townsend, Sr. was the leading practitioner of the craft of carpentry.

In 1881, John Townsend Sr. recorded a bill of sale in the county courthouse records showing that he had sold a gray mare to one Jacob Besson of Hoboken, New Jersey, for $19.58. In March of the following year he bought forty-four and a half acres of a tract known as "Temple Hall," which adjoined his farm. He paid the seller, Littleton D. Brasure, $600.00, or slightly less than $13.50 per acre. During the same period he built a commodious two-story house for his family on the eastern edge of his farm where it adjoined the old state road running southwest from Bishopville.* The house was built in the then- stylish Victorian Gothic manner in a "T" shape. The horizontal part of the "T" faced the road. Across the front of

---

* *The house built by John G. Townsend, Sr. at Bishops is still standing in this spring of 2001, the oldest house in the immediate vicinity. As one travels south along U.S. 113, the rear of the house is visible from the highway on the left, a short distance north of the intersection of U.S. 113 and Maryland Route 367, the main road to Bishopville.*

the house, looking out on the road, was a large gingerbread-trimmed one-story porch. Where the base of the "T" ran back behind the front section, one-story porches were built on either side. Townsend trimmed the eaves with stylish brackets and pierced the shingle roofs with several cross gables. The interior trim was also quite stylish and finely executed. The most notable feature was an unusual, ornately carved newel post at the base of the stairway rising in the front hall to the second floor. To the rear of the house were the usual conglomeration of outbuildings found on every rural farm and even on town properties. They included a large barn in which, according to one account, the elder Townsend maintained his carpentry shop in a portion of the second floor loft. All in all, it was a most imposing house for that neighborhood and served as a fitting testimonial to its owner's skills as a carpenter.

Late in life John, Jr., after a long, full career of many triumphs and many sorrows, fell into the habit of visiting the house his father had built each year on his birthday. He would knock courteously on the door and ask the lady of the house, the wife of one of numerous later owners, if he might come inside and just walk through its rooms. She may have been a bit startled the first time, but obliged. Indeed, she may later have fallen into the practice of putting the place in top shape for what became annual late-May visits. One can only conclude that for the younger John Gillis Townsend, it must in those early days have been a happy home.

When young John reached school age he attended the old one-room Ebenezer School, northwest of Bishop. It stood then and stands today (with a second room added) behind the small country church of the same name. Both school and church are now largely derelict. A mile or two on past the school along Blueberry Road was the edge of the Great Cypress Swamp. Ebenezer was

Ebenezer Church and school house (Sketch by the author)

one and two-tenths miles from home across the fields and through the woods, and just under two miles by road. It is, of course, obvious which way John Jr. and later his sister and brother went, except in cold, snowy weather. Then they may have gotten a lift in the wagon with the wheels taken off and runners bolted on and a few heated bricks wrapped in cloth and placed on the floor at their feet. When they arrived at school on such days the teacher quite likely thrust their hands into a basin of cold water as they came through the door, a curious local custom which was somehow meant to restore their circulation. Like most of the tiny schools in the country districts of the county, Ebenezer had its stove in the center of the room, fed with slabwood from one of the nearby mills, for which the teacher paid a dollar and a half per cord.

Among the best descriptions of the old one-room schools of Worcester County is that contained in *Worcester County– Maryland's Arcadia* by Reginald V. Truitt and Millard G. LesCallette:

> The typical teaching situation was recorded in 1871 by James R. Townsend [probably a brother to John Gillis Townsend Sr.] of Public School # 5, Election District Two [just to the south of St. Martin's] . . . whose school opened in October and ended July 15. Attendance, he recorded, was best in the fall and winter when farm chores were less demanding. Enrollment varied from thirty-five to fifty-two pupils but Mr. Townsend was able to find two older boys to assist him. Teachers then received eighty dollars per quarter and incidental expenses. The school also provided him eighteen dollars for wood, janitorial services, chalk, erasers, and ink. The students purchased their books, such as *Wilson's Advanced Reader* at twenty-five cents, *David's Intellectual Arithmetic* at seventy-five cents, slates and stationery. The classrooms were furnished with unvarnished desks and benches, usually marked with comments and initials. Heat was supplied by a cast iron wood stove, intolerable to those nearby and poorly regarded by those far from its presence. The rooms were equipped also with maps, quickly faded by the sun and . . . eighteen square feet of blackboard . . . Student chores as those of the teacher included drawing a pail of water from a neighboring house, keeping the fire alive in cold weather, and making goose- quill pens for the pupils. Mr. Townsend did not have female students until 1875 and even then the sexes were separated in the room and at recess.

. . . A youth was awakened from a sound sleep before dawn; he raced in his long johns to the kitchen to finish dressing, completed his chores, had a hearty breakfast and then departed for school which was often some distance away . . . To the request for volunteers to prime the pump, some offered to provide the water for the class. Vaccination for smallpox was required but the thought of infection due to drinking from a common dipper was generally overlooked. After all, there was always Barker's liniment, sulphur and molasses, or kerosene and sugar.

Weather permitting, students played outside until the bell called them to line up and march into their assigned seat. Then followed the reading of the Bible, a prayer, and in some schools an enthusiastic, if not always melodic, singing of "America," "Flow Gently Sweet Afton" or "Yankee Doodle." Group by group [they] moved to the long recitation bench close by a platform and the teacher's desk, stacked with lunches, all marked with the pupils' names. The hour of reckoning had arrived, pleasant for those who had completed their assignments, otherwise for some who tried to appear small, if not to disappear completely. In the meantime others labored over their studies, making mistakes and thoughtlessly erasing the errors on their slates with their sleeves. Paper was not always available in large quantities. At last there was recess, fifteen minutes for the girls and fifteen minutes for the boys, separately held, most of which was spent for the girls playing Annie Over, Goosey-Goosey Gander, Hopscotch and Drop the Hankie. The boys preferred baseball, tag, marbles in season, or wrestling, Prisoner Base, and Crack the Whip. The center of such activity was around the coal house or outhouse with its fence separating the males from the females.

One of the few things which can definitely be said of John Townsend as a school boy is that he excelled at arithmetic. He had what might be called a "trick mind" for mathematics, a faculty that was to serve him well in later life. It is very likely that, with his warm and outgoing personality, he was one of the more popular boys at Ebenezer–probably with the teacher as well as with his fellow students. He was even then a natural leader. He probably did not concern himself much with his studies, but absorbed what he needed to know quickly and with ease. Like many men of his day and time Townsend received a minimum of formal education. He went as far as the educational resources of the neighborhood could carry him, leaving school after six or seven years. In the middle 1880s there were already several high schools in the county. The closest of them was Buckingham at Berlin, eight miles away. But to have attended high school would have meant boarding in town. It would have meant that his family would have lost the benefit of the work he could do. Moreover, seven years of education in a country school of the 1870s and 1880s equipped one far better in some respects than twelve years of public school a century later.*

Nearly fifty years after he left school, Townsend was asked by a Washington reporter about his educational background. Having long since proved himself to be a sterling example of the benefits of self-education and an inquiring mind, he replied with a smile, "I'm a graduate of the University of Ebenezer."

---

* *John G. Townsend Jr. was by no means the only product of a one-room school house who found the experience beneficial to his later success. The grandmother of this writer attended a similar one-room school on Maryland's lower Eastern Shore for eleven years before matriculating at Western Maryland College in September, 1904. The first person in her family to attend college, she said in later years that she found the college work so much easier than her assignments in the one-room school that she "thought she'd died and gone to heaven." She sailed through a pre-medical curriculum and graduated four years later summa cum laude–one more product of a country school education.*

Another pattern that manifested itself in his character during those years was a large capacity for hard work. If the man he became in the 1890s is any indication of the boy he was in the 1870s and 1880s, he did not stop at performing those chores expected of him. He went out looking for jobs to do and ways to make a profit by his labors. It is also probable that he impressed his neighbors with the strength of his personality. He may have been picking strawberries for a penny a quart like a farm boy named Orlando Harrison who lived a few miles north in Roxana, Delaware, during the same period and whose later life bore many parallels to John's own experience. He may have worked a yoke of oxen for a local timberman, hauling logs to nearby mills. It was said of him a few years later that he knew how to handle a team as well as any man around.

2.   A Bishops Boyhood

The Townsend family lived about a mile and a half west of Bishopville.   In the 1830s, when an old water-powered gristmill was expanded to handle the sawing of lumber, the village that grew up around it was called "Slabtown." Later the name was fancied up somewhat to "Milltown," by which it was still known to many older people during John's childhood.   By the 1870s, the bustling village had been renamed for the Bishop family, who had established the sawmill and were thus judged largely responsible for the town's growth.   In 1878, Bishopville had a population of 350 persons.   It possessed two Methodist churches, a public school, a post office, a butcher's shop, a blacksmith and wheelwright, and seven stores.   In addition, there were five millers, a justice of the peace, and two doctors.

The St. Martin's River is a tidal estuary running north and west from Big Assawoman and Isle of Wight Bays into the eastern side of the Great Cypress Swamp.   In those years the huge swamp covered more than fifty-thousand acres on both sides of the Maryland-Delaware state line.   Its great freshwater aquifers served as the source of a number of rivers draining both to the east into the shallow inland bays of the seaside and to the west into several major estuaries of the Chesapeake Bay.   The St. Martin's, one of the seaside estuaries, had two main branches or "prongs."

In earlier years the local economy had been based mainly on

timber and its byproducts. Before the use of portable steam sawmills became widespread in the 1860s, the mill at the head of the northern (or Bishopville) prong of the St.Martin's River had been of great importance in the region. Another product of the area was hand-hewn bald cypress shingles, produced to the west of the village in the great expanse of the Cypress Swamp. The finished shingles were then hauled out by oxcart over rough roads to a landing and wharf at a point on the southern prong of the St. Martin's. This branch of the river became known, appropriately, as the "Shingle Point Landing Prong."

In those days, when much of the land bordering the river and the smaller branches and streams which fed it was still heavily forested, the St. Martin's was deep enough to allow for the passage of sizeable seagoing sailing vessels. Among those who owned ships were the Showell family and Captain Peter Whaley. Captain Whaley was the leading citizen of northwestern Worcester County and the man for whom the town of Whaleyville was named. Persistent (though apparently unproven) local tradition held that Whaley was descended from the infamous "regicide," General Edward Whaley, the Puritan leader who had removed the head of King Charles I during the English civil war. It was widely believed in Worcester County in the late 1800s that General Whaley, who was known to have disappeared following the downfall of the Cromwell government, had taken refuge in the Great Cypress Swamp. Whether or not the story is true, General Whaley could hardly have found a more remote haven in late seventeenth century British America.

By the 1860s, the St. Martin's river had silted up to the point where it had become difficult for deep-draft vessels to navigate. A further hindrance to shipping was the closing by shoaling sands of the old Sinepuxent Inlet, some distance north of the present Ocean City inlet, in one of the frequent rearrangements of the coastal barrier. This made it necessary to sail all the way to the southern tip of Chincoteague Island, Virginia, nearly fifty miles distant, to reach the ocean by way of Assateague Inlet. The combination of these factors had done much to hinder the movement of goods before the coming of the railroad in the 1870s.

In spite of the decline in shipping, a seafaring tradition remained alive. Many local farmers were part-time watermen and fishermen, plying the trade during the annual runs of herring, fatback, rock, and other fish. Most knew at least the rudiments of boat building. Young men from the area, with no immediate prospects for making a living close to home, often went to Philadelphia to work on Delaware Bay steamboats and sailing vessels in the coastal trade. The ocean was only a few miles distant across the shallow Assawoman and Isle of Wight Bays. Local men went to Fenwick's Island at certain seasons to fish commercially. This was to provide a part of young John's income in his late teens and early twenties. He was involved in this seafaring tradition to some extent even as a boy. He learned how to handle small craft and was familiar with the many creeks and coves in the river. He knew Lighthouse Cove and Devil Island, Dog and Bitch Island, Porpoise Pond, and other spots in the bays.

In the summertime during the 1880s and 1890s most local families took holiday excursions by sailboat down the river and across the Isle of Wight Bay to the newly established resort of Ocean City. The town had gotten its start in the early 1870s when a group of local businessmen began extolling its virtues as a summer resort. Those virtues did not become readily apparent to most residents of the peninsula until the railroad was extended from Berlin across a causeway to Ocean City in 1878. That did not stop the group of boosters.

They formed the Sinepuxent Beach Corporation and built the new resort town's first large hotel in 1874 and 1875. John G. Townsend Sr. was one of the carpenters who helped to build the huge frame Atlantic Hotel. Thus began an intimate association with the development of Ocean City that was to involve three generations of Townsends in one way or another.

His son's world during those years centered around the family farm. Many smaller farms in the region were operated primarily for subsistence. If there was any surplus it was used for trade, but it was not always central to the family's income, especially in cases like that of the Townsends where the head of the family was a craftsman. Most farms in the area produced a variety of grain and vegetable crops, livestock, eggs, and dairy products.

Families had their strawberry patches, walnut trees, and small orchards of apple and peach trees. Such orchards usually contained a variety of apples—Grime's Golden, Smokehouse, and Red Delicious. Many grew tiny sweet crab apples used for making jelly. There would be several types of peaches such as press peaches and sweet pickle peaches. In the winter apples, potatoes, onions, and turnips were buried in deep pits lined with pine "shats" (needles). A thick layer of pine shats was laid across the top of the pit, which was then covered with dirt, leaving a small opening at the top for access. The contents stayed fresh and unfrozen throughout the winter.

Given his outgoing personality, John Townsend Jr. found numerous excuses to visit neighboring farms and to go into the village. One could linger at the stores or stand around Bishop's Mill waiting for the family's corn to be ground into meal and hearing the news of the district. Many families went visiting in the evenings after supper. In her book, *Folklore of Sussex County*, Dorothy W. Pepper writes of such visits:

They ate corn popped in the fireplace and sometimes apples . . . The children played quiet games such as comey comey in a corner of the kitchen and played outside, but usually ended up watching as their parents played talking tables. To play, four people sat around a night stand or small table, touched the table lightly with all fingers, and rubbed the tips of their fingers very lightly in a circular motion.   One hand went clockwise and the other went counter-clockwise. This was done while all concentrated deeply on a question that had been asked.   Everyone in the room was very quiet.   Sometimes after long concentration and rubbing, a table leg would rise up slowly and tap out the answer. A common question asked was, "How many pigs will my old sow have?" The table leg banged eight times and, sure enough, when the pigs were born there were eight in the litter. Another question was, "Will I get a letter this week? Bang once for yes and twice for no." Before long there would be two taps.

Another great source of social activity throughout Delmarva was the church. In those years the overwhelming majority of the population was Methodist. In the years following the Civil War a new wave of revivalist spirit swept across the peninsula, resulting in the establishment of many new congregations and the growth of older ones. The slavery controversy leading up to the war had caused a deep division within the church resulting in the establishment of two branches: the Methodist Protestant Church (North) and the Methodist Episcopal Church (South). The town of Bishopville had one of each. Ebenezer Church out on the edge of the swamp was also a product of the Civil War era.

During the 1870s, the revival spirit also led to the birth of many summertime camp meetings in Worcester County and throughout the peninsula. Though primarily a Methodist phenomenon, camp meetings were also operated by Baptists and other denominations, white and black. By 1900, there were a dozen camps in Worcester alone and

At Fenwick Camp: *The Townsend family maintained a "tent" at the Fenwick Island Camp Meeting in the early 1900s, just as they had done in earlier years at Sound Camp, several miles inland. In the photo above a group of relatives is seen in front of the Townsend tent. Zare Brasure's tent is at left (Lyla T. Savoy Collection)*

well over a hundred on the lower Delmarva Peninsula. The camps attracted throngs to hear back-country preachers thundering away, working on the salvation of souls, and gospel groups harmonizing. In the early days the camps were just collections of temporary pole structures with tree boughs for roofs, "brush camps" as they were called. In later years they became more formalized, with a large ring of wood-frame, open-fronted "tents" clustered around a central tabernacle building where the preaching and singing took place. The old people sat on their porches, fanning themselves with woven palmetto fans in the still night air, nodding, muttering an "amen" now and again, and gossiping and laughing with their friends and neighbors. The little children, running fast and furiously between the tents, played games and shrieked with frightened glee out in the woods.

Later, after the preaching was over and just before drifting off to the hot tent to sleep for the night or hitching up the Dearborn ("durban") wagon for the trip home, the young men and women would promenade arm-in-arm around the ring in the torchlight. The elders sat thoughtfully on the porches of the frame "tents" enclosing the ring, doubtless pondering the transformation of their sons and daughters into young men and women and remembering their own youth in the flickering firelight cast off by scores of fat lightwood torches. Their children thought other, not unrelated, thoughts as they strode proudly arm-in-arm, partaking of a traditional courtship ritual of Delmarva. In those days of isolation and strict Methodism, young people had relatively few opportunities to discover the delights of courtship except in connection with organized activities like church services and camp meetings. The camps gave young couples a place to meet, to test their feelings and to be seen together.

One of the largest and oldest camp meetings in the area around Bishopville was the one behind Old Sound Methodist Church near the head of Big Assawoman Bay, several miles northeast in the direction of Fenwick Island. The church, located near the Worcester County hamlet of Little Georgetown and the Sussex County hamlet of Williamsville, was the "cradle of Methodism" in the area, having been established by the fiery Methodist circuit rider Freeborn Garretson during the first sweeping wave of Methodism in the late eighteenth century. As such, Sound Church served as the mother church of most Bishopville-area Methodists, even though most attended regular services closer to home. This traditional link had much to do with the popularity of the Sound camp meetings.

During the last quarter of the nineteenth century many children from throughout Baltimore Hundred and upper St. Martin's were baptised during the summer gatherings at Sound. In 1878, young Arthur W. Townsend, the infant son of John's Uncle Jacob, was baptised there, as were members of Mariedith Townsend's family, the Dukeses. During the summer of 1883, John Jr., Mary Elizabeth, and James were all baptised at Sound, even though they had been in regular attendance at their home church for years. Another family who attended Sound camp meeting year after year were Edward and Mary Collins and their children. During the 1870s, they had been neighbors of the Townsends, later moving to a large farm on St. Martin's Neck below Bishopville. The Collins's four children were all baptised at Sound–Effie and Jennetta, who was called Jennie, in the summer of 1874, and their younger sister and brother, Bertha and James, in 1880. Young Addie Bishop, daughter of other Townsend neighbors, James and Mary Bishop, was also baptized that summer.

At some moment during the later 1880s John G. Townsend Jr. looked at Jennie Collins, whom he had known from early childhood, and saw something different in her, and she in him. He was tall and full-bodied with a light complexion and finely featured with a full head of reddish-blond hair. Jennie, an attractive, dark-haired girl, was just two years younger than he. They would have taken their place in the promenades, John performing for her a little, talking big and smiling his easy smile, telling her of his plans for the future. These were grand visions, for by the late 1880s big things were finally happening in St. Martin's. Jennie listened, flattered and charmed by his attention, laughing, urging him on a bit, then shushing him. The same things were happening during those years to James Townsend and Addie Bishop,

John G. Townsend Sr.
in his later years
(Lyla T. Savoy Collection)

and to many another young couple who walked around that circle at Sound Camp. It was happening all over Delmarva in the late 1800s and early 1900s. The young couples who would give birth to the Delmarva of the 20th century, John and Jennie, James and Addie, and thousands of other young men and women of Delaware and the Eastern Shore, promenaded around those camp meeting circles into the future.

Mariedith Townsend did not live to see her children grow to adulthood. Early in September, 1885, she died at the age of thirty-eight, leaving her husband with the three children, aged fourteen, twelve, and nine years. There was something especially poignant about her death, coming as it did on the twelfth birthday of her daughter Mary Elizabeth. In later life the three young Townsends remained especially close. That closeness probably stemmed from their need for each other at the time of their mother's death.

Fortunately there was a large family to see them through. Their father had three sisters and three brothers, all of whom had their own families except Aunt Sarah Covington Townsend, who never married. Aunt Sarah thus occupied the time-honored role in the Townsend family of the "maiden aunt," helping out in the family where she could. She apparently came to live in her brother's household for a time after Mariedith's death to look after things. In later years she possessed a

Ida White Townsend, *the second wife of John G. Townsend Sr.* (Lyla T. Savoy Collection).

sizeable collection of the fine furniture John Sr. made in the shop behind his home.

Some years after his first wife's death Townsend married Ida M. White. The stepmother seems to have gotten on well with the three children. Much younger than her husband, who died in 1918, Ida Townsend lived to a ripe old age, surviving into the 1950s. John Jr. always remained friendly with her. In the years following the death of his own wife it became a regular part of his routine, when he was at home in Selbyville, to stop by her home for breakfast.

After Mariedith Townsend's death, John Townsend Sr. continued to practice his profession. He also added to his holdings during those years in a small but important way. In February of 1886 he bought three acres of land from his neighbor, Charlie Bishop, for $150. This purchase was especially significant because the land adjoined his farm and also fronted on the new railroad. The Junction,

Breakwater, and Franklin Railroad branched off from the main railroad line down the peninsula at Harrington, in southern Kent County, Delaware, running thence over to Lewes at the mouth of the Delaware Bay (the location of the famed Delaware Breakwater) via Milford and Georgetown.* The Junction, Breakwater, and Franklin also connected by means of a spur line running south from Georgetown the towns of Millsboro, Dagsboro, and Frankford. Finally, in the 1870s, the decision was made to extend the southern spur southward through Selbyville to Berlin and beyond. Berlin was already connected to the Baltimore, Chesapeake, and Atlantic Railroad, which ran east through Willards and Whaleyville before reaching Berlin and Ocean City.

With the completion of the north-south line from Frankford to Berlin, St. Martin's finally became, by 1880, a part of the vast national rail system which by that year had grown to 163,562 miles. In later years, after the small Junction, Breakwater, and Franklin line had been absorbed by the Delaware, Maryland, and Virginia Railroad, Berlin and Snow Hill were linked, thus giving farmers and merchants in St.

---

* Tracing the various name changes of early Delmarva railroad lines can be extremely confusing. The railroad which is referred to here for purposes of simplicity as "The Junction, Breakwater, and Franklin R.R." was originally known as the "Junction and Breakwater R. R.." The line later became known as the "Junction, Breakwater and Frankford R.R." when a spur line was extended south from Georgetown to Frankford and later Selbyville. Still later it became the "Junction, Breakwater, and Franklin R.R." when it was extended southward into Worcester County. At that point in its history, the company merged with a Worcester County line and was run southward to Franklin City, Virginia, on the shore of Chincoteague Bay, then the main entry point to Chincoteague Island. This combined entity was later acquired by the Delaware, Maryland and Virginia R.R., a division of the Pennsylvania R.R. Those interested in pursuing the subject further might wish to consult John C. Hayman's Rails Along the Chesapeake–A History of Railroading on the Delmarva Peninsula, 1827-1978 (Marvadel Publishers, 1979) from which much of the information herein contained is drawn.

Martin's easy access not only to Delaware and Philadelphia in the north but to the lower Virginia Peninsula, Norfolk, and the South.

In 1889, Townsend sold just under three acres of land to the Delaware, Maryland, and Virginia Railroad for the construction, at the western side of his farm, of a small railroad station. The station was named Bishops because all the land in that immediate vicinity had first been settled by Littleton Bishop, whose son Charlie was still a prosperous local farmer. It thus became possible for Townsend or his son to walk to the western edge of their farm, board a train, and travel almost anywhere in the North American continent. While they certainly did not avail themselves of that opportunity, the proximity of the railroad had a sudden and profound impact on the thinking of the younger John Townsend. It immediately relieved him of the need to leave home like so many of the young men of the area to seek work in the burgeoning industrial complex of Wilmington and Philadelphia.

By his eighteenth year John already had experience in the timber business working for other men. The coming of the railroad had brought with it the need for large quantities of railroad ties, piling, timbers, and telegraph poles. The station's close proximity to the family farm also gave John a chance to see at close hand how the railroad business operated. Since he had left school, Townsend had been working at odd jobs in the district. The construction of the Bishops Station gave him his first chance for advancement into something more rewarding: telegraphy.

3. Young Manhood

When John Townsend Jr. had a chance to discover the possibilities of telegraphy as the vehicle for moving his career forward, the device was still surprisingly new in the broad scheme of things. An earlier Delaware statesman, Louis McLane, had been the first person in authority to give the telegraph a chance. In 1843, McLane, then president of the Baltimore and Ohio Railroad, approved a request from the eminent portrait painter and would-be inventor, Samuel F. B. Morse, to run the first experimental telegraph line down the B. & O. right-of-way from Washington to Baltimore. Even McLane failed to realize the fabulous potential of the telegraph for railroad operations. In the forty-five years since that time, the telegraph had come into its own as an aid not only in managing railroad operations but in the realms of news, commerce, and finance.

The arrival of the railroad and the construction of Bishops Station were perfectly timed to suit John's ambitions and career goals. In 1889, when the station adjoining his father's farm went into operation, John was eighteen years old and in love with Jennie Collins. He had reached the time for making decisions, not only about whether and when to marry but also about how to support a wife. For a young man desiring to move up in the world the aura of telegraphy, the contact with faraway places that it gave, and the entry it afforded into the world of commerce, must have seemed irresistable. John did not shy away from manual labor, but he already knew that if he wanted to move up in life he must find an alternate route.

He began hanging around the station at Bishops, talking to the railroad men about their jobs and how everything worked. Before long he had learned telegraphy. It was typical of him that while every young man in the community was idling away spare moments at the station, taking in the sights and sounds of the most progressive thing to happen in years, John only appeared to be idling. In reality he was learning. He probably cajoled and charmed the station's telegrapher into teaching him the skill. Within a few months, by late 1889 or early 1890, he had learned it well enough to win a job as a relief telegrapher with the railroad. Although he may have started out working unofficially at Bishops for the experience, his first paid position was twenty-four miles to the north at Millsboro. Little is known about his work there. It is probable that he boarded in the bustling Sussex County town during the week and rode home on weekends on a pass in order to pursue his courtship of Jennie Collins. During his months at Millsboro John was familiarizing himself with southeastern Sussex County, looking at the land with an eye toward its potential, meeting its people. He already had some knowledge of the area from childhood visits to relatives and family friends and trips to haul timber, but the Millsboro job presented him with his first opportunity for close scrutiny.

One of John's closest boyhood friends was young William Jacob Peter White, whose father, William B. White, was a Bishopville businessman. The Whites lived on a farm a half-mile south of the Townsends and young William, who was a year and a half younger than John, was a frequent companion. Evidently, the two young men went to Millsboro at about the same time–John to work as relief telegrapher and Will to work as a clerk in a local general store.

When John returned to St. Martin's a few months later, Will White stayed in Millsboro and applied himself to the mercantile business. His employer, Jacob Reese Godwin, soon became a close friend of White's, as did Godwin's business associate, Henry A. Houston, a member of the prosperous old Dagsboro Hundred Houston family. Houston's father, Robert, had been one of the largest landowners in the area. Henry and his brother, Charles B. Houston, had moved into town and were among Millsboro's up-and-coming young businessmen in the 1880s and 1890s. In 1893, Henry Houston took Will in as a partner in a new general store along the railroad in Millsboro. Houston probably put up most of the money; White put up most of the expertise and the labor. A few years earlier Henry and Charles Houston had established a small box and basket manufacturing company in partnership with John and Vandalia Perry of Wicomico County, Maryland, who were experienced in the field. This firm, which sat across the tracks from the store, prospered along with the store. By the late 1890s, Henry and Will White bought out Charles and the Perry brothers and changed the firm name to Houston-White Company. They set up a steam mill capable of producing not only rough-sawn boards but more finished lumber and millwork as well.

Will remained friendly with the Godwin family. He was especially interested in Jacob Godwin's daughter, Georgina, and in 1898, the year the Houston-White lumber business was formally established, Will and Georgina were married. They acquired a large lot at the corner of Main Street and Railroad Avenue from Mr. Godwin and in the next few years built a large and elegant home befitting the up-and-coming young lumberman. By 1903, they had a son, Jacob Reese, and a daughter, Mary Catherine.

In 1905, the lumber business, which had expanded considerably since 1898, was formally incorporated under the state's new corporation statute. It gradually came to specialize in the manufacture of gum veneer baskets and other containers to meet the needs of the growing fruit and berry trade on the lower peninsula. In 1907, White, Houston, Godwin, and several other Millsboro businessmen went together to establish the town's first bank, the Millsboro Trust Company. Will was active in the Democratic Party in his adopted town. His father-in-law was a Democrat, and his partner, Henry Houston, had been elected as a Democrat to the U.S. Congress in 1902. The young man was also active in St. Mark's Episcopal Church. He was a member of the town commission. Thus, at the age of thirty-five, Will White was a man of some prominence and prestige in the community.

The experience of John Townsend's boyhood friend followed a pattern in motion all over Delmarva in the 1880s and 1890s. Young men were leaving their family farms throughout Sussex and Worcester and elsewhere on the peninsula. Dissatisfied with the subsistence farming and small crafts of their fathers, they were searching out ways to take advantage of the new spirit of progress and opportunity that had come to the region with the railroads and was bursting into full blossom with the tremendous expansion of capital and industry across the continent. A few years later the historian and philosopher Henry Adams, awed by the power of the forty-foot dynamos he had seen at the Paris Exposition of 1900, adopted the dynamo, from which lines of force shot out across the landscape in a barely contained frenzy of energy as the spirit of the age. The old rural ethic of America was giving way to a marriage of technology and capital, joined by the concept of the modern corporation. Those young men of Delmarva did not have the rarified vantage point of a Henry Adams to ponder the deeper meaning of the revolution sweeping the nation but they were afire with its spirit.

After a few months at Millsboro, learning the ropes from an older and more experienced telegrapher, John came back home to work full time for the railroad in Worcester County, and to marry Jennie Collins. The young couple were married on July 10, 1890, at the church in Bishopville. Jennie was seventeen and John nineteen. No record can be found of a wedding trip and it is possible that the new telegrapher was in no financial position to take one. Shortly after they were married the Townsends set up housekeeping in what John later remembered as a "cabin" near the little station at Friendship, midway between Showell and Berlin. Their home was probably a bit more refined than a log cabin, of which there were few remaining examples in Worcester even in 1890. It was probably the typical one-room house with sleeping quarters overhead which had been the standard working man's abode in the area for two hundred years. John's salary as a telegrapher at Friendship Station was $12.50 a week or about $650.00 a year. While hardly lavish, it was a reasonable wage for a young man starting out in a relatively skilled job. Ten years later the average skilled labor artisan was earning from $13.50 to $19.50 a week. The average college professor made $40.00 to $50.00 a week. While money was tight, the young couple had two family farms within a few miles from which to derive some sustenance and a whole host of friends and relatives in the neighborhood.

John's salary was enough to foster his ambitions, but it was not enough by far to make him comfortable nor to lull him into complacency. That he was not satisfied with his salary is evident from one of his sideline occupations of that period. During the late nineteenth and early twentieth centuries many local men who might make most of their living as small farmers or loggers were in the habit of turning their hands at slow times of the year to ocean fishing as an extra source of income. It was not easy money. By the 1890s, most of the early inlets had closed up and the large wooden surf boats the men used had to be hauled down to the beach by horse and wagon. The boats were launched from the beach through the surf. At the end of a night's fishing these craft, now laden with fish, were hauled back through the breakers and pulled onto the beach again by horses. Many fishermen lived for weeks at a time in crude fishing camps near the beach. They were there from Monday morning through Saturday noon and went home on Saturday afternoon for the weekend. The pace was rigorous. When they were not fishing with handlines or nets, they were cleaning, drying, and salting down their catch, packing the fish in barrels, hauling the barrels twelve miles to the railroad, and riding back to the beach to repair nets and start all over.

In the 1880s and 1890s, a sturgeon fishery developed in the Delaware Bay and in the ocean just south of it. Sturgeon caviar had been discovered by America's wealthier classes and had become a prized delicacy, bringing high prices in the marketplace. A few years earlier Worcester and Sussex fishermen had been using sturgeon eggs to bait their Assawoman Bay eel pots, but now suddenly the stuff was valuable. One of those who went after it was John Townsend. In 1890, a bridge had been built across the creek known as Fenwick Ditch that separated Fenwick Island from the mainland. The bridge was built principally as a convenience for the light-station crew who maintained the lighthouse there and for the crew of the nearby lifesaving station. It also made the trip much easier for fishermen and others trying to get to the beach from the mainland. John and a partner would make their way down to Fenwick and set off from there with oars to try their hand at sturgeon fishing. His career as a part-time sturgeon fisherman proved to be a short one. He apparently concluded after too many trips and not enough sturgeon that his time was better spent working with surer things on dry land. The experience showed that while John was willing to work hard physically, he was not willing to do so unless there was a clear chance for making a fair and steady return on his investment.

Friendship was about a mile east of St. Martin's, a substantial hamlet with a larger station on the Wicomico and Pocomoke Railroad and a post office. From St. Martin's and Friendship the two rail lines ran south two and a half miles to meet at Berlin. There they tied into the branch line running east to Ocean City and the newer line running south to Snow Hill, the county seat. It was a good area in which to be an ambitious young man with a responsible job and an interest in commerce. From Friendship, John Townsend's circle of friends grew larger to include people from all over northern Worcester County and southeastern Sussex County.

He was on the lookout for business opportunity. A year after his marriage he found what was to be the first of scores of opportunities in the ensuing seventy years–the timber business. As a telegrapher in intimate association on a daily basis with the railroad business, John could hardly help being aware of the needs of the railroad for which he worked. One constant and growing need was for timbers for railroad ties, for piling for trestles, and for lumber for construction of bridges and other needs. He was undoubtedly aware of the going rates for such material and was familiar with the timber business already. As a young man with a fine head for figures and a growing circle of ambitious young friends, John found a way to make an inroad into the exchange between timbermen and railroad. John's first transactions were on a small scale. He may have served as a middleman in return for a commission. He soon impressed his employers as a person with the right connections to save them money on ties and piling and was doing a regular sideline business in addition to his regular duties.

On August 1, 1891, his father borrowed $700 from Elisha D. Layton of Bishops and put up his forty-four-acre tract "Temple Hall," adjoining Bishops Station, as collateral. Young John used the money and what little he had thus far been able to set aside as payment for a movable steam sawmill and some timber rights. He made the leap from middleman to producer and became a full-fledged capitalist at the age of twenty.

One incentive was the knowledge that he was also about to become a father. On September 16, Jennie gave birth to the couple's first child, a daughter. They named her Edith May Townsend. Eighteen months later another child was born–this one a son, Julian E. Townsend. By then John and Jennie had moved into slightly more commodious quarters at the village of Showell, midway between Friendship and Bishops, where John was still working as telegrapher and was operating an increasingly successful lumber business.

His practice, in common with other timbermen of the day, was to purchase the timber rights to a piece of land for a given period, two or three years, perhaps. He would move his mill to the site with a team of mules and begin cutting. The mill would be set up in the woods some distance from one side of the tract. As the tract was cut, the mill was moved from spot to spot for added convenience. John and his workmen (or, in the beginning, his workman) would begin cutting trees with two-man crosscut saws and axes, hoisting them onto a timber cart, a wooden contraption with massive ironbound wooden wheels six or more feet in diameter. The logs were hauled off through the woods to the mill where they were rough cut to the proper dimensions and hauled off to the landing to be loaded aboard vessels or to the railroad. His first employee in those early days was John Postley, a local black man who became a close friend.

Some sense of those logging days can be drawn from the writings of David J. Long, a Selbyville pioneer who was born in 1846 and whose early career resembled those of both John and his father. Long was first a house carpenter during about half of the year, a trade he followed until 1880. In 1928, Long published his memoirs in a series

of articles in a local weekly newspaper: He recalled that, during his
years as a logger, in winter and spring:

> I worked at getting out vessel keels, keelsons, and
> knees [structural members of wooden sailing ships]. Large
> white oak logs were cut and hewed sixteen, eighteen, or
> twenty inches square and forty to fifty feet long. The ship
> knees were made from large spur roots and large limbs.
> The spur roots were blasted apart by boring a hole in the
> center of the tree stump, pouring in some powder and
> touching it off. While I was getting out ship knees, President
> Grant's brother had the contract to get several thousand
> knees for the government. He and William Reynolds came
> to my house and stayed with us all night and inspected a
> carload of knees which I had ready to ship.

This work was of the hardest sort and involved the hand-hewing
of the great timbers with broad hachets, adzes, and other tools. While
there is no direct evidence that John was ever involved in this phase of
the business, he may have been in his younger days. In 1880, Long
gave up carpentry and the ship-timber business as a profession and
turned to the lumber business. Of this work, which was much nearer to
that done by John a few years later, he wrote:

> While trying to build up the town of Selbyville, I gave
> up carpentering and bought a steam mill. I started in the
> lumber business, bought a tract of timber near White Oak
> Swamp, and built a small house fourteen by sixteen feet.
> We moved in and stayed there four years . . . In 1884, I
> bought a half interest in the steam mill of William R. McCabe
> at Selbyville. We then moved back to Selbyville. In the
> same year I bought a tract of timber and land to make a
> farm near Williamsville [a village several miles east of
> Selbyville]. I moved the mill from the first place to the
> second tract.

We lived in Selbyville three years while I was looking after both mills... In 1886, we moved from Selbyville back near Williamsville, where my first mill was located... We lived there six years while I operated the mill. In 1891, I bought a tract near Johnson's Corner [about a mile north of Williamsville], moved the mill to it and stayed two years. In 1892, I bought the Dr. Mustard tract with part of the land, made a farm and built a house. I moved the mill near Roxana, and operated it there until 1899. I then bought a tract of timber from Jacob Breasure and moved the mill there, near Bayville. In 1902, I bought a tract of timber near Sound Church and moved the mill to that location. While operating the mill at this place, I drove a team of horses to and from home near Roxana and made crates for strawberries. In 1910, I turned the mill over to my two sons and retired from the mill and lumber business.

One of the more unusual phenomena of the timber business of the late nineteenth and early twentieth centuries was the low regard in which cut-over timberland was held. Landowners were often unwilling to sell the timber rights to a tract of land unless the logger would also buy the land. At that time prime farmland was selling for ten or twenty dollars an acre. Timber land was less valuable, often selling for no more than five dollars an acre and, if the land was swampy, even less. Good land was highly valued. Commercial property or land such as that which John Townsend Sr. owned near Bishops Station was still more valuable. Timber was one of the more abundant commodities on the peninsula and the land on which it stood was generally considered marginal. Landowners did not consider it worthwhile to pay taxes on cutover timberland while waiting for it to restore itself, and they generally did not have the time or inclination to clear it of stumps and ditch it to make new farmland. The answer was to sell it, and let the logger worry about the taxes.

Even while this mentality reigned, such an easy disregard for the possibilities of thousands upon thousands of acres of land was becoming an obsolete concept. The revolution in American technology was giving birth to a new nationwide system for the fast, easy movement of agricultural products to previously inaccessible markets. A new technology was developing as well for clearing the land to grow crops and for the growing and processing of these crops. The first decades of the new century were to see an unparalleled expansion of all agricultural activities even as the nation's cities were booming with the expansion of industry.

As the 1890s and the old century drew to a close, John G. Townsend Jr. was slowly being forced into becoming a landowner just to stay in the timber business. Evidence suggests that it was a development he was not unwilling to face. His first two land purchases were made in 1899–one in Worcester County, Maryland, and one in Sussex County, Delaware.

In the meantime, John and Jennie had made a major change in their lives by leaving Worcester County permanently and moving to the new and flourishing town of Selbyville, only about two miles north of Bishopville across the state line. As the old waterborne commerce of northern Worcester was giving way to the railroads, the village of Bishopville was slowly beginning to decline in importance. At the same time, Selbyville was forging ahead. Even in the 1880s many legal deed descriptions did not even mention the place by name but referred instead to "the public road from Frankford to Berlin." Selbyville had gotten its start after 1778 as the crossroads hamlet of Sandy Branch, clustered around two millponds and a rough-hewn cypress log store. Its growth had been slow until the railroad arrived in 1874. Its coming made all sorts of new enterprises possible. Selbyville, on the southern boundary of Delaware, was ready to take advantage of them.

Mule Team: One of John G. Townsend Jr.'s early mule teams is seen about 1900 as it hauled a lumber wagon through the streets of Selbyville. Standing at the end of the team at right is John Postley, John's friend and first employee (Lyla T. Savoy collection).

Thus, by 1894 an ambitious young man from St. Martin's District of Worcester County could see that to progress he would have to turn the focus of his interest either south or north—to Berlin or to Selbyville. John chose the latter, probably for a variety of reasons. His family connections were largely centered in northern Worcester and southern Sussex. Several friends like Will White and Charles Hamblin had already come to Delaware and were doing well there. Berlin was an old, established town with clearly delineated social levels, old families, and set ways of doing things. Selbyville, on the other hand, had never been large enough until recently to worry much about tradition and different levels of society. The spirit driving the community in the 1890s was overwhelmingly progressive. It was a town well suited to a young man like John.

In 1894, John and Jennie loaded up their possessions in an old farm wagon drawn by mules and set out with the two babies for Selbyville with John's friend and employee, John Postley, along to help them. At first they rented a small two-story house in the old part of town along a small stream called Sandy Branch, near one of the old mill ponds that had given the village its start. The place had a one-story rear kitchen wing with additional sleeping quarters overhead and a "catslide" roof sloping down over the back porch. By this time, John owned one sawmill with the help of his father's loan of $700 and had leased others. He had a growing timber business and he had apparently left his job as a railroad telegrapher before the move to Selbyville. That railroad job was the only time he ever worked for anyone other than hemself except when he later held elective office. He never quite forgot how to operate a telegraph key, however, as he proved forty years later to a Washington reporter while serving as Delaware's senior U.S. senator.

According to his own recollection decades later, one of the first things John Townsend did after the move was to stroll around the town, stopping at nearly every house, knocking on the front door, and introducing himself to the occupants, if he did not already know them. It did not take long for word to get around that the Townsend family had arrived. The townspeople were soon impressed with how hard and effectively John worked. He had to work hard and fast if he was to establish anything like a substantial home for his family. It was growing steadily all the while.

On August 27, 1894, a second girl, John and Jennie's third child, was born. They named her Lyla Mariedith Townsend. Fifteen months later their fourth child and second son arrived–John Gillis Townsend III. A few years after John and Jennie moved to Selbyville, they were joined by James and Addie Townsend. The brothers became partners in various enterprises in the late 1890s, but they devoted most of their joint efforts to the lumber business. John also became involved in an enterprise that was to provide him with his first really substantial capital–the strawberry business. The lumber business was potentially profitable, but it required large amounts of working capital to have a chance of real success. The buying and selling of strawberries was a way to raise that capital.

The same David Long who worked in carpentry and sawmilling was one of the local pioneers in the growing of strawberries. In 1871, he bought six thousand strawberry plants from a nurseryman down on Trappe Creek near Berlin. He planted them on a half-acre plot that fall and they promptly died. The next year was more successful. By this time several other farmers were experimenting with the plants. They shipped their berries out from St. Martin's, which in 1872 was the closest rail depot. J. Frank Dukes was the first local grower to experiment with western strawberry plants, which had the distinct advantage of staying firm for shipping in contrast to the older, softer eastern plant strains. By 1880, such Selbyville-area farmers as Ezekiel Bunting, Allard and Arion Lynch, Harb, Bill, George and Levi Holloway, and others were growing strawberries for market.

The new crop helped the local economy in a variety of ways, not the least of which was the creation of a demand for berry baskets and crates. In the beginning, most local growers manufactured their own sixty-quart crates, paid field laborers one cent per quart for picking, and sold their berries for three to four dollars per sixty-quart crate. The farmers shipped the berries to Philadelphia or New York commission merchants who usually returned the crates empty to the farmers for reuse since the farmer's name and address were stenciled on each crate. By the middle 1880s, the strawberry business was becoming very important to the local economy. By now, a new type of middleman, known as the "solicitor," moved into the business. These men, usually local growers themselves, handled sales to the Philadelphia and New York commission merchants, leaving the other farmers free to concern themselves only with the growing. The solicitors received 3 percent commission on all the business they could generate for the various

Strawberries: *In a scene from the days when strawberries were Baltimore Hundred's greatest crop, a group of Selbyville men examine a wagonload of berries along Church Street (Lyla T. Savoy collection).*

commission merchants. They were by this time shipping the berries by ventilated railroad cars, which helped to slow spoilage of the fruit, but which were far from ideal.

This type of work was natural for John with his acute mathematical ability and his knowledge of the railroads and the people who ran them. He soon found himself getting into the strawberry business on several fronts. Not only was he beginning to grow berries on his own, but he was beginning to work as a solicitor. By the time he got heavily involved, a few years after he moved to Selbyville, the solicitors had evolved into strawberry brokers who bought berries from the growers and resold them to commission merchants and confectionary firms in cities all over the East. This expanding market demanded the use of a new development in railroad technology–the insulated refrigerator car.

Townsend has sometimes been credited with being the man who introduced the refrigerator car to the local area, but in reality he was only one of several early local brokers to use them. The first was D.C. Williams, who shipped out the area's first refrigerator car full of berries in 1899. He was followed by Frank Faulkner, a Methodist minister, William G. Williams, the Simpler Brothers, and John. The cars themselves were nothing more, at that stage in their development, than large rolling insulated ice boxes. The brokers packed their berries inside and cooled them at first with ice from local millponds. This was something of a problem since it did not get cold enough some winters to produce sufficient quantities of ice, a fact that made it necessary by 1902, when the quantity of berries being shipped had grown considerably, to bring in large amounts of ice from Maine's Kennebec River. This increased the cost of shipping and reduced profit margins, which were reduced still further by the fact that brokers even had to engage special "icing" firms such as the California Fruit Transport and the Fruit Growers' Express to come in and ice the cars for them. Icing a refrigerator car properly was an exacting process. A poorly iced car could arrive at its destination with its contents a total loss. Such a loss was borne by the broker, who had to assume the risk of shipping the fruit.

In the next few years John and other local men found ways around these technical problems, but one of the greatest hindrances to the potentially lucrative new business had nothing to do with strawberries and refrigerator cars. It had to do with politics. The middle 1890s were years of recession in the country, a recession that was caused largely by the excesses of the railroad barons and the great Eastern financiers and industrialists in their quest for ever-greater profits. The downturn came at a time when southern Delaware farmers and businessmen were just beginning to see the marvelous new opportunities opened up by the coming of the railroads, of which the new strawberry business was just one example.

Forward-looking men like John Townsend could see quite clearly that the age of the old subsistence farms was coming to an end, that the days were past when a man would make a three-day trip with wagon and mules along terrible roads simply to sell a thousand board feet of lumber for twelve dollars to get some hard cash money. But those times were not changing as fast or as equitably as local businessmen and farmers had hoped in the halcyon days of the railroad's first arrival. The rapid growth of the railroads in size and sophistication opened up fabulous new opportunities for truck farming, canning, improved use of timber and fisheries on the lower peninsula. With ready access to rail and reasonable freight rates there was no reason why the economy of lower Delmarva could not become truly healthy and thriving for the first time in its long history.

Southeastern Sussex County was situated perfectly, given the technology of coldpacking, to sell fresh fruits and vegetables, fish, oysters, wildfowl, and other goods in the markets of Philadelphia and New York. A New York banker could be feasting on Sussex County oysters and Baltimore Hundred strawberries in the evening of the day after they had been dredged from Assawoman Bay or handpicked in a Williamsville field, but only if the Sussex Countians could afford to send their produce to New York. Two problems kept this great promise from being realized. In the first place the public roads were so profoundly awful, so rutted, bog-filled, and lumpy, that it was often impossible for farmers five or ten miles from the railroad to get to the depot at all, or for watermen to move their fish and oysters before spoilage set in. The second problem was the railroads themselves, or, more precisely, the railroad management.

Rail lines down the peninsula and across it from east to west were not rated as profitably as the great east-west routes across the continent or those running to the south down the west side of the Chesapeake Bay. While they could have produced an economic miracle on the peninsula with a little far-sighted and creative management, the railroad magnates were less interested in future potential than in immediate profit. The railroads on the peninsula had been built only with the most powerful inducements and concessions from the state governments and with the very limited resources of Delmarva businessmen. Soon after their construction most lines were in financial trouble because of their limited financial backing and because the great railroads with whose lines they had to connect were able to charge outrageous sums for the privilege. To keep from going under, the management of the local railroads were forced to seek outside backing. Naturally enough, this backing came directly or indirectly from the Pennsylvania Railroad, which was interested in expanding its control into the peninsula as a logical extension of its activities to the north and west. In the 1880s and 1890s, the Pennsylvania was moving to absorb most of the peninsula's smaller lines like the Queen Anne Railroad running eastward across the peninsula to Lewes and the Junction, Breakwater, and Franklin Line running through Selbyville. The process happened in stages. The Pennsylvania first set up under its control the Delaware, Maryland, and Virginia Railroad to oversee all the small lines. Ultimately they were absorbed into the Pennsylvania system, or driven out of business.

Many of those who had been the local financial leaders in the growth of the early rail lines in Sussex, men like former Governors Charles C. Stockley of Georgetown and William Ross of Seaford, the Houston brothers of Millsboro, and John Hickman of Frankford, were powerful Democratic leaders in a state that was almost completely in the hands of the Democratic Party in the 1870s and 1880s. It was in the best interests of the railroads to maintain the Democrats in power since so many of them were financially involved with the lines and could be depended upon to see the situation from a point of view favorable to the railroads.

The emerging principle of governmental regulation and oversight of interstate transportation and commerce was in its earliest infancy. Even though the gradual tightening of the railroad monopoly was of direct harm to the newly emerging small businessmen of the lower peninsula, the reigning powers, most of whom were Democrats, by and large supported the goals of the railroad barons. This support came both because most of the elected officials still held to the old philosophy that "that government governs best which governs least" and because it was in their own financial interest to see their railroad investments salvaged.

By the time of John's first involvement in the strawberry business, virtually all the lines on the peninsula were under Pennsylvania control. As that control grew, rates for produce shipped from the lower part of the state and from Worcester County spiralled upward to the point where local farmers and watermen were hard pressed to ship their products by rail and make any profit at all. The Pennsylvania was involved in the great battle for dominance in major east-west interstate commerce and was cutting its rates for those cross-continent runs to rock bottom. To make up the difference they were charging outrageous rates in areas like Delmarva where they held a monopoly. They thoughtfully gave those whom they needed to maintain their tight control, like Delaware's Democratic leadership, preferential treatment. The absurdly high rate schedules in use on the peninsula were directed particularly at fresh fruits, seafood, and other perishables, the very products which Baltimore and Dagsboro Hundreds and Worcester County produced in abundance.

In western Sussex the situation was not nearly as bad because the farmers had easy access to the Chesapeake via the Nanticoke River. In Kent County communities farmers could get either to the Choptank or to the Delaware and its tributaries with ease. They could ship their produce by water to the great markets of Baltimore and Philadelphia. They were thus not under the complete control of the railroads.

Many Baltimore Hundred men tried to escape the railroad rates by shipping from Townsend's Landing (now known as Sandy Landing),

White's Creek, and other Indian River shipping points, but that was a much less certain proposition. The hazards of navigating the shallow Indian River Inlet and the mouth of the Delaware Bay were notorious. For that reason a clamor arose in southeastern Sussex for a canal linking Indian River Bay with the port of Lewes and another canal linking Indian River to Assawoman and the lower bays in Virginia.

Any matter as important to the economy as this could hardly remain nonpolitical and before long this matter of the throttlehold of the railroads led to an epic battle. The political patterns set as a result have lasted for generations, long after citizens have forgotten the reason for them. Anyone familiar with Sussex County politics, for instance, is aware that, well into the 1970s, western Sussex tended to be strongly Democratic in its politics while southeastern and eastern Sussex tended to be more Republican. This is because in 1880s and 1890s western Sussex Countians were not slaves to the railroads while southeastern Sussex Countians were.

As the battle became political in nature, the personable and well-spoken John G. Townsend Jr., already a Republican by family tradition, was among those who stood up to fight for the economic survival of Baltimore Hundred and his native St. Martin's District of Worcester County. The fight was long and hard and of almost unbelievable complexity in its ever-changing alliances. It was to provide the young Townsend with a marvelous political apprenticeship and served as the basis for his entire later career.

Part II:

The Political Background

4.   The Way It Used To Be

W hen young John Townsend was becoming politically active in Sussex County politics in the 1890s, the Reconstruction Era was just passing.   The older generation of politicians had been the men who fought the Civil War. As a Border State, Delaware was a region of contrasts between the attitudes and lifestyles of the South and of the North. New Castle County was essentially a Northern province. Kent and Sussex, along with the rest of Delmarva, were more of the South.

The Republicans of southern Delaware felt little sense of political kinship with their upstate brethren during the 1870s and 1880s. They might as well have inhabited different worlds for all they had in common. Republicans in Kent and Sussex were clearly poor relations, but more than this they lived with harsh political realities absent from the New Castle scene. The lower counties were largely controlled by a Democratic machine that held most of the General Assembly seats and all the courthouse row offices. The Democrats had their problems, of course. Their organization was a frequently uncomfortable union of five or six major families and their underlings. This arrangement often erupted into feuds and bitter wrangling over senate seats and the like. Such Democratic battles provided downstate Republicans with about the only opportunities they had for success at the polls. Even so, those successes were rare.

In Kent and Sussex the Democrats were similar in style and outlook to their counterparts in the Reconstruction South. Many of them had been Confederate sympathizers during the Civil War. Their ranks included many who had themselves been slaveowners or at least found the institution of slavery acceptable. An important part of their heritage was public resentment against what they felt were the wartime excesses of Delaware's Republicans. In a brief few years of power during the war the Republicans had brought federal troops into the lower two counties to "guard the polls" at election time. The Democrats charged that these soldiers were insulting and abusive and that their presence was wholly unjustified. While this was a thing of the past, the sores had not yet healed over.

The national Republican party had been created during the 1850s as an expression of the growing fight over slavery, among other factors. It first achieved national power in the election of 1860 which saw Abraham Lincoln elected as the first Republican president. By the 1870s and 1880s that party also was a union of disparate elements– Western farmers and miners, Eastern industrialists, Wall Street bankers, and others. Just as Delaware was a microcosm of the East economically, it was a political microcosm as well. It contained within its small expanse everything from Northern industrial city to Southern rural farm life. Politically it was much the same. The state leadership came mostly from the wealthier classes of New Castle County–and when one spoke of wealthy classes in Delaware in the late nineteenth century, one was speaking largely of New Castle. It was estimated in 1890 that Delaware had ten millionaires, all of whom lived north of the Christina River (and most of whom were Republicans). A few Kent and Sussex Countians held party leadership positions but it was clear where the power lay.

The New Castle County Republican leadership was drawn basically from three groups. First were the scions of the great industrial and milling families. These included members of the Quaker establishment of the county, the Leas and Bancrofts and others, and such non-Quaker industrialists as the du Ponts. Another group was the county's landed gentry (or that portion of them who were not Democrats). Typical of this group were the Higginses of Red Lion Hundred in the southern part of the county. Finally there were the professional men of Wilmington–the judges, lawyers, and doctors. This was far from absolute, of course. Some party leaders were connected to several of these groups. In at least one case, that of General James Harrison Wilson, a Civil War hero whose wife was from an old Delaware family, none of these categories quite explained him.

The one thing they all had in common was an almost total lack of appreciation for the problems of Republicans in southern Delaware. Most of them seemed to go about the practice of politics with a gentlemanly disdain for the downstaters, or at any rate an indifference to their plight. They sent their children on grand tours of the Continent and summered at Saratoga, Newport, and Mount Desert Island. They knew national party leaders personally and entertained them in their homes. They measured their annual income in tens of thousands, not in hundreds. Many of their deeply-held beliefs were directly at odds with the beliefs of the downstaters. Their state organization seemed at times to be based on the principle of gentlemanly defeat. In 1878 and again in 1886, the Delaware Republican Party did not even bother to nominate state tickets, so sure were they of the futility of the gesture.

An important element in the political equation of the 1870s and 1880s was the effort made by the Democrats to disenfranchise black voters in clear subversion of the 13th, 14th, and 15th Amendments to the Constitution. These measures, approved between 1865 and 1870, provided for the abolition of slavery, extension of citizenship rights to blacks, and voting rights for black men. They were all the law of the land by 1870. It was perfectly clear that the enfranchisement of black voters would be of enormous benefit to the Republican party since the new voters would logically cast their ballots for the party of Lincoln and Emancipation. Therefore, state Democratic parties throughout the South and in most border states where they tended to hold majority power enacted laws designed to keep blacks from voting. This occurred in Delaware where, after the end of the war, the General Assembly refused to ratify the three constitutional amendments. While the state was constitutionally bound like every other to abide by those amendments after a sufficient number of states had ratified them, the Democrats set about subverting them.* A series of laws enacted in 1870 had the clear purpose of keeping blacks from voting in Delaware. As these measures were almost blatantly unconstitutional, they were quickly struck down by the courts. The campaign of 1872 was the first in which large numbers of black voters were qualified and the Republican leadership made a strong effort to bring them out. The result was the only victory, however minor, the Republicans were able to claim for more than twenty years after the Civil War, an outcome that alarmed the Democrats. Still tenuously in possession of their legislative majority, they enacted a new and much more subtle measure during the 1873 session known as the Delinquent Tax Act.

The Delinquent Tax Act was in no way openly aimed at black voters. It stated simply that no one who had not paid his county capitation taxes by a certain date well before an upcoming election would be eligible to vote in the election. This law was hardly

---

In 1901, when the Republicans of Delaware had finally wrested control of the General Assembly from the Democrats they symbolically voted to ratify the three amendments, which by then had been a part of the U.S. Constitution for over thirty years. With this gesture they sought to bring to a close one of the more unfortunate episodes in the state's political history.

unreasonable on the face of it; in practice it kept black voting to a minimum for several reasons. In the first place, southern Delaware still faced a perennial shortage of cash money, making it difficult for the poor to pay capitation taxes at all. Secondly, the Democrats were in firm control of most courthouse offices in Georgetown and Dover and were able to control the process of setting tax rates, naming tax office officials, and collecting tax revenues. This gave them considerable power in determining who was qualified to vote and who was not.

Delaware had no tax collectors as such. The comparable officials were known officially as "receivers of taxes." The distinction was small but important. A tax collector actually went out, tracked down voters and collected their taxes from them. A receiver of taxes sat in an office in the courthouse and waited for citizens to come pay him. If they did not do so they were delinquent. As the law was written, if people did not pay their taxes directly to the receiver of taxes, they were delinquent and could not vote. If the receiver of taxes could not be found for one reason or another as the deadline neared, then that was just too bad for the voter. In practice, of course, Democratic voters never had any trouble paying their taxes and getting qualified to vote. For the Republicans it was not so easy.

One entertaining tale of the day concerned a Kent County receiver of taxes who was even more elusive than most and the efforts of a band of particularly stubborn Republicans to run him down. As the deadline for the payment of capitation taxes neared, the receiver disappeared mysteriously from his office. He was not at home. He was nowhere in town. The Republicans finally succeeded in tracking him to Philadelphia whence, they learned, he had been called on urgent business of an unspecified nature. They followed him to the city and were able after much effort to find out in which hotel he was staying.

After making their way up to his room they bearded him in his den as it were and reportedly found him cowering fully clothed beneath the covers. Cornered at last, he meekly accepted their tax money, thereby qualifying them to vote.

The capitation taxes were quite clearly a political tool and were treated as such. Neither party organization thought anything amiss in raising the necessary funds, if possible, to pay the taxes of their less fortunate members. It had long been taken for granted that both sides would hand out such Election Day favors as a bag of groceries, a pint of whiskey or, much less frequently, a few dollars in cash in thanks for a voter's trouble in coming to the polls . . . vote buying? Not really. Not in those days. It was just a fact of life, as was the common practice of having party functionaries assist illiterate voters in marking their ballots. While it was assumed that no Republican worker was going to help an illiterate Republican voter mark his ballot for Democrats, this was not really considered unusual either. One could reasonably assume that both parties had roughly equal numbers of illiterate supporters and that everything more or less equalled out. Such practices had been fixtures of political life in Delaware and elsewhere since the enfranchisement of nonlandowning whites during the Jackson Era.

At first blacks were not included in this largesse since they always voted Republican and the Republicans had much less money to spend. Later they were included. By the 1880s and 1890s such practices were so common that they caused nary a ripple of concern. And in some respects politicians of that day were considerably less hypocritical than a latter-day presidential candidate who may routinely accept $50 million in campaign contributions from a multitude of special interest groups while steadfastly maintaining that he has not been "bought."

An influx of Irish and European immigrants into northern Delaware soon after the Civil War tended further to strengthen the edifice of the Democratic Party. Just as the Republicans were more hospitable toward American blacks, the Democrats went out of their way to attract these newcomers, most of whom worked in the large mills and factories of New Castle County. Their employers tended to be Republican and capitalist who espoused protective tariffs and low pay for employees, a fact which served to drive those men into the arms of the waiting Democrats. With this added strength and with the Delinquent Tax Act firmly in place the Democrats possessed so much electoral strength during the 1870s and early 1880s that the G.O.P. did not even bother to nominate state tickets in 1878 and again in 1886. The only opposition to the statewide Democratic candidates in those years was that raised by such entities as the Greenback Labor Party and the Temperance Party, which was in its ascendancy during those years. Yet the Republicans still possessed a respectable amount of political power in some sections of Delaware outside of New Castle County. Even as Democrats were victorious year after year in Kent and Sussex, there remained pockets of Republican strength. The old Whig strongholds of Cedar Creek, Indian River, and Northwest Fork Hundreds in Sussex had evolved into Republican areas after the demise of the old party in the 1850s. Northwest Fork bore the distinction of having produced Delaware's first (and until 1894, its only) Republican governor, William Cannon of Bridgeville, who was elected in 1862.

More important to John Townsend's future was the respectable amount of Republican strength in Baltimore Hundred where the railroad issue had alienated many onetime Democrats. The hundred still had its strong Democratic families such as the Dukeses, the Tunnells, and the McCabes but overall Democratic strength was in decline in the area. In 1886, the last year in which the Republicans failed to nominate a state ticket, Baltimore Hundred voters supported the Temperance Party over the Democrats. That reflected not only the anti-Democratic spirit then prevalent but also the area's intense Methodism. A Baptist or an Episcopalian could get elected to office in southeastern Sussex but he had to know how to appeal to Methodists.

The Democratic Party in lower Sussex, successful for so long, was more closed to outsiders than the Republicans, who would welcome anyone–a vote was a vote to them. The Democrats were wrapped tightly in bonds of family association, business arrangements and old-time alliances. Of course, while the Republicans were glad to have newcomers, no newcomer with political ambitions would have seriously considered joining them in the lower part of Sussex until there was some future in it. That future was provided by the growing resentment against the railroads, which were so closely linked to the Democrats.

The Republicans had won their first important postwar electoral victory about six years before John and Jennie Townsend arrived in Selbyville. It was the election of 1888 and it had largely been won for the Republicans by a newcomer to the area named Charles Treat. He had arrived in lower Sussex in the late 1870s and established wood products factories first at Frankford and then at Georgetown where he quickly became the town's largest employer. As a politically-ambitious Republican Treat was naturally interested in promoting the party in the area to the point that he could win office. Through the 1880s he was one of the few local Republicans with enough money to pay any poll taxes for black voters. His efforts were enough to give the Sussex Republicans their first chance for real victory. An intraparty feud erupted within the Democratic Party in 1888 over the U.S. Senate seat. Treat ran as the Republican candidate for U.S. Congress and waged one of the hardest fought and best-financed campaigns in Delaware history up to that time. He was narrowly defeated but his hard work and money enabled the Republicans to win the first General Assembly majority since their creation.*

The 1888 election was a turning point in Republican Party fortunes. Their legislative victory meant not only that they could rid themselves, at least temporarily, of the hated Delinquent Tax Act and that they could at last win a share of state patronage, but that they could elect a Republican United States senator. In those days, before passage of the Seventeenth Amendment to the U.S. Constitution provided for the popular election of senators, the office was filled by majority vote of a joint session of each state's legislature. Thus, control of a majority in the joint session normally insured that a party would elect one of its own to the Senate. In addition to the psychological boost this would give Delaware Republicans, U.S. senators also

---

* *Charles Treat's own story following the 1888 election was a sad one. Soon after his loss in the congressional race his large Georgetown factory burned. He hadn't yet paid off his original mortgages at Georgetown's branch office of the largely state-owned Farmers Bank, the board of which was then firmly in the hands of the Democrats. Being underinsured, Treat was forced to return to the bank in search of additional loans with which to rebuild. Not only did the bank board turn down his application for new loans but they began calling in his old ones, quickly driving him into bankruptcy. After one of the largest sheriff's sales in the history of Sussex County up to that time, Treat and his family left Delaware to seek a new start elsewhere, His later career proved more successful both in business and in politics. Some twelve years after his ignoble departure from Georgetown, Treat was appointed Treasurer of the United States by President Theodore Roosevelt. In what must rank as one of the best instances of poetic justice in the history of Delaware, the very bankers who had forced Treat into bankruptcy were now forced to circulate U.S. currency bearing his signature. Every single dollar crossing the counter in the Georgetown office of the Farmers Bank had Charles Treat's name on it.*

controlled a substantial number of federal patronage positions in the state, serving to further enhance a party's power base.

The Republicans had several highly qualified men, most of whom had never had an opportunity to advance far politically because of the Democratic control in Dover in earlier years. The competition was therefore intense. After much deliberation and some weeks of deadlock the Republican caucus finally settled on Anthony Higgins of Red Lion Hundred and Wilmington. Higgins had served as U.S. Attorney for Delaware during the Grant administration, but he was best known for his prowess as a defense attorney. His reputation stemmed largely from his brilliant defense of a New Castle County black man accused of the rape of a white woman in 1880. Higgins lost the highly emotional case in the lower courts. He appealed it all the way to the Supreme Court of the United States and ultimately won it, making legal history in the process.

By far the most interesting Republican senatorial candidate in that late winter and early spring of 1889, however, was a man who never even ran officially. His name was John Edward Charles O'Sullivan Addicks and he was one of the more intriguing phenomena in the state's political lore. His only involvement in the 1889 Senate race occurred in the barroom of Dover's elegant Hotel Richardson late one night in early January. Various political seers, hacks, and hangers-on were standing around discussing the outlook for the upcoming joint session and the possibility of an unbreakable deadlock between two or three of the leading candidates. A handsome, elegantly dressed man in a great, fur-lined overcoat and high, silk hat spoke up and said that he would be happy to offer himself as a compromise candidate to break any deadlock. No one in the place even knew the man, and his outrageous offer was treated as a joke. Addicks might even have meant it as a joke in 1889, but before too much more time had passed the idea of seeking a Senate seat from Delaware had become his overriding ambition, even his obsession.

At the time of his 1889 visit to Dover Addicks had just returned home from a trip to Europe where he was said to have made more than a million dollars speculating in Trans-Siberian Railroad securities. He was at this time in his career first and foremost an organizer of municipal gas systems and street railways and a speculator in those and other securities. Then forty-seven, he lived on an estate at Claymont, just south of the Pennsylvania state line.*

Addicks had been born in Philadelphia where his father had been a Republican politician, once serving as Republican city chairman. The son had made his first fortune in flour in the early 1870s, married a wealthy wife, gone bankrupt, recovered, been widowed, remarried (to his dead wife's sister), and gone on to make another, much larger, fortune. His wealth, though ample and growing, was not of the magnitude of Jay Gould, the Vanderbilts, or John D. Rockefeller. It was based in no small part on his skill in the fine art of manipulating gas company charters in ways favorable to himself. Gas in the 1870s and 1880s had an importance electric power was later to assume. It was used for lighting, for cooking, for heat, and for some industrial power, among other things. Most municipalities were either unable or unwilling to finance public systems and so they gave franchises to private operators such as Addicks. The gas companies were for the most part stock corporations with both local and larger, outside investors. Though Delaware's classic corporation law was not enacted

---

* *Addicks later confessed to an interviewer that he bought the Claymont estate in the late 1870s and had lived there for several months before he realized that he was living in the State of Delaware and not in Delaware County, Pennsylvania.*

for another decade, the state already had favorable corporation laws and Addicks's trip to Dover in 1889 was for the primary purpose of taking advantage of those. He was seeking to set up an entity known as the Bay State Gas Company, which would own municipal gas systems in Massachusetts as well as being the linchpin of his business empire. He was seeking several clauses in the corporate charter which would enable him to conduct the corporation in ways that might not always be in the best interest of the minority stockholders. For that reason he thought it best not to charter the company in Massachusetts. Delaware was his choice as an alternate corporate domicile. Addicks had just happened by chance to read of the possible deadlock in the Republican Party over the senatorial race. His remark in the Hotel Richardson was just frivolous, loose barroom conversation, but a few years later those who had heard it thought Addicks's statement to have been a warning of future intentions.

The Republicans used their brief moment in control to demolish the Delinquent Tax Law, which, though revived briefly by the Democrats in 1892, never again regained the frightening power it had in the 1870s and early 1880s. They took no action during the 1889 session on Addicks's Bay State Gas Company charter. In 1890 and again in 1892, the Republicans failed to win legislative majorities, working without the aid of Charles Treat downstate. Addicks's only political activity in Delaware during this period was his contribution of $25,000 to the Democrats during the 1890 gubernatorial campaign. He had decided that the Democrats were the probable winners and he still sought passage of his charter, an act which the new Democratic majority in the General Assembly accomplished in short order. In later years Addicks bragged that his investment of $25,000 in the Democratic campaign that year had earned him two million dollars through the gas company–a nice piece of business, he thought. By the early 1890s his business affairs were positively flourishing and Addicks had the leisure to turn his thoughts to serious consideration of a political career in Delaware.

In 1892, Addicks officially registered as a Republican in Delaware. He continued to give both parties generous donations as a means of establishing his credentials, but his donations to the Republicans became slightly larger. Nothing really happened to further his career until 1894, when, faced with another mad scramble to raise poll tax money under the renewed Delinquent Tax Law, downstate Republicans were looking everywhere for financial backers.

The bulk of this effort was undertaken by a young Dover jeweler named J. Frank Allee. His late father had been one of the few Kent County Republicans closely involved with the railroad bosses and Allee was the perfect stereotype of the pragmatic Kent County politician. He made the rounds of all the downstate Republican big shots and got nowhere. On top of other problems was the cash shortage brought on by the 1893 "panic," then in full swing. He went to Washington and sought the help of Senator Higgins, now nearing the end of his first term in the Senate and a logical candidate for reelection if a Republican legislative victory could be achieved. Allee thought that with a good word from Higgins some of the wealthy Republicans of New Castle County would contribute. Higgins refused him. The rebuff permanently embittered Allee against Higgins and was one factor in the party strife which followed.

Allee, now having tried nearly everything he could think of, was close to giving up and accepting the inevitability of another Democratic victory when he suddenly remembered Addicks and his contributions of the past few years. Allee did not then know Addicks except by reputation, but he set off to Philadelphia to see him. When he arrived he found that Addicks was in New York on business. He called him and was told to stay in Philadelphia overnight. Addicks said he would be back the next day. Allee waited for him to return and then explained the problem in detail. Addicks very calmly reached for his checkbook and wrote out a check large enough to pay the poll taxes of most of the poorer voters of Kent and Sussex Counties.

That moment marked the real beginning of what might be called the "Addicks Era" of Delaware political history. Addicks later recalled that in his own mind his claim to a U.S. Senate seat in Delaware stemmed from that day. Though this is by no means certain, one might reasonably conclude that Allee may actually have promised him the Senate seat. Allee was a very cagey and resourceful politician who would have felt few qualms about such a promise. He might well have thought that he could easily deliver Higgins's Senate seat to Addicks during the joint General Assembly session of 1895. After Higgins's treatment of him, he certainly owed the New Castle Countian nothing. Looking back on it from a remove of more than a century, it is easy to see that if Addicks had gotten his Senate seat that year it would have been much simpler for everyone. But he did not and from that failure arose one of the most interesting periods in all of Delaware's long political history.

Without question Addicks's money was an important factor in the decisive Republican victory of 1894. Just as important was public dismay over the serious economic recession then sweeping the country. Democrats had been in power when it arrived and the old "throw the bums out" philosophy was at work. This 1893-97 slump was in some ways harder on Delawareans than the Great Depression. A popular Sussex County Republican, Joshua H. Marvil of Laurel, was elected governor. Marvil was a lumberman, basket manufacturer, and minor mechanical genius, whose brilliant technological innovations had helped him establish one of southern Delaware's leading industrial enterprises. He was only the second Republican in the state's history to win the post. Republicans also won a majority of the legislative seats, though the Democrats held a majority in the state senate, giving them the right to name the Speaker of the Senate.

Most party leaders assumed that Higgins would be reelected without much opposition. He had done a creditable job in the U.S. Senate and was well respected by most of his Senate colleagues, but J. Frank Allee had other plans. Of the thirty legislators in the two houses, nineteen were Republicans. A total of sixteen votes was needed to elect a senator. Addicks had the pledged support of six legislators, most from Kent County. This meant that even if Higgins could succeed in winning the other thirteen Republican votes, he could not win the Senate seat without some Democratic help unless he could cajole three Addicks men into voting for him.

With the convening of the first joint session in January, the balloting began. It stretched on through January and into February and March with no end in sight. Dozens of ballots took place with no break in the impasse. Higgins could not make Addicks's six men budge and Addicks could not sway any of his rival's votes over to his side. At last Higgins faced the fact that he could not win and withdrew from the race in hopes that another candidate might prove more acceptable to Addicks's six supporters. He and the other Republican leaders of New Castle County were already adamantly opposed to Addicks, who in their view had no legitimate right to a Delaware U.S. Senate seat and was therefore unworthy of their support. Most of them were stiffly honorable Victorian gentlemen who found the very

Col. Henry Algernon duPont
(Delaware Public Archives)

thought of Addicks's candidacy repugnant.

The party regulars put up Colonel Henry Algernon du Pont as a replacement candidate for Higgins. Colonel du Pont perfectly exemplified the ideal candidate in the eyes of the party leadership. He was an officer in the family powder company and thus one of Delaware's leading industrialists as well as one of its wealthiest men. A West Point graduate and hero of the Civil War, in which he had earned the Congressional Medal of Honor, he was called by one writer "the Junker of Delaware." He did somewhat resemble a stern-visaged Prussian nobleman with his imperious upthrust moustache, carefully clipped Van Dyke, steel-rimmed spectacles, and brushed silver hair, though du Pont would more likely have thought of himself as a French aristocrat rather than the Prussian variety. In any case, he was unquestionably an aristocrat. He lived amidst mementoes of his illustrious forebears on his elegant Winterthur estate in New Castle County (later turned into one of the nation's greatest museums by his son, Henry Francis du Pont). Colonel du Pont also had the advantage of being more popular with the General Assembly than was Higgins.

By now it was early April and a sudden catastrophe occurred for the Republicans, though it was not immediately recognizable as such. Governor Marvil, in office for only a few months, died suddenly. Though the Republicans had a majority of the seats in the General

Assembly, the Democrats held the majority in the upper house. Under the Delaware constitution of 1831, which was then still in effect, there was no office of lieutenant governor in Delaware. In the event of a governor's death in office the next highest elected official–the Speaker of the Senate–became acting governor. In this instance the speaker was the Milford Democrat William Tharp Watson, who assumed the duties of governor.

Republicans were devastated by Marvil's death, but it did seem as if there might be a "silver lining" in the form of a reduction in the number of state legislators with Watson's elevation to acting governor and a corresponding reduction in the number of votes needed for the election of a senator. With this in mind the Republicans who opposed Addicks set about securing two additional votes, which would give Henry du Pont the total of fifteen he would need to be elected in the absence of Watson. All through the joint sessions, the Democrats had routinely been casting their votes for various Democratic candidates in the clear awareness that none of their candidates had any chance of winning. No Democrat wished to aid the Republicans in breaking their impasse.

At last, on May 9, 1895, the du Pont faction succeeded in winning a commitment from two Addicks men to cast their votes for du Pont. They called for another ballot, confident at last of victory. It was the last day of the legislative session and it was now or never. A failure to elect someone senator that day would leave the state with only one U.S. senator. Just before the votes were cast the acting governor entered the chamber and took his seat with the other senators. He announced to the amazed Republicans that he was a duly elected state senator, acting governor or not, and that he intended to represent his district in the important matter of electing a U.S. senator. Amidst a chorus of protests Watson cast his vote for one of the Democratic candidates. du Pont got his fifteen votes but, if Watson's action was allowed to stand, he would be one vote short of the required majority. The result was absolute chaos, with charges and countercharges flying in all directions. Watson sat quite calmly through the storm, denying the outraged protests of the du Pont supporters that he had somehow been bought off by Addicks to keep the colonel from taking his rightful place in the U.S. Senate.

While Watson could hardly have been ignorant of the lopsided favor he did Addicks, if depriving Addicks's rival of a seat in the Senate could be called a favor, helping the gas tycoon had nothing to do with his motivation. The 56th Congress had just gone into session in Washington (the Congress convened during the first week of March in those days). Not counting the still-to-be-elected Delaware senator, the U.S. Senate had eighty-six members: forty-two Democrats, forty-two regular Republicans and two Western independent Republicans who espoused the radical rural populism then sweeping the Far West. Populists were adamantly opposed to what they saw as the unholy union between Eastern capitalists, supporters of the protective tariff, industrialists, and similar interests that tended to dominate the mainstream of the Republican Party. They saw an alliance with congressional Democrats as being less onerous than voting with the Republican caucus on most issues. They supported the Democrats even to the extent of allowing their votes to be used to give Democrats chairmanships and other majority perquisites in the upper chamber. Election of a Republican from Delaware would throw this fragile balance of power into doubt and could cause the whole Democratic power structure in the Senate to collapse. In voting to keep du Pont out of the Senate, Watson was doing a service of great importance for his own national party. He probably did not even give Addicks anything more than passing thought in deciding to take his action.

du Pont stormed off to Washington in a state of high indignation to place his case before the Senate, which has final authority to settle disputes arising over the seating of its members. The senators kept him dangling for nearly a year and then, voting strictly along party lines and with the populists joining the Democrats, they denied him a seat, leaving Delaware with only one U.S. senator. After the fall elections of 1896, du Pont tried once more to press his claim, only to be turned down again.

The effect this situation had on the political situation at home was explosive in the extreme. It was the direct cause of a major schism in the Republican Party which was the dominant political reality when John made his entry into local politics a few years later. The old Republican hierarchy, then under the leadership of General James Harrison Wilson, bolted the Republican State Convention in the summer of 1896 when it became clear that the Addicks faction had a majority of the delegates. They formed their own Republican Party, seeking to give the impression that theirs was the legitimate and rightful Republican Party of Delaware even though it had been they who had bolted the convention and not the Addicks men. Wilson's faction became known as the Regular Republican faction, or, more often, simply as "the Regulars."

By now, Addicks's supporters were a very substantial group. While the Regulars had sat back awaiting the results of du Pont's Washington efforts, Addicks and Allee had been assiduously courting downstate Republicans. The Addicks faction met in Rehoboth Beach later in the summer to formally establish their own party. This group became known as the Union Republican Party. Both factions held their own conventions and elected their own slates of candidates for the fall elections. By the fall of 1896, Delaware had three major parties, a state of affairs which was to continue for a decade.

Throughout this period the Regulars sought to portray Addicks as the archvillain of Delaware, as a thoroughly unscrupulous and degenerate man intent only on buying votes and corrupting Delaware voters in pursuit of his own selfish ends. Addicks was to some extent his own worst enemy and his later hardships made it easier for this view to become prevalent in subsequent years. The victors, after all, generally write the histories of wars. Yet in this case it was never a simple fight between right and wrong, between good men and bad, between corrupted and uncorrupted. Some of the best and most responsible men in the Republican Party supported Addicks and some of the worst supported the Regulars. Nor, in the context of his day, was Addicks all that unusual. Shortly before his own effort began similar attempts to acquire Senate seats had succeeded in Montana, West Virginia, and Pennsylvania. Men with backgrounds, interests, and outlooks similar to Addicks's were very close to dominating the national Republican Party. Addicks's method of operation, which was to supply large amounts of cash to keep the party machinery well oiled, was more the rule than the exception in 1896 (and it was only when his Regular rivals adopted similar strategies that they finally prevailed). Finally, in his own way J. Edward Addicks was genuinely interested in helping the people of southern Delaware. He was certainly more sensitive to their needs than Colonel du Pont, General Wilson and the other Regular Republican grandees ever were. It is even reasonable to conclude that Addicks would in some respects have made them a better U.S. senator than Henry A. du Pont did when he finally got to the Senate.

General Wilson, who headed the Regulars, was brilliant, arrogant, and abrasive. He had been one of the youngest general officers in the Union Army during the Civil War and had led Sherman's cavalry during the infamous "March to the Sea." He also had an unfortunate talent for alienating many of those with whom he came into contact throughout his career. One such enemy was a frumpy, unimpressive Tennessee senator named Andrew Johnson. When Johnson unexpectedly became first vice-president and then president upon the death of Abraham Lincoln, Wilson's military career began to suffer serious setbacks. He resigned his commission in favor of a career in business. Throughout his career the highly competent Wilson was impatient with the need to consider views contrary to his own and did not mind showing it. This trait was a factor contributing to the Regular–Union Republican schism. While he and the other Regular leaders put forth the impression that downstate Republicans flocked to Addicks because he bribed them, far more joined him because they could not abide the high-handed treatment they received from the New Castle Countians. In the 1880s and 1890s it seemed almost as though the high Republican leadership spurned the winning of elections as somehow ungentlemanly. When the Addicks movement started, they refused any and all proposals for compromise. They fought the Union Republicans with every weapon at their disposal except common sense.

The Democrats used every opportunity to drive the two factions still farther apart. Their ploys were usually petty but still maddening. One example of this sort of thing occurred just before the general election of 1896, the first in which the Union Republicans appeared on the ballot as a separate party. The clerks of the peace of the three counties were in charge of having the actual ballots printed up. All were Democrats and they ruled that the Union Republicans could not use the traditional eagle symbol of the Republicans at the top of the ballot. This symbol would go instead at the top of the Regular Republican column. It could have been argued that the Union

Republicans were the legitimate party and the Regulars the new faction, but the clerks of the peace chose to interpret it the other way in the knowledge that the Union Republicans had a very pronounced majority downstate. Since many, even possibly a majority of voters at that time, were illiterate, the use of these symbols was important and could confuse enough voters to throw the election to the Democrats, or so they reasoned. At the first official Union Republican gathering in the fall the new party adopted the star as its symbol.*

In the aftermath of the same 1896 election the Democrats of Kent County carried out a maneuver which outdid anything the Republicans ever attempted during the Addicks years. Kent County's Board of Elections was controlled by Democrats. Of the fourteen election districts in the county, six in the southern part of the county were clearly carried by Republicans (and most of these were Union Republicans). This would have brought about the election of several more Republican state representatives, enough, in fact, to have given the Republicans a clear majority in the joint session of the General Assembly. The Kent Board of Elections simply refused on the flimsiest of pretexts to certify most Republican ballots in those six districts, throwing out over three thousand votes. Then they announced that the total number of votes cast was nearly three thousand less than the true figure.

The Democrats were well aware that their scheme would be immediately obvious to the Republicans, but they also knew that it would take months to have the Board of Elections ruling overturned in the courts. In the meantime they could proceed to seat Democrats

---

* *The Regular-Union Republican schism and its final settlement is still graphically depicted on modern-day Delaware ballots on which the symbol at the top of the Republican column is an eagle with a star on its chest, first used during the election of 1908 when the breach was finally healed.*

representing those districts in the General Assembly and elect a
Democrat as U.S. senator. Then whatever the courts ruled wouldn't
undo the damage. One of the lawyers for the Board of Elections, a
young Dover attorney named James H. Hughes, freely admitted to an
interviewer forty years later that the whole thing had been a ruse with
no legal justification whatsoever.* The justification was that it worked.
The General Assembly's joint session in 1897 had a Democratic
majority of one as a result of this shenanigan. Even as the litigation
moved through the courts the Democrats speedily elected one of their
own, Richard R. Kenney of Kent County, to the U.S. Senate term
unfilled since 1895, thereby ending du Pont's chances once and for
all. Some time later the courts ruled that the Board of Elections action
had been illegal but by then the damage was done. Kenney served
out the remaining four years of the term.

Such irregularities did have one very positive result: they brought
about a major revision in Delaware's long obsolete 1831 state
constitution, an action that reformers had been seeking for many years.
With the disgraceful antics that had characterized the 1896 election
and the earlier joint session in which Acting Governor Watson had
voted as a senator, responsible politicians could no longer turn their
backs on the need for improvements. The resulting Delaware
constitution of 1897 included many significant reforms. One major
improvement that grew directly out of Watson's action was the creation
of the office of lieutenant governor. Other newly created elective
positions were the offices of insurance commissioner, attorney general,
state auditor, and state treasurer. County offices such as prothonotary,
clerk of the peace, and recorder of deeds were also made elective

---

* *Hughes and John G. Townsend were to have several significant encounters
in later years. Hughes was Townsend's Democratic opponent in the gubernatorial election of 1916. The two men later served together in the U.S. Senate.*

positions in an effort to end the old "courthouse gangs" of entrenched corruption that had enabled the Delinquent Tax Law to succeed in its purpose. Of course, boards of elections were also reformed. The link between payment of capitation taxes and voting eligibility was at last severed. A system of literacy requirements in which one was required to demonstrate an ability to read and write replaced the old Delinquent Tax Act. While the new system was little better, it at least ended the old problem of disappearing tax collectors. The new constitution also strengthened the office of governor, which had been a relatively innocuous one since the creation of the Delaware State in 1776 (at which time it was known as "president"). The governor was now empowered to veto legislation, including appropriations bills, when he saw fit. His term was extended from two to four years and he was now permitted to serve two terms where one had been the limit before. He did, however, lose some old powers. His major appointments were now subject to Senate confirmation where before they had not. In general the governor's executive powers were strengthened. His patronage powers were weakened.

The delegates to the state constitutional convention dealt with several pressing, though politically sensitive, issues. One of these, woman's suffrage, had more supporters, surprisingly enough, in traditionally conservative Kent and Sussex Counties than in New Castle where some of the state's wealthiest and best-educated men, like Judge Edward Bradford, opposed it. When a vote was held in the convention on the question of whether or not to include a woman's suffrage provision in the new constitution, seven men favored it and seventeen were opposed. All of the seven who favored giving women the right to vote were from Kent and Sussex Counties.

Delegates also failed to fully confront the touchy issue of reapportionment, though they made a few gestures in that regard,

such as doing away with at-large, countywide voting for General
Assembly seats and replacing the old system with a new district
structure. It had been well known for decades that the City of
Wilmington was grossly underrepresented in the legislature on the basis
of population. Southern Delawareans and even many rural New Castle
Countians opposed any change because they feared that a political
upheaval might result from Wilmington's large immigrant and black
populations gaining a major share of political power. Another factor
in a convention with a slight Democratic edge was that the more
populous New Castle County was traditionally Republican. The
convention vote establishing a new election districting plan did go more
along geographical than political lines, however, in keeping with the
old Delaware tradition of downstaters and upstaters voting their
respective regional interests regardless of party affiliation.

Now, with the changes brought about by the new constitution
of 1897, a young resident of Baltimore Hundred seeking to break into
politics needed to run only in Baltimore Hundred, where he was
relatively well known, and not countywide. In this sense, the new
constitution was the direct impetus to John G. Townsend's political
career.

5. The Union Republicans Take the Field

One of the first friends John and Jennie Townsend made after moving to Selbyville was Isaiah J. Brasure, who was more generally known as "Zare." He was a native of the central Baltimore Hundred community of Roxana, which had still been called "Centerville" during Zare's youth in the 1860s (in his father's day it had been known by the lively name "Dog's Ear Corner"). Before the arrival of the railroad in Baltimore Hundred, Roxana was the population center of the district. In the 1860s and 1870s the flourishing village boasted several doctors, a school, shops, stores, a lodge hall, several churches, and a substantial population. At this same time Selbyville was a sleepy hamlet clustered around a mill pond and John McCabe's log store house.

Roxana also had several steam sawmills in the 1860s and two blacksmith shops and carriage-making establishments. One of these was owned by William R. Tubbs and the other by Zare's father, William Brasure. Zare had quite naturally picked up the smithing and carriage-making trades from his father. He had worked in the family shop as a young man with his brothers, Willy and George. The establishment was located at the corner of the main road running southeast to Johnson's Corner, Sound Church, and Fenwick Island at the point where a road turned off toward the village of Bayard.

When the railroad line came through Selbyville in the late 1870s the entire pattern of life in Baltimore Hundred began to change. Selbyville was the only town in the hundred with a railroad depot and

Brasure's Store: *Two unidentified young men stand in front of Zare Brasure's store on Church Street (Lyla T. Savoy collection).*

it quickly outpaced Roxana as the principal town in the hundred. In the days before the railroad arrived, Roxana had prospered because of its location midway between the public road south to Maryland, the Great Cypress Swamp, and the landings along the Indian River where most commerce entered and left the area. After the railroad its importance was reduced.

Some Roxana residents moved to Selbyville in the 1870s and 1880s in hopes of partaking of the expected new prosperity. Among them were William R. Tubbs, the Watson family, who operated Roxana's undertaking establishment, and Zare Brasure. His move was further prompted by the fact that his father's business could not support the father and all three sons. Zare acquired a fifty-foot lot in Selbyville fronting on Church Street, the new business street, connecting the old north-south public road, Main Street, with the railroad depot. Until the railroad arrived and a depot was built the whole area of Church Street had been part of the McCabe family farm. The street had been a farm lane with a gate at the Main Street end. The lumberman David Long bought some of the land along Church Street and resold it after subdividing it into building lots. Zare paid Long fifty dollars for his lot, which was on the south side of Church Street three doors down from the Main Street corner and at the center of the new business district. He erected a wood frame building and established a general hardware business with a carriage-making shop on the side. He later rented some space in the back of the building to young W.O. McCabe, who opened a blacksmith and wheelwright shop on the premises. Brasure soon secured the village post office as well. Like all local merchants in those cash-poor years, he was forced to do much of his trade by barter. He once sold Fred Pepper a grindstone in return for a large quantity of eggs.

Zare was involved in many of the cultural activities in the growing town. Selbyville's first musical, "Queen Esther," was given in 1886 at the Methodist Church. Though many of the actors were part of a touring company outfitted with elegant costumes and colored lights, some members of the cast were local. Zare played the part of the biblical character, Mordecai, and did quite well by all accounts.

He was also a member of a newly created fraternal order, the Wissahickon Tribe of the Red Men. The late nineteenth century was the golden age of lodges and other fraternal orders, and almost every man in southern Delaware belonged to at least one–the Elks, the Moose, the various Masonic orders, the International Order of Mechanics, the Odd Fellows, the Red Men. Newspapers had regular daily or weekly columns devoted to their activities. Zare was not a founding member of the Red Men in Selbyville, which had come into being in 1884, but he was active from the late 1880s onward. By 1898, he had been named "Great Sachem" for the State of Delaware. It was often possible to use membership in such organizations as a springboard into politics, not as an intentional exploitation of one's membership but simply as part of a natural process of getting to know one's fraternal brothers around the county and state.

The Red Men in Selbyville built a two-story hall near the Methodist Church which became one of the town's favorite public meeting places and was often the site of public entertainments of one kind or another. They also established a cemetery north of town near the new railroad line, both as a service to the community and as a way of raising operating funds. Like most such groups, the Red Men also did charitable work locally and raised money to help support an old-age home in Newark sponsored by the state order of Red Men. In his own turn, John Townsend also became a member of the Red Men and several other fraternal orders in the area, and the contacts and friendships he made there proved valuable in his later career.

Like most Baltimore Hundred men of intelligence and ability, Zare Brasure was more than casually interested in politics. He was one of those who had seen the promise of the railroads. He was also one of a sizeable group who had been disappointed by the manner in which the combined greed of railroad executives and upstate politicians had kept any real economic transformation from being realized. When this disappointment began to come out politically, Zare Brasure was at the forefront of the movement.

Zare was one of those men who, though he had little formal education, had an interest in ideas and the ability to express himself. He was interested in the young men of the community and served as a sort of intellectual leader for many of them, carrying on long conversations and setting them to thinking about ideas larger than the confines of Baltimore Hundred and Sussex County. Among his more avid disciples in 1894 and 1895 was a young man named Everett Johnson, who had been born in 1877 at the village of Blackwater in the northern part of the hundred. He was the son of Captain Isaac Johnson, skipper of various of the coastal schooners which sailed out of the river up and down the Middle Atlantic coast. Everett had been educated in the local country schools and in Selbyville, where he spent much of his youth. Like most Baltimore Hundred boys, he had numerous relatives in the town and he went there to find work. He got a job as a clerk in the large general store owned by William R. and Caleb L. McCabe. He soon struck up a friendship with Zare and with another new arrival–John Townsend.

Everett Johnson's widow, Louise Staton Johnson, recalled in her memoirs nearly eighty years later that "during his high school days, Everett and most of the young boys became very much attached to a gentleman named Isaiah Brasure. 'Cousin Zare' as Everett called him . . . adopted a number of boys after a fashion."

> For instance, before Christmas he trained a group for a minstrel show and they spent the holidays at Chincoteague Island, where they were heartily welcomed by the people there, who were isolated. They were supposed to have given one show and a repeat, but a real blizzard struck the island. Cousin Zare and his boys were perfectly capable of new dialogues. They gave a new show every evening and the same people attended. It was a week to remember.

The 1890s were a time of great intellectual excitement in Baltimore Hundred and elsewhere as the technological revolution seemed to hold out promise of solving every great social problem. Young men were fired up with the new ideas and Everett Johnson more than most. In 1895, he entered Delaware College at Newark, graduating with the class of 1899 as an honor student. Though most of the remainder of his life was spent in New Castle County, he never lost touch with his Baltimore Hundred friends. His friendship with John G. Townsend was to prove particularly important to both men in the years ahead.

The Union Republican Party waged its first sophisticated election campaign in the fall of 1898, the first election under the guidelines established by the new constitution. The new party fielded a respectable slate of candidates in Kent and Sussex Counties. Among them was a prominent Greenwood farmer named Simeon Pennewill, brother of Judge James Pennewill and a future governor. Another candidate, running for the state senate from the Fifth Senatorial District in southeastern Sussex, was Zare Brasure.

Because of new provisions contained in the 1897 constitution establishing a more equitable system of apportioning legislative districts, five senatorial seats were open in Sussex County. The constitution called for senatorial terms of four years, with three of the five Sussex County senators running in one election and the other two running in the next. To establish the proper system of staggered vacancies, two of the five senators elected in 1898 would be required to run again in 1900 after only two years in office. The persons elected to those seats in 1900, however, would serve a full four-year term. The seat for which Zare was running was one of the two-year terms. John served his friend during the campaign in a capacity which would today be called "campaign manager," though few observed such niceties in politics then. Zare was elected handily, defeating both Democratic and Regular Republican opponents. At that time the overwhelming majority of Baltimore Hundred Republicans were Union Republicans.

John's involvement in the campaign gave him his first direct experience of political life. He went to Dover as Zare's guest and participated in some of the excitement of the inauguration, seeing and being seen. More important to his own success a few years later was the chance to get to know Republicans throughout southeastern Sussex County. The Union Republicans had waged as sophisticated a campaign as the lower part of the county had ever seen and the young Selbyville businessman was an apt observer. While Addicks had provided the wherewithal to run the party in 1896 and afterward, the Union Republicans quickly developed a platform addressing real needs in lower Delaware and John supported this as well. The party became in effect a vehicle for the political liberation of downstate Republicans both from the Democrats and from the upstate Republican organization. Some people joined the party hoping to benefit materially either through anticipated patronage jobs or just by picking up some of the ample funds the tycoon distributed at election time. Most joined Addicks and Allee and their party because they were seeking what a later politician described with masterful simplicity, a "New Deal."

With the outbreak of the Spanish-American War in 1898, General Wilson departed from the Delaware political scene to resume his military career. He was appointed military governor of a Cuban province and was thus absent from the Union Republican-Regular Republican fight for several years. His departure marked the beginning of a new pragmatism among the Regular leadership. Though they still refused to compromise on the matter of U.S. senator, the Regulars now occasionally supported Union Republican candidates for other offices and vice versa. The feeling was that a Republican, whatever his factional affiliation, was preferable to a Democrat. Though the Union Republicans held more strength within the state, the Regulars then had better contacts and more influence within the national Republican Party.

All the while the Republican National Committee was keeping a close and troubled eye on what was happening in Delaware. Senator Marcus Hanna of Ohio, the nation's most powerful political boss, was particularly unsympathetic to the Regulars as the feud continued. He had more in common with Addicks than he did with Wilson or du Pont. He kept urging the two Delaware factions to enact a compromise.

In several instances the Regulars threatened to join the Democrats to defeat Addicks in a senatorial ballot. Invariably the G.O.P.'s national leadership raised a great cry of protest, fearful as they were of altering the fragile balance of power in Washington, which was now tilted toward the Republicans. Through the period from 1900 to 1902 the national leadership was slowly coming to favor the Union Republicans. Not only did they obviously represent a majority of Delaware Republicans but they tended to be considerably more reasonable.

The Regular leaders were now attacking Hanna as a sort of national version of Addicks, which did not help matters greatly. If Hanna and his greatest political creation, President William McKinley, had lived longer, the Union Republicans would likely have found themselves fully recognized as Delaware's Republican Party by 1904 at the latest, but such was not to be. After the assassination of McKinley at Buffalo in 1901 and the assumption of the presidency by Theodore Roosevelt the situation was altered nationally and locally.*

The Regular Republican leadership did not have a great deal more in common with Roosevelt than they had with Hanna (who died himself a year or so after McKinley's death). One major segment of the Union Republican Party was composed of what would soon be known as Progressives. While both Regulars and Union Republicans espoused this philosophy there were many Union Republicans, including John and Zare Brasure and their friends, who welcomed the coming

---

* *Upon hearing the tragic news of McKinley's death and learning that Roosevelt had been sworn in, Hanna lamented, "Now that damned cowboy is President of the United States!" The cowboy did not take long to cut Hanna down to size.*

of Roosevelt. To the extent that Roosevelt noticed the Delaware situation at all in the early years of his presidency, he tended to take much the same position that Hanna did and urged compromise.

The Union Republican State Committee was headed by J. Frank Allee, the man who had brought Addicks into Delaware politics. His subsequent association with his new patron had shown the former Dover jeweler a heady new

Dr. Caleb Rodney Layton
as he appeared later in life.*

world of money and power. Addicks said that he thought of Allee as a son and a political partner and by 1898 he had made him president of the Bay State Gas Company. The jewelry shop was left far behind.

Next in the party hierarchy was the prominent Georgetown physician Caleb Rodney Layton. He served as party chairman in Sussex and as one of the movement's leading public spokesmen. Dr. Layton was then the leading member of that singular Delaware Layton clan who through the nineteenth and early twentieth centuries almost always represented a conservative political philosophy composed of equal parts Jacksonian Democracy, Jeffersonian mistrust of government, Whig politics, and Sussex County cussedness. The

---

* *Photo reproduced from* History of Delaware, Past and Present *(vol. 3); ed., Wilson Lloyd Bevan; assoc. ed., E. Melvin Williams, (New York: Lewis Historical Publishing Company, Inc., 1929.)*

Laytons tended generally to feel that things had been somewhat awry at least since the death of John M. Clayton in the 1850s. Dr. Layton was a graduate of Amherst and University of Pennsylvania Medical School, a classical scholar, irascible sage, and eccentric descendent of various illustrious ancestors. He was an important intellectual force behind the Union Republican movement. That he could be in the same party with fiery young Progressives was evidence that Layton was also at heart a pragmatist. Probably the dominant theme of his political philosophy was a profound and all-abiding pride in his Sussex County heritage. Addicks represented for Dr. Layton a means by which his homeland could free itself from the upstate hierarchy that he so disdained, and to that end he devoted himself.

Part III:

Representative Townsend

6. The Young Businessman becomes a Legislator

By 1899, John had made enough in his timber and sawmill operations and in his early dealings in strawberries to begin buying land. To John and many others in his time and place, land had an almost mystical appeal. They had grown to manhood in the last days of the subsistence farms when families who might only see a hundred dollars of cash money in a year could live decently, if not lavishly, with a little land. It was something that had value and potential. Moreover, in the 1890s it was undervalued in the deflated economy that then prevailed.

John was a man with no hobbies in the usual sense of the word. Throughout his life he loved attending public auctions. His work, his political interests, his family life, and friendships consumed most of his time. But if there was anything left over, it went into looking at land, considering its potential and possibilities, and buying it. He had probably been building this love all his life. Though there is no evidence either way, he probably began attending public auctions and following local real estate transactions while still a boy, years before he actually bought any land.

His first transactions, which were not legally recorded, involved the purchase of timber rights. Frequently, however, when one bought the timber standing on a piece of land, one had to buy the ground along with it. The owners did not want to get stuck having to pay the taxes on a piece of cutover land. By 1899, John had a good enough eye for timber so that he could look over a tract with a close idea of its market value. He could figure how much it would cost him to get it out of the woods and how much he could hope to make on the deal. On the fourth of April in 1899, John made his first recorded purchase of land in his native Worcester. He bought a 300-acre tract of woods near Showell from Mr. and Mrs. Joseph Vandegrift for $1,400. The land was situated on the south side of the St. Martin's River near the Showell Landing. A little over one year later he sold the same tract to Daniel Cathell for exactly what he paid for it. The timber he was able to cut, saw up, and sell in the course of that year was his profit. It is likely that he had not cut all of it and that Cathell was interested in buying it to cut the remainder himself. A 300-acre tract was enough to occupy one small logger for well over a year. Apparently John had found some other need for the $1,400 by 1900.

Just before Thanksgiving in 1899, John made the first of what were to be literally hundreds of land purchases in Sussex County. This transaction was also notable because it was the first farmland he ever bought. At a public auction at the old Clayton House Hotel at the main intersection in Dagsboro, John bought a 115-acre farm situated south of the village for $3,235, or just over $19 an acre. The land was being sold to clear an estate. With its purchase, John had officially become a farmer, or, at any rate, the owner of a farm. By the spring of 1900, he was growing strawberries on it.

In the summer of 1900, he and a partner bought two tracts of timber in the Millville area which together amounted to 118 acres of land. His partner on that transaction was former State Representative George H. Townsend of Millville. They paid $2,530 for the land. It is reasonable to assume that George Townsend put up most if not all of the purchase price and John did the work of cutting the timber and that they split the profits. George Townsend was no direct relative to

John. He was a member of the northern Baltimore Hundred clan of Townsends which, though descended from the same forebears, had settled in that area in the eighteenth century.

George Townsend was well established in business in Millville where he was a partner in a sawmill with Elisha C. Dukes. He also owned part interest in Duke's schooner, the *Lem Lemita*. Dukes was a Democrat and followed George Townsend in the legislature, serving from 1897 to 1899. He was the sole owner of the *Ethel Dukes*, which had been built at Walter's Bluff on the Indian River, and of several other vessels. The *Lem Lemita* was larger than most vessels on the river and had been built by Lemuel Showell at Shingle Landing on Worcester County's St. Martin's River. Her name was a combination of that of her builder and his daughter Lemeta. The vessel proved too large to navigate successfully in the St. Martin's, so Showell sold her to Dukes and Townsend. They used the ship in the Indian River to carry box boards cut at their Millville, Delaware, sawmill across the Delaware Bay to a glass factory in Millville, New Jersey, where they were used in the manufacture of shipping crates. The vessel carried a crew of four men including a cook, who was paid five dollars a month in wages. The owners were finally forced to sell the ship to Frank Maull of Lewes because she also drew too much water for White's Creek, a tributary of the Indian River where Dukes's wharf was located. If a ship drew more than four or five feet, she was no good to the local men. This problem placed the Baltimore Hundred economy even more at the mercy of the railroads. They had water, but it was so shallow and the inlet so treacherous that only small vessels could navigate it, and small vessels did not give local merchants and businessmen enough of an edge to compete with the railroad.

George Townsend was also a Union Republican. He had served in the state house of representatives in the 1895-1897 session and was considerably older than John. The fact that John was in partnership with him shows that even in 1900 he was becoming accepted by the area's leading businessmen as an equal. A picture of his financial situation in that year is revealing of the position of the young man who was about to embark on a political career.

According to the Sussex County assessment records for that period, John's property holdings in the county just after his joint purchase in partnership with George Townsend amounted to about $5,500 in assessed value, or about $11,000 in real value. His Worcester County holdings are not, of course, included here; nor are any cash assets. Adding in these factors, it is possible to estimate that he was worth somewhere in the range of $15,000 to $20,000 in 1900, which was a very respectable net worth indeed for a young man of twenty-nine in Baltimore Hundred. Among his assessed property that year were fourteen mules; two horses, one of which was a mare; and one milk cow.

Early in 1902, John and several of his Selbyville friends, including Zare Brasure, embarked on a new and very promising business venture. They became the incorporators of the Selbyville Telephone Company, which was capitalized at $5,000. This was a new departure for John. Up to that time he had been involved in numerous partnerships but never in a formal corporation. The venture marked a progressive new direction for the town of Selbyville as well. The first telephones had arrived in southern Delaware only a few years before. That same year the Diamond State Telephone Company listed six persons in the Georgetown section of its directory, which included in one book of no great size all telephone customers on the entire Delmarva Peninsula, southern New Jersey, and portions of southeastern Pennsylvania. Most telephones in the area, and they were few and far between, were in hotels or in the offices of the larger mercantile establishments and the more prosperous law firms in the county seat. The establishment of a telephone company in a town like Selbyville was a very ambitious undertaking indeed.

It is revealing of John's character that the first of many corporate ventures in which he was to involve himself in the next sixty years was one that promised to improve the quality of life in the community and one which relatively few men in the town then felt was a reasonable risk. John's progressive instincts were closely tied to his business instincts. Even as early as 1902, he felt that progress was inevitable, that it was desirable, and that when it arrived it would come in the form of a profit-making enterprise that also benefited the community as a whole. He already possessed the brand of free-enterprise progressivism that was the basis of his entire career.

The new company was established in a small building on the south side of Church Street. It was outfitted with a small switchboard operated by the first employee of the firm, Miss Roxie Dukes, a relative of Zare Brasure. Among the few pioneering customers were, of course, the incorporators. Over the years the business grew and in due course it was bought by the growing public monopoly, the Diamond State Telephone Company, which slowly during the first decades of the new century consolidated its control over all telephone networks in the state. While the Selbyville telephone company was by no means a great moneymaker for its owners, they ultimately sold it for a small return on their investment. More importantly, they brought telephone service to Selbyville years before the town would otherwise have had it.

In the early summer of 1902, John embarked on another venture that was to have far-reaching consequences–he decided to run for the state house of representatives from Baltimore Hundred.

He recalled in later years that Zare Brasure was the man who talked him into running, although it is unlikely that Zare had to talk too hard. John's interest in politics had been growing steadily for several years, and when Zare and the other Union Republican leaders in the hundred began to look for a candidate that spring, John Townsend was a name that came naturally to mind.

His formal nomination came at a gathering of Sussex County Union Republicans in Georgetown on Tuesday, August 19. The party leadership, including Addicks, Allee, and Dr. Layton, were in attendance. Georgetown physician and pharmacist Dr. James Chipman chaired the gathering. Others nominated were Simeon S. Pennewill of Greenwood, a candidate for the state senate; Oliver A. Newton of Bridgeville; and, for some of the county's ten seats in the state house of representatives, Dagsboro lumberman Rufus D. Lingo; Frank Lawson of Millsboro; former sheriff Thomas R. Purnell of Milton; and the Lewes pilot Harry V. Lyons. Dr. Layton's son Daniel, a Georgetown lawyer, was the candidate for county register of wills.

Two weeks later the party faithful gathered at their state convention in Dover to nominate the state ticket. The sessions were held in the third-floor meeting room of the Kent County Courthouse facing the Green. Between the working sessions the crowd moved up to the Hotel Richardson three blocks north along State Street, where the Dover Philharmonic Band was assembled on the curving verandah. Allee was reelected party chairman and William D. Denney of New Castle was elected secretary. In his remarks to the group, Addicks praised William Michael Byrne, the party's congressional nominee, and added, "we have a candidate who will give us a whirling campaign, and when we get through we will forgive our enemies," an obvious rebuke of the Addicks-hating Regular leaders. In his acceptance speech, Byrne presented interesting and possibly accurate statistics indicating that the Union Republicans controlled some 90 percent of all Republican strength in Kent and Sussex Counties. A few weeks later the Democratic *Delaware Pilot* estimated more conservatively that the party controlled 75 percent of the downstate Republican vote.

The convention adopted a platform which by Delaware standards was classically progressive. In addition to the obligatory honest government and good roads, they favored improved on-the-job safety for workingmen, servicemen's pensions, strengthened federal antitrust laws, strengthened interstate commerce regulations, fixed salaries for elected county officials instead of the old system of having them draw their salaries from fees collected, and "permanent registration of voters with ample time before elections to correct and amend registration lists." All in all, it was a workable platform that included something for everyone from Civil War veterans to disgruntled Sussex County farmers.

With that and a few closing ceremonies, the delegates adjourned and went home. As they made their way down Loockerman Street in a long procession toward the railroad station they were led by the Philharmonic Band playing such rousing favorites as "Hail, Hail, the Gang's All Here" and "There'll Be a Hot Time in the Old Town Tonight." And John embarked for Selbyville, a full-fledged political candidate.

He was campaigning for the seat held by incumbent Daniel J. Long, a Democrat, who was not seeking reelection. It was the same seat held by his lumber partner, George H. Townsend, from 1895 to 1897, and later by Elisha Dukes. He had nearly a month to campaign before the Democrats nominated a candidate to oppose him, Dr. James Martin of Selbyville. On October 7, the Regular Republicans also nominated a candidate for the seventh district seat, Roxana merchant, Robert Wilgus. By 1902, the Regulars were routinely nominating various Union Republicans to certain county posts and the Union Republicans were doing likewise with some Regular Republicans. So it was that John's Union Republican friend, George Townsend, was the Regular Republican candidate for county treasurer and Dr. Layton's son, Daniel, was the Regular and Union Republican candidate for register of wills.

Of John's two opponents, Martin was the more formidable because there was a strong Democratic hierarchy in Selbyville and elsewhere in the hundred. Martin was a medical doctor who also owned and operated a pharmacy, a common practice in those times. Like Townsend, he was a relatively new arrival, having moved to town in 1890. Wilgus was a member of an old Baltimore Hundred family who had been storekeepers in the central part of the hundred for generations, but as a Regular he was running under a handicap in 1902. The Regulars and Democrats were both so hard pressed that they worked out at least one deal.

The Democrats agreed to pull out their candidates for representative in Northwest Fork and Cedar Creek Hundreds, both heavily Republican, and support the Regular candidates instead. In return, the Regulars agreed to keep their full county ticket in the field even though for many Regular candidates it was an exercise in futility. This maneuver, the Democrats hoped, would split the Republican vote enough to give them a few extra representative seats or county offices.

The average Sussex County voter in 1902 was not giving much thought to such machinations, nor, for that matter, was he thinking of the by now long-standing feud between Addicks and Henry du Pont. Most Sussex Countians would have accepted either man readily enough. What they were thinking about was which of the candidates running for representative would work the hardest and bring home to his district the most benefits from Dover. By that measure, John Townsend was the clear favorite in Baltimore Hundred over Martin and Wilgus. The people had seen at close hand his enterprising spirit and his interest in the economic betterment of the area.

On Election Day, John won handily in his three-way fight. The deal between the Democrats and the Regulars amounted to little in the end. The Democrats won four representative seats in heavily Democratic hundreds in western Sussex and in Lewes and Rehoboth Hundred on the eastern side of the county. The Union Republicans took the other six seats. The Regulars won nothing. Of the three state senate seats at issue, the Union Republicans took two and the Democrats one. In Sussex County in 1902, the Regular Republican Party had almost become an abstract concept.

Another big winner in the November election was Henry A. Houston of Millsboro, the Democratic candidate for U.S. Congress and Will White's business partner in Houston-White Company. Houston had soundly defeated both Republican candidates for the office, illustrating anew that in statewide races the two Republican factions could keep each other from winning but could not win themselves. Houston won with nearly fifteen thousand votes while the total Republican vote of both factions added up to just nineteen thousand.

Two months after his victory, John travelled to Dover for the opening of the General Assembly. In those days in Delaware and in most other states a legislative session lasted only about three to four months every other year. Although John would serve until the next election in 1904, the great bulk of his service as a representative took place during those few months in the late winter and spring of 1903.*

---

* *Such short sessions are still the case in Texas, where the state legislature meets for 147 days every 2 years. One local wag said that many Texans would greatly prefer a system in which the legislature meets 2 days every 147 years.*

Special sessions were rare and without the great machinery of state government that developed in later years it was not essential that legislators meet more than once every two years. When they were in session the pace was frantic, especially in sessions such as that of 1903 when it was necessary to elect one or two U.S. senators.

Most members of the General Assembly boarded in Dover at least part of the time during the session, though with railroad passenger service through much of the state they all got home at frequent intervals. John spent most nights at home in those months both because of his diverse business affairs and because Jennie was expecting another baby. He had always been an early riser and was up and going most mornings by five thirty, so he had ample time to get some work done at home and get to Dover in time for the day's session after lunch. When he did stay over in Dover on nights when the session ran late or when he had committee meetings early the next morning, he probably stayed at the old Capitol Hotel on the Green. Though older and not as stylish as the larger Hotel Richardson two blocks away, it was cheaper and was just a short walk from the old State House which sat at the east end of the Green.

On Tuesday, January 6, 1903, John Townsend joined his fellow legislators in the old gas-lit house chamber of the State House situated along the east end of the Dover Green. That once elegant eighteenth-century building was then nearing its low point. In the late 1870s it had been drastically altered inside and out. The most obvious change from its original Georgian plan was an abominable mansard roof and clock-tower that a well-meaning Democratic legislature had seen fit to fund in the late 1870s. Their attitude about the desecration of the old building is easier to understand when one considers the comment of another Delaware legislator when the General Assembly was preparing to build another large and imposing edifice as a state office building in the early 1960s, this one to be named in honor of John G. Townsend Jr. When told that the building would be of Georgian design, the somewhat irate senator said, "Who is this fellow, George, anyway? He has his hand in just about everything around here."

But on that day in 1903, the newly elected Union Republican majority in the legislature had much more to worry about than the roof style of the venerable old State House in which they met. Their biggest problem was the still unresolved question of the two unfilled U.S. Senate vacancies thoughtfully left to them by the 1901 session, which had proved unable to come to grips with the matter. By January of 1903, the state had been wholly without representation in the United States Senate for nearly two years and for several years before that it had been represented by only one senator in Washington. By now, everyone–journalists, national political leaders, and voters–was clamoring for some resolution of the Addicks-du Pont impasse.

As the General Assembly went about organizing itself, the upcoming joint session was, of course, on everyone's mind, but there was also the routine business of the state to see to. The Union Republicans, with a clear majority in the house, elected one of their own men, Henry S. Anthony, Speaker of the House. The Regulars had a slight majority in the senate, though not in the joint session. They were able, therefore, to name the Regular, Harry C. Ellison of Summit Bridge, as senate president pro tempore.

The Union Republicans named the bulk of the legislative per diem staff appointees for the session. Only one Regular, Edward B. Hazzard of Milton, got a job as reading clerk of the senate. Among the Union Republican appointees was young Asa Bennett of Dagsboro Hundred, a college student in Maryland at the time, who was named enrolling clerk of the senate.

Townsend's place in the organization of the house shows that, although a novice representative, his talents were already recognized. Speaker Anthony named him one of two tellers of the house. In those days before such functions as majority leader and majority whip had been created, the office of teller was one of only two leadership positions in the house in addition to that of Speaker. He was also appointed to the following committees: revenue and taxation, appropriations, public highways, municipal corporations, elections, and revised statutes. On the important appropriations committee, he served with his fellow Sussex County Union Republican Oliver A. Newton of Bridgeville. On revenue and taxation, his fellow Sussex Countians included Rufus Lingo of Dagsboro, also a Union Republican, and Democrat Samuel J. Lowe of Delmar.

As a gregarious and personable young man, John was now in a position to form acquaintances and friendships that were to be of great importance to him for the rest of his life. By 1902, the Union Republican-Regular Republican schism was of long enough duration to be considered an almost normal state of affairs. Though the party leaders still occasionally rose to the heights of vituperative eloquence in tearing down one another, the rank-and-file members had become generally philosophical about it all. That is, a Regular could not be elected in Baltimore or Northwest Fork Hundred; a Union Republican could not be elected in Brandywine or Christiana Hundred. But all were still Republicans and as Republicans they could be friends even if they voted against each other in the joint sessions. This was also true in relations between the Republicans and Democrats, and John made many good Democratic friends in those months in Dover.

In the days that followed the opening session, John and his colleagues considered a great variety of pending legislation, most of which was of no great importance. They passed bills requiring the licensing of chiropodists and allowing illegitimate children to be the legal heirs of their mothers. They raised the salaries of the state's three county superintendents of schools from $1,000 to $1,200 per annum. They acted quickly on a bill to exempt the family Bible, personal wearing apparel, and mechanics' tools from attachment for debt. They passed a bill to prohibit the practice of mutilating horses by docking their tails to make them more stylish in appearance. The legislators passed a bill abolishing the ancient requirement that a witness kiss the Bible when taking an oath. Henceforth it was sufficient simply to rest one's right hand on the book. They authorized an increase in pay for the ten Sussex County Levy Court Commissioners.

A bill was passed authorizing the Town of Millsboro to borrow $20,000 for street repairs, and another bill allowed construction of a new oyster-shell road in Broad Creek Hundred. Representative Newton introduced a bill to appropriate $25,000 a year for a period of six years to pay for improvements to the state's notoriously bad public roads.

For years under the Democrats the railroads had routinely doled out free passes to legislators as a gesture of goodwill. When the Republicans at last gained control of the legislature in the 1890s they did away with this benefit. Henceforth, the only public officials authorized to hold free passes were judges, who, it was assumed, were above any temptation to look favorably on the railroads simply because of such paltry perquisites. When, in the last week of January, one particularly dense representative made the mistake of introducing a bill to give free railroad transportation to all state, county, city, and town officials, the newspapers had a field day. "You wouldn't find a vacant seat on any train in the state," roared the *Delaware Pilot*. "Why, Robbins [a tiny whistle stop north of Georgetown] would be incorporated in twenty minutes after the bill was passed." Not only did the legislators not approve the bill, but Zare Brasure introduced in the senate and shepherded through to passage another bill to deprive even the judges of their passes.

The new state hospital for the insane at Farnhurst was nearing completion that spring and the legislature approved an appropriation of $114,000 in state funds to equip it. Nearly all the members of the General Assembly, Townsend included, travelled up to New Castle County to inspect the new facility. The legislators informed the papers that they were quite favorably impressed by what they saw. With this new institution in mind, they returned to Dover, where they soon found it necessary to appropriate additional state moneys to pay for mentally-retarded Delaware youngsters to attend the Pennsylvania Training School for Feeble-Minded Children, the state having no institution of this type.

This expense started at least one member of the General Assembly thinking about the possibility of building such a training school in Delaware. John thought about those retarded children he himself had seen in southern Delaware who would never be able to attend such a facility even with state help unless there was one available closer to home. He felt deeply enough about the experience to go home and discuss it with Jennie. It is likely that the couple themselves knew of, or may even have been related to, families who bore the burden of "feeble mindedness," because neither John nor Jennie forgot the matter. When, years later, they had a chance to do something about it, they did.

John introduced several pieces of legislation himself. The first of these, which was given the designation House Bill 71, was "An Act prohibiting the manufacture and sale of cigarettes, cigarette paper, and cigarette tobacco within this state." The impetus for this somewhat puzzling measure is not entirely certain, but it may have had something to do with the fact that Baltimore Hundred was a strong Methodist area and the staunch Methodists of the day held cigarette smoking to be an evil closely akin to drinking, dancing, and playing cards. John, himself an occasional cigar smoker, was a strong Methodist.* He may have wished to use his status as a representative to do a service for the church by furthering the cause of clean living. Surprisingly, the bill passed with little difficulty.

Representative Townsend introduced another bill with the ponderous title "An Act to Appropriate Money for the Repayment to Sussex County of the Sum Paid to the State Treasurer by the County Treasurer of Sussex County from the Funds Arising Under an Act Entitled, 'An Act to Equalize Taxation for State and County Purposes' (Chap. 381, Vol. 20, Laws of Delaware) and Acts Amendatory Thereof." Every legislator must perform this type of mundane chore scores of times during his career, boring but necessary. John was as dutiful about it as most other lawmakers, and that was all.

Probably the most important set of bills he introduced during the session were two pioneering pieces of legislation to

---

* *Regarding John's own cigar smoking, his son, Preston, recalled that his father had a fondness for fine Havanas. He continued smoking them regularly until one day many years later, after the conclusion of his term as governor, when he was in Philadelphia on business. As he walked down the street he was approached by an obviously downtrodden man, who told him that he was out of work and needed enough money to buy a cup of coffee. John gave him a dime. As he stood there reflecting on the man's sad tale, watching him shuffle off down the street and puffing on his fancy cigar, he thought, "here is a man who doesn't have enough money for a cup of coffee and I'm smoking a cigar that cost five times as much as I gave him." He threw down the cigar and never smoked again [Interview with Preston C. Townsend, 1978].*

establish much needed regulatory procedures. The bills were entitled acts to "regulate the sale of oil, petroleum, or burning fluid in the State of Delaware," and to bring about "the inspection of oil, petroleum or burning fluid in the State of Delaware." Before that time the state government had been only minimally involved in such matters, preferring to let the citizenry tend to this. The enactment of these bills helped to form the legislative basis for a whole series of later fire and safety laws and, more importantly, for the future taxation of gasoline by the state.

He also worked during those first months of 1903 as a member of the Joint Audit Committee "to audit the Secretary of State, the State Treasurer, and the State Insurance Commissioner." This phase of his duties gave him an overview of the operations of the executive branch as it was then constituted. The experience proved invaluable when, fourteen years later, he was in charge of that government.

The session was not all routine work in the State House. In addition to the trip to Farnhurst, John and his fellow legislators enjoyed some lighter moments during the session. They were invited to social events in the state capital and elsewhere. On one memorable occasion, they embarked on an inspection of the towns of Rehoboth Beach and Lewes. They gathered first in Rehoboth on Thursday afternoon, February 19, as guests of the town council. The councilmen led them on a tour of the town to see all the new growth and expansion in the community.

Late that afternoon, they travelled by train up to Lewes, where again the town officials showed them around the community before entertaining them at a banquet in the dining room of the Virden House Hotel. The Virden House then had an active winter trade consisting of Wilmingtonians and Philadelphians who came down to shoot ducks and geese on Rehoboth Bay. The hotel dining room was more than equal to the task of feeding the state legislature in style.

After beginning the banquet in the hotel parlor with a musical interlude and, as the *Delaware Pilot* put it, "funny stories," they moved into the dining room. They started off with Chincoteague oysters, celery, salted nuts, olives, and pickles and then moved into successive courses of broiled Indian River Rockfish, terrapin Delaware-style, and turkey with cranberry sauce. This, the main course, was accompanied by white potatoes, green peas, asparagus, chicken salad, and Delaware beaten biscuit. For dessert they were served ice cream and cake, fruit, nuts, cheese, raisins, and candy. The meal was washed down by "G.H. Mumm's Extra Dry," and followed by coffee and cigars. At the conclusion of this substantial feast, the group was addressed by former U.S. Senator Richard Kenney of Dover, by former Governor Ebe Tunnell, Lewes's leading citizen, and by Colonel Theodore Townsend of Milford, publisher of the *Milford Chronicle* and highly-placed member of the Delaware Militia, who spoke on the current state of readiness of that organization. It is likely that several, if not all, of the speakers had a largely somnolent audience.

In the midst of these duties Representative Townsend and his fellow members of the house and senate were meeting almost daily in joint session in the house chamber to consider various candidates for the two U.S. Senate seats. Once more, the two leading candidates were Addicks and du Pont. Other names under consideration included Democrat Willard Saulsbury (the younger) and several Regulars. At first, the 1903 session seemed to be a repeat of that of 1901. In December, the *Union Republican* had confidently predicted that "J. Edward Addicks will be elected Senator by the Legislature that is to meet in Dover next month and it may not take more than one ballot to do it, either." But such was not to be.

The Regulars were just as obstinate as ever in their refusal to accept Addicks; but there were several changes in the 1903 session that led the Union Republicans to take the Regular rigidity more seriously than in the past. The most important thing was the clear political necessity for electing two senators regardless of who they were. Then, in the February 7, 14, and 21 issues of the prominent national journal, *The Outlook*, there appeared a three-part account of Addicks's political career in Delaware entitled "Holding Up A State." It was written by the well-known muckraker George Kennan (great-uncle of the prominent diplomat and author of the same name), who had spent several weeks in Delaware following the November election gathering facts and somewhat scandalous assertions about Addicks. Kennan had been a guest in the home of Robert G. Houston in Georgetown while writing the piece.

He painted a picture of Addicks as a robber baron in the style of Jay Gould, and as a political manipulator in the style of Senator Marcus A. Hanna, the great Republican kingpin who had brought about the election of President William McKinley and his own appointment to a Senate seat from Ohio. While many of Kennan's assertions of voting irregularities in Kent and Sussex Counties were undoubtedly true, his articles also contained exaggerations and, more significantly, were characterized by a curious tunnel vision. Kennan wrote nothing about the even more scandalous behavior of the Democrats in the campaign of 1896 and earlier. He portrayed the Regulars as a group of high-minded idealists and crusaders for morality and truth in politics. This last assertion might have been due to the character of his host, Houston, who, more than most Regular leaders, did in fact personify that image. But the narrow attitude of the articles is at least partly explained by the fact that the publisher of *The Outlook*, Lyman Abbott, was both a close friend of the Regular leader, General James H. Wilson, and a leader

of the anti-Hanna wing of the Republican Party. Wilson had been
entreating Abbott for years to assist the Regulars in their fight against
Addicks. That assistance finally came in the form of the Kennan article,
which appeared, conveniently, at the very moment the Delaware
General Assembly was meeting to elect two senators.

It is difficult to escape the conclusion that "Holding Up A
State" was at least in part a masterful political gambit designed to
destroy Addicks nationally just at the time when he seemed to have
reached his point of greatest power in Delaware. Immediately after it
appeared, the Regular leaders had hundreds of offprints of the article
prepared and distributed to Republican leaders around the country.
A year and a half later, when the Republican National Committee's
credentials committee was meeting to determine which of Delaware's
two Republican delegations should be seated at the 1904 Republican
National Convention, copies of the article were given to each member
of the committee in advance in an effort to sway them in favor of the
Regulars.

Whatever its motivation and however unfair it was to the Union
Republican Party, the Kennan exposé had a major influence on the
General Assembly's joint session. That influence was compounded
by some as yet hazy and unclear rumors to the effect that Addicks
was in trouble in his business dealings. Some years before, he had
made J. Frank Allee president of the Bay State Gas Company, a
largely honorary position since Addicks continued to manage the day-
to-day operations of the firm and his other interests. Yet Allee was
active enough in the company to be aware that some of Bay State's
minority stockholders had begun to question Addicks's management.
He knew also that they were considering legal action against the gas
magnate to recover assets which they believed had been diverted
illegally to various of Addicks's other ventures.

The third matter to figure in the considerations of the legislators was related to the recent dramatic changes which had occurred in the power structure of the preeminent Wilmington firm of black powder manufacturers, E.I. du Pont de Nemours and Co. In January 1902, Eugene du Pont, president of the family-owned firm, had died. Though several other members of the du Pont clan were associated with the company (Colonel Henry A. du Pont foremost among them), none wished to take over the presidency. The inclination of most older family members with a say in the matter was to sell the company outright and divide the profits among the various shareholders, each of whom could then turn his attentions to activities more appealing to him. Thirty-seven-year-old Alfred I. du Pont, an engineer who had earlier purchased 10 percent ownership in the family firm, had other thoughts on the subject. He did not wish to see the venerable old industrial concern sold to outsiders, both because of family tradition and because he saw a potential for a much greater and more extensive chemical business with the addition of a little modern management. He approached the other owners with a proposition to buy the company and then, approval in hand, went to two of his cousins, Pierre S. and T. Coleman du Pont. Pierre was the youngest of the three, being only thirty at the time. Coleman, a member of a branch of the family that had settled in Louisville, Kentucky, in the 1860s, was a few months older than Alfred. All three were alumni of the Massachusetts Institute of Technology, and all, it was already evident, were men of impressive vision, ability, and business acumen.

Since, in 1900, Coleman du Pont was both the wealthiest of the three and the most experienced in the management of major industrial enterprises, he became president of the new firm created to buy out the old company. Alfred was named vice-president. Pierre became treasurer, and another cousin, Alexis I. du Pont was named

U. S. Senator T. Coleman duPont, Wilmington

"General" T. Coleman duPont
from a 1920 sketch by the popular
Delaware cartoonist George T.
("Gee Tee") Maxwell*

secretary. Under the terms of the sale arrangement approved by the old owners, the new owners took over management of the company in March of 1902. The new president of the company, Coleman du Pont, found enough free time early in 1903 to turn his attentions to Colonel du Pont's political difficulties in Dover. Before long he had become a major factor in what was to become the beginning of the end for J. Edward Addicks.

In examining the careers of Colonel Henry du Pont and those of his younger kinsmen, Coleman, Pierre, and Alfred, it is evident that the Colonel was a man of the old century while his cousins were just as definitely members of the new age in America. Where Henry was the "lord of the manor," surrounded with faithful family retainers of many years standing, conducting his business and political lives as his father and grandfather before him might have done, the younger men were preparing to move the family company into the twentieth century. They were fully prepared to operate in a business world in which J.P. Morgan was creating the giant U.S. Steel, and John D. Rockefeller Sr. had achieved nearly total control of the multitiered oil industry. They were proud of the

---

* *This sketch and those reproduced on pages 118, 327 and 340 are reproduced from a copy of* The Blue Hen's Chicks in Caricature, Sketches and Captions *by Gee Tee Maxwell, which was published in 1921 in collaboration with the Delaware State News, Dover, and was printed by the Kells Press, Newark (courtesy of Mrs. Lyla T. Savoy).*

family's heritage as the first and greatest of American powder makers, and of their great-grandfather's eminence in revolutionary France and his friendships with the great lights of the Age of the Enlightenment. But they were not of a mind to rest on the family laurels.

Of the three younger men, Coleman was the most obviously aggressive and ambitious, traits which may have stemmed in part from his

Pierre S. duPont as a young man
(courtesy of the Delaware Public Archives).

upbringing away from the old du Pont domains on the Brandywine. His father and bachelor uncle had struck out on their own and gone west in the mid-nineteenth century in search of greater opportunities which they felt were opening up in the upper south with its largely unexploited coal and iron resources. By the time Coleman was a young man in the early 1880s, his branch of the family owned a successful street railway company in Louisville and lucrative coal and iron mining interests elsewhere in Kentucky. Upon his return from M.I.T., where he had studied mining engineering, du Pont mastered the field of surveying and then went to work as a laborer in the family mines, earning fifteen dollars a month and board. He had soon become a proficient miner and blacksmith and had mastered most other occupations related to the business. Though he soon became superintendent of the mines, he was not the typical boss's son doing token service on the bottom before moving into a soft office job. He

Alfred L duPont, Wilmington
Nemours

Alfred I. duPont
from a 1920 Maxwell sketch
(courtesy of Mrs. Lyla T. Savoy).

found that he enjoyed hard physical labor and liked the men who made their livings doing it. Coleman developed a rapport with these Kentucky miners that was one of the keys to his later success both in business and in politics. Even as a young man, he was a commanding figure. Six feet four inches tall, heavyset, and handsome, with a fine sense of humor and an easy charm, he was well suited to the multiple careers he pursued.

While managing the family's mining operations, Coleman also became the Kentucky agent for DuPont Powder, and began an industrial engineering and construction firm. He and his partner specialized in mine construction and surveying, and then branched out into railroad building and the construction of waterworks and reservoirs. He turned his attention next to the establishment of an industrial hardware business.

When all these various endeavors were functioning smoothly, du Pont moved his base of operations to the coal fields of Pennsylvania. In 1889, he had married Alice du Pont of the Delaware clan, daughter of the attorney Victor du Pont Jr. and Coleman's third cousin. Following their marriage the couple moved to Johnstown, Pennsylvania, where the young man took a job as manager of a steel manufacturing company. In the next five years, he bought and sold street railways, manufactured railroad cars and machinery, developed a line of refrigeration equipment, and invested heavily in coal mining operations in Kentucky and elsewhere. By 1900, he had become both a leading industrialist and a multimillionaire.

Coleman and his equally resourceful cousin Pierre both saw themselves in later life as self-made men. To a large extent this image is accurate. Though they had some access to the considerable resources and connections of their family to use as steppingstones to success, both men had built great fortunes largely through their own talents and hard work without depending on direct financial backing from their wealthy relations. Though Pierre du Pont had begun his business career working for the family firm, he had left the business by 1900 to forge his own career in the West. Under the management of the company as it existed in the 1890s, many younger members of the family concluded that they would find greater opportunities elsewhere. Events were to bring Coleman and Pierre back to Delaware, where they would play a greater role in determining the state's destiny than any du Ponts before them.

In 1900, Coleman du Pont's far-flung enterprises had become well enough established that he felt he could give up the day-to-day management and give in to his and his wife's desire to move to Delaware. His ostensible reason for doing so was the establishment of a new button-manufacturing company in Wilmington, but he later admitted that this had only been an excuse. His motivations were doubtlessly complex and involved both family ties and a love for Delaware that he had cherished since his youthful visits with his grandparents. It is reasonable to assume, however, that one factor in his thinking was a desire to involve himself in politics. In this sense he bore some superficial resemblance to Addicks. Delaware, with its small size and political makeup, was indeed a tempting target for a man of resources and political ambitions. Unlike Addicks, however, Coleman had both the background and the ready-made political base from which to operate.

The 1903 joint sessions started out like all the others in the years since Addicks first ran for senator in 1894. The results of ballot after ballot were indecisive. Addicks could not get enough votes to emerge the clear victor in spite of the hopeful predictions in the Georgetown *Union Republican* a few weeks earlier. No Regular candidate could get enough votes to win either. In addition to such names as Colonel du Pont and Anthony Higgins, the Regulars also suggested that of T. Coleman du Pont. Though the new company president did not have much of a chance to win, it is revealing that his name was already being considered only three years after his permanent move to the state.

On the face of it, things were much the same as before except for a few new faces, but that was only on the surface. Behind the scenes, the years-old impasse was on the verge of breaking up. As "Holding Up A State" came out in successive issues of *The Outlook* during February, the Regulars were coming closer and closer to a deal with the Democrats, with whose help they had enough votes to elect a senator without the Union Republicans. By this time no one in the Regular camp seems to have been greatly concerned whether the deal meant the election of a Democratic senator as long as Addicks was beaten. This new pragmatism among the Regular leaders may well have had something to do with the entrance of Coleman du Pont into the fray. The balloting became so intense that one Wilmington Democrat, Representative William M. Connelly, finding himself stuck in the city with no regularly scheduled train to Dover as one of the ballots neared, chartered a special train at a cost of $167 to make certain he would reach the State House in time. He told reporters he did it so that no one could accuse him of missing a vote on purpose.

Finally, during the last weekend of February, a Regular leader came to Allee and Layton and issued an ultimatum. Unless they could talk Addicks into withdrawing by the session of Monday, March 2, and throwing his support to any other Union Republican for one of the two seats and to a Regular for the other, the Regulars were joining forces with the Democrats. For Allee and Layton this was enough. They paid a visit to Addicks at his office and laid their cards on the table. He had to withdraw if he was to retain any political power in the state. Addicks was at this time sixty-four years old. The elusive Senate seat had seemed so near as the year 1903 had dawned, and now it seemed to be slipping away once more. He refused. Layton at his most eloquent presented the matter as a civic duty. At last Addicks agreed to back his protegé, J. Frank Allee, for one of the seats. Since there were two seats and one was for a full six years while the other had only two years to run, the Union Republicans could at least derive some sense of victory by electing Allee to the six-year seat.

The following Monday, Allee was duly elected to the United States Senate. The legislators elected the Regular, Dr. L. Heisler Ball, to the short term. This development must have grated mightily on Addicks, who loathed Ball, the unsuccessful Regular congressional candidate in the 1902 campaign and one of the Union Republican leader's most virulent critics, but he remained outwardly philosophical. As a small consolation, Governor John Hunn appointed Addicks a trustee of Delaware College in Newark. He continued to occupy a central position in Republican politics for several more years, at least in the eyes of the press and the public, but no less an authority than Dr. Layton later marked Addicks's downfall from March 2, 1903.

The legislative session lasted another two weeks, but after the senatorial election it was all anticlimax for most members. For Townsend the most important matter of official business was yet to be done. It was a perfectly routine matter–the chartering of a new bank for Selbyville to be known as the Baltimore Trust Company.

Part IV:

Commerce and Construction

7. Banking and Business

During the second week of March 1903, the General Assembly approved the charter of a new bank to be located in Selbyville and to be known as the Baltimore Trust Company. The charter was duly approved by Governor John Hunn. The constitution of 1897 had removed the requirement for the legislature to approve every new corporate charter, but it was still necessary in the case of banks. In 1903, banks were still scarce in Sussex County. Before the new state corporation law of 1899, they had been almost nonexistent except for the Farmers Bank of the State of Delaware in Georgetown.

Representative Townsend refrained from voting on the charter because he was to be the president of the new bank. The vice-president was Timothy E. Townsend of Sandy Landing near the village of Blackwater in northern Baltimore Hundred. Like George Townsend, Timothy was part of the old Baltimore Hundred branch of the family and was a son of old Captain Ebe Townsend, a prosperous merchant and sea captain who had centered his activities at Townsend's Landing near the mouth of Vine's Creek. Timothy Townsend was also the man who would follow John in the house of representatives. The secretary-treasurer was Isaiah W. Long of Selbyville, a lumberman, merchant and partner in the new Selbyville Telephone Company. Isaiah J. Brasure and George H. Townsend, John's political mentors and partners in various enterprises, were the directors.

Of the initial capitalization of $5,000, John put up the largest share, but each of the others contributed some part of the to-

Baltimore Trust Company: *The second office of the Baltimore Trust Company in Selbyville, shown here, stood at the northwest corner of Church & Main Streets. This building was later destroyed in the disasterous downtown fire of 1916. The third bank building, erected just to the west, is now a clothing store. The bank is now housed in its fifth building near the same site as this structure (Photo courtesy of Dorothy W. Pepper).*

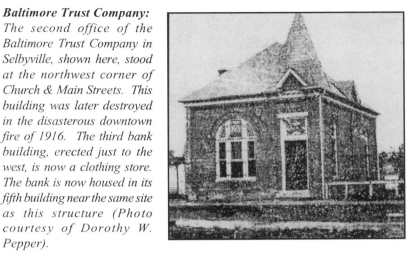

tal. By this time Townsend had been a private banker on a limited scale in the area around Selbyville for several years, loaning out money at interest for short periods of time. He had been a member of the bank board in Georgetown for two years except for the period between his election to the General Assembly in November 1902 and April of 1903. He had resigned before the start of the 1903 session, probably to avoid any conflict of interest between his directorship and his duties as representative. Several weeks after the new bank charter was approved, Governor Hunn reappointed him to the Farmers Bank board. That five-month period was the only gap in his directorship for more than fifty years after 1901. But he was growing increasingly knowledgeable about banking by 1903 and soon showed his affinity for the profession in his organization of the new bank.

Banking was only one of many undertakings which were preoccupying John at that time, however. He was still very much involved with the lumber business, but perhaps his greatest interest at the time was the growing, buying and selling of strawberries. By 1903 and 1904, strawberries were becoming big business in southern Delaware and Worcester County, Maryland. Selbyville, near the center of the growing area, had already established itself as a leading shipping point. The Wilmington *Morning News* commented on this fact in its issue of Wednesday, June 1, 1904, in an article written by the Georgetown correspondent:

> Before noon today considerably more than half a hundred carloads of strawberries passed through here enroute to the city markets. Of that number, 26 carloads were shipped from Selbyville, the principal fruit-growing station of the Delaware, Maryland, and Virginia Branch of the Pennsylvania System.
> Berries at the Georgetown Station sold this morning as low as $1.00 per crate of 32 quarts, barely paying the owner for the cost of the crate, the picking, and conveying the fruit to market. It was learned here that 42 carloads of berries were shipped from Bridgeville yesterday.

But that was still early in the season and the prices were improving as other crops further south were running out. By the morning of June 5, the *Morning News* was reporting that "growers about Georgetown say there is profit at four cents a quart" and added further that:

> Long trains of freight cars loaded with strawberries and ice, the berries enroute for Boston and Canadian markets, pass through here [Georgetown] going northward every day from Selbyville and Frankford. The strawberry season is at the height there and great armies of pickers invade the red-dotted patches about three o'clock every morning, starting to pick by lantern light and continuing until they are almost exhausted. The number of pickers continues inadequate to the supply.

Strawberry brokers: *A group of leading strawberry brokers is assembled near the auction block in Selbyville during the boom days of the strawberry business, about 1912. Mr. Levin Holloway, left, displays a thirty-two-quart crate of prime berries. The only identifiable member of the Townsend family in the photo is Jack, eighth from left, behind man in large white hat (photo courtesy of Dorothy Williams Pepper).*

Rival buyers and shippers vie with each other after every load that arrives at Frankford, Selbyville, and Georgetown; and the farmers keep hurrying them in upon low platform wagons under which fine springs work to protect the delicate fruit from jostling.

At Selbyville the Boston and New York buyers have erected frame tents, in which they live and in front of which they outbid each other for the possession of the hundreds of wagonloads arriving with the sunrise and continuing all day. A wagonload of fancy berries calls forth most spirited bidding. Fine berries sold Wednesday at low prices but the hundreds of farmers who are growing them almost exclusively now see large profits in them at four cents a quart.

In the other major shipping center for berries, Bridgeville, local growers got a total of $30,000 for the forty-two carloads of berries shipped out the following Monday. Of this amount, the farmers paid out $6,000 for the cost of the migrant laborers to pick the fruit and for crates and other expenses. The rest was profit. Bridgeville was said

A view of Main Street, Selbyville, about 1910 (Lyla T. Savoy collection).

to be "crowded with Negroes and Bohemians who come from distant points."

During that period, the pickers were paid one to two cents per quart, and a good picker could pick a hundred quarts a day. But even at a dollar or a dollar and a half a day the field workers, many of whom were immigrants living in inner-city tenements in Baltimore, Philadelphia, and other cities, could earn in a few weeks much more than they could in twice the time in the city.

Strawberries had indeed become big business and Townsend, as one of Selbyville's more active brokers, was right in the thick of it. He had a two-story frame office on Church Street near the railroad. In late May and early June, the streets were filled with the wagons with special springs from early morning on into the evening. Townsend and the other brokers walked up and down examining the berries, assessing their quality, and bidding. In those early years the growers had banded together to form the Selbyville Fruit Growers Association, Inc., and the following year, the Selbyville Produce Exchange, Inc., to help organize things and to get their members the highest possible prices. One of their first undertakings was the construction of an auction shed near Townsend's brokerage office at the corner of Church Street and Railroad Avenue.

Similar organizations were coming into being all over the central peninsula in those years, and all the extra money coming into the area had created a business boom. Though strawberries were one of the most successful crops, they were not the only produce contributing to the new prosperity. Another big crop was tomatoes. As early as the summer of 1903, the *Delaware Pilot* commented on "the alarming glut in the tomato market," and added: "In the last few years tomato acreage has been multiplied time and again. In the vicinity of Lewes farmers have combined and built their own canneries. Every farming center has its own cannery."

And in Seaford that same summer, Colonel James J. Ross, son of former Governor William Ross and one of the state's wealthiest farmers, had had a bumper crop of white potatoes. It was so large, in fact, that a local newspaper reported that the Colonel had harvested "the largest crop ever heard of in Delaware" –3,000 bushels, which Colonel Ross sold for a total of $7,500.

Not only was Townsend directly involved in the strawberry business as a broker and to a lesser extent as a grower, but he was profiting from strawberries and other crops as a banker. Growers needed short-term financing at the beginning of the growing season to carry them until harvest. The growth of related industries like canneries and crate and basket making companies was also creating a demand for financing. As money came into the area, deposits were growing, which in turn created more opportunities for bankers to finance promising new enterprises.

Business ventures were popping up all over the peninsula at a great rate. Most were in some way connected with agriculture, but there were also purely industrial ventures–button factories, new types of machinery manufacture, the beginnings of formal real estate firms, fish-product companies. All of these new businesses needed capital and banks were being established to provide it.

The Selbyville office of Baltimore Trust Company opened its doors in the spring of 1903 in a tiny twelve-foot by twelve-foot wood frame building a few doors down from the intersection of Main and Church Streets. The building had once been part of a private home but the area in which it was located had become the central business district two decades before. The directors hired a young Frankford native named I. Layfield Long as the first cashier. Like many young men in the area, Long had gone as high as he could go in the local public school and then went to the Wilmington Conference Academy in Dover, a Methodist institution, for several years of further education. After leaving the academy, he had become a public school teacher in Maryland and then took a job as mathematics instructor at the Ann Arundel Academy near Baltimore. But like many of those who had left the area to seek work elsewhere, he saw greater opportunity back home with the growth of the local economy after 1900 and returned to southeastern Sussex County.

Business was slow at first and one of Layfield Long's duties was to sweep the street in front of the bank each morning. Things soon picked up, though. By the following spring the bank had deposits of $6,854.05 and was growing steadily. The new bank had missed by a few weeks being Selbyville's, and indeed southeastern Sussex County's, first bank. In January of 1903, Selbyville's leading merchant and lumberman William R. McCabe had organized his own bank, the Selbyville National Bank. In the years that followed it came to be known more generally as "the McCabe Bank," and Baltimore Trust as "the Townsend Bank." Both banks were doing a brisk business in those years of the strawberry boom and, quite naturally, a friendly rivalry grew up between them. This rivalry was heightened by the fact that McCabe and his vice-president Elisha C. Dukes were both former Democratic state representatives while Townsend and several of his officers were former (or future) Republican officehold-ers. McCabe's bank opened its office on the southeast corner of the main intersection. On the north side of Church Street across from the bank was his large, imposing home. Across the other street was the large general store which he had operated before selling out a few years earlier to his younger cousin, Caleb L. McCabe. Of the four corners of the main intersection the McCabes owned all but one.

Possibly because he was immediately faced with competition in Selbyville and thus with the prospect of slower growth than he might otherwise have enjoyed, Townsend took the unorthodox step of organizing two more branches of the Baltimore Trust Company late in 1903. He found other backers to join him in each of the two communities, Camden in southern Kent County and Bridgeville, the other center of the Sussex County strawberry boom. Nei-ther town had any other bank and each was situated in an area of rapid agricultural growth. Though Camden was within five miles of the state capital, there was enough local business activity to justify opening a bank there.

In each of the branch banks, Townsend organized a completely different set of backers, officers, and directors. Townsend himself, the president of all three branches, and the bank's name and overall direction were the only common features. This approach had several distinct advantages over the more conservative one of allowing the Selbyville office to grow slowly for a long period until it was strong enough to open a wholly-owned subsidiary. In fact, most of the early twentieth century banks in the two southern counties which did follow this supposedly safer route never got beyond a single office, which was later bought out by one of the larger upstate banks. By opening three different banks in different locations with different financial backers, he could triple the overall competitive position of the Baltimore Trust Company and give each office the advantages and economies of a larger organization than a single small-town bank could have afforded. Yet, with local directors and staff, each of the three banks functioned in its own community as a local bank, an essential ingredient for success at that time.

Both the locations of the various offices and the speed with which Townsend organized them reflected his knowledge that it would not take others long to start banks themselves. He had learned his lesson from McCabe and it was a good thing he did. Within a few years new banks had opened in Milford, Seaford, Frankford, Millsboro, Georgetown, Milton, Greenwood, Delmar, Dagsboro and Rehoboth Beach. Some towns that were too small for banks had newly established building and loan associations. The concept that he had used in establishing Baltimore Trust was similar to that which had been used by the Farmers Bank of Delaware since its founding a century before. More recently the Sussex Trust Company, which had opened its first office in Lewes in the early 1890s, had opened branch banks in Laurel and Milton in 1898 and 1902.

The Bridgeville branch of Baltimore Trust was capitalized at $16,000. Its cashier was a former telegrapher, station agent, and oyster packer named Charles H. Rawlins. The Bridgeville branch also had two vice-presidents, one of whom, Oliver A. Newton, had served with John in the 1903 session of the General Assembly. The other, Harry W. Viven, was a Bridgeville crate and basket manufacturer. His partner, William Burton Truitt, was a director.

The Camden branch opened in the late fall of 1903. The Bridgeville branch opened in January of 1904 in a temporary building while a new bank building was being erected. The permanent office in Bridgeville opened its doors on Wednesday, June 1, 1904, at the height of the strawberry harvest. The grand opening turned out to be somewhat more eventful than the officers had planned, as an article in Thursday's *Morning News* described:

> The new bank at Bridgeville was entered by robbers last night. They first visited a blacksmith shop where they stole tools with which to accomplish their purpose. The front doors of the bank, which were put in at great cost, were very badly damaged. After gaining an entrance the robbers blew open the vault doors by the use of dynamite. The bank had just begun business in the building yesterday, and had not moved its safe from the old building where they had been doing business temporarily. It is not known how much is missing but considerable specie was stolen. There is no clue to the robbers.

On Saturday, it was reported that one Henry C. Carr, "a tramp machinist of Bridgeport, Conn.," had been arrested in Seaford Friday afternoon by that town's "Officer Thompson," and charged with the robbery. Carr had been caught because he "displayed an unusual amount of pennies, nickels, and dimes."

The mechanism by which Baltimore Trust and all the other new banking institutions were coming into being had been created by the new Delaware Corporation Law of 1899, which helped to establish the state as a corporate haven. Limiting the liability of the organizers of banks and other new businesses helped to create the economic boom of the early 1900s.

The State of Maryland was to follow suit after the turn of the century with its own version, but it had not yet done so by 1904. As a result, there was still only one formally established bank in Worcester County, the Snow Hill Bank, which had been organized in 1887. Yet Worcester was experiencing a boom much like that in Sussex

County and it had its own increasing demand for capital. That demand was met, especially in the northern half of the county, by prosperous merchants and farmers acting as private bankers.

Among the leading private bankers in Worcester at the turn of the century were Elisha D. Layton of Bishops (the man who had lent the elder John G. Townsend the money to establish his son in the steam sawmill business ten years before) and a Berlin lawyer named Calvin B. Taylor. Layton was an old friend of the Townsend family and Taylor was, in the early 1900s, John's lawyer in his extensive real estate transactions in Worcester. These associations aided John's own banking activities since in 1904 and 1905 the demand for loans by Worcester strawberry growers exceeded both Layton's and Taylor's resources. As a result they funnelled much of the overflow to John.

Since Baltimore Trust was chartered in Delaware, it was somewhat awkward to do business across the state line. Thus, virtually all of his Worcester County loans in the early 1900s list John as a private banker with no mention made of Baltimore Trust Company. This business was both a service to the community and a good way to turn a nominal but speedy profit since most of the loans were for a period of only a few months. Even those in which the borrower was purchasing land were usually repaid with the profits from two or three strawberry seasons. By 1908, Maryland's new corporation law was in effect and Layton and Taylor banded together to open the Bishopville Bank. Taylor established independently the Calvin B. Taylor Banking Company of Berlin the same year. Thereafter John's private banking activities in Worcester dropped off. By then his other interests had prospered to the point that he did not have much time to spend on private banking activities in any case.

This sideline illustrates several aspects of John's character at the close of his term as a representative. He had become a remarkably shrewd businessman with an acute sense both of timing and of the chances for success of a wide variety of enterprises. He was constantly travelling around the central peninsula and beyond on journeys having to do with his diverse interests. At each stop he made friends and renewed old acquaintances, assessed the state of the local economy and kept an eye out for a good land deal or for business opportunity. By the age of thirty-five he was reaching his full stride both as a businessman and as a natural politician, though after 1903, he was too busy with the demands of his family and diverse business interests to run for another political office. It was to be more than a decade before he was again an active candidate and by then he had two sons working in the business with him.

John was a "go-getter." He had a direct manner about him. He was not shy; he went right up to people, introduced himself, and began finding out about them—who they were, what they did for a living, who among his growing multitude of acquaintances they might know, what they thought of matters of local importance. One old friend recalled that Townsend "always knew who to ask for information and advice." Most of the time this approach paid off as it had in his dealings with Layton and Taylor in Worcester. He had a way of infusing those who might have a good idea but were timid about pursuing it with the confidence to take the plunge. A large part of his success in this regard stemmed from his willingness to risk his own capital, to "put his money where his mouth was." In establishing the banks in Camden and Bridgeville, he did not have to put up all the money by any means. He had simply had to put together the right combination of men who were willing to go into partnership with him.

By this time, John had also developed a trait that later proved essential as he became more and more the executive—a highly refined talent for spotting intelligent and hard-working young men with a desire to better themselves. It was no accident that many came from backgrounds similar to his own, because they could think in similar ways and had similar motivations. In a sense, by acquiring all these partners, he was only doing what older men for whom he had great respect, men like Zare Brasure, had earlier done for him. His usual approach was, after much apparently aimless discussion about any manner of things, to conceive of a new and potentially lucrative idea. He then found a partner who was capable of running the business with adequate financial backing and a share of the owner-ship. In some cases, the potential partner had the initial idea and came to him with it. If it sounded reasonable and he had the capital to invest, he went with it. In an article written about him in the short-lived *Delaware Magazine* in 1919, halfway through his governor-ship, the author had written that one of his hobbies was partner-ships.

> Probably no man in the State, or in any seven states for that matter, has such a mania for partnerships as has the Governor. All through Delaware he has partnerships of almost every interest. Throughout the South he is a partner in milling and lumber concerns, and in most of those he is president or manager. In the fruit juice indus-try he now works from Louisiana to Jersey, with part-nerships and factories in practically every State between the two.

This, of course, was written years after 1903, but even then his style was well established. He wanted to make money, but money was not an end in itself. He was more interested in the pure dynamics of commerce, of supply and demand, of banking. He had a progres-sive vision of economic development that led him into many of these partnerships. He wanted the region to grow and to prosper and he wanted to be part of it.

Quite a few of his early partners possessed more formal education than he. As is often the case with substantially self-educated men, he had a great deal of respect for education and he was favorably inclined toward men who had come from humble beginnings to acquire an education. In the late 1890s and early 1900s many young men from Sussex County were pursuing higher education at institutions like the Methodist-sponsored Wilmington Conference Academy in Dover (now Wesley College), Delaware College in Newark, Dickinson College in Pennsylvania, and others. Most were motivated by a desire to get away from the depressed subsistence farms of their youth. Many went on to become men of great achievement in their chosen fields. Many of those from Baltimore Hundred had already become friends with John Townsend in their youth and ramained so in later years.

With the conclusion of the 1903 session of the General Assembly most of John's official duties as a representative had come to an end. His term lasted until the beginning of the next session, which was to come in December 1904, but after the spring of 1903 the title of representative was largely honorary. John was not inclined to seek reelection for several reasons, the most important of which was the need to attend to his rapidly expanding business interests. It had become more or less traditional for a man to serve only one session in the legislature and then to step aside to make room for someone else. He had been paid only $300 for his services and it almost certainly cost him more than that to serve. Since his replacement was Timothy E. Townsend, vice-president of the Selbyville office of Baltimore Trust, it is apparent that he had an active hand in finding the Union Republican candidate to run for his seat.

Another factor in his decision to retire temporarily from active politics was Jennie's fifth pregnancy. She was expecting another child in the fall of 1903 and the family had outgrown the old house on Sandy Branch. He needed to do something about building a house. Then, of course, the legislature was hardly the most comfortable place to be, with all the pulling and hauling between the rival Republican factions. A canny politician, which Townsend most assuredly was even in 1903, might have concluded that the prudent course was to remove himself from office until the outcome, which seemed imminent, had been decided once and for all. Zare Brasure also got out at the end of his second term in 1904. Oliver Newton did not seek reelection either. Timothy Townsend was doing John more of a favor by running for his seat, thereby getting him off the hook with the Union Republican leadership, than John was doing Timothy by stepping aside.

John remained powerfully interested in politics, of course, but for a few years that interest was less active. He still had commitments to attend to and did so enthusiastically. In September he and some of the family travelled to Rehoboth Beach to attend what was billed as a "grand reunion of the Delaware Legislature." The event was mostly for fun, though of course there was a constant background hum of wheeling and dealing and gossiping politicians throughout the two-day event. The local people hoped that the reunion would be "of vast importance politically" and noted proudly that the village "has been for many years famous as a political state-making resort." They were probably disappointed since nothing big was coming along in 1904, except for the congressional race. It was already evident that the popular Roosevelt would have little trouble being elected to a full term in his own right. At the end of the reunion, the legislators and their families were guests on the new steam pilot boat *Philadelphia* for a cruise in the bay before going home.

Jennie Collins Townsend
*as a young matron**

Representative Townsend was also expected to join in Baltimore Hundred summer festivities like the annual Fourth of July gathering at Sandy Landing that drew hundreds of men, women, and children from all over Baltimore and Dagsboro Hundreds. It was just after the end of the strawberry season and everyone was in need of a good holiday. Some of the more industrious folks would leave home the night before in horses and wagons or, somewhat earlier, in ox carts and carry up loads of food, ice cream freezers, fireworks, and other items of enjoyment to sell to the crowds the next day. Others would go out with their seines and net fish to fry. The young folks would play baseball and run along the river beach or go swimming and crabbing. The older people would sit under the pines and gossip, brag about how much they made on strawberries that year, tell yarns, and listen to speakers like John and Zare Brasure report on the doings in Dover.

The Townsends would also attend one or more of the local summer camp meetings later in the summer. In the early 1900s there

* *This engraving, which appeared in Volume Three (the biographical volume) of Henry Clay Reed's* Delaware–A History of the First State *(New York: Lewis Historical Publishing Co., 1947) was prepared from a portrait painted from photographs after Mrs. Townsend's death. Her daughter, Lyla, posed for the proper posture and body type (courtesy Lyla T. Savoy).*

was a variety to choose from. Several of the many camp meetings were near Selbyville, including Sound Camp with its old associations and a Baptist gathering just down the road from it. By the early 1900s, most Selbyville people went to the new camp meeting at Fenwick Island, which was held in a grove of trees just south of the Fenwick Island Light Station. It, like most of the others, was a natural magnet for local political figures, many of whom were also ardent Methodists.

John went about his duties as representative, slight as they were after the end of the active legislative session, until Timothy Townsend was elected to replace him. His departure from elective office did not alter his lifestyle greatly, however, since he still continued to get requests for help from people in need and he continued to help them when he could. It was a pattern that he followed for the rest of his life, in or out of office.

By the summer of 1903, John and Jennie were busy planning their new home. It was to be a large one, but with four children and a fifth one on the way it had to be. It was something of a mixture of styles but was basically what later came to be known as "colonial revival." This did not imply that it would look colonial but simply that it had such classic features as paired Corinthian columns on the broad porch that would extend along three sides of the house. The first floor contained a parlor, front hall, dining room, kitchen, and other smaller rooms. The second and third floors were divided into bedrooms with storage space on the third floor and another, smaller, attic above. A small balcony with its own miniature portico led off from the third floor bedroom that would become the boys' domain.

The work was done by local carpenters and many of the materials came from John's own lumber mill. The house with its barn in back and other outbuildings cost about four thousand dollars to build, which seems almost unbelievable by modern standards until one considers the

The New House: *Edith Townsend stands about 1908 with the family's pony and several pet dogs in Main Street with the new family home visible in the rear. A group of boys playing leap-frog behind the hedge and her mother, Jennie talking to a friend at right complete the picture of family life (Lyla T. Savoy Collection).*

chronic shortage of cash money then afflicting the region. It is also probable that the huge house cost less for John to build since he was in the lumber business and could obtain most of the materials at minimal cost. Still, it was one of the more imposing houses in town and it was assessed for the same amount as the equally spacious William R. McCabe House one block north. After the peach boom in southern New Castle County and northern Kent several generations earlier, when the prosperous orchardmen were building themselves great, square, flat-roofed Italianate piles with cupolas on top, people took to calling their houses "peach mansions." Applying the same standard, it would have been only fair to call the new Townsend home one of Selbyville's first "strawberry mansions," though it was only a mansion if one compared it to the old Sandy Branch house or to the first house John and Jennie had lived in down in Worcester.

The new baby was born on October 21, 1903, the fifth child and the third boy. He was named Paul Lockwood Townsend, and he spent his first winter in the old place while the new home was still under construction. By the spring of 1904, the family moved in. The parents and Lyla and Edith had their rooms on the second floor as did the baby. The boys, Jack and Jule, had their own domain up on the third floor. The house soon had one modern convenience then rare in the state–a telephone–one of the most essential tools of John's diverse trades.

In the summer of 1904, Everett Johnson was in town with his wife of just two years, introducing her around to old friends and relatives and showing her his hometown. She was the former Miss Louise Staton of Newark and she had met her husband in 1897 when he had come as a boarder to her mother's home on West Delaware Avenue. Louise had been born in 1882 in the parsonage of the old Welsh Tract Primitive Baptist Church at the foot of Iron Hill outside of Newark, the daughter of the Rev. Joseph Leland Staton, another Worcester Countian who went north with his wife and older children in 1880. After her father's death in the early 1890s, the family had moved into the town. Mrs. Staton had taken in college students as boarders to help make ends meet.

The Johnsons had stopped in to pay a call on "Cousin Zare" Brasure at his home on Main Street. As they sat in rockers on the porch, the men talking about old times, Zare's friend and new next-door neighbor, John, came walking across the lawn to see Everett and meet his new wife. He was carrying the baby in his arms, wanting to show him off to the Johnsons. This was Louise Johnson's first meeting with the man who was later to play a role of great importance in their lives.

Another thing she remembered about that first trip she made to Selbyville when she looked back on it seventy-two years later was travelling with her husband in a buggy over the dusty summer roads of Baltimore Hundred from Selbyville to Bayard. They were going to visit other relatives and friends in that village. "As we pulled up in front of the house, three or four barefoot little boys came running up to the buggy." That, she said, was her first meeting with John J. Williams, who made his own mark in Delaware political history some four and a half decades later.

8. The Dawn of a New Era

The years after John G. Townsend Jr. had ended his brief service as state representative from Baltimore Hundred and before he made his run for the governorship of Delaware were among the fullest in a long and full life. They were years in which four Townsend children grew up, in which two more children were born, and in which one baby died soon after birth. They were productive years for the entire family but most especially for the father who evolved during that period from a reasonably successful young entrepreneur, banker, lumberman, and fruit broker into an executive of statewide and even regional prominence. In politics as well, his horizons expanded from local to national consciousness.

The day-to-day chores of politics did abate somewhat after he left the legislature, but they never stopped completely even when he was working hardest in the businesses. He was always doing little political chores for people who needed help–putting them in touch with the right state official, writing letters for them, keeping in touch with political friends all over the state. These are chores that most politicians do, but which none but the born politician relish the way Townsend did.

Soon after the conclusion of his career as a representative, the Union Republican leadership paid him the compliment of choosing him to be an alternate delegate to the 1904 Republican National Convention. The delegate for whom he served as an alternate was Dr. G. Layton Grier of Milford, president of the L.D.Caulk Company, a manufacturer of dental supplies and one of the largest firms in the town. Most of the delegates left early enough to be in Chicago, where the convention was being held, in time for the Republican National Committee meeting on June 15. Once again they would wage the by-now inevitable battle to see which of the two Delaware delegations would be seated. The feud had become so much a part of national conventions that the newspapers were referring to the Delaware Republican rift as "their old-time enmity."

The Regulars deluged the committeemen with copies of *The Outlook* article "Holding Up A State." They thought they had brought the committeemen around at least to the point where they would vote not to seat either delegation, but when the national committee made its decision on Thursday, the sixteenth, it was overwhelmingly in favor of the Union Republicans. On the same day the committee voted not to seat a group of Wisconsin Progressives led by a man who was then little known beyond his own state–Robert M. LaFollete, Sr. After his election to the Senate two years later he would spring from his relative obscurity to become the fiery leader of the national Progressive movement.

But this convention of 1904 was lacking in the excitement and the intensity of one in a hotly contested presidential year. The only chance that Theodore Roosevelt would be opposed in his bid for a full four-year term had died with the unexpected death of Senator Mark Hanna the year before. Even the Union Republican–Regular Republican feud had about it an air of old-hat boredom.

John went to the convention late. The strawberry season had kept him at home in Selbyville until after the national committee meeting and he went not because he thought his presence was needed but because it was his first chance to observe "big time" politics first hand. For a novice, every national convention is exciting, even when the presidential incumbent is away on vacation and makes his acceptance speech by telegram as Roosevelt did in 1904. John was observing the well-known and familiar Republican leaders he had been reading about in newspapers for years. He was brushing shoulders, if only in a figurative way, with "comers" in national politics like William Howard Taft who would himself be president four years hence.

He was also able to enjoy all the parties and social functions that went along with any convention. Withal, it was an exhilarating week for the young Baltimore Hundred businessman. Little is known about Townsend's experience at the convention beyond the mere facts that he was there and that he did not accompany the main delegation but arrived later. He probably stayed at Chicago's Great Northern Hotel with the rest of the Union Republicans. He brought Jennie and his young family along on the trip. Zare Brasure brought his family as well, and they all took a side journey to St. Louis afterwards to attend the World's Fair being held that summer. Many

Riding a Camel:
When John G. Townsend Jr. and Isaiah J. Brasure attended the 1904 Republican National Convention in Chicago, they took their families along and later went to the St. Louis Exposition where Jack and Jule Townsend got to ride a camel. John and "Zare" Brasure are shown on the ground with the camel driver (Townsend family scrapbook).

other delegates also visited the fair on their way home.

E1isha Dukes of Baltimore Hundred was a delegate at the Democratic National Convention which was held in St. Louis soon after the Republicans held their gathering in Chicago. That event was more interesting to Delawareans than the Republican convention because Judge George Gray of Wilmington, prominent Democratic statesman and onetime senator, was being talked up as a candidate for president. Had he been nominated he would have been something of a sacrificial lamb, but his fellow Democrats chose William Jennings Bryan for that dubious distinction.

Old Paynter Frame of Millsboro, widely known still as "The Watermelon King" for his experiments in propagating the plant at his farm (and distillery) on the Indian River, had attended the Democratic State Convention early in June. He had been to every one since 1847. In 1904, he was loud in his praise of Gray and equally outspoken in his opposition to a second congressional term for his fellow townsman, Henry Houston. As it turned out, a majority of the delegates agreed with him about Houston. In his two years in Washington, however, Houston had made substantive gains in advancing the cause of a series of canals linking Little Assawoman Bay to Indian River Bay and Rehoboth Bay to the Delaware Bay, thus creating a continuous inland link from Fenwick Island to Lewes and the Delaware Bay and ocean beyond. It was perceived that these improvements would bring about great economic progress in Baltimore Hundred in less than a decade.

The 1904 general election was relatively quiet. By now Addicks's business problems were public knowledge. The Regulars and the Union Republicans had joined together to elect a prominent New Castle County Quaker as governor–Preston Lea. Lea was president of his family's large milling business on the Brandywine and also president of Wilmington's Union National Bank. He found a valuable downstate ally and friend in John Townsend. Though nearly thirty years John's senior, the governor and the young former representative had enough in common that a warm friendship grew up between them—warm enough so that when the fourth Townsend son and the last child was born in 1910, he was given the Christian name Preston in honor of Governor Lea.

All Delaware governors devoted part of their first days in office to the naming of a military staff of honorary militia officers. It was a quaint and pleasant custom that had the added advantage of being a simple way of rewarding favored political supporters by bestowing upon them the legal title of "Colonel." The only one of these officers who had any real work to do as a result of the appointment, at least in peacetime, was the man, usually a professional soldier, named adjutant general. The others had the official right, if they desired, to don military uniforms on ceremonial occasions and to bear (for the rest of their lives if they wished) the title "Colonel."

John became a colonel on the military staff of Governor Preston Lea. Lea's successors in the governorship followed suit in honoring a man who was evolving into Baltimore Hundred's most prominent Republican. In 1908, Governor Simeon Pennewill of Greenwood, who had been a Union Republican state senator when John was a representative, also named him a colonel. When Governor Charles Miller was elected in 1912, he continued the tradition, bestowing upon John his third appointment as colonel in as many administrations.

During the nineteenth century there were many men in the state who, having once been honored with a colonel's commission, adopted the title permanently and more or less openly let it be known that they expected to be addressed by their title, though few had ever seen any military service. John never allowed himself to become

Colonel John G. Townsend Jr: *Delaware governors traditionally honored prominent friends and supporters by appointing them to the governor's personal military staff as aides-de-camp and similar positions. The staff of Governor Preston Lea, the venerable gentleman attired in white linen at the center of the photo above, was photographed on an early summer day about 1906, probably at the Delaware Militia's summer encampment at New Castle. Newly appointed Colonel John Townsend stands directly behind the governor. Seated at left is T. Coleman du Pont, who received the title of Quartermaster General, which carried with it a brigadier general's commission. He was known forever after as "General" du Pont. Others in the photo have not been identified (Lyla Townsend Savoy Collection).*

too self-important. He, after all, remembered his days as a farm boy in Bishops regardless of what honors the governor saw fit to affix to his name. For that reason he never used the title in normal circumstances though some formal communications from the governor's office were addressed to "Colonel John G. Townsend" and some newspapers referred to him as such during his gubernatorial campaign.

Governor Lea and his two Republican successors also saw fit to reappoint Townsend to the Farmers Bank Board at regular two-year intervals. These appointments and those to the governor's staff were more than just a recognition that the former representative was a good party man who supported the candidates at election time and could always be counted on for a campaign contribution. They were the outward and official recognition of the growing importance of the Baltimore Hundred Republican in the affairs of the party, and more specifically in the evolution of the Republican Party out of the Addicks Era.

It was becoming clear to the more perceptive politicians of all parties as early as the 1903 session that Addicks was treading on shaky ground, even if he had managed to be named to the Republican National Committee the following year. It was not just his failure to be elected senator. He was finally sued in the Bay State Gas Company case early in 1904. By then the company was almost in ruins and hovering on the brink of receivership. Its majority stockholder had, it seemed, been routinely draining its assets and using them to finance his political career, his elegant homes, his yacht, and all the other expenses that went with his high-rolling lifestyle.

To make matters worse, just as Senator Ball's two-year term was coming to an end in January of 1905, when a majority of Union Republicans had been elected to the legislature and it might outwardly have appeared as if Addicks's election would at long last take place, his third marriage began coming apart in a most embarrassingly public manner. The newspapers were reporting by this time that Senator Allee had turned "state's evidence" in order to protect himself, having once been president of the gas company. Addicks's public image was sliding precipitously downward. Instead of being elected to the Senate, Addicks emerged from the 1905 session with fewer votes than he entered, though he had once again kept anyone else from being elected to replace Ball.

The end was in sight for Addicks. The ultimate collapse of his Delaware political career occurred the following year. In September of 1905, he lost the gas company suit and faced a four million dollar judgement against him. Early in 1906, the same session of the General Assembly that had been unable to replace Senator Ball the year before, met in special session and gave Colonel Henry du Pont a resounding victory on the first ballot. Union Republicans and Regulars alike supported him.

Allee made a point of announcing before the session that he could no longer support the disgraced Addicks and that he was throwing his own influence behind du Pont. If anything, however, Allee was hurt as much by the mess as his erstwhile employer. He was judged a turncoat by press and public for having deserted the man who had done so much to build his political career. After the end of his term in the Senate in 1907, Allee was never again to hold major public office, though he had a few tricks left before he died quietly in Dover in 1938.

Many contemporary journalists quickly concluded that the Union Republicans had been using Addicks only as long as it was convenient for them to do so, and that they had never had any intentions of electing him senator. They further concluded that as soon as he lost his money, his erstwhile followers had deserted him en masse. This view of the Union Republican movement is both oversimplified and somewhat erroneous. It contains some nuggets of truth, but the impression created is false in many respects. It is true as far as it goes that the Union Republicans were happy to make use of Addicks's money to finance their declaration of independence from the upstate industrialists. Some may have attempted to enrich themselves at his expense, but there is no contemporary evidence to suggest that they intentionally kept him from becoming U. S. senator. In fact, many Union Republicans held out longer for his election than was prudent.

With regard to the question of the Union Republicans supporting a scoundrel simply as a way of keeping the campaign money coming in, Addicks was not necessarily any more of a scoundrel than many other politicians and financial manipulators of the day. For that matter, he seems to have been considerably less rapacious than some who got much farther in politics than he did. During the height of his power in Delaware politics, few of his followers were in a position to judge the propriety of his business dealings, even if they had been privy to the details, which they were not. He seemed like any other high-rolling upstate millionaire politician except that he displayed a greater sympathy for the problems in Kent and Sussex Counties.

Politicians were, on the whole, a tolerant lot in the early 1900s, willing to overlook some failings and lapses of taste as long as a man adhered to a certain minimal standard of decency and was not treacherous to his political allies. They could even enjoy vicariously the more picturesque escapades of a man like Addicks, knowing that he came from relatively humble origins and was trying to bluster his way into the Senate and other enclaves of wealth and privilege.

By 1905, however, it was clear to everyone that Addicks had overstepped the bounds with the dual disasters of the Bay State Gas case and his messy divorce. His support had begun dropping off after publication of "Holding Up A State" and this in itself suggests that some of the Union Republicans were shocked by the disclosures, one-sided though they were. Still, even as late as the fall of 1904, as respected a figure as Judge Henry C. Conrad, one the founders of the Wilmington *Morning News*, and later Delaware historian and archivist of note, could serve as the Union Republican candidate for governor. While Addicks lost his political support at about the same time as he lost his money in the gas company suit, it does not necessarily follow that he lost his support *because* he lost his money.

The Union Republican movement did not end overnight. Just as the conditions that brought on the Republican split in the first place had been decades in the making, the concluding chapter of the great fight took years to play itself out. The party was already showing signs of coming apart as early as Townsend's term in the house of representatives for reasons that had nothing to do with Addicks himself. Among those Union Republicans who were beginning to cut their ties from the party before 1905 were Townsend, Zare Brasure, and other more progressive members whose main reason for joining the Union Republicans had been to seek economic progress for their region. Like most American political movements, the Union Republicans were composed of at least two disparate and distinct elements–the progressive bloc who had felt that downstate Delaware was being unnecessarily held back by the upstaters and the railroad men, and the conservatives, of whom Dr. Layton was perhaps the best example.

One of the most visible issues on which the two blocs within the party differed was that of good roads. By 1903, Henry Ford's experiments were well underway at his shop in Dearborn, Michigan, which would soon lead to the first mass-produced, easily affordable automobile. Most of the pioneering motor vehicles one saw on the roads were still the elegant, mostly hand-made machines of the rich. In the cities, where the streets and public roads were generally of a high enough quality to pose no problems, motor vehicles were already coming into use for the transport of goods. But the roads of southern Delaware were notoriously awful. The public road system, such as it was, was the responsibility of the counties to maintain. Their maintenance program left a great deal to be desired.

During John's term in the house, the General Assembly enacted legislation appropriating $30,000 per year for a period of six years for the purpose of paving public roads with a hard macadam surface. This measure, known as the State Aid Law, also provided for a new position of highway commissioner in each of the three counties whose duty it was to oversee the highway work. A central highway administration office was established in Dover to handle the details of the program.

An accompanying measure passed during the 1903 session was designed to regulate "the Use of Automobiles on the Public Highways of this State." The owners of the few motor vehicles in Delaware were thereafter required to reduce the speed of their automobiles when approaching a vehicle drawn by a horse, mule, "or other animal" and to stop completely if the animal became badly spooked. These two laws were the very beginning of the modern highway transportation system of Delaware and John was one of their early supporters. But for a Sussex County legislator to be an avid supporter of such bills was not without some political hazard. The problem was that because of the awful roads downstate and the lack of citizens with the wherewithal to purchase automobiles, most conservative legislators promptly concluded that the appropriations bill was an outright gift to the well-heeled motor car owners of Wilmington and its environs. Where some few automobiles did exist downstate in places like Dover, the city streets were generally good enough to keep them from being bogged down in the mud.

Few citizens downstate, limited in their vision by centuries of bad roads and a depressed economy, could conceive as early as 1903 that motor vehicles would ever be anything more than rich mens' toys. John's genius lay in his uncanny ability to spot a trend or invention of great social and economic value before almost anyone else around. He undoubtedly saw the possibilities of the motor vehicle the first time he went to Philadelphia or Baltimore and saw goods being moved along city streets by some primitive version of the truck. It would not have taken him long to realize that the machines could be perfected to the point where they could be of great value to commerce. This was especially true of commerce as it existed in southeastern Sussex County and in Worcester where the fruit growers were still at the mercy of the railroads and the rivers and inlets were still silted in or rendered almost unnavigable because of shoals. With decent roads linking southern Delaware to the cities, the motor vehicle could be the answer.

Yet there were few, if any, motor vehicles downstate and even the town streets were poor. It was all too easy for those without John's vision to conclude that his support and that of a few other progressive southern Delawareans was, to some extent, disloyalty to the cause. The first annual report of the highway commissioners seemed to confirm the conservatives' suspicions of the new laws. Just over eight miles of public road in New Castle County had been macadamized. Somewhat more than one mile in Sussex County had been done, most of it near the town of Lewes. No roads at all had been hard-surfaced in Kent County because the county government there did not wish to avail themselves of the funds.

This report was not published until the year after the conclusion of John's one session in the legislature, but he was still representative until the end of 1904. This apparent parting of the ways with the mainstream of the Union Republican Party probably had no bearing on his decision not to seek reelection in 1904. He may have been somewhat weary of life as a legislator and he had pressing family and business needs to attend to. Nor, in that era, was it common for legislators to serve multiple terms as has since become the norm. Neither he nor Zare Brasure ran for reelection in 1904. It was clear by then that the progressive ideal espoused by the Union Republicans several years earlier was a sincerely held belief of only a minority of the party. During the 1905 session, which had a somewhat larger number of Union Republicans, the State Aid Law was repealed by a substantial margin. That action marked the end of the state's efforts to build a modern road system until one was given to it, as it were, on a silver platter. Despite this setback, John and a few other downstate leaders remained strong advocates of good roads. In this stand they found their firmest friend in none other than T. Coleman du Pont. By this time the DuPont Company president had moved in Regular Republican circles into a political position best described by the old cliché, "the power behind the throne." His older cousin, Colonel Henry, was at last in position to win his longsought seat in the U. S. Senate, due in no small part to Coleman du Pont's efforts in his behalf. Coleman had become state chairman of the Regular Republican Party.

Quite aside from this political activity, he was a pioneering believer in good roads. He advocated a modern highway system with a missionary zeal unmatched by any other man in the state. Though some opponents later made charges to the contrary, du Pont's belief in good roads had little to do with politics, other than in the broadest sense of his knowledge that the improved economy modern highways would usher in would benefit politically those who had gotten the job done. Long before he had become a politician, he had been an engineer and builder. These occupations were still his first love. He cared more about building than he did about the DuPont Company itself. When he finally gave up the presidency of the company in 1915, a large part of his reason for doing so was to devote more of his time to his various building projects.

John had first met du Pont in 1903, when he was a member of the house and du Pont was managing his cousin's senatorial campaign. At the time they were on opposite sides of the Republican dispute and it is unlikely that their friendship developed immediately. But du Pont spotted the young man early on as a valuable ally in the Good Roads Movement in Delaware. The action of the 1905 session in repealing their State Aid Law had caused John and other progressive downstaters to reassess their positions with regard to Republican politics at a time when the Union Republican leadership was falling into disarray. By 1904, Coleman du Pont had shown himself in his role as the chairman of the Regular Republican State Committee to be an entirely different breed of politician from the stiff, intractable men of the older generation. At a time when the conservative wing of the Union Republican Party was effectively alienating the Progressives, he moved in rapidly to offer men like John Townsend an honorable reconciliation and to provide them with a new political home.

The legislature of 1907 proved more responsive to the opportunities created by the invention of the motor vehicle. It enacted the state's first motor vehicle registration law at a time when there were only 313 motor cars in the entire state, mostly owned by New Castle Countians. Henceforth, owners were required to register them and to pay an annual licensing fee of two dollars. Operators' licenses were issued for the first time, and automobile license plates were introduced, though vehicle owners were required to provide their own.

Though the situation was improving somewhat, it was evident that at the rate things were going it might well be decades before the state could set about building a modern, high-quality network of good roads. The reluctance of the legislature to act was even more of a problem since neighboring states like Maryland and Pennsylvania were already moving ahead with major highway construction programs. Every year Delaware delayed served to increase the already acute economic stagnation in the southern part of the state.

9. The Highway of the Future

At a crucial moment in the history of his adopted state, when legislative inaction could have doomed Delaware to another generation of economic depression, Coleman du Pont stepped in with a remarkable proposal that promised to create a whole new reality. In 1908, he offered to build, at no cost to the citizens of Delaware, the world's most advanced highway to run from one end of the state to the other. Upon its completion, he would donate this magnificent transportation corridor to the state. The public response to this almost incredibly munificent gesture is itself very revealing of the torpid state of affairs du Pont was combatting. While a majority of the state's citizens were bowled over by the offer and accepted it with alacrity, a substantial minority treated it with the same militantly provinical suspicion and distrust with which they viewed nearly anything smacking of progress. Unable to believe that du Pont could be moved solely by altruistic motives to make such an offer, they promptly concluded that he hoped thereby to gain financially or politically. Oddly enough, most of this sentiment was centered in Kent and Sussex Counties, the very areas that would most benefit from a new highway. Though this negative view was held primarily by Democrats, a fair number of onetime Union Republicans were equally suspicious. John, of course, was overjoyed by the offer as were many other southeastern Sussex Countians.

In order to fully understand the negative response from many downstaters, one must know something of the state of philanthropy in Delaware as it then existed, and also something of the specifics of du

Pont's proposal. The first great philanthropic enterprises of the early twentieth century were then in their infancy, their activities confined largely to areas far removed from the state. In Delaware, the only sizeable philanthropy to have been attempted, the efforts of the Bancroft family to create the Wilmington free library and park system, had proved successful. But those efforts were not familiar to most southern Delawareans.

Nor could many downstaters conceive of wealth on the magnitude of that possessed by Coleman du Pont by 1908. Already a millionaire when he assumed the presidency of the DuPont Company in 1902, he had prospered greatly in the years since then as he and his cousins Pierre and Alfred went about the task of transforming the old firm into a modern industrial giant. The federal personal income tax was still, by 1908, five years away from becoming a permanent fixture of American life. When one considers that the steel magnate Andrew Carnegie had a tax-free annual income of $23 million at the turn of the century, it becomes easier to understand how Coleman du Pont could afford to give such a gift to the people of Delaware. It is safe to estimate that his annual income was at least $1 million by 1908, and possibly more.

Just when he conceived of his grandiose gesture is not known, but by 1908, he had been seriously interested for some years in modern highways as a means of economic revitalization. He was among the more active members of the recently established National Highway Association, an organization of which he later became chairman. He had also studied modern highway construction techniques in Europe, where engineers had developed the most advanced methods then in use. du Pont was also personally familiar with conditions on the lower peninsula. He owned an estate on the lower Eastern Shore of Maryland. Travelling there forced him to use the substandard roads of southern

Delaware and Maryland. Nor could he avoid seeing, in these journeys, the economically depressed countryside through which those roads ran. du Pont was one of the first men in the United States, if not in the world, to recognize the future economic importance of the motor vehicle and to envision the highway system that would be required to develop the invention to its fullest potential. The project he proposed in 1908 was so advanced that some aspects of it did not come into widespread use nationally for forty years thereafter. Other features of his plan are still being discussed as futuristic concepts. du Pont was so far ahead of most of his fellow Delawareans in his thinking about the automobile that it is not any wonder many totally failed to comprehend what he was talking about.

du Pont was, of course, actively involved in politics and his political ambitions were no great secret. Many doubters therefore concluded that his highway plan was simply an audacious scheme to advance himself politically. Others saw it as the work of a supreme egotist. One report of dubious veracity current at the time quoted du Pont as saying, "I will build a monument a hundred miles high and lay it on the ground." But all of this talk overlooked the fact that if du Pont had been primarily interested in his political career he could have found a much less expensive and less problem-fraught way of accomplishing his political goals.

All of his subsequent actions lead one to the conclusion that du Pont was indeed sincere in his efforts to build the world's finest highway in his adopted state. If his not-inconsiderable ego entered into it at all it was in the personal and professional satisfaction he hoped to achieve in seeing his grand plan through to completion, and in sitting back and watching the economic transformation that he knew would result. Like most extremely intelligent and capable individuals, du Pont could display at times an impatience that some saw as arrogance, but he seems to have been truly altruistic in his desire to improve the conditions he saw in Delaware.

The plan that he first proposed in 1908, was for something much more ambitious than simply a highway, though that was the heart of it. du Pont set out to build a self-supporting transportation corridor the length of the state. Had it been built as he first envisioned it, the corridor, which he called a "boulevard," would have provided for every type of land transportation except for the steam railroad. It would have been operated by a nonprofit corporation that possessed many of the features of the later metropolitan transit authorities. As originally presented, du Pont's plan called for the boulevard corporation to acquire by purchase, donation, or, if necessary, condemnation, a two-hundred-foot-wide right-of-way from Delaware's southern border with Maryland to the Pennsylvania state line north of Wilmington. In the center of this corridor was to be a hard-surfaced, limited access highway for high-speed automobile through traffic. Running along either side of this highway were to be north- and south-bound trolley tracks for public mass transportation. Outside the trolley tracks were to be located hard-surfaced north- and southbound lanes for heavier motor trucks. Soft-surfaced roadways for horse-drawn vehicles were to be situated outside the truck lanes, with pedestrian sidewalks running along the outside.

du Pont saw the highway as the first step, with the outer trolley lines and trucking lanes coming later as the economic development of lower Delaware progressed. He thought that portions of the extra land should be used during the interim for the establishment of public agricultural experiment stations to promote the development of modern farming methods downstate. The land not used for this purpose was to be leased to public utilities for the running of electric and telephone lines and other utilities, or to commercial enterprises for the development of highway-related businesses.

One of the fullest expressions of his ideas came in an article he wrote for the March 16, 1912 issue of the *Scientific American.* By this time he had been at work for more than a year on the job of acquiring the necessary land for his right-of-way. He had found the process a frustrating one indeed. In addition to those who objected outright to the location of the highway across their property, du Pont encountered some property owners who were quite happy to have the roadway. They realized that the highway would increase the value of their land by at least 100 percent. It was just that they felt they should get an astronomical sum at the outset for the land they sold for right-of-way in addition to the benefit they would obtain from the increase in value to the remainder of their land. Possibly for this reason, du Pont expressed the view that the government that builds a highway should by right be the entity to benefit from increased property values. He advocated acquiring enough land at the outset "to ultimately make the road pay for itself."

> Records will be kept to see if the income from the extra width will in time pay an amount that will, first, maintain the road; second, pay interest on the cost of the road; third, pay the cost of the road; and after this be a source of income that would pay all county or city taxes. The writer's opinion is that it will, and, if so, let the towns or counties or the Nation take enough ground . . . and allow the people who want to use the land to have it on 999 years lease, with certain conditions, at four per cent the value of the land for purpose of paying rent to be adjusted every five years.

The plan suggested the money could be raised without injuring the interests of the users of the land:

> The Government, State or Federal, as the case might

be, would get what it was entitled to from the people who properly should pay it, and the people would obtain land on a four per cent basis. Finally, the speculative value of the real estate near the road should accrue to the Government, to whom it would properly belong.

Sadly, this intriguing scheme of things never came to pass because of the difficulties du Pont encountered in acquiring the necessary right-of-way. du Pont was constantly plagued by this problem. He had hoped that the necessary legislation could be enacted during the 1909 General Assembly Session to allow him to establish his boulevard corporation and to give him the power to acquire his 200-foot right-of-way. When the session began, several months after he made his proposal, the public controversy was still raging over whether or not the state should even accept his offer. Instead of having the bill introduced, du Pont's supporters took the more prudent course of introducing a bill that would authorize the paving of the old oyster-shell public road from Wilmington to Georgetown.

One of the major objections to du Pont's boulevard, even among those who otherwise favored the idea, was the fact that he proposed a route that would carry the road near, but not through, the towns along the way. Local merchants feared that such a route would deprive them of the business they got from passing travellers, who would be less inclined to pass by their businesses if it meant taking a side road off the boulevard to do so. du Pont reasoned that the necessary rights-of-way would be much more difficult to obtain in the towns. Besides, he said, a high-speed highway through the middle of the towns would be much more dangerous than having it at a safe distance outside with side roads leading into it.

The legislation to resurface the old road was used as a test to determine the amount of support for highway improvements, and also to see if the legislators were so strongly opposed to du Pont's plan that they would rather spend the state's money to come up with an alternate idea. When it came up for a vote, the bill was narrowly defeated, an outcome that improved du Pont's chances of getting his own bill through. It would have to wait until 1911. In the intervening period of nearly two years du Pont and his supporters, John G. Townsend among them, worked to sell the plan for the boulevard throughout the state.

During the 1911 session, du Pont finally succeeded in getting the necessary legislation approved, but even then there were problems. Many property owners questioned the new highway corporation's right to obtain a two hundred-foot right-of-way when the first phase of the construction would involve less than forty feet. To make matters worse, du Pont was forced to work under the existing law governing railroad rights-of-way. That measure provided that all litigation arising from a condemnation proceeding for a right-of-way had to be carried to a conclusion in the courts before work could proceed on the condemned land. This problem was potentially the greatest of all since such litigation could drag on for years.

du Pont protested that many states had a system whereby a public utility could place a cash bond in escrow to cover the cost of any award made to a property owner by the courts, but the work could begin immediately upon condemnation. He did not succeed in having the law changed and this problem was to prove the single greatest hindrance to him in the years that followed. In the end it kept him from being able to complete the magnificent transportation artery he had first proposed. du Pont was a realist as well as an idealist and at last he was forced to recognize, as so many other men have, that the political process can rarely, if ever, be short-circuited, however worthy the cause.

Despite these problems, there was a spirit of great excitement in the air in that spring and summer in Sussex County as the newly created Coleman du Pont Road, Incorporated was organized and the job of marshalling the resources needed to build the new highway was begun. The first and most important task was, of course, obtaining the right-of-way. du Pont knew he was going to have problems and he went about the matter in a practical manner. In the first place, he decided that the route should run wherever possible through the area where the greatest number of people supported the road. He already knew the feelings of John Townsend who had been one of the first and most enthusiastic of highway boosters since du Pont first presented his idea to the public several years before.

John had drummed up support all through southeastern Sussex County, which was not difficult considering the problems the residents were having with the railroad. The people of southwestern Sussex were not as interested in the beginning. With the main railroad line down the peninsula running right through western Sussex, area residents felt they were already in good shape. If the railroad did fail them, there was always the Chesapeake Bay, to which they had access through the Nanticoke River. Delmar, the only logical southern terminus for the highway other than Selbyville, was a railroad town. The railroad had founded it and a large part of the populace was supported directly or indirectly by it. Western Sussex was also the most heavily Democratic region of the county, and its residents were among those who suspected du Pont of some conspiracy to profit personally from the road. For all these reasons, among others, it was decided that Selbyville would be the boulevard's southern terminus.

The only instance in which du Pont deviated from his plan to keep the highway away from the center of the towns was in the case of the small southern New Castle County village of Odessa on the

Before...
A typical public road in Sussex County in the days before construction of the du Pont Boulevard–a sea of rutted mud (Lyla T. Savoy Collection).

After:
A section of the newly completed du Pont Boulevard north of Selbyville (Lyla T. Savoy Collection).

Appoquinimink Creek. Here, the citizens of the town were so much in favor of the highway that they volunteered to deed over to du Pont a two-hundred-foot right-of-way straight through the center of town. Even Selbyville was not that supportive, but it was not far behind. In the section of his *Scientific American* article in which du Pont described the route in some detail, he spoke highly of Selbyville as one of the most enterprising towns in southern Delaware and mentioned its flourishing strawberry business as proof of the need for the highway.

John was greatly impressed with T. Coleman du Pont and for good reason. The personable and outgoing millionaire made a profound impression there in 1909, as he went about the job of scouting out his route. Though du Pont could not begin actually acquiring tracts of land until the spring of 1911, he was already hard at work on preliminary surveys and similar chores when he was able to take the time from his other activities.

By this period in his career, du Pont was moving at a furious pace through a whole host of occupations in addition to the road. Soon after assuming the presidency of the DuPont Company he had embarked on a course of corporate empire building, absorbing in the next few years more than ninety smaller powder and chemical firms into the company. In most of these mergers he was able through a combination of great charm and equally large powers of persuasion to acquire the smaller company with a minimal outlay of cash. He was so successful, in fact, that in 1907, the U.S. Justice Department filed a major antitrust suit against the company, charging that the firm was attempting to create an illegal monopoly in the powder industry. Pierre S. du Pont, treasurer of the firm, was spending much of his time during this period dealing with the antitrust suit. That case eventually was to result in the division of the company into DuPont itself and two smaller powder firms, Hercules and Atlas Powder Companies.

At the same time, the company president had taken a large-scale plunge into New York City real estate where he was involved in a partnership with Charles H. Taft, the brother of newly elected President William Howard Taft. Though he was later to extend this enterprise into other regions, Coleman was at this time primarily interested in the creation of a chain of hotels in the city. He built the Hotel McAlpin and purchased large interests in the Waldorf-Astoria, the Sherry-Netherland, and other well-known establishments. He was spending so much time in New York, in fact, that he had been made an honorary police commissioner of the city. In this role, he was later to delight and scandalize New Yorkers by racing the mayor of New York up Broadway in his limousine.

In the period just before and after 1911, Coleman's favorite activity was the road. He spent as much time as possible in southern Delaware, and it was during this time that his friendship with John G. Townsend developed. John had sought out the millionaire to offer his support at a time when relatively few downstaters were doing so. Coleman soon realized that the young Selbyville businessman could be of much more practical assistance to him in ways other than simply as a supporter in the public relations campaign to sway public opinion in favor of the boulevard. By 1910, there were few men in Sussex County who knew more about local land

T. Coleman duPont
on one of his inspection trips in Sussex County (Courtesy of the Delaware Public Archives).

than John—about its types, its characteristics, its value, and about its ownership. Nor were there many Sussex Countians with a larger network of friends and acquaintances.

Though Coleman du Pont was never able to carry out his full plan, it is unlikely that he could have accomplished even as much as he did without John's help in the all-important work of acquiring rights-of-way. This assistance was at first purely advisory and unofficial. On du Pont's trips through the county in his large and elegant Minerva limosine, he often stopped in Selbyville to see John. From time to time the two went on inspection trips together along the proposed route.

One sign of the high regard in which John and Jennie Townsend by now held du Pont came at the birth of their fourth son, Preston, in 1910. As noted, they had named him Preston after Governor Lea, but they also gave him the middle name Coleman after du Pont.

After the Coleman du Pont Road Corporation was formally established in March, 1911, the work on the highway could at last begin. That same month, John and James Covington Townsend entered into one of their innumerable partnerships to form Peninsula Real Estate Company, Inc. The third partner in the company was Orlando Harrison of Berlin, a fruit-grower, orchardist, and nurseryman who was himself something of a legend on the peninsula.

A look at the activities of the real estate company during its relatively short existence suggests that one important consideration in starting it was to offer du Pont assistance in acquiring rights-of-way for the first phase of the road in Sussex County. Just as important was the fact that Harrison, the most knowledgeable man on the peninsula, and one of the most knowledgeable in the country, on the subject of orchards, had gotten the Townsends very much interested in this logical extension of their fruit brokerage business.

Getting the road built was no easy thing to accomplish, even for as formidable a character as "General" T. Coleman du Pont. He had gotten that title at the same time and in the same way as John had become a colonel. He was officially "Quartermaster General" on the staffs of Governors Lea, Pennewill, and Miller. Unlike Townsend, he used the title routinely and so did most everyone else. At that time in Delaware du Pont seemed much like a general as he went about organizing his forces to fight the battle of the highway. After two years of statewide and even national publicity about the boulevard and the man who was proposing to build it, du Pont had only to ride through a Sussex County town to send real estate prices shooting upward at an alarming rate. It did not help that he travelled in an enormous, custom-made Minerva touring car that was designed to be opened out into a sort of tent-like home on wheels. This novel vehicle, which was illustrated in the *Scientific American* article on the road, was undoubtedly Sussex County's first "motor home."

Many property owners were hard at work figuring out ways to profit from the road. du Pont relished the favored treatment he received in his travels around the state, but he was not happy about the price he had to pay for that treatment in the form of inflated right-of-way prices. Townsend proved invaluable to him in this effort because, at least, he was not tied directly to the road effort and had long since established himself as a large-scale buyer of farm land. Even where it was known that he was assisting du Pont, he had the advantage of being a local man with a keen sense of land values and a deep understanding of local customs and traditions. He was also, of course, an expert at dickering with Sussex Countians.

From the spring of 1911 to early 1916, he undertook roughly a dozen land acquisitions for Coleman du Pont Road, Inc. Five of these were conducted through Peninsula Real Estate Company and the others were in Townsend's own name. The road corporation had been granted the power of eminent domain in its charter from the legislature, but the use of that power was something to be avoided except as a last resort, considering the archaic law governing its use. Whenever possible, du Pont sought donations of rights-of-way. Otherwise he was more likely to buy the land than condemn it, in an effort to avoid litigation. Condemnation was a last desperate tool. Townsend aided him mightily in several instances by buying the necessary land when it would have been virtually impossible for du Pont to do so at even three times its true value.

Throughout the spring and summer of 1911, du Pont worked to

build the senior staff and work force necessary for the undertaking. Most of the senior staff were outsiders, but the project also provided jobs for many local men. In that way, the road brought immediate economic benefit to the area even before it was completed. du Pont bought a large old house situated near the route outside Georgetown for use as a field office and headquarters. For the next several years the place was in a constant flurry of activity.

At first he acted as his own chief engineer, but before very long he had hired a New Yorker named Frank Williams to fill the position. Williams was a highway engineer of great experience who had been working as chief engineer of the New York State Highway Department. du Pont also brought in the well-known European engineers Ernest Storms of Belgium and Thomas Aitken of Scotland as consultants. He hired several younger men for the engineering staff who soon became disciples, absorbing "T.C.'s" views of modern highway construction. Since nothing like the boulevard had ever been attempted before in the United States he was providing these men with an unparalleled opportunity to work at the very forefront of their profession. They were working not only to build a modern highway, but to advance the whole state of the art in the United States. Many of their methods were experimental. The same month du Pont's article appeared in the *Scientific American*, the magazine ran an accompanying piece on the then-revolutionary practice of using motor trucks in highway construction work.

Among the younger staff members was Charles Upham, who went on to become the first chief engineer of the Delaware State Highway Department when it was organized in 1917. Another was twenty-year-old Clayton Douglass Buck, a native of southern New Castle County and a great-grandnephew of John M. Clayton. Buck, who had been born at his famous ancestor's country home, Buena

Vista, went to work for du Pont after completing two years of an engineering course at the University of Pennsylvania. He also went on to greater things, becoming in due course chief engineer of the highway department, then governor of Delaware, and finally, in 1937, U. S. senator. In the first two positions, he was to be instrumental in carrying out the dualization of the du Pont Highway between Dover and Wilmington, making it the first dual-lane highway in the United States.

The eldest of du Pont's two sons, Francis V., also worked on the road. He later carried his father's philosophy into the 1940s when he was the prime mover behind the successful effort to build the Delaware Memorial Bridge. In the 1950s, while serving as U. S. Highway Commissioner in the Eisenhower administration, he worked to lay the groundwork for the federal interstate highway system, which his father had envisioned half a century before.

This was a high-powered group to descend on the Town of Selbyville in the late summer of 1911. Their arrival heightened the excitement that had been building ever since du Pont had declared that Selbyville would be the southern terminus. The General's decision to start construction there was partially determined by his success in acquiring rights-of-way in the area. It was also a political decision. du Pont wished to demonstrate as quickly as possible the value of the highway to Sussex County, the area in which he faced the most opposition. Every mile of road he could complete northward from Selbyville was one step toward that end.

He hoped to show the citizens of Sussex that the highway would more effectively link the entire state together than had ever been the case with the railroad. He knew what he was about. When his road was finally finished more than a decade later, the profound isolation that had characterized life in southern Delaware for generations was ended forever. The railroad had lessened the extent of that isolation.

The du Pont boulevard rendered it little more than a historical curiosity.

Though the project was under the nominal authority of the state government, du Pont himself exercised full control over design, route, construction methods, materials, and virtually everything else involved. For him it was a laboratory in which to test his theories. As usual when such a revolutionary undertaking was afoot, John G. Townsend was carefully taking it all in, making mental notes for future reference and learning the practical details of modern highway construction. Ground was officially broken at the Maryland state line just outside Selbyville on the morning of September 18, 1911. From there, through what remained of the warm weather, the first two-lane portion of the boulevard was run north through Baltimore Hundred. Work was also starting along other sections of the proposed route where rights-of-way had been acquired.

It is somewhat ironic, and was probably highly symbolic for John Townsend, that the first transaction he handled for the road corporation was the purchase of a two-hundred-foot strip of land through a farm owned by Captain John Long of Frankford. Captain Long was a prominent Democrat and was the son of the first president of the old Junction, Breakwater, and Franklin Railroad, the line which, when it was run through Dagsboro and Baltimore Hundreds in the 1870s and 1880s, had seemed to hold out such promise for the future. With the act of purchasing that strip of land in February of 1912, Townsend was in a sense writing a conclusion to that long and frustrating chapter in the history of southeastern Sussex and an introduction to the new age. One sad aspect of the story was the death, exactly one year before, in February 1911, of Zare Brasure. The man who had done as much as John Townsend to bring about this moment died just as it was about to happen.

For the remainder of 1911 and the early part of the 1912 construction season, the road moved steadily northward. Then, with the highway completed through Baltimore Hundred and portions of Dagsboro Hundred, the work ran into a major stumbling block. One particularly stubborn landowner refused to sell a section of right-of-way through his farm at any reasonable price. When as a final alternative the corporation condemned the land, the man sued. He charged that Coleman du Pont Road, Inc., should not have the power to condemn a two-hundred-foot right-of-way when, for the first phase, it planned to use only about forty feet. With this question being decided in the courts, du Pont's political opponents took advantage of the situation to hamper progress on the road still further. Very little work was accomplished for the remainder of the year. Matters had reached such a point early in 1913, that du Pont asked the legislature either to affirm that it was in favor of the project, or to repeal the act of incorporation for the road company and to return the $50,000 bond deposited by du Pont with the state treasurer's office. At the same time, he made several major concessions in an effort to defuse some of the opposition.

He agreed to reduce the width of the right-of-way he sought from two hundred to one hundred feet. He proposed that a state commission be created to establish fair rentals for the use of excess lands along the boulevard by utility companies. He offered further to turn over to the state all profits realized from these leases after development and maintenance expenses on the road had been paid. Finally, he took the remarkable step of offering to pay anyone through whose land the road passed five times the present assessed value of their land five years after the road was finished.

The legislature apparently never made any official response to his message, but they never halted work on the highway either. The right-of-way litigation was at last decided by the Delaware Supreme Court in du Pont's favor late in 1914, and the road building began again in earnest in the spring of 1915. Townsend, himself, was deeply involved in this incident and his efforts to help du Pont overcome the hurdle were a major reason for the eventual completion of the first phase of the project. The details of just what happened are not entirely clear, but there are two versions that bear repeating.

The problem with the rights-of-way was centered in the area north of Millsboro where there were a group of hold-outs. The route through that particular area had had to be changed at least once because of the local opposition. The new route had to run through several farms that had originally been owned by the Morris family, which from time immemorial had operated a gristmill on the headwaters of Cow Bridge Branch above Millsboro and Doe Bridge Mill Ponds. Their land holdings extended westward from the branch and ranged out across the proposed highway route. By the time the road was being built several large tracts were still owned by the family. In his 1922 work, *Delaware and the Eastern Shore*, Edward N. Vallandigham, a Delaware College professor and author, recalled the incident:

> [The road] had crept northward twenty miles when it was stalled between two villages by a stubborn farmer who would not grant a right of way. John G. Townsend hastened to Wilmington with a strong delegation of Sussex County men, and in spite of their warning that he promised too much, pledged himself to remove the obstacle. Mr. du Pont had already called off his engineers and workmen in disgust, but his answer was that they should return to the job on Monday, an answer given on Saturday. Mr. Townsend hastened home and bought the farm, wondering

how he should come out whole, and the cement road began again its progress northward.

In this account, Vallandigham exercised considerable poetical license, but it seems accurate in its broad outlines. The other version, which is similar and may have been even less accurate, is more entertaining. It was the story as recalled by an old friend of Townsend's many years later. He said that John went to du Pont to urge him to continue the road, that du Pont pointed out the problem with the farm and then bet the Sussex Countian $10,000 that he couldn't succeed in buying it. Townsend came home, bought the land and won the bet.

The actual facts were probably less dramatic, but they seem unfortunately to be lost with the passing of the men involved. Sussex County deed records do bear out the basic story, however. Beginning in 1913, and extending through 1914 and early 1915, Townsend purchased eight contiguous tracts of land along the route of the highway between Millsboro and the small village of Stockley. The largest, purchased from Samuel H. Morris for $5,850, was a farm of just under 340 acres. That figure represented top dollar at the time. The smallest tract, purchased from Granville A. Cannon, was just under an acre. The eight tracts together amounted to 860 acres and 94 square perches.

All told, the 860 acres were assessed by the county in 1917 at $15,000. Since the county assessed at about 50 percent of real value, this put the true value of the land at around $30,000. It is impossible to say what Townsend paid for the eight tracts since most of the deeds read only "One dollar and other valuable consideration." Under the circumstances, however, it is clear that he paid top dollar and the land may even have cost him more than $30,000. After the purchase of each tract, he turned over to Coleman du Pont Road, Inc., the land it required. For a consideration of $2,000, he transferred the remainder of the land to Peninsula Real Estate Company, of which he was the president. This gesture may have been a way of limiting his personal liability in the property.

This was by far the largest tract Townsend had acquired up to that time, and it was one which he was hard pressed to buy since he was then deep in the midst of an expansion of his businesses. He did not need the land, which was not well suited to the type of farming he did and was far from Selbyville, but he bought it to allow the road to continue.

Though he could not have realized it at the time, that gesture, which was a more dramatic demonstration of support for the highway than any other Sussex Countian ever made, may well have been the single biggest reason why he became governor of Delaware. It was talked about throughout lower Delaware in awed tones. The general conclusion was that anyone who would assume that much personal risk for the road was not only progressive but remarkably committed to economic progress for lower Delaware. Just as important, of course, was the profound impression John's act made on Coleman du Pont, who was thereafter one of his greatest supporters and strongly urged him to make the run for governor of Delaware in the fall of 1916.

Some years later, Townsend as governor was able to find an honorable and appropriate way of getting back his investment in the land. He was finally in a position to establish an institution that he had conceived as early as 1903, a "Delaware Home for the Feeble-Minded." The concept of this institution was that it should consist of a group of detached cottages in a wooded, park-like setting in southern Delaware. The institution should also have an attached farm that could produce most of the food necessary to feed the patients and hospital staff, and could provide work for the more highly-functioning residents.

Such a system operated successfully at the Sussex County Almshouse Farm a few miles to the north and at other similar institutions. When it came time to find a suitable site, Townsend knew just the place. In March 1919, Peninsula Real Estate Company sold to the State of Delaware 800.5 acres of land near Stockley, the same land that Townsend had purchased. The price was $35,000, which represented the initial purchase price, taxes, and other expenses the company had incurred during the years it had held the land. The governor, personally, received little, if any, profit from the transaction other than the satisfaction of seeing the land go toward two good causes.

The legal complications had slowed construction on the highway. It had been finished only to a point near Ellendale by 1917. The complications slowed progress enough that T. Coleman du Pont would never be able to carry out his grandly-conceived plan in its original form. After 1912, in frustration du Pont turned his attentions more and more to his New York City activities. He had also been experiencing increasingly severe illnesses, which had him in the hospital five times between 1907 and 1915. He simply did not have the energy to see the plan through to completion, but what he had accomplished produced remarkable results in southern Delaware.

John G. Townsend's faith in the concept and his labors in its behalf had affected his own career in an entirely unplanned and unexpected way. When he had first announced his support for the road, he had been one of many Delawareans expressing similar views. But when he made his remarkable personal financial commitment to it at a time when it was in danger of coming to a complete halt, he suddenly stood out from the noisy and brawling crowd of downstate politicians as a man with a very special commitment not only to the road, but to the well-being of his fellow citizens.

10. Growth and Progress

During the spring of 1916, John Townsend turned forty-five. He and Jennie had been happily married for twenty-six years and they were the parents of six children. Edith and Julian were grown and had left home. After graduating from normal school, Edith had taught school for several years before marrying John Asbury Tubbs, a young Selbyville lumberman who was also a former teacher. Julian had gone to work for his father first in the lumber business and then in the strawberry business. He was now running the Townsend interests in Georgetown. Lyla and Jack, though still at home, were close to adulthood. Lyla had graduated with the first senior class of the new Selbyville High School in 1912, and had entered the Women's College at Newark after working for her father in his brokerage business during several strawberry seasons. Jack was also employed in the far-flung family enterprises and was beginning to travel further and further afield as the strawberry brokerage business expanded over the peninsula and beyond.

Paul Townsend was thirteen and was attending school in Selbyville. He had already displayed a remarkable mathematical ability similar to that which had played such a large part in his father's success. Preston, the youngest, was just six and would begin school in the fall. The Townsends were active members of Salem Methodist Episcopal Church, where John served as a trustee, and they took part in most of the social events of the town. Grandfather Townsend was living on Church Street with his second wife. Now seventy-eight years old, his health was beginning to fail after a lifetime of hard work.

John's business interests had grown steadily since he left the legislature. Though he was still involved primarily in the lumber business and in fruit cultivation, he had moved beyond his initial involvement at the "grass roots" of the two industries. He was now a manufacturer of lumber products, and of canned and packed fruits and vegetables. The banks were successful at all three locations, and he was continuing to buy and sell timber and farmland. This period of growth in his enterprises had come at a time when the entire peninsula was beginning to experience the greatest wave of prosperity in its history. A large factor was the dramatic improvement in agricultural technology in the last two decades, but there were other reasons as well. The railroads were becoming somewhat more reasonable in the new air of government scrutiny brought on by the Roosevelt administration, and the pioneering efforts of such highway builders as T. Coleman du Pont had made it easier for farmers to get their perishable produce to market.

Improvements in refrigerator cars and in the technology for handling fruits and vegetables had made it possible for Delmarva growers to sell their products not only in the region but through much of the East. As their markets expanded so did the public demand. Incomes were growing throughout the country and with them grew the appetite for the products the peninsula produced. When John had first gotten into the strawberry business as a broker, most of the market had been for fresh berries. It was strictly seasonal, limited for the most part to nearby cities within easy railroad range. But strawberries could now successfully be preserved in various forms and sold all year long. This had the added advantage of providing a good use for those berries that were not of high enough quality to bring good prices in the city markets.

All this set John in the direction of preserving and canning strawberries. Canning was certainly nothing new on the peninsula. Harbison Hickman of Lewes had started a successful cannery before the Civil War, and by the late nineteenth century scores of tomato, vegetable, and peach canneries had sprung up on Delmarva. John was one of the first men in the region to apply the new technology to berries. He was later credited with inventing the strawberry ice cream soda one Saturday afternoon at Blackstone's Drug Store in Millsboro as a way of finding a new use for strawberries. Though this story is difficult to verify, it is quite possibly true. The strawberry soda not only tasted good, but it had the added advantage of providing a new market for strawberries.

Discovering new markets and new uses for strawberries was one of the challenges brought on by John's success as a broker. By 1910, his territory had expanded well beyond Delmarva. He and his agents were now travelling south in the early spring to buy up the first berries ready for market in Louisiana and Tennessee. They followed the harvest north through the Carolinas, up the peninsula, and into New Jersey. At some time during this period John began the practice of renting small canneries and packing houses along the route during the harvest season and putting up his own strawberries for sale to the confectionary trade. He had a crew who travelled from place to place during the season to oversee the work.

Another early diversification was a 1908 venture into the ice business. Refrigerator cars were still just giant ice boxes

The Townsends at home:

Pictured above is one of a series of summer cottages the family rented at Rehoboth. At left are Lyla and Jack about 1910 with their father and an unidentified young lady who is seated on the children's pony (all photos from the Lyla T. Savoy Collection unless otherwise marked).

Preston and his cousin, Covington Townsend, are seen playing with their friend Dorothy Williams in 1911 in the yard of James Townsend's home on Church Street, Selbyville. The dog was Covington's (photo courtesy of Dorothy Williams Pepper).

**The young
Townsend
Ladies:**

*Lyla, at right, as a
college student,
about 1916.*

*Edith, below, swimming
at Rehoboth shortly
before her marriage to
John Asbury Tubbs.*

On Indian River:
*Julian and Jack
Townsend are seen
with a friend aboard
the family's motor
launch about 1912.*

without their own built-in refrigeration equipment. Having access to large quantities of ice at the right times was essential to a successful brokerage business since the railroad cars that carried fresh berries to market had to be packed with ice. In 1908, John entered into another of his numerous partnerships with Zare Brasure and a third man, D. W. Campbell, to form the Selbyville Ice Company. They were able with their own ice plant to produce enough ice for John's own needs and to sell the excess to other brokers in the area. Before this time, local brokers and growers had been forced to purchase most of their ice from large ice-making companies in northern Delaware. Now John and his partners could produce it locally and sell it for less. For some two years, they had a near monopoly in the Selbyville area, but by 1910, another ice company had opened up in town. After the death of Zare Brasure early in 1911, John made the decision to move the ice plant to Chincoteague Island, Virginia, where great quantities of ice were needed for the shipment of oysters. This arrangement worked better because the oyster season came during the off-season for strawberries. Since there were many berry and fruit growers on the Eastern Shore of Virginia and in southern Worcester County, the ice could be sold to them during the summer and to the oyster packers in the fall and winter.

The big development in his career came late in 1911, when John became a cannery owner himself by purchasing the already well-established Calhoun & Jones Cannery along the railroad track in Georgetown. His partners in this new enterprise were his brother James Townsend and Vollie Murray of Selbyville, who had been working with him for several years in the brokerage business. With this purchase, the Townsends were in a position not only to can and pack strawberries but tomatoes, peaches, and other fruit and vegetables produced in the area.

Early in 1913, the same three partners started the Atlantic Canning Company in Rehoboth Beach. This new cannery came about as a direct result of the completion the year before of the new Lewes and Rehoboth Canal, which had been built by the federal government. The canal had been a pet project of businessmen in the area for decades–ever since the Assawoman Canal had been finished in the late 1800s, linking Indian River Bay with Little Assawoman Bay. The new canal was a continuation of this effort and gave Baltimore Hundred and northern Worcester county growers a link with Lewes and the Delaware Bay.

Fruit and vegetable growers in northern and eastern Baltimore Hundred, on Long Neck, and in Indian River and Lewes and Rehoboth Hundreds had been far enough from the railroads that they still faced major difficulties in getting their crops to market. Construction of the new canal and the dredging of a channel across Rehoboth Bay meant that now they could load their produce on large, shallow draft barges and tow them by water to the railroad at Rehoboth or Lewes.

The Atlantic Cannery was situated just south of the new railroad bridge crossing the canal into Rehoboth Beach. A siding was built into the cannery yard itself so that produce could be brought to the cannery wharf, processed in the cannery, and loaded into railroad cars for shipment. Within a year or two, a competing cannery, the Rehoboth Cannery, was built just north of Atlantic, but there was ample business in the area to keep both operating at full capacity during the growing season.

By 1915, a third Townsend cannery had been established in the town of Selbyville itself. This operation was situated along the railroad at Hoosier Street. Though John had handled much of the management of all three canneries himself at the outset, it had become too big a job for one man, especially one with so many other interests. In that year he incorporated the Georgetown cannery as J. G. Townsend, Jr. & Company, with himself as president, James Covington Townsend as vice-president, and his son, Julian, as secretary and treasurer.

After finishing his studies at the Wilmington Conference Academy (now Wesley College) in Dover and the Beacom Business School (now Goldey Beacom College) in Wilmington, Julian had returned to Selbyville and gone to work with his father in a newly created lumber company, J. G. Townsend and Son. After several years, he had concluded that he was more interested in the newly acquired canning operations and shifted into that. With the formal incorporation of the Georgetown cannery much of its operation soon fell under his management. John plainly did not believe in coddling his children when they were old enough to go to work.

Thus, when the growing and canning seasons were at their height, the Townsends employed as many as five to six hundred men and women in their various enterprises. John in all his various partnerships was becoming one of the county's larger employers. It was a status he would enjoy for the rest of his life.

Strawberries remained John's mainstay in his canning operations and in his brokerage business, but he was beginning to branch out into other areas as well–especially into the development of orchards. This interest came about primarily because of his friendship with one of the most remarkable "agriculturalists" in Maryland, Orlando Harrison of Berlin.

The Townsend brothers' partnership with Harrison in Peninsula Real Estate Company had played an integral role in the construction of the du Pont Boulevard, but that was only one purpose of the firm. The other was the acquisition of land suitable for orchards, which was an all-consuming passion with Harrison at the time. He knew more about orchards and about the cultivation of trees and shrubs than any other man on the peninsula and had become an international authority on the subject by 1910.

Harrison's origins and early development were similar in many ways to that of the Townsend brothers except that he had started out in Baltimore Hundred and gone south to Worcester. Four years older than John, he had been born on a farm near Roxana and had moved with his parents to Berlin in 1884. The elder Harrison had started a small orchard and tree nursery there, but it had been his son who moved it beyond the realm of a small family operation. In the late 1890s Orlando Harrison embarked on a study of orchards and nurseries that consumed much of the next decade. By 1906 he had travelled widely throughout the United States studying growing methods, tree strains, and fruit growing. By this time he had spent years working on experiments in orchard development on his lands in Worcester County. He had acquired additional land in Western Maryland (where he planted 50,000 fruit trees), Delaware, and West Virginia. Harrison spent several months in Europe in 1908, studying the propagation of evergreens and shrubs and purchasing new base stocks for the expansion of Harrison Nurseries, Inc., near Berlin. By 1916, they were the largest general nurseries in the world.

John and James Townsend were more interested in Harrison's skills as an orchardist and it is safe to say that John owed his early education in the propagation of apple and peach trees to Orlando Harrison. By 1912, Harrison was already involved in such Sussex County ventures as York Imperial Orchard Company and the Woodland Orchard Company. In January of that year, Orlando Harrison, John Townsend, and Albert W. Sisk of Preston, Maryland, incorporated Eastern Shore Orchards, Inc. and listed themselves as the stockholders. Later that same year John was listed as "resident agent" on a new Harrison venture, Stayman's Winesap Orchard Company, although he was not listed as a stockholder.

In 1913, he was one of the original stockholders of the Berlin Orchard Company. By 1915, he was also a partner in Harrision's Pomona Orchard Company, Bay View Orchard Company, Redlands Orchard Company and Riverside Orchard Company. Harrison also had several other orchards in the county in which John was not involved. The largest of these, the Indian Swan Orchard was located on the north side of the Indian River a few miles east of Millsboro. It took its name from its location on the river and on Swan Creek, which branched off from the river and served as the eastern boundary of the orchard. Even though John was not involved in the Indian Swan Orchard, he early marked it as a prime piece of real estate. A decade later, he bought it and it became one of his most important acquisitions.

By this time, John was a principal in something like ten or more separate corporations, including at least six orchards. The reason for this profusion of corporations, company names, and separate sets of stockholders was a practical one. The Delaware Corporation Law as then written stipulated that one's liability in a corporation extended only to the amount of one's interest in that corporation. Thus, if Redlands Orchards failed, the stockholders could lose their investment in it, but their other interests were not affected. In high-risk agricultural ventures this provision was especially attractive and it led men like Harrison to incorporate many of their riskier ventures in Delaware. When that provision was later changed, it made for fewer corporations of greater value. It also meant that a multitude of marvelously creative and optimistic company names passed from the state's rolls of active corporations .

In the course of this growing involvement in canning and orchards, John had by no means lost interest in the lumber business. He was, in fact, expanding his interests there as well. He and James were still active in numerous timber ventures and operated several sawmills. John was moving farther and farther afield in that area as well and had at least one partnership in North Carolina with his old Worcester County friend George Bishop under the name Townsend and Bishop Lumber Company. Bishop moved down to operate the business at first hand while John kept an eye on it from home.

After involving himself briefly with Julian in J. G. Townsend and Son, he and James consolidated their lumber operations in 1915 under a new corporation, Selbyville Manufacturing Company, with an office and a lumber yard at the corner of McCabe Street and Railroad Avenue in Selbyville. John's son-in-law, Jack Tubbs, had worked with his father William R. Tubbs and other members of his family in the Delaware Lumber Company for several years, but when Selbyville Manufacturing Company was incorporated, he came into the new business as secretary-treasurer. Not only did they continue the sawmills under the new arrangement, but they also established a millwork department and became building contractors.

The "Machine": Lyla, Jule, and Jack Townsend are seen in the family automobile in Selbyville about 1916. It was one of the first motor vehicles in Baltimore Hundred (Lyla T. Savoy Collection).

All of this diverse activity, including the banks and canneries, kept John on the go much of the time, throughout Delaware and the peninsula. He took frequent trips south to run his brokerage business and to keep an eye on his lumber venture in North Carolina. He also visited many cities in the Northeast and Midwest arranging for the sale of his cannery products and to keep in touch with large customers.

That he also found the time to conduct an active political career and to raise a family seems quite remarkable until one realizes that he was a gifted natural executive in the truest sense of the word–he had a talent for getting things done and for making decisions quickly. He was able to judge the abilities of his friends and employees skillfully and had, by 1915, developed a team of able managers and assistants who carried out much of the day-to-day operations of the companies. His active involvement in many of his smaller partnerships was minimal. He picked his partners carefully, put up the financial backing, and gave them their heads. Yet in his larger enterprises he was by no means an absentee boss. His correspondence for this period reflects a remarkably detailed knowledge of the most minor aspects of his various businesses.

In a morning of discussions, letter-writing, or telegraphing, he could discuss knowledgeably the color and texture of the tomato puree being produced that week by the Georgetown cannery, the construction details of new sheds at Atlantic Cannery, the price of sugar in Chicago versus that in New York, the availability of timber for pilings in obscure points in the Carolinas, the railroad freight charges between Selbyville and a score of cities, the doings of the Salem Methodist Church, aunts' and uncles' banking problems, his children's school work, choices for Christmas presents, the political make-up of Brandywine Hundred, and an abundance of other matters as well.

John owned one of Baltimore Hundred's first automobiles. He enjoyed the impression it made, especially on children in the area. He often gave them rides in his "machine." He was more than ever in the habit of introducing himself to everyone he encountered, great or small, young or old. By 1915, he probably knew as many of his fellow citizens as any man in Delaware. He enjoyed robust good health and had a full shock of reddish-blonde hair that the press would soon take great enjoyment in referring to as "strawberry blonde." This, then, was the man who announced his candidacy for governor of Delaware in the summer of 1916.

Part V:

The Race for Governor

11. The Campaign of 1916

In the course of a long and varied political career, John was involved in many campaigns under many different sorts of conditions. His very longevity as a political leader qualifies him as an uncommonly successful member of the profession, but his successful passage through the shoals and rapids of the 1916 campaign in Delaware qualified him as a true master. The possibilities for failure were unlimited. Not only were there three separate and distinct Republican factions in Delaware, none of which fully trusted the others, but the Prohibition Party and the smaller Socialist Party were at their respective high-water marks that year. The situation was further complicated by the intense fight the Democratic Party was waging to retain the tenuous hold on the General Assembly it had achieved four years before. Last but not least, for the first time in American history U.S. senators were being popularly elected.

The 1912 campaign had been a watershed in American politics. The Progressive movement, which had been building in strength nationally for years, made a hard fight for power and nearly won the presidency. In the course of that fight the G.O.P. had undergone the kind of split that had been plaguing Republicans in Delaware for nearly twenty years. The Roosevelt administration, begun in the aftermath of the McKinley assassination in 1901, had easily been the most dynamic in American history. The brilliant and mercurial Theodore Roosevelt had succeeded in changing the "gilded age" atmosphere of the federal government. He had replaced the old air of tired corruption with a fresh breeze of Progressive reform. In so doing, he had become the most personally popular president in decades and the model for many younger politicians, among whom was John Townsend.

Roosevelt had decided in 1908 to honor his 1904 pledge not to run again. Instead he supported the candidacy of his amiable and rotund secretary of war, William Howard Taft. It was his belief that the Ohioan would carry his unfinished Progressive program forward. With Taft's victory accomplished, Roosevelt made a graceful exit, departing on an African safari. He soon saw, however, that Taft was more conservative than Progressive. In 1912, Roosevelt broke with his erstwhile protegé and announced his own candidacy.

Taft controlled enough of the party machinery by then to secure the G.O.P. nomination for a second term, whereupon the Progressives with Roosevelt at their head bolted from the party and formed what came to be known as the Bull Moose Party behind TR's third party candidacy. An insurgent leader of this magnitude had the effect of polarizing the G.O.P. throughout the country. In Delaware, the regular Republican machine formed by Coleman and Colonel Henry du Pont after their defeat of Addicks six years earlier worked for the national Republican ticket. In doing so, they created a rebellion among many Delaware Republicans who were already chafing at the bit under the dominance of the du Ponts.

Georgetown lawyer and newspaper publisher Robert Houston, who had fought on the du Pont side to oust Addicks in the 1890s and early 1900s, now emerged as one of the chief Progressive leaders and became state chairman of the newly formed Progressive Party. His *Sussex Republican* was one of the few newspapers in the state carrying the Progressive message in 1912, but even so many Delaware voters heard the call and heeded it. Another publisher in favor of the Bull Moose ticket was Everett Johnson in Newark.

Many onetime Union Republicans used the Bull Moose campaign as an excuse to leave the domination of the du Ponts and to rally around the new Progressive cause. John tended in this direction himself, but he was careful then as in the past not to use his support for Roosevelt as a podium from which to direct attacks at the du Ponts. Old Dr. Caleb R. Layton was not so restrained, however, and soon Houston found himself in the unlikely position of being on the same side as his former bitter enemy, Layton, and in opposition to his former allies, the du Ponts.

The Delaware Progressives were poorly funded and poorly organized that year, but still they made enough of a showing at the polls to have a major influence in the coming General Assembly. Nationally, the Republicans had gone down in defeat to a Democrat, Governor Woodrow Wilson of New Jersey. The Democrats had been able to agree on a candidate with just the right combination of attributes. Son of a long line of Virginia clergymen, former president of Princeton University, and moderately liberal governor of New Jersey, Wilson also had the advantage of an undivided Democratic Party. Even so, he scored only a narrow victory over Theodore Roosevelt, marking the only time in the twentieth century in which a third party candidate outpolled a major party nominee. Taft, the Republican nominee, came in third, though he managed to carry the state of Delaware.

Delaware Democrats had won a majority in the General Assembly and they used it to elect Willard Saulsbury Jr. to the U. S. Senate. Saulsbury, son of former U.S. Senator and Delaware Chancellor Willard Saulsbury, was a native of Kent County and had led the Kent County Democrats through the halcyon days of the Addicks period. He had since moved to Wilmington, where he had married May Lammot du Pont, a sister of Mrs. T. Coleman du Pont, and established a successful legal practice. Despite marrying into the family, Saulsbury had remained an arch political foe both of Coleman du Pont and of the old senator. The enmity between Saulsbury and Senator Henry du Pont was so deep that the latter refused to perform the customary duty of the state's senior senator in escorting the junior senator to the front of the U.S. Senate chamber to be sworn in.

Another Democratic leader then emerging, Thomas F. Bayard, was also married to a member of the du Pont clan. He was almost as much at odds politically with the family as Saulsbury. It could already be seen that the du Pont family and the political life of Delaware were irrevocably bound together. When things were relatively tranquil within the family, the political situation tended also to be more calm. It was even more obvious that when the du Ponts were feuding among themselves, state politics reflected the storm.

The session of the General Assembly that began in January of 1913 saw many Progressive developments, the most dramatic of which was the creation of the Women's College as an adjunct of Delaware College in Newark. This action came largely through the efforts of Everett Johnson, who laid the groundwork during his term in the legislature from 1910 to 1912. He had been advocating a Women's College for years and now succeeded in obtaining passage of enabling legislation in March 1913, after leaving the General Assembly. It was the result of several years of concerted effort by woman's clubs and by many of Delaware's more enlightened citizens. The new college was seen by most citizens as a long overdue improvement. Delaware State College in Dover, which in those days of segregation was the state's college for blacks, had been coeducational since it was established in the 1890s. Delaware College itself had experimented with coeducation when it reopened after being closed during the Civil War. It had accepted female students from 1870 to 1885 but after this trial period the college had returned to its former all-male status. John had become a firm supporter of the Women's College after a lobbying effort by his younger daughter, Lyla, who had just graduated from high school and thought it deplorable that the opportunity for a young woman to attend a public institution of higher education in Delaware depended upon her race. Her father's close friendship with Everett, one of the leading proponents of the Womens' College, was also an influential factor.

After his graduation from Delaware College in 1899, Johnson had gone to Johns Hopkins University for two more years of post-graduate study in history and political science. He had remained there for several years after his marriage to Louise Staton, working as a teacher at the Johns Hopkins preparatory school. He had always been in somewhat delicate health. After a near-fatal illness in 1903 and continued ill health thereafter he gave up his teaching job and returned with his wife to the Newark area. Soon after their return, the Johnsons were able to purchase a small farm in Pencader Hundred. The new home, once the parsonage of the nearby Welsh Tract Primitive Baptist Church where Louise and Everett had been married, had great sentimental appeal because it was the house where Louise was born. For the next several years Everett made a living raising vegetables and selling them at the King Street Market in Wilmington, while trying with only partial success to learn the complicated craft of farming. In fact, he endeared himself to members of the local Grange with his hilarious accounts of his trials and tribulations as a farmer. Despite his best efforts to master agriculture, he remained an intellectual and an idealistic and dedicated Progressive with an avid interest in politics.

In January of 1910, he founded a weekly newspaper in Newark, the *Newark Post*, which served as a forum for his philosophy. He had become by now a polished public speaker and was much in demand in Pencader Hundred, where he was well liked even by those who did not accept his political views.* For that reason, he was drafted as a Republican candidate for the legislature in the fall of 1910. Johnson was none too comfortable in the role of candidate. For one thing, his Democratic opponent, Roseby McMullen, was a good friend and fellow farmer. But, as Louise Johnson later wrote, Everett prevailed. His most successful ploy during the campaign was using his own well-known shortcomings as a farmer to combat McMullen. "Mr. McMullen was the prize grower of sweet potatoes in the district, and Everett succeeded in convincing the voters that he (McMullen) would be needed more for that purpose than in Dover! Everett won."

Ever since his graduation from Delaware College, Johnson had been firmly committed to improving his alma mater, of which he was an active and dedicated alumnus. During his term in the General Assembly, he succeeded in obtaining passage of legislation to create a state-supported Delaware Chair of History. He also brought about passage of the first bill for state financial support for the college's agricultural extension service. Johnson declined a second term in 1912, but he remained vitally interested in the women's college and, as a former legislator, led efforts to bring about enactment of the bill in the 1913 session, speaking convincingly in its favor. Aided by the Progressive

---

* *In his preface to a recent biography of Johnson entitled* Press, Politics, and Perseverance - Everett Johnson and the Press of Kells *by Robert C. Barnes and Judith M. Pfeiffer (Wilmington: Oak Knoll Press, Cedar Tree Books, 1999) eminent Delaware historian John A. Munroe quoted an oldtime Delaware journalist as saying that Johnson was the finest orator he had ever heard–and that in a day when oratory was greatly prized.*

explosion, his efforts to achieve passage succeeded.

Following his brief legislative service, Everett returned to Newark to devote all of his time to building up the *Post*, adding a job-printing business and increasing the newspaper's circulation. Yet, almost in spite of himself, Johnson was becoming more and more influential in Republican politics. He was also seeing more of John and talking with him about Delaware's needs and how best to accomplish them. Well before the 1916 election campaign, he had become the leading promoter of John's candidacy for governor.

In December 1914, a situation arose within the du Pont family which at first glance seemed entirely unrelated to politics but which quickly became central to Republican Party matters. T. Coleman du Pont had by now been president of the family firm for twelve years. He decided to resign and to sell his stock in the company. His reasons for doing so were reasonable enough. He had been in failing health for some time, suffering from the early stages of what was later diagnosed as throat cancer. His business activities outside of Delaware, chiefly in New York City, were consuming more and more of his time and dwindling energy, even as he continued to press ahead on the Coleman du Pont Road. He also harbored serious, though still confidential, political ambitions. He hoped at least for a seat in the U.S. Senate and thought that he might even have a chance at the presidency. The outbreak of war in Europe made it clear to everyone in the company that DuPont might soon need to undergo the largest expansion in its history. Coleman had neither the time nor the interest to direct this expansion. The moment had arrived for him to step aside and let someone else take over.

Alfred I. du Pont, who, with Coleman and Pierre, made up the company leadership, had become more and more alienated from his cousins in recent years. Like them, he was a remarkable person of many and varied interests. He was a musician of considerable renown locally. He had started Wilmington's first symphony orchestra in the 1880s and had served as conductor and composer (Pierre was the pianist). But Alfred was also well known for his eccentricity and for his stubborn independence. Most members of the family, including Pierre and Senator Henry du Pont, had been shocked by the manner in which he had divorced his first wife in 1906 and involved himself in a notorious romance thereafter. As the disapproval of the clan became more evident, Alfred's defiance increased. In the end even Coleman, a well-known bon vivant himself who was generally quite tolerant of the peccadilloes of others, began to gaze askance at his cousin's behavior. Largely as a result of this situation, Pierre had engineered a reorganization of the company management in 1911 which had the effect of removing Alfred from his duties as general manager of the black powder division. He remained a major stockholder and continued to serve as a vice-president, but powder production was his first love and Pierre's action infuriated him. Nothing occurred within the next three years to heal the breach.

When Coleman announced his plans to retire and sell his stock back to the company, Alfred objected strenuously, contending that the asking price was too high. He probably sensed that any purchase of Coleman's stock by the company would further erode his own position. Shortly thereafter, Pierre quietly organized a group of family members and close friends, including his brothers Irénée and Lammot du Pont and his former assistant, John Jacob Raskob, for the purpose of buying the shares and holding them intact as a means of acquiring control of the company. The syndicate he created later became known as Christiana Securities Company and served as the foundation upon which Pierre built the modern DuPont chemical empire. When he heard about this development, Alfred was livid. He promptly filed suit, seeking to have the sale overturned by the courts. He failed in this attempt. Though he continued to be a major stockholder, he withdrew from active participation in the company. Thereafter, he embarked on a campaign of political vengeance against Senator Henry du Pont and against Coleman, the two members of the family most politically active and therefore most vulnerable to attack. Alfred had always been a political idealist and was generally more aggressive about pursuing his beliefs than either Senator du Pont or the more moderate Coleman. But his remarkably bitter fight against them in 1916 was prompted, it seemed, more by a thirst for revenge than by the strong social conscience he later displayed. Aside from his substantial wealth, the most powerful weapon in his arsenal was his ownership of the Wilmington *Morning News*, which he had quietly purchased in 1911. He also set out to subsidize, and in a few cases to purchase, weekly newspapers throughout the state. With these organs he embarked on a propaganda battle against what he fondly termed the du Pont Machine. He also brought about the creation of two groups, the Independent Republicans and the Voters' Non-Partisan League, which sought Progressive reforms and the defeat of Senator du Pont.

Alfred's most important ally in this fight turned out to be J. Frank Allee, who was still smarting from the treatment he had received at the hands of Coleman in the wake of the Addicks affair. Well-financed by Alfred, Allee was out drumming up support throughout Kent and southern New Castle County for the battle against the machine. Alfred also sought to assist the already established Progressive Party of southern Delaware. While they were mildly receptive, Houston and the other leaders carefully refrained from becoming too closely aligned with him.

By the late spring of 1916, John's gubernatorial ambitions had become common knowledge among Republicans of all persuasions. Close friends like Everett Johnson were hard at work talking up his candidacy in New Castle and elsewhere. The Regular Republican State Committee was agreeable in principle to the idea of a candidate from lower Sussex. Simeon Pennewill, the last Sussex Countian to hold the office, lived so close to the Kent County line in northwestern Sussex that he had been little known in central or southern Sussex. Never, in fact, had a Republican from the lower part of Sussex County held the office of governor, with the unfortunate exception of Governor Marvil of Laurel, who had died very soon after taking office, thus helping to precipitate the split between the Union and Regular Republicans.

The state committee was also generally agreeable to the idea of John G. Townsend Jr. as the gubernatorial nominee quite apart from his geographical origins. Not only had he been a faithful Republican of many years' standing, but his work as a peacemaker during the Addicks period was well known and much appreciated by Republicans of all factions. Nor did it hurt John's chances that T. Coleman du Pont had come to admire him greatly for reasons quite aside from politics.

In view of the atmosphere of factional dispute that spring, it is probable that the committee hoped to use the Townsend candidacy to defuse some of the fiery Progressive sentiment threatening to tear the party apart. If that was their hope, however, they were soon to be disappointed. The regular Republican State Convention was held in Dover in May and it nominated a slate that contained few surprises. The ticket was headed by old Senator Henry du Pont who, at age seventy-eight, was seeking his third term. John was nominated for the office of governor with a minimum of discussion, since he had been the favorite in the months leading up to the convention. New Castle Countian George M. Fisher was nominated for lieutenant governor.

The congressional candidate was incumbent Thomas W. Miller. The only other Sussex Countian on the state ticket was John's former colleague in the state legislature, William J. Swain of Bridgeville, the candidate for state auditor.

A few weeks after the regulars had concluded their business and gone home, the Progressives also met in Dover to nominate a state ticket. This event was more exciting all the way around than the regular convention. The Progressives had a strong feeling that this was their year at last. With all the extra press coverage as a result of Alfred du Pont's interest and the general optimism among the delegates, "a good time was had by all." The Progressives nominated Dr. Hiram Burton of Lewes for U.S. Senator. This onetime Union Republican leader was well liked in the state and had served two terms in the U. S. House of Representatives from 1905 to 1909.

When the Progressives got around to deciding on a gubernatorial candidate, however, they arrived at a choice that confounded the regular Republicans: John G. Townsend Jr. John was, after all, enormously popular in the downstate precincts where the Progressives had their greatest power. They felt that his nomination by the regulars had been a clear attempt to preempt them. They would not be preempted. To further confuse things, they also nominated Swain and the regular candidate for attorney general, David Reinhardt of Wilmington, for their respective offices. The ball, as it were, had been knocked back into the regulars' court.

It did not take them long to respond. The day after the Progressive convention the regular Republican State Committee announced that unless Messrs. Townsend, Swain, and Reinhardt withdrew from the Progressive ticket, they would be dumped from the regular ticket. Though John's reactions to these developments

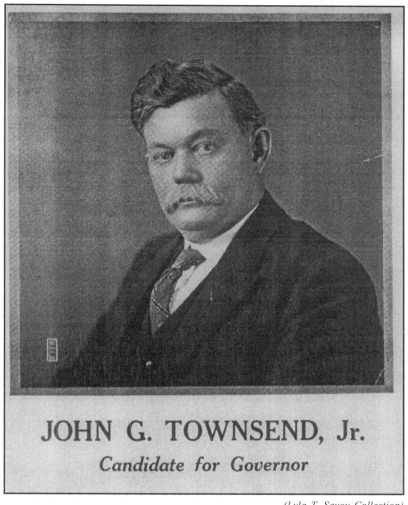

JOHN G. TOWNSEND, Jr.
Candidate for Governor

(Lyla T. Savoy Collection)

have not survived, it is not hard to imagine what they must have been. He suddenly found himself in a position in which his very popularity could lead to his political demise before his candidacy even got off the ground. It seemed like a no-win situation. If he threw over the Progressives and continued on the regular ticket, he would destroy his own downstate power base. Yet, if he refused to do as the state committee demanded, he could find himself without the support of the organized party around Wilmington where he faced his toughest fight. It was a hard decision. It was arguably the hardest decision of John G. Townsend's political career (although some of those in the four years that followed would have run it a close second).

Like the master politician he was, John made the right choice. He announced that while he very much wished to remain on the regular Republican ticket, he would not throw over the Progressives under any circumstances. Swain and Reinhardt concurred. Then they all sat back and waited to see what would happen. Behind the scenes, of course, John exerted every bit of influence he had with the regulars to make them see that their action would hurt themselves at least as much as it would hurt Townsend, Swain, and Reinhardt.

The front pages of the daily newspapers were frantic. The editorial columns–especially those of Alfred I. du Pont–were outraged. In the days that followed, the regular state committee refrained from making any decision, waiting to see which way the public was swinging. They swung, upstaters and downstaters alike, into the Townsend column. Without even trying, John became the hero of the moment, even overshadowing the larger political story of Alfred I. du Pont against Coleman and the senator. The final result was anticlimatic. The regulars decided it would be unwise to carry through with their threat and so they ultimately did nothing. In one sense, they had become the ones who could not win. When the public realized that the Progressives and the three candidates had made the regular machine back down it was a turning point in the political history of Delaware. The battle in the du Pont family that fall received the lion's share of the publicity, but the battle over the candidacy of Townsend, Reinhardt, and Swain had a more profound effect on life in Delaware.

When, soon after this victory, John was also nominated for

governor by the Prohibition Party, it was the icing on the cake. He won this honor because of his strong Methodism and because he had agreed not to oppose, if not strongly favor, the campaign for a prohibition amendment, which was then gathering strength throughout the country for a final fight toward passage. He was a moderate on this issue, but he came far enough over to the prohibition side to win their endorsement. Though the Prohibition Party nominated some candidates from the regular Republican ticket and others from the Progressive ticket, John Townsend was the only candidate to appear on all three. He did not win the support of the Socialists, who were also active that year, and neither did any other candidate from either Republican or Democratic ranks.

John's Democratic opponent was Dover lawyer James H. Hughes, the same man who had defended the Kent County Board of Elections some two decades earlier when it had conveniently failed to count some three thousand Republican votes. Though this incident had happened long before, many downstate voters had vivid memories of it. It was difficult, under the circumstances, for Hughes to establish himself in the eyes of the voters as a statesmanlike figure of gubernatorial timber.

The Democrats nominated Josiah O. Wolcott, a prominent attorney, to oppose Senator du Pont and Dr. Burton in the U.S. Senate race. Their candidate for lieutenant governor was a respected southern New Castle County farmer named Lewis F. Eliason. They were optimistic as they entered the fall campaign behind the incumbent candidacy of a popular Democratic president, Woodrow Wilson, and a split in the Delaware Republican Party that was a potential advantage for their side.

The U.S. Senate battle overshadowed the Townsend-Hughes race and every other political event in Delaware that year. It was the first time Senator du Pont had ever had to face a popular election. He had been safely ensconced in the Senate when the 17th Amendment had been ratified three years earlier, bringing about the popular election of U.S. senators. Had it been simply a matter of fighting for votes in a joint session of the legislature as in the old days, it is unlikely that the battle between Alfred I. du Pont and his kin would have been so public or so prolonged, but the popular election threw things into a whole different light.

The pages of Alfred's Wilmington *Morning News* were filled daily with stories about the impending defeat of the old senator and the dirty deals of the "du Pont Machine." The *Evening Journal* was just as intense in its support for Senator du Pont and its opposition to Alfred. Curiously enough, neither paper had much to say about the other races. Alfred's staff would print flattering reports about John Townsend and his fellow Progressives in passing, but they did not devote much space to them. They reserved their energies for the job of defeating the old senator. It also became clear that they did not care greatly whether the people cast their votes for Wolcott, Dr. Burton, or the Socialist candidate as long as they voted against Henry A. du Pont.

John spent the campaign in the traditional manner, attending political rallies and other gatherings of Republicans of whatever persuasion. He also used the extensive network of contacts he had built up in the preceding twenty years in his many businesses. Among those contacts were many downstate Democrats.

After being forced to back down on the matter of Townsend's dual candidacy, some members of the state Republican hierarchy, according to the *Morning News*, were not working as hard for his candidacy as they might have been. In its editorial of Tuesday, October 31, the *Morning News* pointed out that it had taken the regulars nearly

Campaign Car: *John G. Townsend Jr. used this Buick touring car to travel across Delaware in search of votes during his 1916 campaign. Note the cut-out photos of John set into the headlights and the American flags flanking the hood (Lyla T. Savoy Collection).*

to the end of the campaign to place John's name on the banner of the Kent County Republican Club, the Dover headquarters of the regular Republican organization.

Senator du Pont made a rare foray into Sussex County on Wednesday, November 1, hoping to generate some excitement for his candidacy. The result, according to the *News*, was depressing. "No doubt," it reported, "the Colonel (du Pont) thinks it would have been much better if he had never come down to Sussex . . . than to meet with such a cool reception."

Although Colonel John G. Townsend Jr., candidate for governor, David J. Reinhardt, candidate for attorney general, and Congressman Thomas W. Miller, who is seeking reelection, were present–the first two seated in the stand with Senator du Pont . . . none of them was called upon to address the crowd, much to the surprise of all . . . The meeting was evidently a frame-up on the part of someone solely for the benefit of Senator du Pont, and little consideration was given the candidates whom the organization so vainly tried to get to withdraw from the Independent Republican ticket.

If John had been hurt by the treatment he had received at the hands of the regular organization, he was to have the last laugh. It came less than a week later when, in an outcome largely lacking in dramatic sweeping victories, he defeated Hughes by the largest plurality of any statewide candidate of any party–2,581 votes. Ironically, the Democrat Josiah Wolcott defeated Senator du Pont by 2,522 votes. The voters of Delaware that fall were obviously voting for the man and not for the party.

The election of John G. Townsend Jr. was among the very few times that a Republican candidate had been elected governor without the strong support of the regular party organization. It was true, of course, that the organization did not actively oppose his candidacy during the fall campaign, but whatever support they could be said to have given him was given only grudgingly. John was also the first true Progressive to be elected governor of Delaware. Not only had he run as a Progressive on a Progressive platform, but he had a long record of support for Progressive causes. Robert Houston and Dr. Layton, the downstate Progressive leaders, were elated. Not only had Townsend, Reinhardt, and Swain been elected by comfortable margins (significantly, John's margin of victory had been almost twice as large as Swain's and three times that of Reinhardt), but no Republican on the state ticket who had not also been endorsed by the Progressives even got elected. The final crowning glory was a sweeping Progressive

Downtown Conflagration: *A short time after John's victory in the guber-natorial race, Selbyville's downtown business district was destroyed by fire. Among the casualties was the main office of Baltimore Trust Company, the ruins of which are visible at left center, above, and in detail below. The large home of John's banking rival, William McCabe, at center, above, survived the fire as did McCabe's bank, the Selbyville National Bank at right, above. A new Baltimore Trust office was soon built at approximately the same location (courtesy of Dorothy Williams Pepper).*

victory in the Sussex County courthouse races over the entrenched Democratic "courthouse ring."

Despite his problems with the regular party organization during the campaign, John remained a loyal Republican Party man thereafter.

He was never blindly obedient to the organization in any sense, however. He did learn one very important fact of political life from observing the ignoble fate of old Senator du Pont: while a good organization can do much to help a strong candidate, it can do very little to carry a weak one. The key to having a successful political party was fielding the best available candidates.

Part VI:

The Townsend Administration

12. Taking Command

On Tuesday, January 16, 1917, at the stroke of noon, John G. Townsend Jr. placed his right hand on the "ancient Latin Bible" of the State of Delaware, that had been used to swear in every governor since 1849, except Governor John Hunn in 1901. Hunn, a Quaker, would not swear on a Bible. The oath of office was administered by Chief Justice James Pennewill on the stage of the Dover Opera House as an enormous crowd of people looked on.

John had arrived in Dover at 10:00 in the morning with Jennie and all six children, his father and stepmother, Edith's husband, John A. Tubbs, and other relatives and friends. Another train arriving in Dover in the morning from Wilmington brought Mr. and Mrs. Everett C. Johnson, their daughter, Marjorie, and Everett's father, Captain Isaac Johnson. John had announced several weeks earlier that Everett Johnson would be his secretary of state. His formal appointment of Johnson was the first act of his new administration.

This appointment, which was to be of such importance in the lives of both men, was very typical of John's management style in both business and politics. He had known Everett from his first days in Selbyville. This was the boy who had accompanied "Cousin Zare" Brasure to Chincoteague to put on amateur theatricals one Christmas back in the 1890s. Everett had gone to Delaware College in 1895, to a new world of great ideas and intellectual excitement, a world for which his friendship with Zare had prepared him. He studied under such professors as Edward Vallandigham, whose own parents were natives of Worcester County. His friends included many other young

A newspaper cartoon showing the new governor and some of his interests at about the time of John's inauguration (Lyla T. Savoy Collection).

men from Sussex County who were embarked on the same course of self-improvement, men like Hugh Morris of Northwest Fork Hundred and H. Rodney Sharp of Seaford. Morris later became a leading attorney and federal judge and Sharp a high-level executive with the DuPont Company. All three of these former Sussex Countians worked in their adult lives to improve the quality not only of Delaware College but of the entire state. Johnson, as he began to make a name for himself in his adopted New Castle County, preserved his strong sense of home. He worked to nourish his roots so deep in the soil of Baltimore Hundred. He well remembered his dynamic friend, John Townsend.

As John became more and more interested in statewide politics, he and Everett Johnson built an alliance of enduring strength and dedication. In Johnson he found a "partner" of the highest order who brought to his own political skills and native progressivism much of the high ideals and guiding philosophy that made the Townsend administration one of the most dynamic in the state's history. He knew the talents of Everett Johnson and of such other younger friends as Harry V. Holloway, whose services he would utilize later in his administration. He had spotted these young men early on and observed their progress with the passing years. He knew they could manage the changes that he felt had to be made without riding roughshod over the independent and conservative southern Delawareans to do it. If this ability to recognize talent could be construed as "cronyism," it was on such a high order as to make cronyism a political virtue.

All the living ex-governors were in attendance at the inaugural ceremonies, and quite a few future ones as well. William D. Denney of Dover, the man who would succeed John four years later, was parade marshall. John's inaugural address had been a collaborative effort with Everett Johnson. John supplied the thoughts and Everett refined them into a melodious whole, which John then reviewed and converted into phraseology he found most comfortable. One of the first paragraphs was pure Townsend philosophy:

> I believe statecraft today, at its best, is administration, based on scientific and practical business methods, In the major portion of our work, party politics has but little to do.

A vote cast with an eye on its influence in the next campaign is very seldom the most deliberate for the public good. To put it concisely, if we are to attempt a business administration, we shall consider the material welfare–the greatest general good to the greatest number of people at the least possible expense. To do this effectively we shall have to adopt the principles in use by those successful in private or corporate business. This can best be begun by the adoption of what is known as the 'budget system.'

He went on to propose a restructuring of the state's tax system to spread the burden more equally among all citizens and to propose that the state operate on a balanced budget. Looking back on this speech eighty-three years later, it is difficult to appreciate just how revolutionary these proposals were in Delaware in 1917. The state government's financial structure, though updated somewhat after passage of the 1897 constitution, had not been greatly altered for a century. The General Assembly regularly and routinely enacted spending bills without the least idea of the availability of revenues to pay for them. The state government was a vast conglomeration of petty fiefdoms, each jealously guarding its own small power over its own bit of turf.

The new governor was proposing a radical restructuring of this administrative nightmare into a more efficient system. The idea of running government like a business did not originate with him, but it was still new in 1917. The speech was a classic statement of Progressivism. He was Delaware's first (and as it turned out, her only) Progressive governor and he was setting a new tone for his administration. How much of this was his own wording and how much was Everett's is unknown, but the two men were in such close accord that it did not matter greatly. The listeners were transfixed. In his eloquent comments, John was the classic Progressive crusader giving the battle call, however festive the occasion. The address also gave him a chance to voice his philosophy concerning the importance of good roads and his support for the T. Coleman du Pont Boulevard:

> Following education nothing so aids the development of a commonwealth as good roads. Not only do they affect the business and material welfare of a people, but they create a betterment of the social life itself. Good roads bring the rural home in close touch and cooperation with the town and city. They create a closer relationship of sympathetic thought and business interests between the different sections. . . Today good roads are a practical part of education as well as a part of increasing the material interests of the citizens.
>
> In our own State we have had a striking example of the need, of the benefits derived and of the interest created. Through the generous gift of General T. Coleman du Pont, Sussex County has seen demonstrated the practical advantages that would result from a development of a system of good roads throughout the State. This Boulevard extending from the Maryland Line at Selbyville to Georgetown, and ten miles north graded for early completion, has so opened the vision of the people of the southern county that there is today a very definite and urgent demand . . . I am confident that I express the sentiment of those who are acquainted with the possibilities when I say that no one thing since the building of the railroad has had such potent influence on the welfare of the people as the construction of this highway.

He went on to call for the creation of a State Highway Commission and for construction of a statewide network of highways to tie into the boulevard. The new governor was trying to extend to all Delawareans the new prosperity sweeping Sussex County:

In all our deliberations we must not forget our agricultural interests. Agriculture is the basic industry of our people. Location, proximity to the country's greatest markets, variety of soils, climatic conditions–all should encourage this industry. The possibilities of Delaware in fruit growing, truck raising, and dairying have not approached realization.

In these interests I doubt if any section of the country offers such striking opportunities. Our small fruits, apples and peaches have, during the past few years, attracted favorable attention in our markets. But even yet we have scarcely tapped our resources. The opportunity is here for Delaware to become the orchard and garden of the east.

The other two major points made by the new governor were a strong endorsement of "woman suffrage" and a call for major improvements in Delaware's notoriously bad public school system. Whether or not he was aware of it, and it seems likely that he was not–at least not fully–these "hot potatoes" would prove to be the two most controversial issues of his administration. In this section of the speech, Governor Townsend included a line that gently pointed out the manner in which Delawareans raised great havoc about new developments before they occurred, only to realize a short time later that they were good ideas. He referred to the new Women's College in Newark, which "four years ago (was) a very seriously questioned theory, (and) is today a vital, practical fact in the life and development of the state."

The governor also spoke in favor of state aid for the draining of low-lying areas, a subject very dear to the hearts of his neighbors in southern Sussex County, where one of the dominant features of the landscape was the Great Cypress Swamp. He called for a new workmen's compensation act to provide increased on-the-job

Inaugural Parade: *The somewhat fuzzy photo above, from the Townsend family photo album, shows the governor-elect's car in the midst of the parade through downtown Dover on January 16, 1917. Governor Townsend is seated in the rear of the car, being handed a baby to kiss by someone in the crowd (Lyla T. Savoy Collection).*

protection for the state's industrial and farm workers. As a reflection of the support he had received from the Prohibition Party, he called for a law to restrict the shipment of alcoholic beverages from "wet" areas of Delaware into "dry" areas, or, in other words, from New Castle and the City of Wilmington into Kent and Sussex, that had been dry under Delaware's local option law for some years. Though the General Assembly had given the counties and the City of Wilmington the right to decide for themselves whether or not the manufacture and sale of alcoholic beverages was legal, they had not said anything about

143

INAUGURAL CEREMONY

—of—

Governor-Elect JOHN G. TOWNSEND

AT DOVER OPERA HOUSE

Tuesday, January 16th, 1917

Admit Bearer—Private Entrance.

Inaugural ticket from Mrs. Lyla
Townsend Savoy's scrapbook.

persons buying whiskey in wet areas and bringing it into, or through, dry areas. This loophole the governor proposed to plug.

Just before the inaugural ceremony took place, the traditional inaugural parade had wound its way on a lengthy route through the streets of Dover. The procession was led by Governor-elect Townsend, outgoing Governor Charles R. Miller, and Brigadier General I. Pusey Wickersham, state adjutant general, in the lead carriage. The Delaware Militia missed the event for the first time in decades. It had been activated the year before by President Wilson to guard the U.S. –Mexican Border in New Mexico against raids by the audacious Mexican bandit-revolutionary Pancho Villa. The militia's usual place was filled by several troops of Boy Scouts and by the mounted parade marshall and his aides, one of whom was the young Dover city solicitor Daniel O. Hastings.

In the afternoon, Governor Townsend presided in his new offices in the State House on the Dover Green. Most of the visitors in town that day went in to greet the new governor and his predecessor before walking out to the Green for a concert by the Delaware Militia First Division Band. At eight o'clock that evening, Governor and Mrs. Townsend, who were staying with their party at the Hotel Richardson, held a reception in the State House. Afterwards, the company moved over to the Dover Armory for the inaugural ball and danced into the wee hours. Twenty-two years after John and Jennie had brought their babies and their few belongings up the old road from Bishops to Selbyville, John had assured himself of a place in the history of Delaware. Only in the coming weeks and months would it become clear that Governor John G. Townsend Jr. would have a very large place in that history.

The first weeks of the Townsend administration were given to such routine tasks as creating a governor's staff and filling the small patronage jobs for which office seekers had been clamoring since the election. Most vacancies were for such relatively minor positions as magistrate, notary public, cannery inspector, public health official, or meat inspector. The governor generally took the recommendation of local Republican party functionaries in filling them and concerned himself with the very few substantial jobs.

As governor, John at last had a perfect opportunity to utilize the services of some of those young Sussex County men whose friendship he had been cultivating for many years. Two of these were his old friends from Selbyville, Everett Johnson and Harry Holloway. To Everett went the honor of being his first gubernatorial appointment. It is very likely that Holloway would have been among the earliest appointees as well, but for some political hurdles.

Harry V. Holloway, four years younger than John, was the son of a local lumberman who, like others in the area, would move his steam sawmill from tract to tract and move his family with it. For several years in Holloway's boyhood the family lived west of town on the edge of the Great Cypress Swamp. It was here that Harry Holloway started his education, attending the one-room White Oak Swamp School. This institution was nearly inter-changeable with Ebenezer, the school John was attending at the same time a few miles south across the state line, and with scores of other schools in the region. Several years later the Holloway family moved back to Selbyville

John G. Townsend, Jr.
Governor of Delaware, 1917
(Lyla T. Savoy Collection).

where Harry went through as much public schooling as there was to be had, working in his father's sawmill in the summers.

At the age of sixteen Harry went off to Chestertown, Maryland, to attend Washington College. When he came home in the summers he continued to work at the mill. Later, his uncle, William M. Morris, the local telegrapher and station agent, taught him telegraphy and allowed him to help out at the station. At college he managed to pick up enough knowledge of surveying to pursue this occupation as part of his summertime employment. After graduation in 1895, he returned, briefly, to Baltimore Hundred to teach at the one-room Lizard Hill School near Bayard. In 1896-97, he taught at Bethel, a boat-building village on Broad Creek near Laurel. A year after that he went to Greenwood in Northwest Fork Hundred to teach and to work as principal. During these summers he was back at Washington College to work on his master of arts degree. With degree in hand, he went to New Castle in 1902 and took a job as superintendent of schools there. He was as knowledgeable about the condition of public education in Delaware and about the state's people as any educator in the state.

Governor Townsend could not utilize the talents of Harry Holloway immediately, even though he had clearly hoped to. The office of state commissioner of education had few powers in January 1917, but the governor realized that if his hopes of revitalizing Delaware's sagging public schools were to be realized, this appointment would be crucial. Harry, who now possessed a doctorate of education and served as superintendent of a large New Jersey public school system, was one of the applicants. In his response to Holloway's letter, Townsend wrote, "Dear Mate: I want you to know that I am giving consideration to the fact that it may be possible to make a good Delawarean out of you yet. If I am not too far prevented you may hear from me in the future." As it turned out, the governor was "prevented" by a large groundswell of influential support for the popular New Castle County school superintendent, Arthur Spaid, who ultimately got the job. The governor was able to put in a good word for Holloway with the Kent County Board of Education, however, and he became Kent school superintendent. It was well that Holloway did return to the state, because in the next four years John was to need every bit of help he could get in his campaign to reform Delaware schools.

When Spaid resigned in 1919, John immediately knew the person to take his place: Dr. Harry V. Holloway of White Oak Swamp School, Lizard Hill School, Bethel, Greenwood, and New Castle, as well as major school systems in New Jersey and Kent County.

Holloway was named to the position and went on to propel the state's public school system into the top 25 percent in the nation where formerly it had been among the worst. At first glance it might have seemed that John, who lived two doors down Main Street from Holloway's parents, was guilty of that sometimes elusive political crime known as "cronyism." But his knowledge of Harry Holloway's character came from twenty-five years of friendship and he knew he had appointed the best person for the job.

The General Assembly still officially held one legislative session every two years as it had during the governor's days as a representative. But governors often exercised their option of calling them into special session between times. The first formal session of the Townsend administration had gotten underway in January, and in the next few months the legislators were involved in such a flurry of activity that one Wilmington newspaper editorialized in late May 1917, that:

> Not only did the recent Legislature pass more progressive laws than any previous General Assembly in the history of the State, but practically every suggestion that Governor John G. Townsend made in his inaugural address relative to new legislation was carried out. This was largely due to the close cooperation between the executive and legislative departments during the entire session of the Legislature.

In particular, Governor Townsend's proposed budget system for state government was adopted. Laws were enacted creating the state's first income tax (one percent on all income with no exceptions) and its first inheritance tax. Another new law was designed to increase school tax revenues by basing assessments on the real value of property rather than on a vague and nebulous "rental value" as the old law had done.

The governor was able to bring about passage of laws to increase the salaries of rural school teachers and of county superintendents. At his request, the General Assembly enacted a bill authorizing the state to pay the expenses for teachers attending summer training schools at Delaware College in Newark and at Delaware State College in Dover. This later proved to be a major step in improving the quality of public school teachers. At the time many, if not most, Delaware teachers had little more than high school educations and there were relatively few with four-year degrees or specialized training in teaching methods.

That session of the legislature also approved the first appropriation in the state's history for vocational education. With the additional tax revenues, the governor also increased the appropriation for regular schools from $107,000 to $250,000. He increased appropriations for Delaware College, the Women's College, and Delaware State. In addition to this, the Women's College received another $125,000 for construction of a new dormitory.

As far as educational reform went, however, those measures were the merest tip of the iceberg, a fact not fully appreciated at the time by anyone in the state, Governor Townsend included. The shape that "iceberg" would take in the next few years was soon to be determined by the work of a committee of five persons appointed by the governor to survey all existing schools in Delaware, to study school financing, teacher quality, administration, curriculum, and the whole educational situation in the state. The committee members were also directed to recommend improvements to the present state school law and, in short, to redesign the whole state system of public instruction. The group appointed included Caleb E. Burchenal, chairman, John S. Mullin, Frank L. Grier, Joseph Frazier, and L. Scott Townsend. The latter, a New Castle County businessman who was not directly related to the governor, was later replaced by Wilmington executive Henry P. Scott. They were given two years in which to do the job. It was clear from the outset that these five men, acting alone at periodic meetings, could not have begun to carry out the task imposed on them, but the existence of the committee created a mechanism whereby the state could get some expert assistance and that was what the governor was after.

In that first session the governor also turned his attention to the questions of highway improvement and prohibition, both of which had figured largely in his campaign. During the session, the legislators passed legislation creating the first Delaware State Highway Department, to be directed by the state's first state highway commission. This Highway Act of 1917 also included the essential provision enabling the commission to issue bonds on the credit of the state "to the extent that the income of the department would pay the interest and sinking fund charges, after all the regular expenses of the department had been provided for." This bonding provision was the mechanism with which the modern highway system of Delaware was built. It meant that work could proceed at a rapid and regular pace without having every proposed highway improvement bottled up in the legislature for years. Though such authority is now a universal cliché of government, the concept was then quite new.

The 1917 highway act became a model of its kind and was copied in the next decade by many other states. It was, of course, no secret to anyone that the concepts it embodied were largely those of T. Coleman du Pont. It was fitting, therefore, that he was appointed to represent the City of Wilmington on the commission. The other three regular members were Josiah Marvel for New Castle County,

Walter O. Hoffecker for Kent, and Joseph E. Holland for Sussex. At their first meeting, these four commissioners elected Governor Townsend himself commission chairman.

During the 1917 session, the legislature also finally accepted "General" du Pont's offer to give the state strips of land along the du Pont Boulevard right-of-way for use as agricultural experiment tracts. And, on May 24, 1917, the governor travelled to Georgetown to make formal acceptance on behalf of the state of the first twenty miles of the du Pont Boulevard from Selbyville to Georgetown. It was one of the sweetest moments of John G. Townsend's long life. Before a large crowd of dignitaries, the governor told du Pont, "We are living in advance of our time by your generosity," and went on to say:

> The difficulties of travel have made us strong advocates of good roads, yet few of us saw the possibilities to be gained. Only by having the advantage given us here did we realize the full advantages of good roads. Today, through this gift, Sussex County is thoroughly aroused.
>
> We realize the economic as well as the social and educational values. We see the wisdom of construction and maintenance of roads by business methods. A million dollar bond issue [that had just been approved by the legislature for Sussex County highway improvement] for Sussex County would have been scoffed at before experiencing this road.
>
> Were a vote taken today by Sussex County on what its citizens most wanted it would be a landslide for boulevards such as this. You have given us what we most needed and what we now most want.

To help the state get the modern highway system that citizens at long last desired, the legislature had set aside a portion of the new income tax revenue for highways. At the governor's direction, they

*An early Gee Tee Maxwell cartoon of Governor Townsend
(Lyla T. Savoy collection).*

also created an automobile licensing fee to go with the older requirement
for license tags. During the first year of the new highway act, the
department had an income of somewhat more than $82,000. By
1918, it was nearly three times that much and it continued to grow.
The du Pont Boulevard was the essential framework. Through the
remainder of the Townsend administration and in the next two decades
afterward that framework expanded into an interlocking network of
paved highways ranging over the face of Delaware. Fifty years later
few people remembered the great outburst that had attended du Pont's

efforts to give his state the boulevard, but they never forgot the gift.

On the matter of prohibition, the governor fulfilled his campaign pledge that spring. Under the terms of the 1897 state constitution Delaware had been divided into four local option districts–the three counties and the city of Wilmington. Each was authorized to hold its own election to decide the matter of whether or not licenses should be granted for the manufacture and sale of alcoholic beverages. Kent and Sussex had both voted in 1907 to outlaw "license," thereby becoming dry counties (and, incidentally, wiping out, at least officially, the old Sussex County apple and peach brandy industry). The loophole in the 1897 provision, which had been a campaign issue in 1916, was the lack of any provision barring the shipment of alcoholic beverages into or through the dry parts of the state. This the governor asked the legislature to change.

Many states had already adopted local option laws similar to Delaware's as an outgrowth of the prohibition movement that had been growing nationally for fifty years. Even as the General Assembly considered Townsend's request to tighten the Delaware law, Congress was preparing to pass the resolution calling for the states to ratify the Prohibition Amendment. The General Assembly not only gave the governor the law he wanted to prohibit shipment of "intoxicating liquors" into dry areas, but set elections in Wilmington and New Castle County on the local option question. When they were held in the fall of 1917, voters in New Castle decided against license, leaving Wilmington a wet island in a dry sea. Even that was temporary. By 1918 the whole country had gone dry by constitutional amendment.

Finally during that monumental session the General

Assembly enacted a new workmen's compensation law and established an industrial accident board to administer it. A commission was established to study the existing level of care for the state's "feebleminded" citizens. It was to make recommendations for improvements. Like the educational commission, it was a preliminary to the much more ambitious task of creating the state's first modern facility for treatment and care of the mentally retarded, but that came later in the Townsend administration.

Governor Townsend's first four months in office had been gratifying, a brilliant beginning, but the governor was too much of a politician to expect that things would always be so smooth. He and his chief aide, Everett Johnson, were already at work on a score of different programs, but he had the satisfaction of knowing that he had gotten off to a good start.

13. War and Sorrow

Even before adjournment of the 1917 session, Delaware and the rest of the nation were overtaken by an event that was to have a radical impact on the nature of American life. During the first week of April the United States entered the World War on the side of the Allies. Hostilities had already been raging in Europe for two and a half years. It came as no great surprise to most Americans that the U.S. had finally been forced to enter the conflict. German confrontations with the neutral United States had been increasing steadily. Some Americans were already at war, fighting with Allied units.

On February 19, the Delaware General Assembly had voted a resolution of approval for President Wilson's handling of the increasingly touchy situation. The resolution read in part, "We pledge him our loyal support now and in any eventuality." On April 2, the president requested that Congress approve a declaration of war against Germany, but by then many states, including Delaware, were ready. The week before, the General Assembly had mobilized the newly named Delaware National Guard which had, until the year before, been known as the Delaware Militia. The guardsmen had returned home only in late February from a year's active duty along the Mexican border under the command of General John J. Pershing. Now they were directed to protect bridges, highways, and other strategic points, such as the Du Pont gunpowder mills, from possible attack by enemy saboteurs and enemy agents.

On the day of the president's speech to Congress, the

The War Governor: *Governor Townsend stands on the portico of the Delaware State House in 1918 with members of his State Council of Defense and a group of ladies involved in the Liberty Loan Drive. Secretary of State Johnson is standing fourth from left in the top row. Lyla Townsend, Liberty Loan chairman for Sussex County, is sixth from right in the front row (Lyla T. Savoy collection).*

legislators directed Governor Townsend to mobilize those portions of the National Guard that were not already on active duty, and to prepare them for service either at home or overseas. He was further authorized to equip them at state expense and to conduct a military census of the state to determine the number of eligible men and the quantities of potentially useful war material.

Soon after Congress formally approved the declaration of war on April 6, the Delaware guardsmen were nationalized and ordered to Camp McClellan, Alabama, for training. They, like most other state troops in the country, were eager to sail to France to "teach the Hun a lesson." It was to be more than a year, however, before most Delaware boys finally got there. The delay was caused by well-intentioned state pride that led Delaware's congressional delegation to insist that the state's troops be kept together as a separate unit. The usual practice was to break up units from smaller states without enough men to make up an entire division and attach the soldiers to larger units with vacancies. Because of strong opposition to this idea among Delawareans, the state's national guardsmen were kept sitting around Camp McClellan, and later Camp Dix, New Jersey, for months. While still in Alabama they were designated the 59th Pioneer Infantry Regiment and given a combined mission of combat engineering and infantry, though by the spring of 1918 many of them were wondering if they would ever get a chance to use their training.

Some Delaware soldiers tried to arrange transfers to other units that were on their way overseas. The governor and Secretary Johnson were kept busy in the first year of the war writing letters of recommendation for these men. Finally in August 1918, a scant three months before the Armistice, the regiment embarked for France, arriving there on September 15. Despite their late arrival, the men of the 59th saw combat in the Meuse-Argonne sector and at Verdun. The regiment remained in Europe after the Armistice as part of the American occupation forces in Germany. When they returned home in 1919, they returned as combat-hardened veterans in spite of their late arrival in battle. They also left behind more than two hundred Delawareans who had fallen in France.

Some years later, after the end of the Townsend administration, the trustees of the recently designated University of Delaware were preparing to erect an elegant classical rotunda in the center of the university mall to serve as a library. They decided to call it Memorial Hall in honor of Delaware's war dead. Everett Johnson, who was one of the university trustees, had become a printer and publisher of elegant and finely crafted books. He designed and printed a particularly large and sumptuous volume, bound in leather, that he called "The Book of the Dead." It bore the name of one of the state's war dead on each page. When the building was finished, the book was placed in a case at the center of the rotunda and for many years thereafter someone would turn one of its pages each day.

As Delaware's war governor, Governor Townsend served as both the symbolic commander of Delaware's war effort and as a coordinator of that effort, overseeing the smooth operation of the state's draft boards and the flow of communications between state agencies and the federal government. One of his more publicly visible duties was leading Delawareans in supporting the various Liberty Loans, the forerunners of World War II's war bond campaigns. He would be photographed purchasing the first bond of each new liberty loan and of the postwar Victory Loan. He enlisted his daughter Lyla's help in this effort by making her the Sussex County chairman of the Liberty Loan committee.

In the early days of the war some Delawareans were certain that the fight would be brought home to their state in the form of spies and saboteurs. This was not entirely wishful thinking in view of the location in the state of the DuPont gunpowder mills and the fact of Delaware's location on a major shipping route. The scare was to a large extent, though, a reflection of the public need to be involved in the great conflict being decided "over there." In the early months of the war the governor received a steady stream of letters and telephone calls from citizens in out-of-the-way places like Kitts Hummock and Slaughter Beach, reporting on the activities of those they considered suspicious-looking characters. Former village eccentrics now suddenly became, in some people's minds, potential spies and saboteurs. Such letters were dutifully sent along by the governor's office to Adjutant General Wickersham, who would investigate the charges and invariably find them groundless. While no German spies were ever found in the state, some Delawareans refused to quit hoping.

A governor in action:

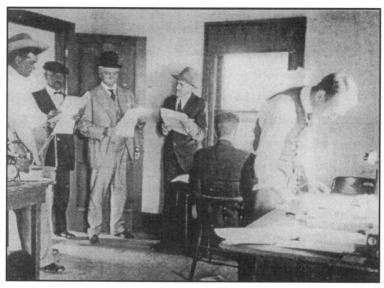

The Office: *The interior of the Townsend office in Selbyville is seen as it appeared in 1917. The photo was taken during strawberry season as a crowd of brokers and employees were going over paperwork.*

Politicking: *This 1917 view of Governor Townsend leaning against his automobile outside his Selbyville office as he talks to friends shows his casual, genial style.*

(Both photos from the Lyla T. Savoy collection)

Young Jack Townsend enlisted and went off to New Jersey for training. Like many other Delaware soldiers in the war, he never managed to get to France. Instead he was sent to the comparatively boring confines of the Raritan Arsenal in Metuchen, New Jersey. In 1918, while on a work detail, the middle finger on his left hand was crushed and had to be amputated below the first joint. The accident, which came right in the midst of one of the busiest moments of his father's administration, caused the governor to drop everything and head for New Jersey. The oldest Townsend boy, Julian, the only other son of enlistment age, was by now married. He was kept at home to manage the family's cannery business in Georgetown while his uncle, James Townsend, ran the other operations during the governor's absence.

The war brought many extra demands to the governor's office. Yet in one sense it was a blessing in disguise. Governor Townsend saw his election as a mandate for reform. Reform of any kind had never come easily in Delaware, nor did it now, but the spirit of cooperation and public-mindedness resulting from the war made it easier to accomplish fundamental change.

Soon after the American declaration of war, the governor had created the Delaware State Council of Defense and appointed Everett Johnson the director. While much of the council's work was directly supportive of the war effort, other aspects were only indirectly connected to it. These operations–programs to educate immigrant Delawareans in English and in the ways of American culture, surveys of public health facilities in the state, and a women's council designed to involve women in the war effort–fit quite easily into the major reform campaign of the Townsend administration. The governor and Secretary Johnson clearly realized that they had an unprecedented opportunity to achieve some long-lasting good because of the national emergency and they made the most of it.

Before the First World War the office of governor had been a relatively leisurely undertaking. While governors were expected to attend to the honorary functions relating to the office, to be in more or less regular attendance in the State House during legislative sessions, and to see to matters of hiring and firing of state employees, drawing up budgets and the like, the pace had been far from rigorous in the old days. For one thing, most governors in the past, or at any rate since the Civil War, had been creatures of the party machines who sought as their greatest goal to preserve the often-fragile peace within their various parties. Things had begun to change slowly under Governors Lea, Pennewill, and Miller as the size of state government had grown. None of those men had been reformers, however, and their programs required little work to achieve success in the General Assembly.

Governor Townsend still had time during most of his administration to concern himself with the general management of his far-flung business enterprises, but he was able to do so only by putting in what often amounted to eighteen-hour days, leaving home soon after sunrise and arriving back there some nights after midnight. His growing office staff in Selbyville, employees of his own company, was often used for official business matters while at the same time the secretaries in his State House office routinely found themselves mixing correspondence concerning the canneries in with letters concerning affairs of state. Though the governor, who owned one of the first automobiles in Baltimore Hundred, enjoyed driving up and down the du Pont Boulevard, he regularly used the services of a chauffeur so that he could find extra time to read correspondence and draft replies. Not only had the war increased his official workload dramatically, but as the administration wore on the job of putting his progressive program across became massive.

The rigorous pace of the job became something of a godsend to the governor in 1918 and 1919 because his duties kept him from dwelling too much on what must have been the greatest tragedy of his life–the death of Jennie Townsend in an automobile accident late in the fall of 1917. The day of the accident, October 27, 1917, had begun as a pleasant family outing. It was Founder's Day at Delaware College, an event filled with speeches and festivities at the Newark campus. The governor had already done much for the college in his nine and a half months in office and he was to be the featured speaker.

Governor and Mrs. Townsend started off early from home in their large touring car and stopped in Georgetown on the way to pick up Julian and his new wife, Mildred. That afternoon, the governor made a speech hailing the great strides the college had recently made and outlining his hopes for further gains during his term in office. It was a festive occasion despite the threatening weather, made better for the Townsends by the fact that they were able to spend it in the company of their daughter, Lyla, who was attending the Women's College. During the afternoon the family also socialized with many of their upstate friends and acquaintances before preparing late in the day to start out on the trip home.

Even in 1917 driving the length of the state was a somewhat uncertain undertaking in bad weather and Lyla urged her parents and their party to spend the night in Newark. But they felt that they had to get home and so set out. By the time they reached Georgetown darkness was rapidly approaching. After dropping the younger Townsends off at their home, Governor and Mrs. Townsend set off on the last leg of the trip to Selbyville in an increasing downpour. By the time they were passing the turnoff into Dagsboro it was dark and the visibility was made worse by the rain. The events that followed are best summed up in an account that appeared in Monday morning's Wilmington *Morning News* following the Saturday evening accident:

> They were proceeding along the du Pont Boulevard and, handicapped by the storm, they came upon a [horse-drawn] carriage proceeding in the same direction, just after leaving Dagsboro, but did not see the carriage until very close to it.
>
> Governor Townsend was not thrown from the machine, but Mrs. Townsend was jolted from her seat, and despite his injuries, the governor lifted the machine from her. The car was not resting on her body in such a manner as to crush it, and apparently her only injury was a fractured collar bone.
>
> About this time a motorist named Truitt from Millsboro drew up and, learning of the accident, left his party along the road and started for Selbyville with the governor and Mrs. Townsend in his car. Mrs. Townsend spoke one or two words after the accident, and it is believed that she did not live over ten minutes.
>
> Arriving at the Townsend home in Selbyville, Drs. H.E. Evans and George E. James [who was married to the governor's sister] were summoned, and following an examination they expressed the opinion that Mrs. Townsend died from shock. The governor's injuries consisted mainly of bruises and he was not seriously hurt, although it is said, suffering from shock.

As the news of Mrs. Townsend's death spread through the state that night and the next day, the result was an immediate spontaneous and massive outpouring of grief that has only rarely been equalled in Delaware. It was not just that she was the First Lady, or that she had died in a tragic accident, but also that she was the young and popular wife of a popular governor and the mother of six children,

Mrs. Jennie Townsend
about the time her husband became governor. This is one of the few photographs of her to have survived (Lyla T. Savoy Collection).

two of whom were still at home. Mrs. Townsend's funeral was held in Selbyville on October 31. According to the account of it that appeared in the *Evening Journal* the next day:

Seldom has lower Delaware been the scene of such a tribute as was that expressed yesterday afternoon by the presence of thousands of the foremost residents of the State to attend the funeral of Mrs. John G. Townsend Jr., wife of the Governor of Delaware, who lost her life in an automobile accident on Saturday night. Men of all political beliefs of all three counties journeyed here to be present at the funeral services.

To their close friends and neighbors the devoted home and family life of Governor and Mrs. Townsend always was pointed to as ideal, hence the grief of the father, sons and daughters who have suddenly been deprived of wife and mother is all the deeper. And thus it was that tears of the hundreds and hundreds of strong men who came from all parts of the state silently flowed with the tears of the big, sob-rocked man whom they all revere as a friend and Governor of the Commonwealth, as they assembled in the Salem M.E. Church for the obsequies yesterday afternoon. Governor Townsend sustained no serious physical injuries in the accident that suddenly ended the life of his wife, but he is suffering from shock and a nervous reaction that will grip him for sometime.

A special train brought many from Wilmington and

intervening points, including Delaware Railroad officials, members of the Governor's military staff and other friends of the Governor and Mrs. Townsend. From all parts of Sussex County came friends by trains, automobiles, and teams. It was estimated that one thousand automobiles, many from Maryland, were parked throughout the town.

Every bank, store, and other place of business in the town was closed out of respect to the deceased. It was a beautiful testimonial of neighbors to one whose memory they revered.

The procession from the house to the church was the most remarkable of its kind ever witnessed in Sussex County. From the Governor's home to the Methodist Episcopal Church where the service was held, a distance of perhaps four city blocks, each side of the street was filled with friends of the Governor and his stricken wife, who stood with bared heads as the funeral cortege slowly wended its way over the streets.

When the great funeral was over and the crowds of mourners had departed, the family went home to be alone with their private grief, to cope with their loss. They pulled together to help the little ones. Lyla withdrew from college and returned home to help raise her two youngest brothers. The governor returned slowly to his official duties and to his business activities but he spent as much time as possible with his children. When he could, he took them with him on his travels around the state and beyond. When they were away from home, as both Jack and Paul were the following year, he wrote them frequently and took much more than casual interest in their activities. His own loss can only be imagined. Suffice it to say that, though he was a vigorous and attractive man of forty-six at the time of Mrs. Townsend's death and remained so for many years thereafter, he never remarried.

14. The School Fight

The political life of a state and the workings of government are no respecters of loss. Events roll on unabated beyond human ken. Before the tragedy of Jennie Townsend's death had been fully comprehended, the governor was planted firmly in the midst of his greatest controversy to date. The once-glowing editorials of praise for his reform program were now careful appraisals of its chances. The governor could quite easily and honorably have avoided the turmoil simply by conducting himself in the manner of his predecessors, particularly in view of his personal loss. He could have paid rhetorical homage to Progressive ideals and then refrained from pushing too hard for their implementation. Instead he resolved to lead the battle for his program.

The fight centered around two large and emotional issues– school reform and, later, ratification of the "woman suffrage" amendment to the U.S. Constitution. Though most realized that Delawareans were conservative, few, the governor included, realized just how hard the extreme conservative elements would fight until the "Great School Fight" opened their eyes to the strength of reactionary fury. As the battle wore on through 1919 and 1920, the governor saw the coalition of factions that had elected him crumble away. The du Pont feud also threatened at times to hinder the accomplishment of goals that all the warring family members supported, though in the end they were able to unite in their support. The Progressive Party also ceased to exist as a formal entity during the struggles of those years.

Most accounts of this period of the school fight devote their attention to Pierre S. du Pont, mentioning Governor Townsend only in passing. It is entirely true that du Pont was the leading architect of the new philosophy of public education in Delaware and his millions in contributions were essential to its implementation. Moreover, du Pont's effective leadership and direction of the reform movement was a key factor in bringing the new school system into being. Yet all of this overlooks one important point–the governor's support and commitment were invaluable. Without them, du Pont's money and his leadership–his very philosophy of education–might not have been enough. At best, the new school system would have been delayed for four more years.

The reformers had vision. The governor possessed the political skills needed to transform their visions into reality. Reformers had recognized the evils of the old system since at least the turn of the century, but they had been unsuccessful in moving the state government. The four twentieth century governors who preceded Townsend had all made paltry and feeble gestures toward school reform but their efforts had been mostly for show. John G. Townsend Jr. was the first governor with the courage to place his political reputation on the line in support of the new philosophy and the energy to fight the battle necessary to implement that philosophy. He was the only important figure on the side of reform to take that direct political risk, since none of the others, du Pont among them, held elective office.

By 1917, Delaware's system of public education had become an embarrassment to many of the state's citizens, not the least of whom was the new governor, who had resolved in his inaugural address to lend his influence to the task of reform. The faults were many and varied but nearly all stemmed from the same root cause. The public education system had been established in 1829. While new law after new law had been enacted since that time, no meaningful attempt had ever been made to bring any kind of order or central control to a mishmash of laws, customs, and traditions that was a system in name only.

With a population of less than 250,000 people, Delaware had 424 separate and distinct school districts. Every little country one-room schoolhouse had its own elected board of education with almost total local control over teacher qualifications, salary, educational standards, curriculum, school building, equipment, books, attendance, and virtually everything else. The problems wrought by such a system were by now notorious and efforts had been underway at least since 1900 to bring about meaningful reforms. In Delaware in the early years of the century virtually absolute local control of public schools was considered to be among a community's birthrights. And this was local in the most extreme sense of the word. A community like Millsboro or Georgetown, which in the 1930s or 1940s had one or two schools would, before 1918, have had ten or fifteen schools, one at every country hamlet and crossroads, and some with only five or ten pupils. Each of these schools would have been its own school district with autonomous local control. The system was so deeply ingrained that most politicians would have nothing to do with attempts to modernize.

Some changes had come over the years but they were more in form than in substance. In 1907, the General Assembly had enacted a compulsory attendance law requiring students to go to school 160 days a year. They did not provide for truant officers or other forms of enforcement, however. Attendance at most rural schools continued to lag far behind the standard, especially during the fall harvest and strawberry season in the spring. The law provided for elected county boards of education and an appointed state board. There were also three county superintendents and, after 1913, a state commissioner of education, but their powers were few.

The U.S. government released a report on the state of American public education in 1915. This document indicated that Delaware ranked thirty-sixth among the forty-eight states in its overall performance. In some areas the ranking was even lower. It was thirty-ninth in average annual teachers' salaries (excluding Wilmington); forty-fifth in capital expenditures for buildings and equipment. This report fell on the state like a bombshell and did much to increase public awareness of the seriousness of the problem. Coming just as the 1916 campaign was getting underway, the report made it easier for Governor Townsend to declare his strong support for true educational reform. Partly because of this new awareness and partly because of the dramatic Progressive showing in the 1916 election, Townsend was the first governor to call for substantial reforms in the existing system. He began early in the 1917 General Assembly session with his proposal for teacher salary increases, greater appropriations for public schools, and similar measures. The most important of these was a bill creating a five-member commission to study the state of public education in Delaware and to recommend improvements. The improvements were to be mandated by a proposed new school code containing broad and far-reaching provisions to modernize Delaware's schools, creating, in fact, a true public school system for the first time.

In working for these reforms, Governor Townsend was motivated by past experience with the country schools of Sussex and Worcester. Another factor was his close friendships with a number of Delaware's more forward-looking men and women. Most important, he had raised his own family in an area where high schools were few and far between. Neither of his older children, Edith or Julian, had been able to attend public high school in their hometown. They were fortunate that their parents were affluent enough to send them to board in larger communities to complete high school and to receive a few years of college. Those less affluent, as John and Jennie had themselves been, were forced to do without. Lyla was the first of the Townsend children to attend high school in Selbyville, where she was a member of the town school's first graduating class.

The educational reform process had been underway for some years and a growing constituency of articulate citizens had been working for change through such organizations as the General Service Board since about 1910. The cold reception with which their initiatives were invariably met by most legislators had caused them to devote most of their efforts to the largely autonomous Wilmington school system and to schools in a few of the other large towns.

One of the best-informed and most committed private citizens in the area of school reform was Pierre S. du Pont, the quietest and least public of the three du Pont cousins who had assumed control of the family company in 1902. Though Pierre was by now nearing the climax of his brilliant business career, heading not only the DuPont Company but General Motors as well, he had found the time to become more and more involved in the management of public schools in Wilmington. He did not marry until 1915 and had no children of his own, but he was sincerely concerned that the children of Delaware receive the best education possible.

In 1917, as the governor's newly appointed educational commission began its work, he stepped forward as the acknowledged leader of the reform movement. He announced that he would personally fund much of the commission's work. Had he not done so, the educational commission report would have amounted to little and accomplished even less. With his help, the opposite occurred. That he came forward when he did was due in large part to private pleas from the governor.

The study he financed, the first of many, was conducted by experts from the private General Education Board of New York City, which had been established by John D. Rockefeller Sr. in 1902. The two men chosen to conduct the study, Abraham Flexner and Frank P. Bachman, had published a similarly comprehensive study of Maryland public education the year before.

The governor and Secretary of State Johnson were also aided in a very real way by, of all things, the war. Early in 1918, they received federal funding to establish the State Council of Defense. Though receiving its overall direction from Washington, the council was autonomous up to a point. Townsend and Johnson soon had the council involved at the very center of Delaware life with its work with women's clubs, its work with industry, the surveys of public health facilities, and even an efficiency study of every one of the hordes of public agencies in state and local government.

One of the most successful council programs was its Americanization adult education classes. That program offered a marvelous opportunity to establish training programs for Delaware school teachers aimed at equipping them with new methods for teaching adults. Since very few Delaware public school teachers in 1918 had any teacher training, this had the inevitable effect of improving their performance in their regular classes as well. By the middle of 1918, Americanization classes were going on in many parts of the state and the concept of teacher training was identified in the public mind with a practical and patriotic purpose.

The momentum for progress and public acceptance of change that had come with the war was of necessity a limited thing. It was becoming apparent, even in the early spring of 1918, that the war would not be much prolonged even though some of the worst fighting for American troops lay ahead. The group of progressive citizens who were working so closely with the Townsend administration realized that they would have a hard time maintaining their momentum in the postwar period. Temporary agencies like the Council of Defense would be disbanded and most people would be clamoring for a return to "normalcy." The mechanism this group devised for keeping the reform movement alive after the war was known as The Service Citizens of Delaware.

The private General Service Board had been organized in 1914 for the task of recording and publicizing conditions in need of reform. Most of the board's efforts were concerned with education. When the Council of Defense was created, it took over much of the work done previously by the General Service Board, which was phased out of existence. With the council itself facing impending demise, the Service Citizens organization was designed to pick up where it had left off. Etta J. Wilson, later executive secretary of the Service Citizens, wrote that the four men who actually came up with the idea for the new organization were Charles Warner, former head of the General Service Board, Everett Johnson, P. S. du Pont, and du Pont's close friend and business associate, John J. Raskob.

By June of 1918, the Flexner-Bachman study of the public education system was nearing completion. Its general outlines were well known to the four men as they met in Wilmington. Dr. Robert J. Taggert, an educational historian writing in *Delaware History* (and on whose richly detailed account much of this chapter is based), believes that Raskob convinced du Pont in the early summer 1918 to make his major commitment to good schools in Delaware at that time.

In any case, when the first organizational meeting of the Service Citizens of Delaware was held in Wilmington on July 9, 1918, du Pont had already established a $1.5 million trust fund and had made Raskob its trustee. The income of $90,000 a year was to go to the Service Citizens until 1924 (du Pont later extended this deadline by several years) to finance its activities. Since he was underwriting the entire cost of the organization and its campaign for school reform, he had no qualms about naming himself its president at the first meeting. He also appointed three vice-presidents, one for each county, and a secretary and a treasurer. The vice-president for New Castle was the Wilmington executive Henry P. Scott. The prominent Dover attorney Henry Ridgely represented Kent. Dr. Rowland G. Paynter, a wealthy Georgetown physician and banker (and son-in-law of Dr. Hiram Burton), was named vice-president for Sussex County. Raskob was treasurer and du Pont's brother-in-law, H. Rodney Sharp, served as secretary.* Both Governor Townsend and Everett Johnson attended the meeting. The governor made a short speech at the beginning in which he stressed his support for school reform and offered the services of his administration in helping to achieve it. The statement itself was far from radical. He was, after all, in the presence of some of the wealthiest and most influential men in the state. Yet earlier governors had made such statements and later been slow to come forward with the support they offered. Townsend was with them all the way, even when it became politically uncomfortable downstate to stand by the cause.

---

* *Hugh Rodney Sharp was a native of western Sussex County and graduate of Delaware College. He had worked for several years as a public school principal and teacher in Odessa before his marriage to Pierre du Pont's sister.*

At the outset, the activities of the Service Citizens were not confined to education. They took over most of the work of both the General Service Board and the Council of Defense. Thus, by the fall of 1918, virtually the entire Progressive movement was managed by one very well financed and directed private organization. It was a situation unique in the history of Delaware. Unlike his cousins Coleman and Alfred, Pierre du Pont was neither flamboyant and eccentric nor particularly domineering. He was quiet and mild-mannered but his mild exterior disguised a man of great idealism and forceful conviction. It also disguised his genius for administration and organization. He faced the accumulated conservatism of generations as well as an element of anti-du Pont feeling. He knew that it would take all the skill he possessed to bring about major changes, regardless of his wealth.

The Service Citizens organization was a mechanism for social change independent of the General Assembly. Although its members did not then have time to think of it in such philosophical terms, the Service Citizens of Delaware represented capitalism at its finest and most fully realized. All the members of the Service Citizens had stood by for years, in some cases for decades, and seen how, in most cases, new ideas were given cursory discussion in the legislature before being adopted in name only or rejected outright. The founders of the group, who had only a few years before seen T. Coleman du Pont reduced to fighting the legislature and rival politicians for the right to give his state the gift of a $4 million highway, sensed that the time had come to push the state into the realm of modern education. P.S. du Pont said in a speech as the new organization started, "our aim is to give assistance, to offer our experience, knowledge, and financial power for the support of those who are in charge of public affairs, but are handicapped by the meagre resources of the state treasury."

They intended to use their own private resources to prove to the people of the state that they, through their own taxes, should support educational improvements. The Service Citizens had probably the most sophisticated expertise in public relations and self-promotion to be found in Delaware in 1918. An important function of the organization from its inception was the selling of its ideas with as high a degree of salesmanship as its business executive members used in the marketing of their products.

The Service Citizens quickly assumed responsibility for the social programs earlier operated by the Delaware Council of Defense. The Americanization program operated under the auspices of the Service Citizens led to the establishment of sixty summer scholarships for teachers at the Women's College, funded directly by P.S. and by his brothers, Irénée and Lammot du Pont. The Service Citizens operated a state research bureau that had been started by the old General Service Board and continued under the Council of Defense. They undertook other functions as well, but most of their efforts centered around the reform of the public schools. du Pont in particular devoted almost all of his attention to the schools, calling them "a state and national scandal."

He had hired a full-time staff for the Service Citizens headed by the Rev. Dr. Joseph H. Odell, the clergyman who, three years before, had officiated at his own marriage to Alice Belin. Odell and his staff did the day-to-day work of the organization while du Pont and the other officers concentrated on strategy. Later du Pont and everyone else moved out into the small towns and villages of Delaware to sell the new concepts to the people.

In the late fall of 1918, the Flexner-Bachman Study was complete. Also finished was a new model school code written by Dr.

Bachman. The study was published as the official report of the state Educational Commission appointed by Governor Townsend. After being presented to the legislature on February 12, 1919, the study was made public. Seventy-five hundred copies of it were distributed around the state by the Service Citizens. The governor proclaimed the next week Educational Week and urged all Delawareans to study the condition of the state's schools with a fair and objective eye. During Educational Week the Service Citizens asked the help of virtually every community and club group in Delaware in arranging forums to discuss the proposed new school code and the entire subject of education in Delaware. More than fifty meetings were held in rural communities. The *Evening Journal* and the *Every Evening* featured detailed coverage of the code. The Service Citizens had in effect conducted the state's first successful media blitz.

By April 1, the house had approved the new school code by a substantial majority. The senate held off passage for several weeks as senators argued its merits. They, too, passed it in mid-April, though with only one vote to spare. Governor Townsend signed the code into law on April 14, 1919. Soon afterward he appointed a new State Board of Education to administer the central authority embodied in the code and to operate the newly created State Department of Public Instruction. The president of the board was George Miller of New Castle. P.S. du Pont agreed to serve as vice-president. The title was a bit disingenuous since it was no secret that he was by now the driving force in education in Delaware.

Events had proceeded with remarkable ease up to this point. But du Pont, Governor Townsend and everyone else involved in the campaign to pass the new code realized that the fight had not yet started. As the hundreds of rural school commissioners came to

understand just how much of their former power would be transferred
to the state, they could be expected to erupt into a fury of protest.

Even as the new law was being enacted du Pont knew that the
support offered by the Service Citizens, impressive though it was,
was not sufficient in itself to win the battle. He was quietly preparing
to launch an even more effective campaign tool. On July 28, he
announced the creation of the Delaware School Auxiliary Association,
the function of which was to distribute funds given by du Pont for
"rebuilding the schools of Delaware." The following day he established
a trust fund sufficient to yield $2 million for the purchase of new building
sites and construction of new school buildings. In the next four years,
this initial effort grew to a total of six trust funds yielding nearly $4
million.

The catch was that the money would go only to those school
districts that accepted the provisions of the new school code. If the
code was repealed, any unappropriated funds would revert to the
trust unspent. School districts seeking funds were required to submit
their plans to the auxiliary's board of managers, which would decide
how much money to give based on the merit of the plans submitted.
Nor was it any secret that the more progressive plans would receive
the most money. du Pont also required that the districts receiving money
raise some funds of their own by bonding themselves to the extent
allowable by law. No school district, of course, was required to take
the money.

At first many districts in the state rebelled against this frontal
assault on the educational status quo. They loudly refused to apply
for any of the building funds. But du Pont had laid his groundwork
with exquisite care. Even before the passage of the new school code,
he had financed the extensive remodelling and enlarging of the twenty-

five-year-old Alexis I. du Pont High School in Wilmington. He had also paid the cost of constructing southern Delaware's first consolidated high school, Caesar Rodney near Dover. These two structures were designed to serve as showcases, to give people an idea of the kind of school buildings du Pont wanted to help Delaware school districts build.

That was not his only stratagem. Now that he had shown people what their schools could be like, he set out to demonstrate in surprisingly objective terms what the old schools really were like. Once again the outside experts were called in, this time to conduct a critical analysis of every school in the state outside of Wilmington. The results, which were made public just as the first school year under the new code was starting in the fall of 1919, were clearly alarming. The state's schools were almost universally substandard. Some were in ruinous condition with holes in the floors and walls, unfit even to keep out the harsh winds of winter. Sanitary conditions were often primitive. So was school equipment. Many school buildings were situated in undesirable locations because local school boards had been able to get these sites cheaply. The survey included information on some 400 school buildings. The experts considered only 8 of the 400 even worth fixing up. The remaining 392, they concluded, should be replaced.

This bombshell was not received peacefully by those school districts whose buildings were deemed worthless. School commissioners were now becoming familiar enough with the details of the new code to realize that they were being ordered to surrender much of their former local control to the state board of education. Worse still in the eyes of many rural residents was the mechanism suggested as the fastest way to bring rural schools up to minimal standards. Many of the old one-room schools, the experts said, should be closed down and larger consolidated primary and secondary schools built in the towns and villages. Students would have to be carried into school by school buses, to be paid for with local taxes. School years would also be longer, a provision that angered many farmers dependent on the help of their children in the fields in the spring and fall.

The final blow was that school taxes would be raised in nearly every district in the state. In most cases they would double and in some instances they were tripled or quadrupled. This came at a time when in the aftermath of the World War, the economy was being plagued by one of its then-rare periods of inflation.

In the late summer 1919, just before the start of the school year, opponents of the code discovered what they thought–and hoped –were legal irregularities in its passage. They began a loud demand to have the code thrown out.

Confident of their own position, Governor Townsend and the State Board of Education requested that the Supreme Court rule on the questions that had been raised. The justices did so, meeting in Dover on September 12 amidst a great outpouring of more than 700 persons. Most of these opposed the code and wore special lapel pins signalling their disapproval. The court was filled with dignitaries from Governor Townsend on down. Each side was represented by prominent attorneys. The arguments of code opponents were presented–and were demolished. The court ruled unanimously that the code was constitutional and that it had been passed legally.

The governor and other code supporters may have had a brief hope in the first flush of their victory that the worst was over. They quickly learned that it had just begun. One of the most vocal opponents of the code was Landreth Layton of Georgetown, a Frankford native who had known the governor for years. He had worked as a clerk in the McCabe Store in Selbyville back in the 1870s and 1880s before establishing his own wholesale grocery business in Georgetown, where by 1919 he was a leading citizen with a grand home on North Bedford Street. He was well-connected politically as the nephew of Dr. Caleb S. Layton, former Union Republican leader and later Progressive Republican leader, and, since the 1918 election, Delaware's lone congressman.

Immediately after the favorable ruling on the code, Landreth Layton presented a petition to the governor urging him to call a special session of the General Assembly to reconsider the code. The petition had been signed by 5,453 Delawareans, most of them from the southern two counties. This placed the governor in an awkward situation. While a special session held at that moment, before the code had even been tested, would clearly have led to its complete ruination, it was equally clear to Townsend that many, if not most, of those who had signed the petition were old Sussex County friends and supporters. Yet, without undue hesitation, he made up his mind to refuse. He said publicly that he was doing so because the state constitution did not allow a governor to call a special session for a specific purpose. This excuse was transparent, of course, since, if called into session with the governor's recommendation that they consider changes to the new code, there is no doubt that the General Assembly would have done just that. The governor's refusal infuriated Layton who, though he had never been among the governor's close personal friends, had generally supported him. But Townsend knew that the new code must be given a chance to work.

In 1919, it was still almost unheard of for Delaware governors to serve more than one term in office, though there was no constitutional prohibition against multiple terms. It had only occurred in one or two instances in the state's history. Nor is there any reason to suspect that, had things been different, Governor Townsend would have tried to run for a second term. Therefore, in making his unpopular stand regarding the code he was not constrained by any concerns for his political future. Even so, it was difficult for as good a party man as Townsend to take an action that he knew would shred whatever fragile Republican Party solidarity could be said to exist.

The political atmosphere now began to get oppressively hot, especially in the two extremes of Delaware–Sussex County and the City of Wilmington. Wilmington was a hotbed of opposition to the new code because it would end the almost complete autonomy they had enjoyed in running their city school system. The Wilmingtonians had a horror of being controlled by a state board of education whose majority was made up of rural Delawareans. Sussex Countians, on the other hand, were not only ruggedly independent but distrustful of anyone from northern Delaware, especially if his name was du Pont. Landreth Layton and his allies began spreading the rumor that the governor had become the tool of the "du Pont machine," a term that was meant to impart vaguely sinister connotations.

Both sides in the school fight spent much of the fall in a battle "for the hearts and minds" of Delawareans. Although P.S. du Pont easily qualified at this time as one of the busier executives in America, he announced that he was taking several months off from his business duties to fight for acceptance of the school code. He said that he would travel anywhere in Delaware to speak in its defense. From September until nearly Christmas he did just that, speaking dozens of times, mostly in Sussex and Kent Counties and usually before hostile audiences.

An ability for dramatic rhetoric was something of a family trait with the Laytons and they used every rhetorical flourish they possessed to fight the new code. Landreth Layton publicly accused du Pont of attempting to subvert the American democratic system with dictatorial tactics. During one memorable address, he even charged that the Wilmington industrialist was somehow leading a German front against American democracy, leaving his somewhat puzzled listeners to conclude that the Kaiser, having lost the Great War, had shifted his attentions to subverting Delaware's public school system.

Landreth's cousin, Daniel J. Layton, the congressman's son, was deputy attorney general for Sussex County and chairman of the state Republican Central Committee. He also spoke frequently against the code, though in a somewhat calmer manner. The congressman remained quietly on the sidelines, deeming it inappropriate for an elected official to openly take sides, but he left little doubt that he was in sympathy with the younger generation of Laytons.

The Layton family was joined in its campaign against the code by such other prominent downstate figures as State Senator Issac D. Short of Milford, president pro-tempore of the state senate, former Congressman L. Irving Handy of Dover, and others. As the battle heated up, Sussex County Progressive Leader Robert Houston, who had originally favored the code, began to publicly oppose certain sections of it.

Always hovering in the background of the opposition was Alfred I. du Pont who was still at war with the rest of his clan. His now strong opposition to the school code was particularly ironic since he, himself, had been an advocate of public school reform for at least a decade. One could only conclude that his cousin's leadership in the crusade for better schools was enough of an affront that it overcame his more liberal principles.

Throughout 1919, as it became clearer to Alfred that Governor Townsend was not only a friend of Coleman's but also allied with Pierre in the school fight, his original support for the governor began to wane. In reading the editorial columns of his papers for the period, one almost concludes that his editorial writers were under directions to find anything wrong with the governor's performance they could, especially if it could somehow be tied to a fumble by another du Pont or his associates.

Typical was his attack on the governor in April 1919, soon after passage of the new school code, for his appointment of P.S. du Pont to the State Board of Education. By this time Pierre's principal residence was his Longwood Farm, just over the state line in Pennsylvania, but he continued to claim Delaware as his home of record. Though his status as a legal Delawarean was well known, the *Morning News* took the governor to task for his appointment of a Pennsylvanian to the Delaware State Board of Education.

An even more serious attack came in the aftermath of the great influenza epidemic, which had swept Delaware and much of the rest of the country in the fall of 1918 and winter of 1919, killing scores of people in Delaware alone. When the outbreak began in September 1918, the war was still raging in Europe and the State Council of Defense and its affiliated agencies were still in full operation. The epidemic quickly became a public health problem of unprecedented severity. Regular state and city agencies were not equipped to deal with a challenge of this magnitude.

Late in September, the Wilmington financier John J. Raskob (who, as a close friend of Pierre's was automatically an enemy of

Alfred's) attended a meeting of the Wilmington City Council held to discuss the medical emergency. The epidemic was serious throughout the state but it was especially acute in the city with many thousands of people living in close quarters. Most of the city's poor were completely unable to pay for any medical treatment. They were the hardest hit segment of the population. The hospitals were accepting them but they were growing increasingly concerned about the mounting unpaid bills. Carried away perhaps by the seemingly insurmountable problems of the moment, Raskob, a member of the State Council of Defense and chairman of its committee on public health, volunteered the services of the organization in managing the emergency. He went further and committed the State Council to paying the costs of the epidemic, even though he had not previously cleared the matter with the full council. Thousands were sick and possibly dying. The city's facilities were taxed to the breaking point and beyond. It seemed like the only quick way to deal with the matter.

By the time the influenza had died down in the early spring of 1919, the outstanding unpaid bill in Wilmington was between $25,000 and $40,000. The war had since come to an end and the Council of Defense was about to be disbanded without ever having officially endorsed Raskob's commitment to the Wilmington City Council. The city council publicly refused to pay the bills, saying that they were obligations owed by the Council of Defense.

It was an embarrassing situation for all concerned, especially for Raskob. With the Council of Defense out of money or very nearly so, Governor Townsend took the position that it was the duty of the Wilmington City Council to pay the influenza bills. He went to Wilmington and told them so personally in the plainest and most unequivocal terms. They refused him to his face, whereupon the normally cool governor intimated that he had sitting on his desk in Dover unsigned several just-passed revenue bills for the City of Wilmington. He implied that unless the City Council altered its refusal to pay the influenza bills he might not sign the revenue bills. This created a great stir as Wilmington city councilmen went yelling to the papers that the governor was trying to browbeat them into paying the influenza bills.

The governor had not criticized Raskob publicly for making the commitment in the first place because it was an understandable thing to have done in the midst of the epidemic, especially since the war was still going on and, for all anyone knew, the Defense Council would have plenty of money. But the governor's threat to hold up the city's revenue bills was a definite miscalculation and Alfred's newspapers made the most of it.

Yet even here the governor had a definite point in his favor. The epidemic had affected not only Wilmington, but the rest of the state as well. His own father's death at the age of eighty late in 1918 had been hastened by it. Young and old alike had been taken with the flu and perished that fall and winter. Only in Wilmington was the city government calling on the state to help it out of an unfortunate situation and then only because of the ill-considered remarks of one man. After thoroughly castigating the governor and Raskob, the *Morning News* announced in a loud splash of headlines that Alfred I. du Pont would pay the city's influenza bills out of his own pocket.

So it went through the summer and into the early autumn of 1919, when, with the real onslaught of the school fight, Alfred's newspapers had a field day reporting on the antics of the code opponents. That opposition consisted of several elements. One segment made up of thoughtful men like Robert Houston favored improvements in the educational system but balked at the need for tax increases which, in some cases, would be huge and would, they feared, fall heaviest on those districts least able to afford the increased cost. Farmers were against the code because the new system would require a longer school term, starting earlier in the fall and lasting later in the spring when the children were needed in the fields. Many of them also objected to the closing of the rural schools which, they reasoned, had been good enough for them and should be good enough for their children as well. Others railed against the increased costs because the nation was in the midst of a period of spiralling postwar inflation, a phenomenon then comparatively rare in the American economy. They could not do anything about the burgeoning prices elsewhere in the economy, but they thought they could do something about higher school taxes. Then there were the true demagogues who were opposed on all those grounds and more and who resented any such "foreigner" as P.S du Pont coming downstate to tell them what to do. While these latter opponents made the most noise and got the most publicity in the opposition papers, they were also the easiest to defeat with logic.

In the fall, the governor remained officially above the battle, though he spoke out publicly in support of the school reforms when he could do so without being dragged into a shouting match. More importantly, he went ahead with the work of implementing the provisions of the new code. P.S. du Pont went to the public meetings, often with Dr. Odell and other staff members of the Service Citizens in tow. He would spend hours in advance carefully preparing himself with facts and figures. These he would deliver quietly and unemotionally after the opponents had had their say.

With the exception of the Laytons and a few others, most code opponents were careful to avoid criticizing du Pont personally. They were content to argue with him on the merits of the case, realizing that any man who contributes more than $2 million for the betterment of public education without any desire for personal gain is hardly a villain even if one does not happen to agree with his approach. Much of the lingering personal animosity toward him was silenced in mid-October when he announced that he was giving an additional $500,000 to rebuild all the black schools in Delaware at no cost to the state's taxpayers. $400,000 of his original $2 million contribution had been set aside for that purpose, but it had become obvious that that wasn't enough to complete the necessary work.

That news was very satisfying to Governor Townsend who had taken the issue of black schools personally to heart. In an interview many years afterward, his two daughters, Edith Townsend Tubbs and Lyla Townsend Savoy, recalled that their father had asked du Pont specifically to make this gesture and that he had convinced him of the need for it. Not only were the black schools the worst in a state filled with bad schools, but black taxpayers were the ones least able to cope with the increased taxes the new school code would demand. When opponents spoke of the inability of poor districts to pay the higher taxes they were referring primarily to the black districts. He also sensed that if the tax problem could be overcome the state's African American citizens might well be some of the biggest boosters of the new code.

Still the opposition had strength and they used it to organize one last public meeting at Milford on November 18. du Pont had been warned in advance by his friend Frank L. Grier that the code opponents were trying to set up the meeting in such a way as to make him look his worst. He advised du Pont to stay calm, to use reason on the reasonable opponents and to ignore the rest. When the meeting began du Pont was slated to speak before the leading opposition speaker, Daniel Layton, who, it was hoped by the organizers, could then leave du Pont's argument in ruins. But Pierre had heard the opposition argument enough times to be able to plan his attack accordingly. Without seeming to do so consciously, he was able to demolish each of Layton's arguments without even acknowledging them. The contrast between his quiet logic and the heated rhetoric of the more rabid opponents as they ranted about secret plots and foreign intrigues swayed many in attendance. They began to see that the problems could be worked out without destroying the whole edifice. For a time after the Milford meeting the pro-school code side seemed to have won. Even Alfred stopped his editorial attacks against Pierre and the governor and seemed to accept the new code, thereby leaving the Laytons and other prominent opponents high and dry. Yet despite these signs the fight was far from over. It was, in fact, still going on when the governor's term ended a year later.

By the spring of 1920 moreover it was becoming clear that Delaware's school fight was but one aspect of a much larger struggle between the conservative old ways and the progressive new ways. The Progressives had been marching nationally for a decade but the end of the war had brought in a new era of retreat from many of the earlier Progressive gains. Some Americans began to hark back to the parochial old ways. During this period the Ku Klux Klan began a brief but disturbing resurgence in the South, the Middle West, and even on some parts of the Delmarva Peninsula. Some state governments reinstituted repressive measures against labor unions, minorities, and radical leftists. U.S. Attorney General A. Mitchell Palmer began a series of witch hunts against the supposed "Red Menace" that served as a kind of precursor to the excesses of U.S.

Senator Joseph McCarthy a generation later. In the realm of diplomacy, Congress refused to allow American participation in President Wilson's idealistic creation, the League of Nations, thereby plunging the nation into two decades of isolationism in international relations.

In Delaware, where progress had come relatively late and then only grudgingly, it was hardly surprising that the new school code had created such an enormous ruckus. By early 1920, after the public battle of the fall, an uneasy truce seemed to prevail. But the governor and the pro-code forces had a problem. They realized that some adjustments needed to be made in the manner in which the school system was financed if the new system was to succeed. They needed to increase the state's support for public education as a way of reducing the school property tax burden somewhat. This would require the action of the General Assembly. Since it still met officially only once every two years the governor would be forced to call a special session less than six months after he had refused Landreth Layton's call for one. Nor was there any guarantee that, once in session, the legislature would not go ahead on its own initiative and radically alter the school code. Under the state constitution the governor could call the special session but he could not dictate its agenda. He could only recommend. Even knowing that the changes were needed, he might have held off but for two other matters that required attention–raising additional bond moneys for construction of a bridge across the Brandywine in Wilmington and a vote an the Women's Suffrage Amendment to the U.S. Constitution.

If possible, the question of whether or not women should be allowed to vote was even more fraught with emotion than the school code issue. Congress had approved a resolution calling for ratification of the woman suffrage amendment two years before and sent the matter on to the states for their action. By the spring of 1920, the amendment had been approved by thirty-four of the thirty-six state legislatures required for passage. As the different legislatures met to consider the amendment, the national suffrage battle became something of a travelling road show, a sort of socio-political carnival, moving from capital to capital with a new round of debates at each stop. Mrs. Carrie Chapman Catt, the national leader of the suffrage movement, would appear in one large hall or hotel ballroom. Across town equally prominent "antis" would address equally fervent crowds on the opposite tack. As the amendment neared passage the heat of each successive debate grew more intense.

Governor Townsend was sincerely committed to woman's suffrage and he realized that most of the states that had not already approved the amendment were not likely to do so. Thus, if the women of America were going to be able to exercise the basic right of citizenship it might be up to Delaware to get the job done. Once again he faced a challenge he could not have avoided even if he had wished to.

In Delaware, the suffrage fight made for some very strange and curious political alliances and some equally unusual disagreements. According to the Philadelphia *Bulletin*, Delaware Democrats tended to oppose suffrage in the apparent fear that its passage would lead to the enfranchisement of ten thousand black women, all of whom would vote Republican, thereby making Delaware a G.O.P. stronghold along the lines of Vermont. Yet one of the emerging anti-suffrage figures in the state was Daniel J. Layton, Republican state chairman. If that were not odd enough, Dan Layton's father, the congressman, was a staunch supporter of the amendment.

Two years before, President Wilson had urged all Democratic U.S. senators to vote in favor of the suffrage resolution in Congress. At the time Delaware was represented in the Senate by two Democrats–Josiah Wolcott and Willard Saulsbury. They both voted against the resolution. Mrs. Thomas F. Bayard, wife of the eminent Democratic attorney and politician, was said to be against suffrage. Mrs. Florence Bayard Hilles, Thomas Bayard's sister, was the leader of the suffrage cause in Delaware.

The leader of the anti-suffrage movement in the state was the formidable Mrs. Henry B. Thompson, daughter of old General James Wilson, Civil War hero and Addicks foe. With such an able instructor, Mrs. Thompson's views were solidly against anything as dangerous as voting women. She contended that the women of Delaware were opposed to suffrage by a ratio of eighteen to one. Her charge was that outsiders were trying to push the vote on Delaware women against their will and at one memorable session in Wilmington she thundered:

> Since that day when the illustrious Rodney rode through Wilmington on his way to form the great union of independent States, Delaware has led in every patriotic move. Delaware will not fall now. She will not place the yoke of political slavery upon our shoulders; she will keep alive the spirit of our independence and protect the liberty of the sovereign people of Delaware. As long as the stars shine upon the blue, Delaware will remain among the immortal thirteen upon our undefeated flag.

While Mrs. Thompson refrained from saying a great deal about the specifics of her opposition to the vote for women, she could declaim such stirring phrases for hours on end and frequently, in those heady days, did so. But the governor could be equally stirring in his support for the amendment. In his speech to the legislature at the opening of

A Formidable Adversary:
The redoubtable Mary Wilson Thompson of Wilmington was Governor Townsend's implacable foe in his 1920 fight to win approval of the Women's Suffrage (19th) Amendment to the U.S. Constitution by the Delaware General Assembly. Mrs. Thompson won the battle when the General Assembly refused after a protracted struggle to ratify the amendment. The governor won the war when, a few months later, another state voted to ratify, thus providing the necessary vote to bring about its adoption (Photo reproduced from the Wilmington News-Journal *which in turn reproduced it from Charles Reese's* The Horse on Rodney Square*).*

the special session on March 22, he said:

> Women suffrage has been a subject of public discussion for over half a century. It is not an agitation of the moment. The right of equal franchise has been granted and exercised with success in several states for years. It is not a theory or untried experiment.
>
> No amendment to the Federal Constitution has been so long discussed. The resolution passed by Congress was the result of long deliberation. The action was not due to the excitement of the hour.
>
> [Suffrage] is not an expression of local or sectional view. It represents a national trend of thought, founded on deliberate thought and successful experience.
>
> The question is not one of political expediency but an interpretation of social justice. It is the world-old question of right and wrong.

If expediency be considered, however, we reflect on womanhood if we refuse her right to express practically by ballot what she now influences by mere persuasion.

Those who would withhold franchise today are descendents in thought of those who refused woman the position in the school, in the office, in the hospital. All those campaigns for reform, civic advance, and protection of the woman who earns her living, have been consummated by the votes of those who today are favoring political as well as social rights.

To you men, I present this responsibility. Your oath of office prompts you to represent the State as well as the constituency of a single political precinct or division. Your supreme duty is to think and act for the good of your State and Nation—and the influence of woman is for good. The eyes of a Nation rest upon you. The responsibility is yours.

As usual, he left little doubt where he stood on the matter. One may also detect the talented hand of Everett Johnson at work behind the governor's fine phrases. In a replay of the school fight of the year before, his stand infuriated many downstate Republicans. The governor had let it be known that he would very much appreciate a chance to represent his party at the upcoming Republican National Convention. Among other reasons, there was a boom of sorts behind the possible presidential candidacy of T. Coleman du Pont and the governor very much wished to be able to help his friend's candidacy. But as he stood before the General Assembly to plead the suffrage case some Sussex County Republicans had already met to figure out how best to hurt him and they had taken aim at his hope of being a delegate.

The governor was well aware of the undercurrent of revolt against his leadership, but he was equally aware that the special session very probably marked his last chance to influence the course of his program in the legislature and he was ready to sacrifice his popularity in furtherance of that goal. His state of mind as the special session began was expressed in the conclusion of his speech to the legislators:

> We are living in stirring times. For my part, I am giving my best thought and energy to my day and generation. The force of all the Truth, as is given me to see the Truth, is given to the problems of the day. Understood and misunderstood, I intend by the grace of Him who rules eventually in the Courts of men, so to continue.
>
> The tasks set before you are charged with vital results. The Ideals conceived in the word 'America' are not yet fully realized. The problems presented are not personal, political, or sectional. Upon your acts here today depend largely the welfare of tomorrow. They challenge your best thought. Upon you depends more than ordinarily comes to a representative of this Assembly.

Governor Townsend was too much a politician ever to lose sight of political considerations, but these were the words of a man who had moved beyond the realm of everyday politics into statesmanship. He was concerned that spring with larger issues of right and wrong and with his own place in history. Unfortunately, few of the men to whom he spoke shared those concerns.

Immediately before the special session began many downstate legislators who opposed the school code were busy dickering with anti-suffrage legislators trying to work out a deal to block ratification of the amendment in return for the "antis" help in repealing or greatly altering the code. Code supporters were just as busy trying to work out a deal the other way-they would support the suffrage amendment if the suffragists would support them in voting for only minor changes to the code. But as the session began, neither side had a deal completely worked out.

Writing in his *Sussex Republican* just before the start of the session, Robert Houston summed up the middle-of-the-road view on the code when he noted that "ninety per cent of the objection to the new School Code is based on the increased taxation necessary to its maintenance." But he wasn't against the code because of the tax problems. He simply hoped to see a plan to divert other state revenues to the schools:

> This is the first time a legislature in this state has had the opportunity to relieve real estate of some of the burden of taxation. The State has several sources of income. The income is large. Can it be expended more wisely than for the benefit of our schools?

When the session finally began there proved to be too many diverse interests among the legislators to put together any sort of coalition for rapid action on the two issues. Many school districts had submitted lists of hoped-for changes to the new code, most of which were aimed at lowering the property tax burden and returning powers to the local districts. A nine-member Commission to Consider Amendments to the Delaware School Code of 1919 was appointed on April 14, a few days after the anti-code forces had lost a crucial vote to repeal the code. Their loss was a personal victory for the governor.

Though a majority of the commission members favored

major changes, their eventual report to the General Assembly favored an altered code that was still intact in its major points. Both the governor and P.S. du Pont found it acceptable and it was adopted formally as the School Law of 1920.

That was hardly the end of the matter. Sentiment still ran deep and it lasted for several more years. Changes were still being made in the code early in the administration of John's successor, William Denney, but the basic code survived and became the basis for a modern system of public education. Through the 1920s P.S. du Pont and his allies continued the work they had started. The system had far to go, but Governor Townsend had been the trail-blazing elected official who took the first and largest step. That step was one of the most important things any Delaware governor has ever done for the lives of his constituents.

15. The Battle Over Suffrage

Very few issues could have been found in the spring of 1920 with more emotional impact than the question of the new school code, over which controversy still raged in much of Delaware. The question of whether or not Delaware's General Assembly should provide the last ratification needed to bring about adoption of the woman's suffrage amendment was, if possible, even more inflammatory. It brought about one of the two or three greatest battles in the history of the Delaware General Assembly. It was directly linked to one of the larger political battles in Governor Townsend's career, which was also fought out that spring.

As the March 22 starting date of the special session neared, thirty-four of the necessary thirty-six states had voted to ratify the proposed 19th Amendment to the United States Constitution giving all American women the right to vote. That week it was learned that Washington had become the thirty-fifth state to ratify. Only one more ratification vote was needed to make equal suffrage for women the law of the land. If Governor Townsend and many other Delawareans had anything to do with it, Delaware would be the state to put woman's suffrage over the top, thus writing a happy ending to more than half a century of struggle. After the ratification vote in Washington State, the national spotlight turned to Delaware.

Hundreds, even thousands of letters and telegrams poured in from all over the country, urging the governor and legislators to ratify or to defeat. Prominent persons of all descriptions from President Wilson on down contacted the governor and the legislators. The

Delaware's statehouse–
as it appeared during the Townsend administration
(Courtesy of the Delaware Public Archives).

Democratic and Republican National Committees had endorsed the amendment and the national chairmen had contacted their Delaware counterparts. Legions of suffragists descended on Dover, wearing yellow jonquils as their symbol. Equally imposing legions of anti-suffragists appeared with red roses on their lapels. The factions marched through the streets of Dover, singing marching songs and chanting slogans. Their banners stretched across city streets and they commandeered large halls for rallies. They marched around the Dover Green and into the State House where they buttonholed legislators and argued their case. The house and senate chambers were beginning to resemble florist shops, buried as they were under increasing quantities of jonquils and roses.

At the beginning of the special session, Mrs. Hilles and her suffragists hoped for an early victory. They had been working throughout the state ever since the suffrage amendment had been approved by Congress two years before, preparing for the inevitable ratification struggle in Dover. They had wanted to bring it to a vote in the fall of 1919, but Governor Townsend felt that he could not risk destroying the school code by calling a special session at the height of the school fight. Now that Delaware seemed to be the deciding factor in the national suffrage battle, the suffragists knew it would be harder.

The special interests were out in force, their interests sometimes obvious, sometimes obscure. The diehard prohibition "wets," still hoping for a fast repeal of the 18th Amendment, opposed ratification. They were convinced that millions of new female voters would be such an immense force in favor of continued Prohibition and against demon rum that repeal would never come. Railroad magnates opposed it, though their reasons for doing so were not entirely clear. Some Democrats were against it, fearing that the Democratically-inspired "Jim Crow" laws of the 1870s and 1880s would make life-long straight-ticket Republicans of all the newly enfranchised Negro women voters. Other legislators were trying to trade their votes on suffrage for concessions on other legislation.

Strangely, some of the stauncher liberal supporters of the new school code were arch-opponents of suffrage. Prominent Wilmingtonians Col. and Mrs. George A. Elliott opposed it. Mrs. Henry P. Scott, wife of one of the leading members of the Service Citizens of Delaware, opposed it as did Mrs. David Reinhardt, wife of the attorney general. Miss Emily P. Bissell, who was already known nationally for her charitable work, was an opponent, as was Delaware's grand old Democratic statesman, Judge George Gray of Wilmington.

Generally speaking, the pro-ratification side had the more prominent supporters both in and out of Delaware. At one point in the proceedings Delaware Democrats even received a visit from Eamon deValera, first president of the Republic of Ireland, urging them to support the amendment. But the suffragists were finding it necessary to contend with one immensely damaging secret weapon of the anti-suffragist cause against which even telegrams from Woodrow Wilson and visits from Eamon deValera proved ineffective. The weapon was none other than Mrs. Henry B. Thompson, the Wilmington socialite and civic leader who went about the task of defeating suffrage with all the skill and gusto her prominent father, General James H. Wilson, had displayed in leading Sherman's cavalry through Georgia (and, it might be noted, considerably more political acumen than the general had shown in his efforts to contain J. Edward Addicks). From March until the end of the special session early in June, Mrs. Thompson was everywhere in Dover and Wilmington, manning the barricades against the suffragists and whipping her troops into line to defeat ratification. She proved to be brilliant in her use of charm, cajolery, press-agentry, and dramatic speechifying.

One of Mrs. Thompson's more successful tactics was to turn the suffrage issue into a question of states' rights. Delaware legislators should not allow themselves to be swayed by the views of outsiders. They should confine themselves to considering how Delawareans felt about suffrage, and Mrs. Thompson was prepared to tell them how Delawareans felt about it. THEY WERE AGAINST IT, GENTLEMEN! ! ! More importantly, Mrs. Thompson said, the women of Delaware were against it! They opposed it by a ratio of at least eighteen to one, she charged, citing the questionable results of a somewhat less than objective survey her forces had conducted the previous year. One outspoken anti-suffrage leader in the house, Rep. John E. "Bull" McNabb, a Wilmington Democrat, said he was certain there could not be more than twenty-five pro-suffrage voters in his entire district. He was abashed to receive a pro-suffrage petition signed by some five hundred of his constituents, but only momentarily.

After the state senate voted for ratification on March 27, Mrs. Thompson and her allies went to work on the house with a vengence almost unequalled in Delaware history. That they ultimately succeeded was no surprise to those who knew her. The great irony of the fight was Mrs. Thompson herself. Her whole career, not only in this fight, but in her many civic endeavors as well, was one continuous testimony to the equality (if not the superiority) of women. She was a person of almost ferocious competence and skill. Had she lived in a slightly later age she could easily have won election to high political office (had she wished to pursue it). Yet she refused to consider that women should be made the political equals of men. She was a paradox of the passing of the Victorian era from Delaware. She was a highly appropriate symbol of the best of the old ways that were passing from the scene, even as men like Governor Townsend sought to bring an end to the worst of the old era. Mrs. Thompson would fight progress ably and nobly on an issue like suffrage even as she sought to bring progress about in other areas. She was an enigma, but one thing was clear: if all American women had been like Mary Thompson, the suffrage amendment would not have been needed. They would have run the country without it.

She succeeded in holding off a pro-ratification vote in the house until adjournment of the special session on June 2, 1920, at which time she proudly announced, "The death knell of women's suffrage has been sounded." Writing about the event fifty-six years later, *Morning News* columnist William P. Frank recounted, and when the House of Representatives adjourned on June 2, Mrs. Thompson and her supporters cheered so loudly that Speaker Alexander P. Corbit almost broke his gavel in a frantic effort to restore order to the lower chamber.

After the session, Mrs. Thompson, who could be most elegant and genteel as a hostess, held a reception in the corridor of the old State House. The *Morning News* stated that she greeted her "champions" with her sweetest smile and hailed the anti-suffrage legislators as symbols of Delaware's chivalry.

But, the *Morning News* bitterly said, Mrs. Thompson [and] her cohorts . . . had "thwarted the wishes of hundreds of thousands of women in the factories in the country who are demanding the right to participate in the making of the laws under which they live."

All that was still in the future as the special session began. Before the session finally ended on June 2, the governor was embroiled in a personal fight nearly as lively as the suffrage battle, to which it was indirectly related. It had to do with Sussex County's Layton family and their battle for dominance in the county's Republican Party. They had been at least nominal supporters of the governor's candidacy in 1916. Since passage of the school code they had taken to abusing him as the worst sort of turn-coat traitor against the people of Sussex because of his efforts on its behalf. Daniel Layton and his cousin, Landreth, had been the leading Sussex County spokesmen against it. They had invested a great deal of their personal prestige in the fight, at least in Dan Layton's eyes, only to be more or less beaten at every turn by the combination of Pierre du Pont's maddeningly effective facts, Coleman du Pont's influence with upstate politicians, and Governor Townsend's skillful fight for the code in Dover. Worst of all, the Laytons' erstwhile political patron, Alfred I. du Pont, had apparently mended his fences with his family and climbed aboard the school code bandwagon, leaving the Laytons high and dry. Daniel Layton seems to have been motivated by a simple desire for revenge.

The most accessible foe was Governor Townsend. They began trying to hack away at his political underpinnings in Sussex County by spreading stories about his activities as governor that showed him in an unfavorable light. Most of them were half-truths. Some were complete fabrications. One example of the latter was the story that he had secretly fought behind the scenes to defeat Dr. Caleb R. Layton in his successful 1918 bid for Congress. In fact, the governor had personally contributed $500 to Layton's campaign fund. In Sussex County in 1918, $500 was far more than a token gesture of support.

The Republicans held two state conventions during general election years in those days. The first, held in the spring, was for the purpose of electing a state delegation to the Republican National Convention. In 1920, the convention was to be held in Chicago in mid-June. Sussex had two of the six Delaware delegate seats. The major task facing the delegates was the election of the state's Republican National Committeeman. The incumbent was T. Coleman du Pont, who very much wanted to be reelected (he still harbored presidential aspirations at that time, though ultimately his health failed him before he could go very far with them). du Pont had asked Governor Townsend to seek one of the Sussex delegate positions and to try to line up support for his candidacy. This was logical enough since the governor had been one of du Pont's more avid Sussex County supporters for years, occasional political differences notwithstanding. He had also been a previous delegate.

At first John tried to work out an arrangement whereby he and Congressman Layton, the heads of the two main Sussex County

Republican factions, would each serve as a delegate and would each give his support to du Pont at the convention. He hoped thereby to avoid the factional strife that so often kept the Republican Party in a state of near chaos during election years. After some consideration, Congressman Layton took the governor up on his offer and all was seemingly set for the two men to go to Chicago in June.

That was before Daniel Layton entered the picture. Though the congressman was still the titular head of "the Layton Faction," he had been in Washington and elsewhere for much of the past two years. His son, who was around the courthouse in Georgetown in his guise as deputy attorney general for Sussex, had plenty of time to run the family political enterprise. He was able also to work on the loyalties, such as they were, of the current county Republican chairman, Elijah Lynch. Lynch had been appointed Sussex County's lone state detective by Governor Townsend. As such, he owed his job to the governor but he worked out of Layton's office and the relationship between the two grew close. As the local *Evening Journal* reporter put it, ". . . he has 'flopped' and is now a right-hand man of the Layton Machine."

Layton obviously refused to accept his father's understanding with the governor to serve as a delegate and to support Coleman du Pont. He insisted on pursuing a campaign to deprive John of the delegate seat he wanted. As the first step in that campaign, he got Lynch to call a meeting of the county Republican committee in Georgetown on the night of March 14, a week before the opening of the special session in Dover and about five weeks before the state convention to elect the national delegates. The meeting was ostensibly one of the Republican county committee, but was attended solely by the governor's political enemies. Neither he nor his friends had been invited, but the word got out and John "crashed the party." What happened then was the subject of an extensive story in the next day's *Evening Journal*:

> The meeting in itself was a succession of highlights and political sensations. The purpose of the called meeting was to "set up the pins" against the governor. All his opponents in Sussex County were present. He was not invited. However, inasmuch as it was a meeting of his own party committee in his own county, and he had not missed attending such meetings for years, he did not feel he would be intruding if he attended.
>
> . . . the meeting was in full blast when the Governor "dropped in." He arrived in the midst of a very vigorous attack which it is said was prematurely stopped by the Governor's unexpected appearance.

To make things even more interesting, Congressman Layton was in attendance, probably trying to protect his own interests as much as anything. At this point he was still officially committed to his agreement with Governor Townsend to serve as a pro-du Pont delegate. It was a classic case of a skillful politician caught between a rock and a hard place:

> [Congressman Layton] was called on for a speech. He told the committee it is the especial wish of National Chairman Will H. Hays that General T. Coleman du Pont be re-elected national committeeman from Delaware . . . Immediately following his speech he called Governor Townsend aside and made him a proposition . . . that both withdraw [as candidates for the delegate seats]. The Governor's reply was delivered to the meeting and those who heard it say it was a "knock-out."
>
> He told the committee he was for party harmony and had always been so. He expressed the opinion there

was no genuine reason for Congressman Layton's offer to withdraw . . . He gave the committee to understand that he and his friends were supporting Congressman Layton's candidacy for national delegate . . . But the Governor also gave the committee to understand that he and his friends did not regard party harmony as a jughandle affair and they expected the same spirit of fairness from Congressman Layton and his crowd that was shown to Congressman Layton.

The Governor took up the charges made against him and his administration and announced his intention of going before the people of Sussex County and making a finish fight in defense of his administrative acts. He announced there would be no compromise but a fight that would compel everyone to stand up and be counted.

Throughout the course of his fight against the governor, Daniel Layton said publicly that he was carrying on the feud because of Townsend's efforts on behalf of the school code. While there was no doubt something to that, there was more. The governor had a way of out-maneuvering Layton politically without seeming to be maneuvering at all. Even when Layton apparently won, the sweetness of his victory was often lost by the time he finally won it.

During the General Assembly session of 1919, Layton had strongly supported a poorly-conceived bill (and possibly even authored it) that would have given the Delaware Attorney General or any of his deputy attorneys general the authority to hire as many additional state detectives as they saw fit. Each person with this authority, moreover, could have decided who would be hired, as well as how many. A rider to the bill would have given existing state detectives pay raises. This last provision was reasonable and probably had much to do with the passage of the overall bill through both houses of the legislature in the final moments of the session. Then as now, representatives and senators found themselves at the last minute voting for any number of bills they had not scrutinized too closely. When the bill reached the governor's desk he promptly vetoed it.

Layton had used the governor's veto of this bill, which would have given a pay raise to Lynch, the reigning county Republican chairman, as futher evidence of Governor Townsend's treachery. Detective Lynch maintained a stolid silence on the subject. During his appearance before the committee in Georgetown on the night of March 14, the governor also brought up this matter. According to the account of the meeting in the *Evening Journal*, he told the crowd he had vetoed the bill:

> because such power in the hands of the Attorney General, or any of his deputies is not necessary to the protection of the state or the maintenance of law and order in the first place. While it might not be abused by any Attorney General or any of his deputies who would have had (if the bill had become law) a power of espionage or blackmail or personal or political persecution that would terrorize individuals, communities, or parties.

As his detractors digested this statement, he turned the meeting on its ear by announcing that he had realized the merit of the proposal to give the state detectives a pay raise. He had in fact given them the pay raises the bill had called for out of his own discretionary funds. Thus, the whole time Layton had been berating the governor, Detective Lynch was drawing his higher pay–a fact he apparently kept to himself. The only one in Sussex really hurt by the veto was Layton.

If anything, this meeting only strengthened Daniel Layton's resolve to get Townsend. It also brought about a most amazing transformation in his views on woman's suffrage. The Congressman had long been on record as favoring ratification and it had generally been assumed that his son concurred. He was, after all, chairman of the Republican State Committee, which had passed a resolution favoring ratification. Yet when the intense lobbying effort for and against ratification began in Dover the week after the Georgetown meeting, Layton turned up as one of Mrs. Thompson's most loquacious allies. He began addressing rallies, making speeches, collaring legislators, and otherwise making himself useful to the anti-suffrage cause. The confusion this stance created in the minds of some legislators was aptly illustrated by this Philadelphia *Bulletin* piece form late March:

> The conflicting attitude of the two Laytons continues to be a disturbing factor. Caleb R. Layton, Congressman, is here [Dover] avowedly working for ratification under instructions of national leaders in Washington. His son, Daniel J. Layton, chairman of the Republican State Committee had indorsed ratification.
>
> A State Representative, present at a Republican conference, following adjournment of the legislature Friday, narrates:
>
> "Papa Layton told us the Republican Party is looking to us to ratify the Suffrage Amendment and we must do so. Son Layton told us he has been for woman's suffrage for years, but now is obliged to oppose it because of feeling among his constituents. Son Layton made a sharp attack on Papa Layton's attitude. After it was all over, Papa Layton kissed Son Layton good-bye."

More seriously, "Son Layton" also began spreading the rumor that many Sussex County Republican representatives on record as opposing ratification were voting against it to get back at the governor for his refusal to withdraw from the delegate race. This charge was clearly spurious, but for several days it succeeded in adding to the hysteria that was already sweeping Dover. The governor held a meeting in his office on March 31, attended by leading spokesmen for both sides in the suffrage battle. The purpose of the gathering was to explore ways of bringing about calm so that the house could get on with its deliberations in relative peace. One reputed "anti" who attended, the prominent Philadelphia lawyer and Milford resident, Ruby Vale, suggested one course of action to clear up the so-called anti-Townsend factor. After the meeting John offered publicly to withdraw from the delegate race if the house would vote to ratify that day (the senate having already done so).

The House did not take the governor up on his offer. Early the following week an effort was made by pro-suffrage forces to bring the matter to a vote. The representatives were not voting on ratification itself in this case. They were voting on whether to bring it to a vote, or to hold off still longer. The motion was defeated and the ratification vote delayed. After that action all but two of the Sussex County Republican representatives joined in an open letter to the governor. They assured him that they opposed the suffrage amendment because of their own beliefs and those of their constituents and not because of any feelings of animosity toward him. "Your offer of withdrawal," they added, "while meritorious, is not pertinent to the question, nor did it in any wise influence our vote. Whether you are or are not a candidate to represent the party has nothing whatever to do with our vote on this question."

"Naturally," Governor Townsend responded, "I am pleased at this statement. It is, however, no more than I expected. Few men today elected to office of Representative would allow a personal prejudice to influence their vote on a matter of such importance. I am human enough to appreciate the fact that my record and personality has not been such as to merit such a rebuke by the members of my party."

So one more rumor came to an end–almost. Probably the last word on the matter appeared in the Sussex County weekly, the *Seaford News*, a strongly anti-Townsend paper that never missed a chance for a dig:

> It is amazing to think that the Governor of any state would in cold blood and calm mind expose himself in this manner, even though he was so vitally interested in a cause that he might be willing to sacrifice any of his personal holdings . . . for the Governor to try and sell a personal ambition to gain only for himself in the eyes of those favoring the cause that he advocates, it is surely enough to bring down the most bitter criticism upon his head.

Fortunately, most Delawareans understood the spirit in which the governor's offer had been made. Townsend did not bother to reply to what had by now become an almost standard editorial style at the paper.

In April with suffrage still undecided and the decibel level in the State House still high, the two Sussex County Republican factions prepared for an April 17 primary to elect delegates to the state convention, which would in turn elect the national delegates. Both sides fielded a full slate of candidates for each of the county's election districts. Julian Townsend ran on his father's slate for the Georgetown district. Traditionally each county caucus at the state convention elected the delegates for that county, so the primary outcome was decisive.

When the vote came on April 17, the Layton faction won by a slight majority. When the convention was held in Dover four days later, Governor Townsend was defeated by one vote in the Sussex County caucus. One possible consolation was that Congressman Layton was also denied a delegate seat. But Townsend came out of the convention with his own prestige enhanced and with many of his enemies in Sussex feeling a bit chastened. In the first place, many of the governor's Kent and New Castle friends had urged him to allow the delegate matter to come to a vote on the floor of the convention. They were certain, they said, that he would be elected by a hefty margin. He refused, saying that he would stand by the traditional caucus vote. Secondly, the two men elected in place of Townsend and Layton, former Governor Simeon S. Pennewill of Greenwood and Robert B. Elliott of Seaford, were both known to be supporters of Coleman du Pont.

In the afternoon, when the full convention turned to the matter of the party platform, the delegates gave a strong endorsement to the policies and accomplishments of the Townsend administration. In particular they emphasized the accomplishments made in public education. Then the governor was accorded a standing ovation and a full fifteen minutes of applause, "during which most Sussex County delegates squirmed uncomfortably in their seats."

Though the governor was ultimately defeated on the suffrage issue as well, even that defeat was only temporary. Several months after the Delaware legislature adjourned without making a decisive vote for or against ratification, the ratification vote of the Tennessee state legislature gave the needed thirty-sixth vote. On August 26, the U.S. secretary of state formally signed the proclamation making the amendment a part of the U.S. Constitution. That evening the Wilmington *Every Evening* ran a cartoon depicting a beautiful, seated woman attired in an elegant gown to which a price tag was affixed bearing the label "27,000,000 Votes." Approaching her with gazes of worshipful awe were a donkey and an elephant, each bearing large and gorgeous bouquets. The cartoon was entitled "Love at first sight." Several days later the same paper in an editorial column assured its readers that the election of a woman to high office would not change job titles: "For instance, if she should be elected as head of the State, she would be a governor, not governess; nor would she be a sheriffess, nor judgess, just as in later day usage the woman physician is a doctor and not a doctress as she used to be designated in the days when women were almost unknown to the profession."

In September, Governor Townsend declined to call another special session to change state election laws to accommodate women. It was his view that "existing laws are ample for the women to vote." By October 20, 884 of the 47,218 registered voters in the City of Wilmington were women, and by December the first women jurors had been called for duty in the city's U.S. District Court.

In June, T. Coleman du Pont had been reelected to the Republican National Committee with nary a ripple of discontent. Mrs. Thompson had had the pleasure of seeing ratification defeated in Dover. Townsend had seen it carry nationally. Daniel Layton had kept the governor from voting for his friend at the Republican National Convention, but du Pont had been elected just the same. Townsend's opponents in those days had a way of winning battles, but he had a way of winning wars.

16. The Other Side of Being Governor

Many chief executives would have been totally preoccupied with the raging brawls that confronted Governor Townsend during the last half of his administration. He did not take them lightly, but they did not dominate his life. He had too much else to do to worry overmuch about all the controversy with which he was surrounded in Dover. Even as he was devoting time and attention to running the State of Delaware, he was still the single head of a large family and was running the far-flung Townsend enterprises.

Days and weeks of more or less normal routine between legislative sessions gave him time to attend not only to his personal interests but to the more satisfying aspects of being governor. Much of his official correspondence in this period deals with the minutia of the job; helping Milford high school girls get permission to hold basketball practice in the town's National Guard armory; helping a University of Delaware student from Sussex County arrange a banquet of the "Down-homers' Club"; writing letters of recommendation for young Delawareans for jobs in cities beyond the state's borders; and attending meetings of the dozens of committees and commissions of which he was a member.

John used much the same style of business management in running the state as he did in his own enterprises. That was natural enough considering that he still exercised much of the day-to-day control over his business during his years in Dover. Many elected officials or, more accurately, would-be elected officials, have talked

A Family Outing: *Even when John was governor, a significant part of the family's social life centered around the church. The photo above, taken about 1920, shows members of the family in a group at a Methodist event in Easton, Maryland. Preston is at right in the front row. Just above him is Edith, holding her son, Bill Tubbs. Lyla sits on the next step above her sister beside "Grandma Townsend" (Ida), who is holding young John Townsend "Towny" Tubbs on her lap. Edith's husband, John Tubbs, stands beside Ida Townsend. Governor Townsend and his son, Julian, are second and third from left in the top row (Lyla Townsend Savoy collection).*

about the need to run government with the same efficiency and style used to manage successful private corporations. John is one of the few who came close to realizing the ideal. That was a notable achievement considering the degree to which his initiatives were hampered by the General Assembly.

His style of governing was to know as much about as many phases of the operation as possible. He strove to stay aware of the fine details of many agencies even as he directed the broad programs.

The Younger Generation: *Seen during a summer outing are Edith and Jack Tubbs, seated, and Julian Townsend and his wife, Mildred Evans Townsend. All had recently been married or were about to be (Lyla T. Savoy collection).*

In the midst of his marathon battles over suffrage and the school code he was corresponding at length with George Marx, the superintendent of the Ferris Industrial School, a state-run reform school near Wilmington, about a tract of woodland on the school grounds. Marx was preparing to have the tract logged. He was trying to get the governor to come up and appraise the woods beforehand to give school trustees a better idea of what they should get for it. This might have been an effort on Marx's part to ingratiate himself with the governor, but if so, he picked an interesting and illuminating approach. The governor liked nothing better than appraising tracts of land, whether for himself, for a friend, or for the State of Delaware. Being at that moment engaged in the greatest political and legislative battles of his career, he was unable to get to the Ferris School to look at the woodland, but he took the trouble to advise Marx at length about the sale.

Governor Townsend was even more interested in the planning and land acquisition for the new Delaware Home for the Feeble-minded during 1919. This project was officially being carried out by a citizen's commission appointed by the governor, but John himself did the majority of the work. His interest stemmed primarily from the fact that the home had been a pet project of Jennie Townsend's before her death. Perhaps for that reason he became almost too involved in the work of locating a proper site for it in the spring of 1919. As it turned out, the best parcel of land he could find was a large piece of the huge tract he had bought years before near Stockley to expedite the construction of the Coleman du Pont Boulevard. His idea (which still has a great deal of merit though it is no longer widely practiced) was that such institutions as the Home for the Feeble-minded could save taxpayers money and provide healthful work for residents if they had their own farm attached to the institution. The Stockley Home was planned to have its own dairy herd, its own swine, laying hens, poultry houses, vegetable gardens, and field crops. What could not be used right there at the institution could be sold to raise money for operating expenses. While the Home was not entirely self supporting, every little bit helped, to John's way of thinking. This concept was not new with Governor Townsend. The Sussex County Almshouse Farm near Georgetown had operated that way for generations, and it had saved Sussex County taxpayers money. Even when the almshouse property was taken over for use as the Sussex Correctional Institution years later, officials of the new prison continued to operate the former almshouse farm. Hundreds of acres of farmland remain in state ownership at what has come to be known as Stockley Center. The land is now rented out to area farmers for cultivation of corn and soybeans as the farm has succumbed to present-day bureaucracy.

John looked at sites all over the state, and at their prices. He concluded that his own property was the best suited for the institution and he sold it to the state at near cost. Some years before this he had transferred the tract to Peninsula Real Estate Company, a firm in which he had majority interest, but of which he was not the sole owner. Others included his brother James and Orlando Harrison of Berlin. He had acquired the property for just under $35,000. Peninsula Real Estate sold it to the State of Delaware seven years later for $40,000. This amount represented a small profit, which was divided between expenses on the land, such as taxes, and the other two stockholders in Peninsula. The governor received nothing from the sale. In addition, he raised the money from private benefactors to buy the land and build the first buildings on it. He succeeded in getting $5,000 contributions from old Senator Henry A. du Pont, T. Coleman du Pont, and Mrs. T. Coleman du Pont (who was wealthy in her own right), among others. Years later while serving in the Senate he gave another tract of land to the institution free of charge.

In the course of all this, the governor had looked at a farm in southern New Castle County that had been offered by its owner for sale to the commission planning the home. This man, possibly reading his own meaning into the governor's remarks, thought John had told him that his farm looked like the best choice for the commission. When he heard some weeks later that Townsend's own land at Stockley had been chosen, he was infuriated. He was certain the governor at the least had lied to him and that he might even be guilty of a conflict of interest. John invited him down to lunch in Dover to discuss the matter. The landowner wrote back a stiffly formal letter of refusal, saying he could not possibly accept an invitation to eat with a man who had treated him so badly. Since this whole matter occurred right in the midst of the school fight John clearly expected the man to go to the papers and charge that he had been wronged. He wrote instructions in pencil on the bottom of the man's letter, "file this where you always know where it is," and waited for the worst to happen, but nothing did. Either the governor's detractors among the Delaware press were fair enough men to realize that the State of Delaware had gotten a much better bargain, or the angry landowner cooled down and saw the light.

Such a transaction as the Stockley land sale would probably be impossible in light of today's painfully ambiguous attitude toward conflict of interest, but it was perfectly straightforward and acceptable in 1919. Another practice that would be somewhat questionable today, but which was then accepted with nary a second glance, was the conduct of public and private business out of the same offices. Even in the midst of the furious legislative battles, John's private businesses went on as usual and as usual he had to tend to them. At that time, the governor's office was in a state of transition between the part-time job it had been in the eighteenth and nineteenth centuries and the more or less full-time job it was to become. The governor spent most of his weekdays in his Dover office in the Statehouse or travelling from meeting to meeting around the state. But he also stopped most mornings in either the Selbyville office or the cannery office in Georgetown (one of the advantages of starting one's day at 5:00 a.m.). He routinely devoted some of his time in Dover to the running of his private businesses. His official secretary typed both public and private correspondence, just as his secretary in Selbyville spent some of her time doing unpaid work for the governor's office. He often combined official functions and business visits into the same out-of-state trip, but he kept separate expenses.

Townsend, the consummate businessman, and Townsend, the skilled and committed governor, were one in the same. He could not have kept these two elements in himself separate even if he had wanted to. Nor was there any particular need to do so in an age before public officials began resorting to increasingly elaborate contortions to keep their public and private selves separate. It was then naturally assumed that high-ranking elected officials were gentlemen, and gentlemen did not betray the public trust. Though the exceptions to this unwritten code of official conduct in Delaware have gained notoriety, there have been surprisingly few of them, withal. John G. Townsend Jr. was a gentleman, and not even a detracter like Daniel J. Layton was prepared to suggest that he was not.

State government was far less involved in the day-to-day conduct of America's private enterprise system than it has since become. Of all Townsend's many businesses, the only ones exposed to any real degree of government oversight on a regular basis were the banks and the canneries. Even those areas faced much less regulation than would later be the case. The state cannery inspector and the U.S. Department of Agriculture kept a close eye on the cleanliness of the canneries, also making spot checks on the quality of the products. Townsend's canneries were among the best equipped in the state at this time. This was not entirely a matter of pride. The Atlantic Cannery along the Lewes and Rehoboth Canal had burned late in 1917. The Townsends rebuilt it and found it necessary to completely reequip it. Since he was already getting a large amount of new equipment for Rehoboth, Governor Townsend went ahead and upgraded the Georgetown and Selbyville operations at the same time.

One of the interesting ways in which his public and private selves came together in the period of wartime hardships was his practice of selling his excess supplies of sugar to the public at the end of each strawberry season. According to one 1919 account:

> While practically every section in lower Delaware
> is experiencing a sugar shortage, Georgetown through the

generosity of Governor John G. Townsend Jr. has the largest supply within a year. Governor Townsend is one of the most extensive operators of syrup factories in the east, having about fifteen plants that are devoted in the spring to preserving strawberries for the large syrup, extract and jam manufacturers of the Country. Hundreds of barrels of sugar are used annually in preserving the berries, and at the close of the season it has been the custom of Governor Townsend to release the surplus for the accomodation of the people, especially during the shortage of the past three years.

For the past two days his employees have been busily engaged disposing of the commodity to the residents here, and those who desired to purchase could obtain from five to one hundred pounds. There is such a clamor for the sugar that those in charge of distributing it are kept busy from morning until night disposing of it.

Practically 20,000 pounds have been distributed within the past two days at 22 cents a pound, thus meaning a saving to the people of 6 cents a pound. It is stated that the reason for the large surplus this year is due to the fact that the crop of berries in the central part of Sussex was not as large as the firm anticipated and therefore they did not have occasion to use up the supply.

The governor could not have served effectively from 1917 to 1921 either as governor or as head of his numerous businesses had those enterprises not already functioned under the direction of a family team. John kept a remarkably close eye on many details even as he spent much of his time away from home. The day-to-day control of both the lumber operations and the Selbyville canneries were handled by James Townsend and several assistants including Edith's husband, Jack Tubbs, who was now working for Selbyville Manufacturing Company. His son, Jule, was the manager of the Georgetown cannery and his son, Jack, was both a banker and an increasingly skilled fieldman in the berry business. The governor's close friends and associates Vollie Murray and Lee Stevens helped run all three canneries. In the spring and early summer daughters Edith and Lyla went to work in the home office at Selbyville, helping to manage the increasingly complex strawberry business. By now Jule and Jack Townsend, Murray, Stevens and others were going south each spring to manage the strawberry crop.

Interviewed about Townsend in 1979, former U.S. Senator John J. Williams of Millsboro summed up the family team as he knew it in the 1920s and 1930s but his description shows the relationship that was already developing a few years earlier:

> You never could really distinguish whether it was the sons or the father. It was teamwork and the old man was in there on all of it. He was there and knowing what was going on and active. He was a respected factor in the management of the business.

One of the harder things Townsend had to learn in those years was the art of delegating authority. He was so interested in everything about the businesses and carried so many facts and figures around in his head that it was almost impossible to explain the total picture to anyone else. As the sons gained more experience this became easier. He made a point of letting his sons work in several different areas of the business at once, though in the gubernatorial years the father still had to keep a fairly tight rein on them.

The worst time of all for him was in the spring when the legislature was in session and the strawberry crop was coming on. In the period before 1922, strawberries and tomatoes were probably the most profitable areas of his operation, with lumber running close behind and the banks some distance behind that. So he could not ignore the canning and packing seasons even though they could not have come at a worse time of year for a governor. Anyone seeking evidence of his extraordinary abilities as a businessman and politician need look no further. While somehow managing the legislature, holding off his enemies in the school and suffrage fights, and tending to all the other headaches of office, he was also overseeing the Townsend Company's complicated dealings throughout the strawberry- and tomato-growing regions of the South and Middle Atlantic states.

His men went south in January and February to arrange for the growing season a few months later. The strawberry harvest started in Florida in January and progressed with the coming of spring in an irregular curve through Louisiana, Tennessee, North Carolina, Maryland, Delaware, New Jersey, Long Island, and finally into southern New England by midsummer. The advancing season generally meant that one area would be in direct competition with the area just to the north of it. While the berries were at their height in Louisiana, they were just coming on in Tennessee. When they were about finished in North Carolina they were at their height on the lower Eastern Shore and were just starting to come on in Delaware. The first pickings of any particular variety in any given area were usually superior to later pickings of the same variety. The market consisted of fresh-packed berries that were speeded overnight to nearby cities, and of berries that were preserved in various ways. By this time the Townsends were beginning to concentrate on packing and preserving berries for the confectionary trade, though they were still heavily involved in shipping fresh berries to market. The berries that were less desirable in appearance or too ripe to survive the trip to market were either juiced or packed in sugar in wooden barrels. The business was incredibly competitive as buyers went about trying to obtain the best fresh berries at the best prices.

One reason why preserving and packing was becoming more attractive was that it enabled the company to line up customers in advance. They could contract to supply a major confectionary firm with a large part of their output the fall before the season began. They would then know about how many berries they needed to purchase, how much of a supply of preservatives, sugar, and barrels they needed, and so on. It was much less uncertain than simply acting as a middle-man for fresh berries. The Townsends sometimes bought a farmer's entire crop in advance, though this was risky. They would rent local packing sheds and canneries as they went along with the harvest, packing the crop in the tiny farm towns of the Deep South.

To be a successful broker and packer one had to be able to juggle a mind-boggling array of figures and calculated risks: the timing of the crop; the weather; the availability of packing facilities and local labor and their cost; the size, taste, and quality of the berries in a particular area; the demand in particular cities; the supply of sugar and barrels one could assemble; the cost and scheduling of transportation; and how good a deal one could work out with customers for packed berries. If, for instance, the Townsends were canning tomatoes or packing strawberries in Accomac or Exmore on Virginia's Eastern Shore, they might have to send a man down to Norfolk to hire some temporary help and bring the workers back across the ferry to Cape Charles and then up the line. They would have to arrange to have all their supplies sent down to the village they were working in. They would have to have a man close enough to the local scene to know what to pay for berries. Perhaps most difficult of all was that these complex equations had to be worked out between the governor and his various agents as the latter sat in railroad stations and dusty hotels and rented packing sheds in unfamiliar farm towns all across the South. The two major differences between Townsend and his contemporaries in the business and today's modern "agribusinessmen" are that the oldtimers were without computers to ease their calculations and they had much more competition in their decentralized age.

A surprising amount of Governor Townsend's business correspondence survives in his official files in the Delaware Public Archives. In reading through it one begins to get some idea of the complexity of his enterprises. One also sees just how spread out the family could be during the strawberry season. By 1918, both Julian and Jack had been going south every spring for several years. Julian was often accompanied by his wife. He would handle things in one southern state while Lee Stevens or Jack would go to another region to prepare for the season there. William B. Chandler Jr., a Dagsboro resident whose father was in a similar business during the same period, recalls that his family actually packed up and moved south each winter in order to be close to the southern growing season. They would settle temporarily in some centrally located southern town. The children would go to school there. Then in the late spring they would return home to Sussex County, remaining until the following winter, when the cycle would be repeated.

This almost nomadic existence became the rule for Jack. Before his marriage, the life on the road had considerable appeal for the handsome young man. He often made Norfolk his headquarters for the early spring, taking side trips further south to buy berries in Tennessee, North Carolina, and other areas. In the years before his marriage to Daisy Rayne, he became something of a local swain in Norfolk, squiring such local belles as the actress Laura Sullivan.

After he settled down with Daisy, he continued to travel during the strawberry season and she usually accompanied him. It seemed at times as if everyone in the family was moving in different directions at once, looking after their increasingly far-flung interests.

In the days when the cultivation of vegetables and fruits and the production of lumber were the backbone of the Delmarva economy, the peninsula seemed a part of the South to a much greater extent than is true today. Not only were large packing firms like the Townsend Company working throughout the southeast, but the major lumber companies were starting to buy into mills and timber stands in Georgia and the Carolinas. The governor's old friend Will White, now the president of Houston-White Company in Millsboro, had bought the Stantonsburg Lumber Company in North Carolina in 1909. With that purchase he had also acquired the company's large stands of gum and other timber. By 1918, Houston-White Company was the second largest producer of fruit and vegetable baskets in the state of Delaware, second only to the Marvil Package Company in Laurel.

The manager of the company's Stantonsburg mill from 1910 until it closed in 1920 was George S. Williams, an Ocean View native who also served as president of Stantonsburg's Planters National Bank. Williams was typical of the group of young Baltimore Hundred men who had sought higher education, thinking they wished to become teachers but becoming instead very competent businessmen. He was a graduate of Wesley Collegiate Institute and Dickinson College, from which he received both bachelor's and master's degrees. In 1919, Will White's son, Reese, also went south to work in the Stantonsburg operation before coming home to become vice-president of the Millsboro mill.

The basket mills were hard hit by the war when both labor and raw materials were hard to get and many were forced to shut down.

Houston-White was big enough to survive, but in 1920 they shut down the Stantonsburg operation and moved all their milling machinery and equipment north to Millsboro. Reese White bought out old Congressman Henry A. Houston, who was ready to retire, and entered the business. One of the major moneymakers for the firm was strawberry quart containers and crates; another was tomato baskets and Townsend was one of their largest customers. After the war, Houston-White began a ten-year effort to mechanize their operations. They were manufacturing a range of produce containers that included square and oblong berry boxes, climax baskets for grapes, hampers, stave baskets, and web-bottom baskets for larger fruits and vegetables. Their products were used everywhere east of the Mississippi.

John himself turned his attention to the south in those years as far as the lumber business was concerned. George C. Bishop of Selbyville, another former schoolteacher, went to work for the Townsends in the lumber business in 1910. In 1914, he went south to North Carolina and established himself as the resident manager of the firm Townsend & Bishop–Manufacturers of North Carolina Pine Lumber.

Several years later, the company relocated in a small mill at Lanes, South Carolina. Typical of the sort of arrangement John had with Bishop and other partners was an exchange of letters between the two in February 1919. On the first, George Bishop wrote:

> Dear John:
>   Please keep in touch with the P.& R. C. & I. Co. [a mining company] for mine plank orders. Would suggest you try Lehigh Valley Railroad people also. Have shipped L.V. a few cars through Cranston and I believe they are more liberal in their measurements and grading than P.& R. as they have never taken a foot off my measurement as yet.

We have about 200,000 [board feet] fir mine plank on the yard and are anxious to turn it into money. Several cars [are] dry enough to ship.

Would much rather make mine plank than boxes at prices we have been getting–Just received check from Cranston for car that netted us a little over $22.00 per [thousand board feet] f.o.b. Lanes–sold at $28.50 f.o.b. mines.

To which the governor responded on February fifth:

I have your letter of the first, and replying beg to say I will take up the matter with the Lehigh Valley people, and also the P.& R. C. & I. Co., for mine planks. I do not think it wise to push too hard for the next six weeks or two months, as it seems to be very quiet.

I would not sell very much to Cranston at the price you quoted yet awhile. Jule is on his way south and I told him to stop to see you, and he will tell you about the car he went up to look about.

It is apparent that while Bishop was in day-to-day control, the governor kept a close eye on the overall market outlook and handled many contacts with larger customers. This was much the same approach he used with all his businesses. He was also particularly resourceful during the wartime days of rationing and shortages in acquiring the chemicals and other supplies needed for the canneries. Much of his business correspondence during his term as governor was devoted to efforts to acquire such ingredients. In October of 1918, for example, he went together with one of his major strawberry customers, J. Hungerford Smith Co., of Rochester, to stock up on benzoic acid, a preservative. Several weeks later he learned through his contacts in the E.I. du Pont de Nemours Company in Wilmington that another preservative, toluel, would be both "plentiful and cheap" and wrote suggesting that Hungerford Smith sell the 2,000 pounds of benzoic acid. "I think it will be perfectly safe to sell ours [benzoic acid] and take the loss and buy back later."

At about the same time he also found himself facing a scarcity that had nothing to do with the war effort–a shortage of barrels or, as they were known in the trade, "cooperage." Since packers of strawberries and other berries packed them in wooden barrels between layers of sugar, enormous supplies of the containers were required. Barrels were expensive if purchased new, and strawberry packers and confectionary firms were major customers for second-hand whiskey barrels. Under federal law distilleries could not reuse the barrels originally used for the aging of bourbon and rye whiskey, so they routinely sold them. When Prohibition went into effect the market in secondhand "cooperage" folded almost immediately. John was able to buy a large supply of barrels in 1918, but this only held him for a year or two and then he was forced to buy new barrels in which to pack the berries. Thus, in addition to all his other concerns he found it necessary to become, at least to a limited extent, a commodities trader as well.

At this same time he was also involved in a Ford automobile dealership in Selbyville–Townsend & Williams. His partner, William G. Williams, ran the agency out of a building on Church Street, but he sometimes sought the help of the governor when he was dickering with Ford over supplying new cars and other details of the operation. John's expertise was especially valuable in contacts of this type with major corporations. They generally seemed to approach small businessmen with a condescending and paternal air, often forgetting many of the small concessions their salesmen and "travelling men" had made when they had earlier visited the businesses in search of orders.

John had a remarkable memory for the details of such deals. He commonly quoted word for word complicated agreements he had worked out weeks or months before with field representatives for the firms he dealt with. Moreover he had a way of putting executives rapidly in their places. If necessary, he was not above using his title in business correspondence, though ordinarily he avoided doing so. Invariably the response would be much more respectful. That, of course, was why he did it that way.

Another of the commodities in which he dealt at the time was money. He had little to do with the routine operations of the banks, but he kept a very close eye on "the big picture." He sometimes found himself involved in the minute details, however. One interesting case that came up in 1919 had to do with the rivalry between two small banks in the flourishing fishing village of Chincoteague Island, Virginia. John had been an occasional visitor to Chincoteague for years. He may even have accompanied Zare Brasure on one or another of his trips to the island and he had a large circle of acquaintances there, especially after moving his ice plant down after 1910. One acquaintance and friend was D.J. Wheaton, president of the Bank of Chincoteague. His was the older of the town's two banks. The newer Marine Bank of Chincoteague was trying various ways to hurt Wheaton's bank and help itself. The situation was comparable to that in Selbyville where Baltimore Trust Co. and the Selbyville Bank (known locally as "the Townsend Bank" and "the McCabe Bank") were involved in a similar rivalry, though without the apparent skulduggery that Wheaton reported in a letter to Townsend in 1919.

Wheaton's stationary was highly illustrative of Chincoteague's economy at the time. In addition to heading the bank, Wheaton was a merchant. He owned Wheaton Merchantile Co., "Wholesale and

Retail Dealers in General Merchandise." He also owned and operated Wheaton's Oyster Company, "Shippers and Planters of Shell and Opened Oysters, Terrapin, Game, Etc." This was in the days when such fashionable establishments as the Plaza Hotel and the new Grand Central Station in New York maintained elegant oyster bars and did a brisk luxury trade in fresh "Chincoteagues," which went up by refrigerator car daily to the vast Fulton Fish Market in lower Manhattan. Chincoteague Island was not yet connected by causeway to the mainland and the only contact with the railroad at Franklin City across the bay was by boat.

The governor also served as a member of Wheaton's bank board and owned some stock in the institution. Wheaton clearly placed a high value on his expertise. In his old age Townsend used to tell a tale of being roused out of his sleep one night by a frantic telephone call from an officer of the bank telling him of its impending collapse unless he could come immediately to its rescue. The by-then ex-governor climbed out of bed in the wee hours, got dressed, and made his way to Franklin City. He finally succeeded in lining up a boat ride over to Chincoteague. He spent the day wheeling and dealing on the bank's behalf by telephone and telegraph. By evening, having succeeded in saving the Bank of Chincoteague from an untimely end, he made his way back to the mainland, back to Selbyville, and so home to a well-deserved rest.

But all this was still in the future when he received Wheaton's letter in the winter of 1919. It seemed that many of the checks written on accounts at Wheaton's bank were sent in payment for items purchased in various mainland cities in the region–Richmond, Baltimore, Wilmington, and Philadelphia. Banking procedure called for these checks to be sent back for payment by the bank in Chincoteague from which they had come. But Chincoteague's Marine Bank had contrived a way to work a little needle into its competitor. First it opened small accounts at the major clearing house-banks in surrounding cities. Then it got these large banks to do their customer a favor. Whenever a check came through for payment to either of the Chincoteague banks, the large banks sent it directly to the Marine Bank. If the check was drawn on one of Wheaton's accounts, the Marine Bank sent it to him for a small fee. It was not much but it was a hindrance nonetheless and made the Bank of Chincoteague just that much less competitive. The worst problem was with checks received by Baltimore's Merchants, Mechanics First National Bank and it was compounded by the fact that several other major banks, including Wilmington Trust Company, sent their Chincoteague checks to Merchants, Mechanics as well. After explaining all this, Wheaton went on:

> Now my object in writing you is to learn if you cannot help us out through your bank, that is if you do much business with the Merchants, Mechanics First Nat. Bank, in getting them to remit such items as they may have on the Bank of Chincoteague . . . direct to us instead of their sending same to [the Marine Bank]."
>
> I did not care to take the liberty of writing direct to your Mr. Long [cashier of Baltimore Trust Co.] in reference to this matter . . . Hoping you may be able to assist us in getting this matter straightened out as I feel sure . . . that some of the would-be managers of the Selbyville Bank has [sic] been making suggestions in aiding the Marine Bank to get after us.

John could only be of limited help, but he agreed to do what he could. "I will endeavor to help you out with the Wilmington Trust Company," he wrote. "I feel confident this can be done," but he could not do much with the Merchants, Mechanics Bank of Baltimore because Baltimore Trust had no dealings with them.

By now it was beginning to occur to people that John G. Townsend Jr. was a very good person to have on a board of directors if he could be persuaded to accept. He turned down most such appointments, but he did accept a few, usually from worthy causes. He served as a trustee of the Salisbury District of the Methodist Episcopal Church and helped them raise money for the new District Superintendent's Parsonage. He served as a director of the Wesley Collegiate Institute in Dover and helped it raise funds for a new building in 1918, hitting up the long-suffering T. Coleman du Pont for $5,000. As noted earlier he raised more than $30,000 for the Delaware Home for the Feeble-minded. His prowess as a fund-raiser for his own church, Salem Methodist in Selbyville, is still legendary among older members of the congregation. When Governor or later U.S. Senator Townsend was standing there asking in a charming but forceful way for a contribution to a very worthy cause, most people not only came forward with some money but thought it a decided compliment even to be asked.

In contemplating John G. Townsend at this period in his life one should not forget that he was also the sole surviving parent of a large family. Though four of the six children were now grown, Paul and Preston were still young. Paul was something of a problem. He had attended several schools and was now a student at Culver Military Academy in Indiana where he was not very happy at first. He had been just fourteen when his mother was killed and was having a hard time recovering from the blow. He was a brilliant boy with the same quick mathematical mind his father had, but he found it hard to buckle down to his studies and apply himself. His father knew what he was capable of and was stern with him in his frequent letters, urging him to excell. In one letter of March 1919, he wrote:

> My dear Son,
>   I received your letter and was very glad to hear from you. Was up all night last night, got to bed at 6 o'clock, had two hours' sleep, and back in the office at work.
>   I have read your letter very carefully. . . I cannot find any just reason for you to dislike the school. You don't give me any reason except you say you simply dislike military drilling. This you will like more when you make up your mind to do it without murmuring or complaining. I know that you feel that I have nothing but your interest at heart all the time, and I feel confident that it will only be a very short time before you agree with me . . . sincerely hope I will be able to get out and see you at some early date . . . The fact that other boys stay in the school and graduate convinces me that you can do it as easily as any other boy, and I sincerely trust you, will get right down to hard work and let your marks come up to where they belong.
>
>   Your loving father

Paul later became happier at Culver and did better in his studies. His father stopped by to see him in the spring while on a trip to Chicago. He met all of Paul's friends and instructors and generally checked the place out, finding it to his liking. That summer he took Paul with him on a trip to the far west for a national governors' conference in Salt Lake City. Interestingly, a very detailed account of the trip survives, kept in the form of a trip diary by Governor Townsend and later typed out by his secretary. It is filled with the kind of detail that he could not help noticing wherever he went:

Left for Chicago Saturday, August 16th, 1919, arrived in Chicago Sunday 5:45 p.m. Left Chicago 7:10 over Chicago, Northwestern and Union Pacific for Salt Lake. Arrived Salt Lake at 4:30 p.m. just in time to get out of coach and join the Governors' party going out to Saltair. This is a picturesque resort, built up by the Mormon Church, and has all the attractions usually seen at any of the seaside resorts of the East. The Scenic Railway is made of wood, and probably cost $100,000. The dance hall was one of the largest I ever saw.

There was a dining room that probably would seat 500 or more, where we took dinner. While going from Salt Lake out to Saltair we could see the great salt levels and how the salt was made. The flats were so arranged that the water could not run off and then they used force pumps to pump the water of Salt Lake out over these flats and the water was allowed to evaporate until the salt was probably 18 inches deep.

There were railroads built all across these lands and cars distributed along on these tracks so there were about forty or fifty cars being loaded at the same time all over these lowlands. When loaded there would be probably fifty to seventy-five cars a day picked up and taken to the refinery up in New York State to be refined for table use. This may be changed in the future so that the refining will be done there and save freight.

Down at Saltair we donned bathing suits and took a bath in Salt Lake where it is impossible to sink. You can lie down on your back and float around like a cork, but if you are not careful you will duck your head under when you try to get your feet down, and this is very bad on the eyes. The salt accumulates on your flesh like a crust if you remain in the water for a long time. . .

[Wednesday] we were at the Governor's Conference. At ten o'clock we left the conference to dine with the mayor and other city officials of Salt Lake City, after which we took a special train . . . and from there motored down the canyon in the evening, going through some of the most beautiful scenery in Utah. We visited the point where artesian wells had been driven and the city's water supply was gotten. This was quite a sight for Eastern people to see a city of fifty thousand people supplied with water from artesian wells driven in the side of a mountain.

The people of the city all turned out and offered their cars. The man who drove the car in which I rode and who also owned the car, was named Browning and was the brother of the Browning who made the Browning Gun and made a great many machine guns that were used during the War and before. The whole family of Brownings live in the City of Ogden. . .

The next day [Thursday] was devoted to the Governor's Conference and a trip to the offices of the Mormon Church. After this trip I broke away from the crowd and with Governor Frazier of North Dakota I went over to the Mormon Tabernacle to hear the organ recital, which was wonderful. This building is [huge] and you are able to hear a pin drop at the farthest end as distinctly as if you were within five feet of it. The acoustics in this building are supposed to be the best of any building in the world, and this is probably on account of the construction of the roof. This roof is built perfectly round and is five feet thick. To find out just how it was built I asked the man in charge if we could get up and see. He took Governor Frazier and me up in the roof. There are no nails in the roof and all the rafters and timber used for bracing it are put together with pegs.

The timber is tied together with rawhide strings about 3/4 of an inch wide. This was tied on when the hide was green and now that it is dry, it is as hard as wood. There are thousands upon thousands of these strings used in the roof. We walked up inside of the roof to the top and it is the most wonderfully constructed roof I have ever seen. There have been other roofs built just like this, using steel and wood but are failures as far as acoustics are concerned. This roof, being made entirely of wood with the five foot space in it is probably the reason for the acoustics being perfect.

Later in the trip the governor's party went to Yellowstone National Park:

> All day until one o'clock we were shown scenery. This it is difficult to describe. Streams, canyons, geysers, these are very wonderful belching forth hot water that builds a lime foundation or crust. These geysers gush up just as regularly as the clock ticks so you can learn just what time each geyser will go off.
>
> We landed at night at Old Faithful Inn. There is a searchlight here which at night throws light on the water as it goes up in the air, and is very beautiful. The Old Faithful Inn is made from native wood notched [together] and is finished inside in the same manner. All the fences are crooked and there seems to be thousands of them. You would wonder where so many crooked trees could be found for fences. There is an old chimney and large fireplace in the hotel, where fire in the evening adds very much to the attractiveness and comfort of the place. It was here that we saw our first big black bear. They come up in the evening to eat off the garbage piles from the Hotel . . . Paul was so anxious to feed the bears. We saw two old bears and two cubs, all stopped and petted them.
>
> All along the route, during the day we saw hundreds of automobiles camped along the streams with people fishing or preparing meals, and getting ready for the evening. Every kind of automobile imaginable was there, and cars from almost every state. Most of the people, both women and men wore khaki suits, almost all the women wearing pantalettes. . .
>
> [We saw] the most beautiful lakes, ten to fifteen miles in width, in which there is an abundance of fish. Here you can catch fish standing on the shore and drop them in a geyser on the other side and boil them in boiling water. . .

One of the more interesting acquaintances Paul and his father made on this trip was Joseph M. Carey of Cheyenne, Wyoming.

Carey, the first governor of the State of Wyoming, had recently been elected U.S. senator from the state and his son, Robert, was now the governor. The thing that most interested John was that the elder Carey was a native of the little Sussex County town of Milton. The son of a prominent merchant of the late 1800s named Robert Hood Carey, Joseph Carey had gone west as a young man and done just as well by the move as Townsend had done by moving across the state line into Delaware a few years later. The two men had hoped to travel east together and so deepen their acquaintance, but somehow they missed each other at the railroad station. Later Carey sent Townsend a gracious note in which he invited him to pay a fall visit to Wyoming "when the weather becomes bearable." Governor Townsend replied in a similar vein:

> My dear Governor - Senator:
>   What shall I call you? Just the big man of Wyoming
> . . .
> I shall certainly always remember my trip west and the pleasant people that I met out there, and most especially the extreme pleasure of meeting a man from my own state who has done such wonderful things for the West.

The governor and Paul were not the only travellers in the family that year. Nine-year-old Preston had gotten to take off early from school in April to accompany his sister Lyla and Jule and his wife down to Louisiana by way of Washington, D.C., the Carolinas, and Tennessee to prepare for the strawberry season. In the first of many letters to his youngest son, the governor wrote to him in Hammond, Louisiana:

> I am mighty glad you didn't go down on the boat, because of the terrible storm that has been raging all along the coast. It would have made a very rough voyage to say the least.

You had better run over to see the Governor of
Louisiana while you are there and tell him who you are,
but I suppose you will be busy trying to make money
capping strawberries. . .

Toward the end of 1919, the governor's stepmother, Mrs. Ida
Townsend, took a long trip out to Hannibal, Missouri, to visit relatives.
John G. Townsend Sr. had died the year before and she evidently felt
a need to get away for awhile. Soon after her arrival she received this
chatty letter from her stepson:

My dear Grandmom:
I received your card stating that you had arrived
and were enjoying yourself, and I am most delighted that
this is the case, but you missed a lot down home. Since
you left, Mr. Hastings and his wife have come home and
they have had a real serenade. I don't know whether
they are all going to land in Court or not. I suppose when
you come back, if you bring a fellow with you, we will
give you a royal reception.
Volley, Lee, Jack and I are leaving for Rochester
[New York] tonight to be gone for three or four days . . .
Please remember me to all your relatives and friends
in the West and tell them I hope they will be able to make
a trip East and visit us in the near future.
Wishing you a pleasant stay and assuring you you
need not worry about the things at home, we will take
care of them, I am,
Your son,
John

Later, the elder Mrs. Townsend returned to her home on Church
Street in Selbyville, without a new "fellow." She stayed there for the
rest of her long life, living on into the 1950s. Her stepson continued to
be loyal, stopping by her house on his early morning and evening

walks and stopping by for breakfast one or two mornings a week.

John also tried to remember his friends when he could. In the summer of 1919, his old Selbyville friend, D. Casher Williams, owner of the Selbyville Hotel and a local lumberman, was in Wilson, North Carolina, preparing to open a new lumber mill there. He needed some assistance and did not hesitate to ask for it:

> I want to ask you for a favor . . . now is there any way you could let me have Frank LeKites for a short time, as we need him very bad to put our machinery in our new plant at Wilson, as we can't get anyone down here to put it in. We have got all buildings [finished] and boilers all built.
>
> There is nothing to do only to put machinery in. I would think he could do this in a short time. Now if you can spare him, I will pay you the price and will pay all transportation expenses and board him, as we can sell everything we can make for a Big Price if we can get our machinery put in now. If you can make out without him please send him at once to Wilson, N.C. I see where strawberries sold very high and hope all farmers got rich on them. Please let me hear from you . . .

Frank LeKites was a member of that skilled and essential fraternity that went by various names in the small factories of the day —engineer, machinist, millwright. They were craftsmen, technicians, and designers who had come up through the time-honored apprenticeship system. Without them, no large mill could function successfully. They specialized in the applications of steam power and in its harnessing to machinery, whether it be wood-working, basket-making, machine-tooling, or canning. Both Williams and Townsend knew how valuable LeKites was.

My dear Casher:

Your letter has just come to my hands and think we can arrange to have Frank LeKites go down and help you out for a while. I will take this matter up with him and shall be very glad if we can accomodate you, but he has both factories torn up at the present time and is trying to get them fixed up for tomato season. Strawberries were very high and everyone who had them made lots of money. Wishing you every success . . .

The picture of the man afforded by his personal correspondence during his years as governor shows a person very intimately involved in his far-flung business enterprises and in the lives of his large family circle and his community, even as he worked as the most active and accomplished governor Delaware had produced in at least a generation. He was, during those years, at the very height of his powers.

17. Summing Up

During the influenza epidemic of 1918-1919, Governor Townsend received a very personal and touching appeal concerning his closest friend and associate. It came from Mrs. Lee Cooch of New York City, a former resident of Cooch's Bridge, near Iron Hill:

> My dear Mr. Townsend,
> I have just made a little visit at Dover with Mr. & Mrs. Everett Johnson after not having seen them for five months. You have seen them right along, and so may not have noticed what I did. That man is a sick man - and it came over me as a shock how very tired and sick he really is. I believe he is keeping up entirely on his will power and is trying to bluff us all into thinking he is well. You are the only person in the world who can send him away for a rest of several weeks. I believe he would go if you insist . . .
> . . . Please regard this as confidential, Mr. Townsend. They do not dream I am writing. Nor do they know I noticed what a brave fight he is making to keep going . . . There are ocean trips advertised to Jamaica & Panama. I enclose a clipping from yesterday's paper.
> If I have done the wrong thing please forgive me. It is prompted by a deep interest in the Johnsons–and I can't help appealing to you . . .

The governor was a little embarassed by the note, but he responded quickly:

> My dear Mrs. Cooch:
> Permit me to acknowledge receipt of your letter of April 24th, and to assure you that the same has been

carefully noted. Mr. Johnson has had some neuralgia lately, which has caused him to look badly, and I am insisting on him taking a vacation at an early date, which I think will help him considerably.

The fact was that Everett Johnson had one of the strongest minds in Delaware, but his physical strength was sadly lacking. John and all his closest friends knew that he was a man who fought daily against his own infirmities to find the strength to work for what he believed in. That knowledge gave them a feeling of affection and respect for him that bordered on love. Everett Johnson survived that terrible winter of the epidemic as he had survived so many illnesses before. He was able to complete his four years of service to his friend's administration and to his state, but with each illness he was just a bit weaker. It was not a matter of the governor or anyone else keeping him hard at work. Johnson's mind and character simply do not seem to have been able to adjust to a frail constitution. At times it seemed as if he was being consumed before the eyes of his friends, but he kept on. His ideals and principles remained steadfast.

Photographs of the two men taken during that period are revealing of the contrast between them. The governor stands tall, strong, robust, fairly bursting with vitality. Johnson is thin, looking slightly wizened, but with a clear intensity of gaze that seems to show something of the remarkable man within. In later years when historians looked back on that period of Delaware history, they generally focused on the achievements of P.S. du Pont or on those of Coleman du Pont, or on the governor himself. But the men who were there at the time seemed to feel that Everett Johnson embodied the best of their generation.

John Townsend's later actions and his respect for the Johnson family throughout his life showed clearly that in his view Everett Johnson

Friends: *Everett C. Johnson and John G. Townsend Jr. are seen during a visit to a Delaware National Guard summer encampment near New Castle, probably about 1919. The camp was officially named "Camp Townsend" in the governor's honor. Johnson and Townsend were fine friends and the closest of political allies (Lyla Townsend Savoy collection).*

had been every bit as responsible for the achievements of his administration as he had himself. The partnership between governor and secretary of state is one of the least known but most remarkable relationships in the political history of Delaware. Between them they encompassed nearly the whole diversity and breadth of the state from humblest swamp logger to the grandest powder-company tycoon, from summer camp meeting to Wilmington symphony. John and Everett

Johnson accomplished things together that neither could have done separately with three times the effort. Those accomplishments helped to foster a sense of state pride in the average citizen that lasted for more than a generation. Equally remarkable, given the quirky regional pride of Delawareans in their own counties and communities, was that it was pride in the entire state. For a time there was a lessening of the old "upstate-downstate" friction that had characterized Delaware life for 150 years. Johnson died while still a comparatively young man in the mid-1920s, before he had had a chance to make his full contribution to the life of his state. But his powerful blend of idealism and practical ability had profoundly influenced friends as different as John G. Townsend and Pierre S. du Pont. Unfortunately many writers on the state's history have overlooked him, not only because of his premature death but because of his personal modesty. But Townsend, du Pont, and other friends never forgot their debt to that singular man.

After the special session of 1920, the governor and his administration officially entered that strange limbo of American government known as "lame duck" status. Townsend remained very busy, however–especially politically. Evidently feeling that he had a few things to settle with the Laytons, he set about opposing them in a second round of primaries after the first Republican convention in April. The first convention was held for the election of national convention delegates. Later in the summer was a second convention held to nominate a state ticket. In anticipation of this event the Townsend faction put up a group of candidates for Sussex County delegate seats to oppose a similar slate of Layton candidates. This time the outcome was different. Townsend men won in a majority of the election districts (though the Laytons claimed victory for public relations purposes). Suddenly, as the *Evening Journal* put it later, "it was up to the governor whether or not Congressman Layton should be the caucus nominee for a renomination." By extension the governor controlled more than just the Sussex Republican caucus since he had already showed his influence with a majority of the Kent and New Castle Countians at the April convention. His decision was typical of his stance in similar situations before and after. He took the position of a good party man:

> Treating Congressman Layton like unto the small boy who was about to step upon the grasshopper and crush out its life, but out of his tenderheartedness had compassion on it, Governor Townsend, believing he had given the Layton faction a sufficient "spanking," was willing for the sake of party harmony, to let by-gones be by-gones. He therefore consented to the re-nomination of Congressman Layton. While no doubt it was a bitter pill for the governor to accede to the wishes of the State leaders, his many friends concede that he acted the part of a good Republican. The Layton faction, while claiming they had a majority of the delegates in the State convention, evidently feared a showdown, and since the governor consented to the nomination of Congressman Layton, are acting the "Betsy and Bear" stunt.

The next showdown came during the first week of October when still another primary was held, this time to elect a slate of Sussex County candidates for levy court and courthouse office jobs. Once again both factions put up competing candidates:

> The Townsend faction, however, slipped a cog in their primary organization machinery by having too many candidates, which meant division of their vote, and this helped the Layton faction to dominate the situation. The result was that the Laytons succeeded in nominating

men of their choice for the several offices; but the Townsend followers now say the next thing for the Laytons to do is elect them, which they are not going to do because the Townsend faction does not propose to support them.

With that intelligence, the clearly pro-Townsend correspondent of the *Every Evening* closed with this bit of subjective reportage:

> The county ticket is looked upon as a Layton hand-picked one from beginning to end, and is distasteful to the better element of the Republican Party. "It's the poorest ticket the Republicans of Sussex County have nominated for years" is the way many of the voters express it, and there is every indication at this time that many Republicans do not intend to support it.
> If Representative Layton can derive any real pleasure in accepting a renomination to Congress by grace of Governor Townsend, he is welcome to save him from the wrath of Sussex Republican voters who were betrayed by Layton's renomination.

As usual with such predictions, the outcome in November was not as dramatic as the newspaper readers had been led to expect. Though the Democrats did somewhat better in local Sussex County races than had been the case in recent elections, Congressman Layton was reelected to a second term. In fact, the entire Republican state ticket was elected. It was headed by the popular gubernatorial candidate, Kent County businessman William D. Denney, who defeated Georgetown lawyer Andrew J. Lynch, the Democratic candidate. But the congressman and his son knew they could not have done as well as they had without the aid, or at least the neutrality, of the man they had just spent many months vilifying. Whether or not this made any impression on them is unknown since Townsend and the Laytons were never again placed by events in direct opposition with each other.

When Congressman Layton ran for a third term in 1922, he was soundly defeated by Judge William H. Boyce of Georgetown whom he had beaten two years earlier. In later years Layton charged that he had been beaten by Delaware blacks who were angered by his refusal to support an antilynching measure in Congress. By this time Layton had been a widower for some years. As if to put to rest once and for all the widespread doubts about his commitment to woman's suffrage, Dr. Layton married Miss Fannie S. Herrington. She had served for twenty-five years as the chief deputy in the office of Delaware's secretary of state and had become at the time of her marriage to the former congressman the state's first female secretary of state, a status that Layton took great pride in pointing out.

Daniel Layton, his renowned temper seemingly little altered by his long battle with Governor Townsend, went on to a relatively distinguished career in the law. His career was capped by his appointment as chief justice of the state supreme court some two decades after his furious fight

Hon. William D. Denney, Governor of Delaware

Governor William D. Denney,
Governor Townsend's successor,
from a Maxwell caricature, 1920
(Lyla Townsend Savoy collection).

over the school code. He was never to realize any higher elected office. Nor did he ever undo the great strides made in public education by his nemesis. The most interesting aspect of the affair in one sense is that it does not seem to have led to any permanent feud of the sort which had sometimes gone on for generations in Delaware politics in the old days. Townsends and Laytons saw each other socially before and have regularly seen each other since with no apparent problems. One wonders, however, if Daniel Layton ever forgave John for opposing him and winning.

The closing weeks of the administration were a time for final ceremonies and closing remarks. John went off to a governor's conference at Harrisburg, Pennsylvania., with his successor, Colonel William D. Denney, in tow. He was one of the leading speakers at the conference, choosing as his topic "The Budget and State Business Methods." Sounding somewhat prophetic, he said in part:

> People are demanding elimination of useless offices and commissions, simplification of governmental process, full value received for taxes paid, fixation of administrative responsibility and introduction of business methods into public affairs.
> Illinois furnishes the most distinguished example of this trend by consolidation of 125 administrative agencies into nine departments, and Idaho, Nebraska and Massachusetts have accomplished much . . .
> The result of the creation of scores of bureaus and commissions has been competition in expenditures rather than in economy. More power, more money. As a consequence we passed through a period of years in which the outstanding feature of government has been its rapidly mounting expenses . . .
> The efficient and successful corporation today is the one which plans years ahead and formulates a financial policy that will take care of its plans without needless outlay,

> on the one hand, or financial embarrassment on the other.
> The efficient businessman or farmer today is the one who
> looks ahead two, three, five years and arranges his finances
> to carry out his plans . . .
>> Why should a state be any less farsighted? For
> what purpose do we have a government if not to provide
> for the future of its citizens?

The editor of the *Delaware State News*, who attended the conference, lauded Governor Townsend's speech and his obvious influence with his fellow governors. He made the somewhat unusual observation that Delaware's outgoing governor also sized up well from a physical standpoint:

> It is surprising how many states are represented by
> little runts, or insignificant-looking men who appear to be
> anything but governors. Governor Townsend and Governor
> Campbell of Arizona were among the few who . . . really
> looked the part. Delaware may be a mighty small state,
> but it played an important part in the proceedings of the
> conference.

On their return from Pennsylvania, Townsend hosted Denney at an enormous reception and dinner in the Hotel du Pont's duBarry Room, followed by a special showing of "The Love Birds" in the adjoining Playhouse. Amidst the speeches and accolades, Major J. Danforth Bush, Denney's running mate and lieutenant governor-elect, presented Governor Townsend and Everett Johnson with 10 x 14 inch bronze medallions containing bas relief portraits of the late President Theodore Roosevelt and the inscription, "Aggressive fighting for the right is the noblest sport the world affords."

Seemingly every civic group in the state was in a rush to present awards and letters of commendation to the outgoing governor, or to fete him at dinners and celebrations. One interesting aspect of all this to-do

Hon. John G. Townsend, Jr., Selbyville

IF any one man deserves the highest place of honor in this or any other book concerning Delaware's activities during the period of the War, and the reconstruction period which immediately succeeded the great conflict, that man undoubtedly is John G. Townsend, Jr., of Selbyville, our War Governor. Governor Townsend served during the most trying period of Delaware's history, when our State sent its soldiers to the front, and when numerous war movements were launched and successfully conducted in the three counties. And his record, during that period, is a remarkable one. Although he met with some opposition of a factional nature at the very beginning of his term, Governor Townsend's administration proved so fair and admirable that when he retired from office at the end of 1920 the entire State was united behind him, and all factions and parties joined in praise of his splendid work. His record as War Governor of Delaware shines as a bright star in that long, dark period, and future generations will honor his name even as we honor it today. If Sussex county had nothing else to boast of, it can always be proud of the fact that it gave John G. Townsend to Delaware. It is a name that will be cherished by Delawareans so long as history endures. Governor Townsend is a Republican and one of the most prominent canners of lower Delaware.

Gee Tee Maxwell caricature of Governor Townsend, 1920,
(Lyla Townsend Savoy collection)

was that most observers thought Governor Townsend was at the end of his political career. It was widely perceived that he had stood up for what he believed in at the expense of his political future. Even Townsend himself may have felt that way to some extent as he decompressed after four years of conflict.

A surprise party was held for Mr. and Mrs. Everett C. Johnson by their Dover friends as they made preparations to move back to Newark. The governor was the guest of honor at that event. At another function he and Johnson were given elaborate letters of praise by the Associated Women's Republican Committees of Delaware. Even such stalwart enemies as State Sen. Isaac D. Short of Milford turned out to make complimentary remarks about the outgoing administration.

He also came in for elaborate praise in the editorial columns of some of the same newspapers that had been heaping abuse upon him frequently during the past four years. They now seemed to be hedging their bets for posterity by allowing as how he had been pretty good after all. Other papers, which had been pro-Townsend all along, were even more generous in their praise. In most cases they pointed out that Governor-elect Denney had pledged to stand by the major Townsend programs and that there would be a minimum of upheaval in state government.

Of Townsend, one Wilmington daily had this to say:

> On January 18, Governor Townsend will lay down the reins as Chief Executive of Delaware and will be succeeded by Col. William D. Denney. It will be the passing of one good governor to make way for another who may be depended upon to give Delaware an equally acceptable administration. To the retiring chief executive we say truthfully, "Well done, good and faithful servant, you have fully vindicated the confidence and trust imposed in you by your fellow citizens."

Everybody, even those hostile to Republican control, including the sometimes captious *Every Evening*, concedes that Governor Townsend has given us an admirable administration, that he has arisen equal to every emergency and has turned every opportunity to account for the advancement of the State. . .

Mr. Townsend, as war governor, had a term of unusual activity. He has been busy almost every minute of that period. . . As the war governor of Delaware, Mr. Townsend will long be held in grateful esteem by the people of this state, both for his splendid achievements and for the example of unflagging patriotism. . .

No governor since the civil war has had half the responsibility nor problems of moment that came to Mr. Townsend in his four years of service as the state's head. In the future estimate of the services of those who have filled Delaware's executive chair we will find Mr. Townsend's name writ large and bright, for he served the State with ability, fidelity to his ideals and with unfailing regard for the welfare of the people.

Governor Townsend's strong and persistent advocacy of a modern school law in face of the manufactured hostility directed against it in his own county among his neighbors and closest friends, illustrated the high courage of the executive when still he was representing the best interests of the state. His insistent work in behalf of suffrage, his willingness to sacrifice all hope of a political future, in espousing the cause of equal rights showed him again to be ready to hazard self-interest for what he believed was right.

Governor Townsend is a true and typical Delawarean of the old school, unassuming, genial, cordial in his relations with his fellow citizens. He is and has been at all times approachable, always open to suggestions and counsel, and the people have generally felt nearer, and actually kept closer to him than they have to any other executive for half a century, for everyone knew him to be sincere, capable, and without ambition other than to serve his fellow Delawareans according to his best lights and counsel, and his administration will stand at the very top in the list of successful ones. . .

On the afternoon of January 6, 1921, Governor Townsend delivered his Farewell Message to the General Assembly, in which he summed up the accomplishments of the last four years and spoke of his hopes for the future. He began by recalling the "program of construction" he had asked for in his inaugural address and said he felt that though the work was "in no wise complete, certain foundations have been made that seem worthy of note."

During the course of his long speech, the governor noted the passage of the new school code and the history of its development. He praised Pierre S. du Pont for his gifts to education, which at that time stood at $3,700,000, and spoke of the work left to be done on public school reforms.

> To you [the members of the General Assembly] comes the responsibility of interpretation of [public] thought on education. Your oath of office and presence here will demand that you no longer think, alone, in terms of local knowledge and conditions, but in terms of the state's best interest at large. A vote in terms merely to satisfy a local constituency at the expense of another community's opportunity is not serving the state's interest. And education, today, is a state and not a local issue . . .

He also praised the contributions of T. Coleman du Pont to Delaware's highway system and urged the creation of a "Coleman du Pont Chair of Highway Engineering at Delaware College." He called for long-range planning for good highway maintenance, for automobile safety legislation, for the creation of a Delaware State Police force, and for a tightening of regulations concerning the issuance of drivers' licenses.

The governor spoke of the work that had been done in health, in child welfare legislation, in the creation of the state industrial accident board, the establishment of the "Home for the feeble-minded," the creation of a program of "mother's pensions," the creation of a state banking commission, the reform of the state tax system, and the survey of all state agencies with an eye toward restructuring. He urged legislative consideration of his plan for instituting a state budget (which was done several years later). He also lauded the passage of the woman's suffrage amendment nationally. He took justifiable pride in having amassed a surplus in the state treasury of $1,700,000, the largest in the state's history. It compared very favorably, John noted, to the surplus of $194,106 he had inherited from his predecessor.

One editorial characterized the speech as "one of the ablest documents of its kind ever promulgated by a Delaware executive" and said it was "patriotic in spirit, broad in conception, intelligent in expression and framed in such clear and simple phrase that no person can plead inability to understand its meaning."

Governor Townsend ended his speech, and his administration, by reminding his listeners of his Maryland birth and saying:

> I am just a Delawarean by choice. The state has signally honored me, and I feel it far more deeply than you perhaps realize. It has been my personal and civic ambition to live up to the duties imposed by the oath of that honor.
> These four years have been hard, hard years. Problems of State, strains of the war, have tested the strength of us all. I have felt the responsibility with a keenness known to but few. This state, with such a glorious record in the nation's history, was expected to measure

up. You expected it. The nation expected it. The inspiration of the past led me on, yet at the same time startled me with duties I was called upon to perform with thought at high tension under the strain of the war, criticism–some fair, no doubt, and some unfair, I think–was often severe and hurt. But again, when almost at the breaking point, the spirit of Delaware called, and differences, political, religious, and sectional, were swept away. You came to my aid. No administration in our day has had the problems that were ours. No man ever had, it seems to me, the loyalty of friends that has been mine. Without this I should have failed utterly. . .

At times, as I look back, you reflected well and truly the heroic ages which your fathers made by their blood. To have lived with you and been a part of it all has been a wonderful experience. Again, and I must speak of it, our success, yours and mine, has been guided by a controlling Destiny, higher than human thought and power. That Divine Providence, to whom in stress we must all appeal, has been the strength to me that makes this day possible. Without that I could not have endured.

I am through, gentlemen. I have given of my thought, time, and energy to serve the State and the truth in the light that was given me to see truth. Standing here four years ago in the shadows of the History of Dover Green, there came to me a realization of the great work of those who made this State possible. Today I am dreaming of the Delaware of tomorrow. Facing the future, I present its possibilities to you.

Part VII:

The Twenties

18. Southern Highways

The four years of John's administration as governor marked a major watershed not only in his own life but in that of the entire nation. Postwar America was not the same place. The Age of Progressivism had given way to the antiliberalism of Attorney General A. Mitchell Palmer's raids on "communists" and radicals, and popular fears of bolshevism and revolutionary upheavals. The League of Nations pact had been rejected by the U.S. Congress, and its architect Woodrow Wilson was an invalid. Eight years of Democratic rule in Washington had given way to the election of the genial and attractive Ohioan Warren G. Harding.

After the initial postwar slump, the economy was picking up. American young people, released with the ending of the war from so many of the old constraints of custom were kicking back their heels and dancing their way into the Jazz Age of F. Scott Fitzgerald's creation. The nation's great industries had embarked on the decade of enormous expansion that in a very tangible way moved the American infrastructure into modern times. So, alas, were America's criminal elements, which had already begun to capitalize on the magnificent opportunity for gain created by passage of the Prohibition Amendment (though this was not yet evident to the amendment's supporters).

In his philosophy of government, John had been the perfect exemplar of the Progressive ideal. Because of the efforts of a few men of wealth and vision like Pierre S. du Pont, that ideal lived a decade beyond the end of the Townsend administration as an important force in state government. Yet even as it came to be honored as the reigning ideal of Delaware government during the administrations of Governor Denney and his successor, Governor Robert Robinson, the fire was going out of it. Their administrations were less a continuation of the new directions begun by Townsend than a consolidation of the gains he had made. The relaxed chamber-of-commerce boosterism of Harding and Calvin Cooledge came to dominate life in Delaware as elsewhere. The moment, it seemed, had passed for the new directions Townsend had symbolized. When they stopped cussing John G. Townsend and Pierre S. du Pont in the Delaware General Assembly and started praising them, that meant the politicians had come to terms with their ideas. This is a process that traditionally makes idealists cynical but it is one Townsend understood perfectly. In his understanding he was able to bring lasting good to Delaware.

The former governor himself had little time or inclination to dwell on such things. A few months short of his fiftieth birthday when his term ended, he was becoming already the family patriarch he would remain for the rest of his life. This role was heightened with the passing of his own father several years before and even more with the birth of several grandchildren. Early in 1918, Edith had had a baby boy, John Townsend Tubbs. Less than two weeks later Julian's wife, Mildred, had her own baby boy, who was named John G. Townsend II.* Then in 1919, another Tubbs baby, William

---

Keeping the various John G. Townsends straight can be a bit confusing to non-Townsend family members. To briefly summarize it, John G. Townsend Sr. was the governor's father. The governor was John G. Townsend Jr. His son, Jack, was John G. Townsend III. Julian, apparently wishing to name his own son directly after his father, named the baby John G. Townsend II. This made for the somewhat confusing state in which John G. III, was the uncle of John G. II. When, years later, John G. II, grew up and fathered his own son, he and his wife managed to get everything back on an even keel by naming their baby boy John G. Townsend IV.

Riley, was born. Lyla Townsend was still at home managing the household and helping to raise Preston, working part-time in the family business and involving herself in a variety of community activities. Occasionally she served as a travelling companion for her father in these years when her sister was occupied with her babies and her oldest brothers with the family businesses. Paul had graduated from Culver Military Academy, to which he had eventually become more or less accustomed. Preston was also beginning to get out on his own in the world. The summer before he had attended a summer camp in the Hudson River Valley. The owner of the camp, a German immigrant named Dr. Paul Kyle, issued regular press releases on the activities of the camp. In one memorable example, issued when Preston was in attendance, the worthy doctor commented in florid prose about a visit by Preston's father:

> Last Sunday, August 14, Governor Townsend of Delaware visited his boy, Preston, at the camp. The boy's father is a most democratic and interesting man. He is a man of commanding height and personality. He made a tour of the camp and remarked at the ideal location, cleanliness, and the sanitary conditions . . . From his son he learned that it was just the place that a real, live, 100 per cent American boy would like to spend his vacation.
>
> The Governor would like to have tarried at the camp but the pressure of business would not allow him to do so. The boys gave him a real Kyle Camp "yell," which pleased him immensely. Turning to Dr. Kyle he said, "Good-bye, Pop! I am glad to have met you and am immensely pleased with the Kyle Camp."

And with that the press agent (whom one suspects was probably Dr. Kyle himself) really hit his stride:

Dr. Kyle has been known as "Pop" ever since he first took hold of his own school at Flushing, L.I., in 1890. All the boys call him "Pop" and it is very easy to do so for on first meeting his fatherly interest and affection for the boys is easily apparent, and when Governor Townsend said "Good-bye, Pop" after his first meeting with the Doctor, it was plain that he, too, was impressed with the magnetic personality of the Director of the Kyle Camp.

John was almost like a boy himself for the first few months after the end of his term. Freed from what had been almost continuous battles with adversaries over woman's suffrage, the school code, or dominance in Republican politics, he took off on a lengthy and meandering junket through the South. It was meant to be restful, but like most Townsend vacations it was filled with activity.

All of his various enterprises had done well during the years he was governor except for the lumber companies, and they had at least held their own during the postwar slump. He had money to devote to new enterprises and in that spring of 1921 there were many to be found. Everyone knew that President-elect Warren G. Harding was inclined to be friendly to business. The economy was definitely on the upswing, especially in Florida and other deep southern states where an actual boom was in progress.

Immediately after leaving Delaware during the week after Governor Denney's inauguration, he stopped off in Washington to pay a visit to Delaware's Republican senator, L. Heisler Ball, and other friends in the capital. It was an exciting time. Republicans were pouring into the city from all over the country in the wake of Harding's election. Presidential inaugurations were still held during the first week of March and job hopefuls had gotten into town in advance in search of patronage plums. The Washington correspondent for the Wilmington

Every Evening speculated in print that the ex-governor was himself angling for a job. "Governor Townsend's visit to Washington," he wrote, "has started some interesting gossip concerning an important mission said to be in store for him." The story continued,

> He was entertained Monday by Senator Ball and had conferences with other senators, and the story went round that he would probably be offered some diplomatic post abroad.
>
> The former governor of Delaware smilingly denied that his visit had any political significance, but his friends say the Republican leaders who had an opportunity to look him over were quite favorably impressed and would certainly give approving mention of him to President-elect Harding.
>
> It is expected the former governor will pay a visit to the Good Roads Bureau of the Department of Agriculture, with a view to impressing the authorities with the claims of Delaware to a substantial portion of whatever money is finally appropriated for Federal aid to States.
>
> He said he had always been interested in good roads, and though out of office he would continue, as a private citizen, to urge better and more extensive highway construction.

Had the correspondent but known it, former Governor Townsend was being completely candid both about his present lack of interest in a political job and about his serious interest in good roads. Heretofore, his interest and involvement in the Good Roads Movement, as it was still known, had been largely a local thing confined to the efforts of T. Coleman du Pont and his own newly-created Delaware State Highway Commission. But he had followed with avid interest the growing consciousness at the federal level of the need for a national highway system.

The Lincoln Highway concept, a forerunner of the later interstate highway system, was being much talked about in Washington and in the various state capitals. It called for a major coast-to-coast highway with connecting links to states not on the direct route. The route had already been laid out, though in 1921 it was gravel, dirt, or rutted mud for much of its course. The first pioneer coast-to-coast motorists were forced to spend as much as two months at the task, but that did not stop thousands of them from trying it. As a result of this new exodus, California and the Far West were enjoying their own real estate boom. A steady stream of Midwestern retirees was flowing into such formerly small southern California cities as Los Angeles and San Diego. They were well on their way toward becoming new American metropolises amidst the orange groves.

In his four years as governor, John had seen the public in Delaware come around to a new awareness of the benefits of highway building. Now he was seeing the same thing occur on a national level. The process had speeded up even more with the development of relatively inexpensive Ford Model Ts, Maxwells, and other automobiles well within reach for most middle-class families. America was highway crazy and all the excitement was setting John's gears to turning.

After leaving Washington, he made his way southward to Raleigh, North Carolina, to visit his former chief highway engineer, Charles M. Upham, who now held a similar position in that state. A North Carolina newspaper account of the former governor's visit noted that the distinquished visitor found Upham "doing almost undreamed-of things in the matter of building roads." The article went on to say that former Governor Townsend had been known at home in Delaware as "the Road Governor."

> Visiting at the offices of the [state highway] commission last night, Governor Townsend had an opportunity to observe something of the plans that are under way for roads in North Carolina. He was frankly amazed at the program and enthusiastic when the details of the highway organization were explained to him.

While it is probable that John had long since dreamed of all the things Mr. Upham was building in North Carolina, it was interesting to see how a state much larger than tiny Delaware marshalled its resources. He also doubtless talked over some ideas of his own with Upham before moving on down through the Deep South. He visited friends and canning business contacts in South Carolina, Georgia, and other southern states before venturing into Florida. What he found there was one of the most remarkable chapters in the whole history of America's "boom and bust" economy.

At the time of John's 1921 visit, Florida had been firmly established for decades as a leading winter resort for the wealthy. That status had been immeasurably improved by the early efforts of Standard Oil tycoon Henry M. Flagler and Southern Express Company executive Henry

Charles M. Upham, Dover

Charles M. Upham from a 1920 Gee Tee Maxwell cartoon (Lyla Townsend Savoy collection).

B. Plant to build major railroad lines throughout the state to link it with the mainstream of American transportation. Flagler's Florida East Coast Railway and Plant's Atlantic Coast Line vied with each other for the tourist trade by offering strings of elegant new hotels at newly established resort towns. Flagler's Palm Beach and Plant's domains in the Tampa-St. Petersburg area were soon attracting throngs of wintertime visitors, many of whom had begun building their own winter homes in the new resort cities by the immediate post-war years. These railroads also made possible the first major development of Florida as an agricultural center, as Flagler and Plant promoted the cultivation of citrus fruits and winter vegetables to make their railroad operations more profitable. Flagler's visionary "Over-the Seas Railroad" constructed on trestles from Miami to Key West quickly became one of the construction wonders of the world after its completion in 1912.

Other millionaire developers joined Flagler and Plant before long. Prominent among them was Carl G. Fisher, whose fortune stemmed from automobile parts. He came from Indianapolis where he had recently helped found the Indianapolis Speedway. He promptly set his sights on the development of a stylish beach resort along the narrow sand spit-cummangrove swamp across the bay from Miami known as Miami Beach. Fisher was also a renowned highway advocate who did for Florida highways what Plant and Flagler had done for its railroads. His major achievement in this regard was pioneering a somewhat circuitous route south from Chicago to Miami to be known as the Dixie Highway.

Another developer, George Merrick, created the city of Coral Gables just south of Miami, designing its structures along an imaginative neo-Venetian motif, complete with gondolas in its dredged canals. To the north similar works were occurring in Fort Lauderdale, and west coast resort cities were also springing up. In addition to Merrick's fake Venetian villas, there were elegant mansions and immense resort hotels being built in fanciful interpretation of Spanish colonial, beaux artes, Dutch, and a host of other styles. A common design element was the use of stucco, tile, and acres of palm trees. With the end of the World War the Florida land boom really took off. Millions of dollars were pumped into national publicity designed to make the state's exotic wonders, both natural and man-made, an integral part of the American dream. Journeys to the land of sunshine and orange groves became the wintertime fantasy of millions.

John's travels had brought him to Florida on several occasions in the past, but his leisurely 1921 visit gave him the chance to look the state over with a new and critical eye. Fresh from his visits with the Good Roads Bureau in Washington and with Charles Upham in Raleigh, he arrived at the outset of the greatest chapter of the "Great Florida Boom," the period between the beginning of the Harding Administration and the devastating hurricane of 1926. Florida was packed with audacious millionaires from all over the eastern half of the country and beyond, all seemingly bent on expanding their fortunes while enjoying balmy winter weather. Building of all types was going on everywhere.

By now quite a few Delaware businessmen were discovering the possibilities of Florida. Among them were several members of the du Pont clan including John's friend, Coleman, and his cousin, Alfred I. du Pont. Within a few years Alfred would more or less permanently abandon Delaware and transfer his interests to northern Florida. It was here, in and around Jacksonville, that he spent most of his last years before his death in 1936, investing heavily at postboom bargain prices in railroads, paper companies, and other enterprises. Coleman

Two Views: *Two very different views of John G. Townsend Jr. during Florida visits in the early 1920s are shown here (both from the Lyla T. Savoy collection).*

du Pont came down after the war, still troubled by his health–fleeing it, perhaps. He arrived fresh from real estate, insurance, and hotel investments in New York City, where he had served Mayor Jimmy Walker as honorary police commissioner. During one memorable episode he and the bon vivant mayor had raced their limousines up Fifth Avenue.

In Florida, du Pont became involved with one Addison Mizner, a very polished architect and real estate developer with an almost fanatic devotion to the sort of Spanish colonial architecture he had known during his childhood in California. His appreciation for this style had developed further during a sojourn in Guatemala while his father had served as U.S. minister. Mizner got his start in Florida before the war working for a wealthy patron, Paris Singer, heir to the sewing machine fortune, in the rebuilding of Palm Beach. Mizner's pièce-de-résistance, the Everglades Club, still stands as a monument to the glory days of pre-hurricane Florida. Until his association with Coleman du Pont in the early twenties Mizner devoted most of his efforts to the design and building of a succession of fantastically ornate mansions in Palm Beach and, later, Boca Raton. Built for families like the Biddles, Wanamakers, Vanderbilts, Phippses, and Stotesburys, the huge limestone and stucco piles dripped with, in the words of one writer, "Moorish patios, neo-Byzantine loggias, baroque staircases and colonnaded orangeries." One house featured an entrance hall lined with medieval choir stalls. The dining room of another was built around a semicircular gothic chapel. All this grandeur was, of course, dropped however incongrously into the Spanish-Moorish motif that poured forth so freely from Mizner's subconscious. With names like "El Sarmiento," "Sin Cuidado," "Lago-Mar," and "Villa Tranquilla," the great mansions were synonymous with the golden age of the Great Florida Boom.

Mizner conceived of Boca Raton as his grandest project yet. It was to be an entire planned community similar to but grander than Palm Beach. With du Pont's financial backing he hoped to create the finest project Florida had yet seen. To set the scene Mizner designed and built a magnificent cloistered administration building. The future seemed limitless, not only for him but for all the others who were making fortunes out of oceanfront land that only a few years before had been worth next to nothing. Through the promotional efforts of men like Mizner and Carl Fisher one seemed to hear of nothing but Florida in those years in magazines and cocktail party conversation. Even former swamps were becoming valuable.

As John had proved early in his career he was an example of a rare type that might best be described as the "prudent risk-taker." He was a gambler but he was not compulsive. A flashier entrepreneur would have jumped into the Florida Boom with both feet and started fighting for his share of the loot. A more conservative businessman would have taken one look at what was going on in Florida and caught the next train home to Delaware. Townsend took neither course. Instead he found a prudent way of cashing in on the boom without overextending himself. He became a highway builder. He quite properly reasoned that he was as well qualified as any man in America for that occupation with the exception of a few titans like Coleman du Pont. Building roads in Florida was a relatively safe undertaking, much safer than getting involved in some grandiose development scheme.

It is probable that John decided on the road-building business while still serving as governor. His decision would have been carefully thought out in advance. His stops in Washington and Raleigh on his way south in 1921 were for the purpose of checking out the "big picture" and letting friends in appropriate places know of his interest. He returned to Delaware in the late winter of 1921 and almost immediately incorporated the Highway Engineering and Construction Company.

Though this firm was relatively short lived, lasting only until about 1940, it was among his most profitable ventures. As he had by now done with so many other businesses, he quickly organized a small cadre of dependable men drawn from his circle of employees, family, and friends in Sussex County and sent them out in the field to carry out the work. The usual practice was to line up local labor at the site of the job. When it was available, equipment was leased locally to keep the overall investment as small as possible. In the beginning

John lined up most contracts himself and sent his team out to do the work. Gradually he built up a talented staff of engineers, superintendents, and managers who ran most of the operation for him. Thus, many young men from Selbyville and elsewhere in Sussex found themselves off to Florida and other states along the eastern seaboard, building roads through the lowlands, the swamps, forests and rolling piedmont of the southeast. Most would work for the company for a few seasons and then return home to Delaware to find work closer to home. Some few stayed in various southern points where they might have met local girls and married. Even now some Selbyville families have relatives in places like North Carolina and Florida who got there in the 1920s and 1930s with the highway construction company.

In some respects the Highway Engineering and Construction Company was one of the Middle Atlantic area's first modern road-building outfits. Several of its principal employees, men like John R. Hitchens of Georgetown, had learned their trade from Coleman du Pont when the du Pont Road was built through Delaware. Others had worked in the new highway department for the "highway governor" and switched jobs to keep the same boss when he left office. In the early days John, as was his custom, prevailed on Julian and Jack to help run the company, but apparently neither relished the work. Jule already had one child with another on the way when the company started and had no desire to be off in Florida or North Carolina building roads. Jack, though he had no children, was also married and already spent much of his time on the road with the strawberry business. Though both helped to ride herd on the road work, it did not become a major activity for either of them.

In the meantime young Paul Townsend had graduated from

Culver. He attended briefly both Cornell and Delaware College in deference to his father's wishes, but Paul was not the type who could adapt himself readily to the constraints of a college classroom. Paul made a deep impression on his contemporaries wherever he went. Many of those he met during his brief stays at Delaware and Cornell remained friends for the rest of his life, but he was just not the scholarly type. Finally he and his father faced the inevitable. Paul left college and joined the road-building company, for which it turned out he was perfectly suited.

A large, stocky, handsome young man, Paul was exceptionally personable with an easy convivial manner attractive to nearly everyone. He was, like his father, a natural politician in the sense that dealing with people was his true element. Again like his father, he was a natural moneymaker with the same ability to figure complex mathematical concepts on the run in his head, a quality that served him particularly well in the construction business. Within a few years Paul had assumed a major management role in the road-building enterprises.

By 1924, when the Florida boom was at its peak, Paul was living more or less permanently in Florida, overseeing the various jobs the company was involved in there. When he was not working, the attractive bachelor spent most of his free time pursuing a sport in which he would later achieve national and even international recognition–big-game fishing. During these Florida years Paul developed a love of the sea, of boating and deep-sea fishing that grew to be one of the dominant interests of his adult years. His brother Jack also became an avid fisherman during his frequent visits to Florida on business.

John had become something of a national spokesman for the Good Roads movement in the wake of his gubernatorial accomplishments. His later private road-building activities only heightened this renown. Everywhere he went in the suddenly highway-conscious eastern U.S., he was the subject of newspaper articles and other official interest. Invariably he was asked to comment on the road-building plans of whatever state or city he happened to be visiting. In the winter of 1924, for example, he spent six weeks in Tampa as Paul's guest "making a survey of road conditions on the west coast." A Tampa daily newspaper printed a story about him entitled "Delaware Ex-Governor Lauds Florida's Highway Program." It was noted that he was Delaware's "Good Roads Governor" and that his state now had more paved highways in proportion to its population than any other state in the union. John was quoted as saying that Florida's extensive highway construction program of those years was the single most important factor in that state's phenomenal growth. He noted further:

> Florida has great possibilities and she is taking advantage of them. A state cannot develop rapidly without good roads and it appears that Florida is doing everything possible to connect itself by a network of fine highways. A great city will be built at Tampa because of its strategic location, its port, and its manufacturing plants.

The next day, the newspaper repeated his remarks in an editorial:

> John G. Townsend, former governor of Delaware, was eminently correct...when he said that Florida's extensive highway construction program is probably doing more to develop the state than any other single thing. Our location has been the same since creation. Our soil and our climate have been since the beginning. Still people were never attracted to Florida much until after we began constructing good roads upon which thay might travel. Today those sections of the state that have the best roads and the most

T. Coleman duPont
during a visit to
Florida in the early
1920s (Lyla T. Savoy
collection).

roads are the best developed. All of this is a mere repetition of facts. The lesson is that we must keep on at road building until every portion of Florida is traversed by as good roads as are to be found anywhere.

As usual, John was in the right place at the right time. In choosing road construction as his major form of involvement in the Florida Boom, moreover, Townsend had picked virtually the only form of development not completely decimated by the traumatic ending of the boom a few years later. In fact, the road-building company not only stayed in business through the late 1920s but even flourished during the Great Depression of the 1930s when publicly-funded highway construction became a major component of the New Deal strategy of using public works projects to put America back to work.

The thing that finally ended the Great Florida Boom was the equally grandiose hurricane of 1926, the first severe tropical storm to hit South Florida in a decade. Coming just at the outset of the 1926-1927 tourist season, the storm destroyed 5,000 homes in the Miami-Fort Lauderdale area alone, damaging another 9,000 heavily and leaving 25,000 residents of the area homeless. Then, just as the state was beginning to recover from that severe setback, another violent storm hit in 1928, raising the water level of Lake Okeechobee so drastically that it flooded its low banks and drowned more than 2,000 people. It appears in retrospect, however, that the boom had already started to go bust before the hurricanes arrived. One of the first to pull out was T. Coleman du Pont, who had apparently become disenchanted with the whole shaky edifice of South Florida development in early 1926. He and John Townsend were even closer during these years than they had been ten years before and together they surveyed the spectacle of the overripe boom with a growing sense of foreboding. As a result neither man was caught in the aftermath.

While John's interests were primarily confined to road-building, he did get into one or two ventures in real estate with his old friend William J.P. White of Millsboro. They were not in deep enough to be hurt by the bust, and when White died in 1936, his remaining Florida holdings were valued at a very considerable sum. One thing both Townsend and White realized was that, bust or no bust, there were very sound reasons why economic growth in Florida was inevitable. They continued to have faith in the state when the boom days were gone and they both lived to have their faith rewarded. In another of his Florida newspaper appearances, this time soon after the boom ended, Townsend attempted to build the morale of local people. He was quoted by a Miami paper thus, "It has been a revelation to see this community grow during the last five years into the city that it is today. Having seen this great development I have become very much impressed with the type of people here."

Despite his generally positive outlook toward Florida and its people, John did have one difficulty during the bust. Much of his work before 1926 had been done for private developers and consisted of building development streets. The standard procedure was for an

William Jacob Peter White
of Millsboro, Delaware
(*Reproduced from W. L. Bevan's*
History of Delaware Past and Present)

escrow account to be set up pending successful completion of the road-building contract. When the development firm for which Highway Engineering and Construction was working when the boom ended experienced serious financial difficulty they attempted to renege on payment for the work the Townsends had done. John had to fight the matter at some length through U.S. District Court in Baltimore before finally getting his money. This experience may have soured him on working for private companies. Most of his road-building thereafter was under contract to various state and local governments. After 1926, the focus of the company's efforts turned from Florida to the Carolinas and the Delmarva Peninsula. Much work was done in the late 1920s in central North Carolina.

Early in January 1929, John was the keynote speaker at the twenty-sixth annual convention of the American Roadbuilders' Association in Cleveland. By this time he was Delaware's United States senator-elect and his topic was "The Pan-American Highway– the Road to Friendship." The speech concerned a plan to link North and South America with a modern highway (a project later carried out). In the audience were representatives of thirty nations. The man who had spontaneously embraced Coleman du Pont's boulevard proposition some twenty years before had now reached the pinnacle of the road-building profession.

19. Family, Business, & Politics

Through the early 1920s former Governor Townsend was still routinely referred to by the Delaware press as being retired from politics, which, at first, he considered himself to be. The retirement was only temporary, but the eight-year pause after January 1921, gave him an opportunity to reorganize his entire enterprise. One of the first things he did after returning from Florida in 1921 was to pay a lengthy visit to Rochester, New York, the home office of J. Hungerford Smith, Inc., the largest wholesale confectionary company in America. Hungerford Smith had been one of his largest strawberry customers for years. Now that he had the time to devote himself fully to such matters, he was able to work out a very favorable contract to sell them virtually his entire output of preserved strawberries for several years. With this contract in hand he set about a rapid expansion of the strawberry preserving plants to meet his guaranteed demand.

The Atlantic Cannery in Rehoboth Beach was now in top condition. It had been extensively rebuilt after the fire of 1917. Though it was in good shape it did not fit particularly well into current plans. Rehoboth was not a large strawberry-growing area. Nor was it close to one. John negotiated a sale of the cannery to Stokely Van Camp, a major national canned food company, and plowed his profits from that sale into the acquisition of more strawberry preserving plants. At the height of the strawberry operations in the 1920s, the Townsends operated twenty-three preserving plants from Tennessee northward.

In 1925, he actually owned (as opposed to leasing) plants in Norfolk, Virginia, Salisbury and Berlin, Maryland, and Seaford, Bridgeville and Millsboro, Delaware, in addition to the two large canneries in Selbyville and Georgetown.

He had time now to turn his attentions to orchards, an area of his operations that heretofore had been pushed into the background. His friend, Orlando Harrison, was in poor health (he died in 1928) and was also spending more of his time on his own political activities and other interests, so John bought the Harrisons' interest in several of the orchards they had begun as partners a decade before.

With the many different varieties of apples and peaches available, it was possible to have an early apple crop come on before strawberry season had hit its peak on the peninsula, then concentrate on strawberries, then peas and tomatoes and other early- to mid-summer crops, then peaches and finally late apples. In this way while the Townsends were packing strawberries in the south they could be canning apples on the peninsula. When strawberries were done their laborers could move on to the harvest of tomatoes, peaches, and apples. The integration of orchard crops into the

Chief Executive Officer: the former governor grew increasingly busy during the 1920s operating his far-flung enterprises. He is seen here in front of his Selbyville office about 1925 (courtesy of the Delaware Public Archives).

overall picture was the logical next step in the growth of the family business, but it was a step that could not be taken until John's temporary retirement from politics.

By now John was known on the peninsula, to his considerable amusement, as "The Strawberry King," a sobriquet that was to stick with him for the rest of his life. But strawberries went into gradual decline

Presidential visit: Ex-Governor *Townsend is shown with President Warren G. Harding at Milford in 1921. The president had been invited to be inducted into the newly established Delaware Masonic order, the Tall Cedars of Lebanon (courtesy of the Delaware Public Archives).*

locally in the late 1920s and 1930s for several reasons including a devastating pest known as the red stele fungus disease. Problems with growing practices in use among local farmers also contributed to the decline. The crop continued to be of major importance to the local economy until the World War II labor shortage dealt it its final blow, but after the mid-1930s strawberries were clearly on their way out. This was nothing new to Delaware farmers. The history of Delaware agriculture is one of successive waves of boom and bust as one crop dies out and another comes in.

The 1920s and 1930s were clearly the days of orchards in Delaware and the "strawberry king" was right in the thick of it. From 1920 to 1929 Delaware was listed as the most concentrated apple-growing area in the United States. This was largely because of the enormous number of Kent County orchards but the Townsend orchards and others in Sussex were growing in importance as well. By 1930, J.G. Townsend, Jr & Co., as the family's canning operations were now known, had closed more than half of the strawberry packing plants of a few years earlier. They now operated only those on the peninsula and the one in Norfolk.

In September of 1921, John and Julian Townsend incorporated the Indian Swan Orchard Company. This company was started when the family bought out a group of out-of-state orchardists who had started a large orchard at the confluence of Swan Creek and the Indian River just before the war. Located some two miles east of Millsboro, it was one of the largest orchards in Sussex County. By the time the Townsends had fully developed Indian Swan Orchard, it had 65,000 apple and peach trees of various types. Several years later John also bought out an enormous orchard near Bridgeville at a tax sale, setting it up as the Delaware Apple Orchard Company. It had originally been planted by Orlando Harrison who had had to let it go when he suffered some reverses on other enterprises. Townsend added to the already large number of trees in the 1,000 acre orchard. It eventually amounted to 85,000 trees, making it one of the largest single orchards in the United States. The third major orchard the family developed during the 1920s was the Delmar orchard, which was officially incorporated as the Townsend Orchard Company in 1925. These three operations qualified John as America's second largest orchardist (in terms of number of orchard trees under cultivation) by the late 1920s. In one of the more interesting coincidences of his career, the largest orchardist at the time was one Harry Flood Byrd who grew apples in Virginia's lower Shenandoah Valley. A few years later, when both men were serving in the U.S. Senate, they became the best of friends and remained so for the rest of their lives.

The center of the orchard operations was Swan Creek since it was midway between John's home base in Selbyville and Jule's headquarters in Georgetown. In the summer months the boss spent as much time there as possible. Mary Williams, who began working at Swan Creek as a youngster in 1922 (and who continued to work at Swan Creek, now Townsend's, Inc., for some seventy years) recalls that the orchard consisted of little but a tiny office, a few sheds, and acres and acres of trees. The business hours were from six in the morning to six at night and any young person from the community who wanted a summer job could get one. When Preston was a student at the University of Delaware after 1928, his father gave him the responsibility for managing the Delmar orchard during the summer— superb training for an agriculture student, but a bit nerve-wracking nonetheless. The family was then spending summers in Rehoboth Beach and Preston was expected to get from there to Delmar by seven o'clock to open the orchard for business. By this time John would have been on the go for quite a while himself and he would call up to check on things every so often. For all his easy-going exterior, he could be a firm taskmaster with his offspring. Years later people who had known the family well then and earlier used to talk about this fact with some bemusement. By this time John had more than enough money to have allowed Preston to enjoy a leisurely summer vacation, but, as it was said, "Those Townsend boys worked!"

The lumber companies, too, took a great step ahead after the war, though this was largely the achievement of "Mister Jim Townsend" and of John's son-in-law, Jack Tubbs. Every Sussex County town is filled with houses built between World War I and the early 1930s. Many in southern Sussex were built with lumber milled in the family's lumber mills and with millwork—door and window units, stair parts and other materials—that they turned out in their shops. The houses were built by carpenters working for one or the other of the two family lumber companies. The older and more established firm was officially incorporated in September 1923 as the Selbyville Manufacturing Co., Inc. On the same day John, James, and Jack Tubbs incorporated another business, the Townsend Lumber Company of Laurel in western Sussex. George Bishop, John's old lumber partner and a relative of James's wife, Addie, came back from the Carolinas to manage the Laurel operation. Jack Tubbs had most of the day-to-day control over the construction operations. James Townsend more or less ran the whole show from Selbyville.

Tubbs's construction crews were particularly active in the rapidly developing resort town of Ocean City, Maryland. During the 1920s Selbyville Manufacturing built many of the huge wood-frame hotels, the three- and four-story boarding houses, and the spacious private summer homes that gave the pre-World War II Ocean City its distinctive character. The company's crews were also active along the Delaware coast and throughout southeastern Sussex County, but the Ocean City work was the "bread and butter." As the beach town grew, Jack and Edith Tubbs came to feel that they had a major role in the creation of the resort. They summered there for most of their married life and other members of the clan followed.

The banks also enjoyed a slow, steady growth during these years, headed by such able managers as Raymond Morris and Layfield Long who ran them with skill and restraint. Their growth was not as dramatic as that of the other enterprises, but it was perhaps more solid. A few years later Baltimore Trust Company was able to weather the worst of the Depression when some other local banks did not fare so well. In one pre-Depression retrenchment, the company closed its Camden office in the late 1920s. That branch had never done as well as the other two because it faced a great deal more competition. The

Cannery: *The Townsend cannery along the railroad in Selbyville during tomato season in the early 1920s. This operation was typical of several that the family owned and operated during this period, including those at Georgetown and Rehoboth Beach. This facility was later sold and was converted for use as a poultry processing plant. Mountaire Foods is located on the same site today (courtesy of the Delaware Public Archives).*

decision was made to close it before it became a drain on the overall operation; the move proved fortuitous.

John's family life during these busy years was for the most part happy and fulfilling, but there were great sorrows as well. On New Year's Eve, December 31, 1923, James C. Townsend died at the age of forty-seven of tuberculosis, leaving his wife, Addie, and his fourteen-year-old son, James Covington Townsend, Jr. (known in the family as "Covington" or "Cub") to survive him. So ended a partnership between the two brothers extending back through their whole lives. James Covington Townsend had in a sense made his brother's successful political career possible. Had he not been there to manage the businesses in John's absence, the latter could never have taken the time to be governor. Had James and John not worked so well together, there might not even have been the businesses at all –at least not the multi-faceted enterprise which the Townsend interests had become by 1923.

Less than a year later, in September 1924, the loss was made complete when Addie Townsend passed away also. John took in the fifteen-year-old Covington as another son. Lyla, who was running her father's household at the time, remembered that "we just made room for one more." In the summer of 1925, she embarked on a tour of Europe with Covington and Preston in tow. Lyla had had a very pronounced streak of independence and adventure even as a child and this was one of her prime characteristics in later years. A decade later, she and Preston took off on a world tour lasting for months and ranging through Europe, the Far East and South America among other points.

The passing of Jim and Addie was not John's only loss in these years. Everett Johnson, his close friend and advisor, had been subject to respiratory problems for many years. Early in 1926, Everett passed away, his great willpower no longer able to overcome his physical weakness. After leaving Dover in 1921, Everett had poured all of his none-too-abundant energies into the development of his newspaper and his Press at Kells. By the time of his death the press had grown and evolved from its humble beginnings as a typical smalltown newspaper job-printing shop into a small press capable of producing books of extremely high quality. Everett was a lover of fine books and of the fine craftsmanship that went into their making, and he poured this love into building his Kells Press.

A devotee of the Arts and Crafts Movement of the late nineteenth and early twentieth centuries, he saw the acts of writing, editing, book design, printing, and binding as an integrated whole. In this he was similar to William Morris and the Pre-Raphaelites of sixty years before.

He was directly inspired by Elbert Hubbard, whose Roycroft Press became the basis for a community of craftsmen known as the Roycrofters, established by Hubbard in East Aurora, New York, in 1895. Louise Johnson recalled many years later that her husband had made a pilgrimage to East Aurora to visit the master and seek inspiration from the community, as thousands of other devotees were doing in the years before Hubbard and his wife perished in the sinking of the *Lusitania* in 1915. The very name "Kells," though it was coined by an assistant, harked back to the premier illuminated manuscript of the Irish golden age. As such the word was symbolic of Johnson's approach to his profession.

The Kells building, which served as Everett's newspaper office and publishing house in Newark, had been designed by him as an almost medieval, castle-like structure built of stone from Iron Hill, the high mass of land rising southwest of Newark near his and Louise's farm. It was tied closely to the artistic vision that had guided so much of his adult life. The stone residence that he built next door to the Kells building was an extension of this spirit.* The sturdy house had bald cypress doors and other interesting reminders of Johnson's Sussex County boyhood. Among its distinctive features was a carved rendering of the Cape Henlopen Lighthouse in bas relief on a wooden mantelpiece. Everett was especially fond of the venerable lighthouse. As chairman of a state commission devoted to its preservation, he had led public efforts to save it from the relentless approach of the sea.**

Under Everett Johnson's direction Kells Press produced many

---

* *The Kells Press building is still standing, though substantially altered, at the corner of South College Avenue and West Park Place in Newark, where it now serves as the local Y.W.C.A. The Johnson home also still stands next door on West Park Place, though no longer in the possession of the Johnson family.*

** *See note on following page.*

Everett Johnson: *shown clowning with a family friend on the steps of the stone building he erected at the corner of Park Place and South College Avenue in Newark to house the* Newark Post *and Kells Press (courtesy of Judith M. Pfeiffer and Robert C. Barnes).*

fine books during the early 1920s. Among them were sumptiously bound editions of biographies of Pierre Samuel du Pont de Nemours and Eleuthere Irénée du Pont (founder of the du Pont powder mills), which had been commissioned by Pierre S. du Pont, a close friend of Everett's and a fellow lover of fine books. Had Everett Johnson lived another decade, the Press at Kells might well have become a very profitable enterprise, but at the time of his death he was still overextended financially and in considerable debt. It was the kind of business that really required "the master's touch" in order to thrive, and the master had just departed.

A group of Everett's friends got together at the instigation of John G. Townsend and tried to keep the firm afloat by providing the overall direction themselves and trying to find competent managers to

---

** *The effort of Johnson and his lighthouse commission ultimately failed. The Cape Henlopen Lighthouse fell into the sea in April 1926, only about a month and a half after Everett's death at the age of forty-eight on February 20, 1926. It toppled from its location atop the Great Dune on a brilliantly clear day following the end of one of the large nor'easter storms that often strike the Delaware Coast.*

see to the company's day-to-day operations. The main principals in this effort were John and Pierre du Pont. Their view was that if the company could be kept going a few years longer it could be sold at a profit, thereby helping to ensure the future financial support of Johnson's widow, Louise Staton Johnson, and their daughter, Marjorie, who was a student at the Women's College at the time of her father's death. This venture was fraught with problems, however. Neither Townsend nor du Pont entirely understood the printing business, particularly the somewhat rarified branch of it which the Kells Press occupied. They had difficulty finding good personnel. The press was losing money regularly. Finally after several years they were forced to shut it down and to sell the printing equipment.

Everett had lived to see another of his pet projects to fruition. This was the construction of the Memorial Library (now Memorial Hall), the central structure on the mall of the University of Delaware. Everett was a very active and dedicated member of the board of trustees and had served as chairman of the committee that oversaw the design and construction of the building. It was intended in part as a memorial to the Delawareans who died in World War I, but it is fair to see it as well as a memorial to Everett Johnson, one of the most remarkable men of early twentieth century Delaware.

Through the 1920s, an unbroken succession of Republican presidents and Republican majorities in Congress presided happily, perhaps a trifle smugly, over the nation's affairs as America enjoyed the greatest period of prosperity it had yet experienced. Times were so good that America's leaders, Republican and Democrat alike, misread the increasing danger signs given off by a horse-and-buggy economy struggling to keep up with high-powered growth. With the exception of a few groups, like the periennially depressed farming community, the bad times were still in the future. When most Americans looked ahead during that wonderful post-war decade they saw only bigger and better and more, more, more. The Harding and Coolidge Administrations were wonderful times to be a Republican and to feel that the government was being run on a sound business basis.

Delaware became more Republican than ever during the 1920s. At last, the various G.O.P. factions were at peace–most of the time. As late as September 1921, one could read editorials like the one in the Dover *State Sentinal* on September 7, which began, "One of the outstanding political topics of the past week in this city is the likelihood of the bringing together of two political forces that have heretofore been working against each other . . . the Henry A. du Pont faction and the Alfred I. du Pont faction." Even then, this kind of talk had become old-fashioned. The intensely emotional battles of the Townsend administration slowly receded into memory.

John's own "retirement from politics" never amounted to much. It did not last much longer than the time it took him to rest up from the rigors of office. By 1922 he was right back in the middle of the action and learning to savor the special status accorded ex-governors who had served honorably and well. Though only fifty, he assumed a sort of elder statesman status in party circles, chairing committees, presiding at state conventions and hosting eminent visiting dignitaries. By the mid-1920s columnists writing for Wilmington and Dover newspapers had begun to reminisce about the good old days under "Delaware's War Governor." All the major programs the former governor had advanced amidst such storm and strife were now commonly accepted parts of everyday life. People had a warm feeling for the irrepressible ex-governor who went about the state talking to everyone he saw and remembering most of them by name. He did not engage in useless vendettas against men like Daniel Layton who had fought him. He let bygones be bygones and this was appreciated.

The speed with which change occurred in those postwar years was striking. Not only did the events of the years just before World War I already seem like ancient history, but political reality had altered almost completely. Progressivism had died during the war as a driving force of government. In Delaware many of the movement's goals had been met or exceeded by the unparalleled union of private philanthropy and state government that characterized the Townsend years. Elsewhere, the Progressives were not always so lucky. Everywhere their time seemed to be passing, their principles submerged under a great tide of fears unleashed by the war and its aftermath, and by the desire of a war-weary nation to stop the crusades and turn to more pleasant pursuits.

Passing as well were many of the faces that had characterized the Delaware scene in the years before and during the war. Old Colonel du Pont, who had still nominally headed a faction of Delaware's Republican party as late as 1921, passed on in 1926, the year of Everett Johnson's death. In 1922, Congressman Layton was forcibly retired by the electorate, soundly defeated in his bid for reelection. Many others, friend and foe alike, though still in good health, now turned away from public life.*

---

* *Typical was John's old adversary, Mrs. Henry B. Thompson. While still a leading Wilmington socialite and civic leader, she had given up crusading for the most part. She was never again to charge into the fray at the State House at the head of a grand cause as she had done so skillfully during the battle against suffrage. She turned her attentions now to the development of the arts, culture, and civic pride of Rehoboth Beach, where she maintained a large summer home—and where she and her family inevitably encountered the Townsends socially. While there are no reports that Mrs. Thompson and John Townsend were particularly friendly, their offspring did maintain friendly relations.*

(continued on following page)

The three du Pont consins, Alfred, Pierre, and Coleman, were still very much alive and still very active in their various causes and roles. Pierre had become the state school tax commissioner, in amongst overseeing the operations of General Motors and the DuPont Company (though now in primarily an advisory capacity). He was still building schoolhouses throughout the state, while at the same time creating one of the world's great gardens at his Longwood, Pennsylvania, farm.

During the 1920s, Alfred patched things up to some extent, both politically and socially, with his cousins Pierre and Coleman and with other family members. By the middle of the decade, he was shifting his operations to Jacksonville, Florida, where he was to spend much of the ten years remaining to him with his new wife, the former Jessie Ball, member of a prominent Virginia family. He still devoted much of his time and energy to the improvement of life for those Delawareans less fortunate than himself. So frequently the idealistic trailblazer, Alfred still had several major initiatives ahead of him, the grandest of all being his posthumous benefactions to the Nemours Foundation with its Alfred I. du Pont Institute. His widow, who outlived him by many years, followed his lead by establishing the Jessie Ball du Pont Foundation, which still funds many worthwhile causes. These charities continue to play an important positive role in the lives of both Delaware and Florida down to the present day. It is

(continued from preceding page)

Mrs. Thompson's son, James, became internationally renowned as the "Thai Silk King" when, after service in southeast Asia with the Office of Strategic Services during World War II, he settled in Bangkok and established a highly successful business marketing and exporting Thailand's native textiles. Mrs. Lyla Townsend Savoy, who had been friendly with Jim during Rehoboth summers, visited him at his lovely home on Bangkok's Klong River during the 1950s. Tragically, James Thompson disappeared while traveling in a remote area of Thailand in the early 1960s and the case has never been officially solved, though various theories still circulate as to his fate.

entirely fitting that Alfred, idiosyncratic though he was, is primarily remembered today for his many acts of charity.

In 1929, even before the stock market crash and the ensuing Great Depression, Alfred began working to establish an old-age pension system for the State of Delaware. When legislation to accomplish this failed to pass the General Assembly, he decided to go ahead with his own private pension plan for elderly Delawareans in need. A hired staff had compiled a list of names of needy individuals by November 1929, and 800 checks were sent out. By the time the program came to an end in 1931, after a shamed General Assembly finally enacted a state program, Alfred was sending out 1,600 checks each month and had expended $320,000 of his own money.

Coleman du Pont meanwhile was in and out of Florida real estate, New York hotels, and other interests. He at last achieved one of his goals by entering the U.S. Senate as senator from Delaware, though not quite in the manner he might have wished. In the spring of 1921, Governor Townsend's successor, William D. Denney, also a close friend of Coleman's, was faced with the need to fill several judicial appointments. Among them was that of chancellor of the state's venerable Court of Chancery, a job then held by the generally competent and respected Charles M. Curtis. His term was due to expire in June 1921. He was only sixty-two and most members of the Delaware bar assumed that he would routinely be reappointed by Governor Denney. Denney decided to do things differently. The chancery court appointment soon mushroomed into a full-blown melee of the kind that appears so often in the long political history of Delaware. The precise details are a bit uncertain, but it happened more or less the way it was recalled many years later by former U.S. Senator Daniel O. Hastings in his political memoirs. Hastings, who was then serving as judge of the Wilmington City Court, was another of the group of young and ambitious men from the lower Eastern Shore of Maryland who had come to Delaware at the turn of the century. An able attorney, he was active politically and by 1921 was becoming quite influential in Delaware Republican circles. At the time of the chancery court incident, Hastings was a very close advisor to Governor Denney.

According to Hastings, he first broached the idea to Denney of appointing someone other than Curtis to the court. He said that the suggestion was made to him by R.R.M. (Ruly) Carpenter Sr., brother-in-law of Pierre du Pont and a close friend of U.S. Senator Josiah O. Wolcott. Wolcott, a Democrat, had defeated old Senator Henry A. du Pont in 1916 to become the first popularly-elected U.S. senator in Delaware history. He was a well-respected attorney and the son of a former chancellor. It was well known among Wolcott's friends that the senator had a strong desire to serve as chancellor himself. The office was and is greatly coveted, easily qualifying as one of the most interesting and influential state judgeships in America. The chancellorship had risen to this lofty state in the aftermath of the enactment of Delaware's landmark corporation law at the turn of the century. As Delaware's reputation grew as a corporate domicile of choice for many of the nation's largest companies, the practice of corporation law began to assume a dominant position in the work of the chancery court, whose judges found themselves ruling on some of the most important corporation law cases in the world.

In light of these realities, it is understandable that a man of Wolcott's family heritage and deep interest in the law would willingly vacate a U.S. Senate seat to become chancellor. And this, Ruly Carpenter suggested to Hastings, is what should be done. If Wolcott were given Curtis's job as chancellor, Governor Denney would be able to appoint a Republican to fill out the year and a half remaining in

Wolcott's U.S. Senate term. The Republican so chosen would then be in a good position to run for reelection in 1922 with some of the advantages of incumbency.

Denney liked the idea. Not only was Wolcott a friend of his, but he was not particularly impressed with the performance of Delaware's other U.S. senator, Republican L. Heisler Ball, in obtaining federal patronage jobs for Delaware Republicans. He expressed the view that Judge Curtis was too old at sixty-two to be reappointed, though this was probably just rationalization. Most of the other Republican leaders with whom Hastings discussed the matter also supported it. In view of what happened later it is interesting that a minority view was expressed by Coleman du Pont, who was cool to the whole idea. He thought that pushing Curtis out and trying to appoint Wolcott would only create problems when the newspapers learned of it. Eventually, however, he gave in. Apparently Denney's original intention had been to appoint Daniel Hastings to fill the Senate vacancy, or so a biographer claimed in an account of Coleman du Pont's career written in 1928:

> The governor's acceptance of the suggestion and his intended appointment of Judge Daniel O. Hastings to the Senate vacancy, had the support of more than ninety per cent of the Republican leaders. Both of the appointees [Wolcott and Hastings] and their supporters were influenced by the approval of eminent legal and judicial authorities without respect to party, which approval was regarded by the leaders as justifying the partisan advantage to the Republicans.
>
> As was well known among Republican leaders, Coleman du Pont had no personal interest in the Senate vacancy, nor had he been considered for the appointment. At the exigency of the party he now accepted the office.

This last statement was somewhat disingenuous since du Pont had long sought either a U.S. Senate seat or the presidency. In fairness, however, he had largely abandoned hope by 1921, and was not actively seeking the office. News of the proposed appointments was broken in the Philadelphia *Record*, a Democratic newspaper whose editor tended to dislike Wolcott. The *Record* turned it into a major uproar, calling it "the dirty deal" and generally castigating everyone remotely involved in it. This went on for weeks and the Wilmington dailies also got involved. Even old Senator du Pont's *Morning News* opposed it.

At last, after he had taken about all the public abuse he could stand, Wolcott let it be known that he would not resign from the Senate to take the chancellor's job. He apparently expected Denney to proceed with Curtis's reappointment and just let the whole mess die down. So did Curtis's friends, but they misread Denney. Having once decided not to reappoint Curtis, he refused to reconsider the decision. He began looking around for another lawyer to appoint who would be acceptable to the Delaware bar. By this time the legal community was adamant that Curtis should be reappointed and no reputable attorney would accept the appointment. Denney refused to give in and resolved finally to send Senator Wolcott's name to the state senate for confirmation as chancellor, with or without Wolcott's agreement, along with his other judicial appointments. This development set off another round of protest in the papers, but Denney's staff did its work well and eventually his entire list of appointees, including Wolcott, was confirmed. His confirmation now an accomplished fact, Wolcott promptly resigned from the Senate and accepted the chancellorship. He went on to serve for more than seventeen years, proving to be one of the finest chancellors in Delaware history. While in that high post he earned the distinction of having only one of his rulings overturned by a higher court. For him, at least, the "dirty deal" had turned out well.

Coleman du Pont was not so fortunate. The fact that Denney appointed him rather than Hastings to fill the Senate vacancy a month after Wolcott's appointment as chancellor convinced many Delawareans that du Pont had engineered the entire incident. He was a convenient target in any case, known to all as the kingpin of the Republican Party and as one of the wealthiest men in the state. It was simply assumed, quite unfairly according to all the evidence, that he had simply bought himself the senate seat. This was typical of du Pont's luck in politics—or, more correctly, his lack thereof. In 1920, the year John was defeated in his campaign to be a delegate to the Republican National Convention, du Pont had hoped to stage a serious run for the presidency. As if it had not been bad enough to have the governor, one of his chief strategists, tangled up in the woman's suffrage fight and in his battle with the Laytons, du Pont ran into other problems at the convention. He had expected the firm support of Delaware's Senator Ball, only to have Ball desert him after the first ballot. du Pont was left with little more than a favorite-son candidacy and the strong feeling that Ball had aided his defeat, rather than using his contacts among Republicans from other states to further Coleman's candidacy. It was doubly frustrating to lose out to the likes of Warren G. Harding, who even then was seen by du Pont's friends as being a far weaker candidate than Coleman would have been.

When the 1922 campaign season approached, now-Senator Coleman du Pont announced his candidacy for a full six-year Senate term. The man chosen by the Democrats to oppose him was Thomas F. Bayard, a prominent Wilmington attorney who just happened to be married to one of Mrs. Coleman du Pont's sisters. The intimacy of

Delaware political life is the stuff of legend, but running against one's own brother-in-law for a U.S. Senate seat was extraordinary even by Delaware standards. Bayard was by no means a sacrificial lamb; he was a formidable and creditable candidate. Among other attributes, he possessed what had to have been one of the finest political pedigrees any candidate ever enjoyed. His father had been both U.S. senator and U.S. secretary of state. His grandfather, his great-uncle, his great-grandfather, and his great-great grandfather had all served as U.S. senators from Delaware and several had served as its representative in Congress as well. One of these illustrious ancestors had cast the deciding vote for Thomas Jefferson (and against Aaron Burr) when the presidential election of 1800 had to be decided by Congress. Thomas Bayard thus had a considerable amount of name recognition, but it was nothing compared to that of Coleman du Pont, whose name had by this time been a household word in Delaware for nearly a generation. Despite his opponent's greater visibility, Bayard beat him by 325 votes, an incredibly close outcome considering the more than 70,000 votes cast. It was obvious to most observers that the voters had not so much voted *for* Bayard as *against* du Pont in a major backlash against his popularly-perceived central role in the "dirty deal" of the year before.

Another factor that hurt Coleman was that his Republican running mate, old Congressman Layton, who was seeking his third term, managed to alienate Delaware's black voters. He had loudly opposed a new federal anti-lynching law being considered in Congress in the wake of several notorious hangings of black men by white mobs in the South. With that gesture, Layton lost a major part of the traditional Republican voting base. The effects of his actions were felt not by himself but by the entire ticket in those days of widespread straight ticket voting. This disaster did not serve to endear the Layton clan to du Pont's wing of the party, since they had also played a large part in the destruction of Coleman's presidential hopes in 1920. Daniel Hastings, whose brief memoirs are among the more revealing political documents to deal with this period, felt that Coleman's refusal to spread the traditional large sums of money around the state also hurt him badly.

Gee Tee Maxwell's caricature of James M. Tunnell Sr., circa 1920 (Lyla Townsend Savoy collection).

According to Hastings, du Pont thought that financing the buying of votes in the manner his less savory supporters had come to expect represented conduct unbecoming a U.S. Senator. Though Coleman had been a major source of political largesse for decades, many turned against him over his refusal to participate in such activities in 1922.

Though he might well have felt like giving up after his agonizingly close defeat, Coleman came back with renewed vigor in 1924 to challenge incumbent L. Heisler Ball for the Republican nomination for Delaware's other Senate seat. This was something of a grudge match for Coleman, who felt he had a score to settle. He was convinced that Ball had worked against him in 1922 as well as deserting him at the 1920 convention. This time he was well prepared in plenty of time and was able to make the state Republican convention exceedingly uncomfortable for Ball, whose candidacy was overwhelmingly rejected by the delegates.

Coleman's opponent in the general election was the Baltimore Hundred native and Georgetown attorney James Miller Tunnell. The forty-five-year-old Tunnell, whose name later figures very prominently in this story, was born and raised in the neighborhood of Blackwater, a hamlet near the present-day village of Clarksville. He was a relative of old Governor Ebe Tunnell, who had operated the general store there before moving both home and business to Lewes. His ancestors on both sides of his family had farmed and fished around Muddy Neck and Miller's Neck for more than two centuries. Tunnell had moved beyond his rural Baltimore Hundred roots and gone off to college in New Athens, Ohio, in 1896. After graduating in the Class of 1900, he had read law first in Ohio and then back in Georgetown, where he studied under the prominent attorney, Robert White of Broadkill Hundred. He appreciated farmland and forest almost as much as John did and was already becoming a substantial landowner in Sussex. His race against Coleman du Pont for the U.S. Senate seat was Tunnell's first foray into statewide politics. He clearly had little expectation of winning, but was running at least in part to build political capital for the future. The race was an opportunity to achieve statewide recognition, and, of course, there was always a chance, however slight, of winning.

The old warrior knew that it was now or never and he pulled out all the stops. Where he had lost two years before to Bayard by 325 votes, this time Coleman won by nearly 20,000.

The congressional race was of special interest that year for Sussex Countians, since two of their own were running. William Boyce, who had spent many years as a judge in Georgetown before moving up to Dover, had beaten Caleb R. Layton in 1922. Boyce was not a very flashy congressman and he had gone to Washington largely because Layton had managed to anger so many different sections of the electorate, but he was well respected around the state. His Republican opponent was Robert G. Houston, also of Georgetown, publisher of the *Sussex Republican*, attorney, and a leading pillar of the community. He was about as close to a crusading journalist as Sussex County ever had. As a young man in the 1890s, he had led the fight locally against J. Edward Addicks. He had run for Congress on the first Regular Republican ticket in 1896. When George Kennan was researching his piece on Addicks for *The Outlook* in 1903, he had stayed in Houston's East Market Street home. Later Houston had founded a group dedicated to cleaning up Delaware elections, and in 1912 he became state chairman of the Progressive Party.* Congressman Boyce was well-respected to be sure but Houston was one of the most respected men in Delaware and he defeated his former townsman handily.

In the off-year election of 1926, Houston ran for a second term and handily defeated a relatively unknown Democrat, Merrill H. Tilghman to win a second term. As the 1928 presidential election year approached, there were few in the Republican party displaying much eagerness to step forward and oppose U. S. Senator Bayard, who was now nearing the end of his first term and was known to be interested in running for a second term. Yet there was one Republican, respected throughout the state, removed from the most recent inter-party squabbles, who, after some six years out of office, was hungering for another plunge into the political waters: John G. Townsend, Jr. of Selbyville. 1928 was to be his year.

---

* *As an example of the sometimes surprising connections of Sussex County's leading lights, one of Houston's daughters, the late Mrs. Mary Houston Robinson, possessed a photograph showing her father entertaining a group of young people at the family's Georgetown home in the years before World War One. Among those in attendance, in addition to herself and other family members, was an out-of-town college friend of one of the guests, a youthful Westerner named Ezra Pound.*

20. Rising from the Ashes–
The Run for the Senate

Through all the Republican party battles in the early and middle 1920s John had maintained a low profile. He had plenty of business interests to keep him occupied when he wished to keep out of the heat of political infighting and that was something he succeeded in doing. He had been in the eye of enough hurricanes as governor. Politically he remained a stalwart supporter of Coleman du Pont and he generally supported Republican tickets, which he aided both financially and by lending his still considerable prestige to campaign events whenever possible.

His was the kind of genial presence that led men of all political stripes to let down their guard and relax when they saw him coming, knowing they were in for a few minutes of generally priceless conversation. He was happy to exchange all the latest and spiciest political gossip but not to engineer Machiavellian deals aimed at some dubious end. In this Townsend was refreshing and almost unique. He was no paragon of virtue, but he simply did not play the game in such a way as to leave casualties–or enemies–lying about wounded in his wake.

By this time his incredible memory for names and family connections had been raised to an art form. It had been said of him a decade before that he knew more people than any other man in Delaware. Now he knew all those he had known in 1919 plus their brothers, sons, daughters, wives, and grandchildren. His practice of strolling the length of every train on which he happened to find himself, introducing himself to all and sundry, was legend. Almost everyone who remembers him as a mature politician brings this up. He would say boldly with his easy smile and his very considerable presence, "I'm John Townsend. Who are you?"

And they would tell him who they were and what they were thinking and where they were from and who they were related to that he might know. And they would remember him–his height and his strawberry-blonde gray hair, his easy smile, and that very singular presence. Where this had routinely gone on up and down the length of Delaware day after day in the early years before he did a great deal of motoring around the state, now it went on from Delaware to Florida and back, out to Chicago, up to New York, and everywhere else he went.

The remarkable thing is that John listened to all of this and he remembered the important parts of it for future reference. In this essential political art he is unsurpassed in Delaware history. According to some accounts, a possible equal was John M. Clayton, another man with roots deep in Sussex, but this claim is hard to verify from the existing evidence. Moreover, while many politicians are exquisitely skillful at appearing interested in the manifold comments of the multitudes of potential voters, John did not have to pretend to be interested. He *was* interested.

During the 1920s he became easily the busiest former Governor Delaware had ever had. No one before, or for that matter since, had been as successful as he was at handling the sometimes difficult role of former governor. Not old enough to be truly an elder statesman, he found it comfortable to assume a more active stance. One of the few official pleasures he had had during his term was the opportunity for friendly social and political contacts

Gubernatorial miners: former Gov. Townsend, second from left in front row, is seen with a group of hard-hatted governors at a 1923 governors' conference in White Sulphur Springs, West Virginia (photos reproduced from New York Times clippings in Townsend family scrapbooks).

with his peers in other states at national governors' conferences and similar events. His political interests had long since ceased being confined to just Delaware and such junkets gave him a chance to find out what other "big men" were doing elsewhere around the country. During the terms of both Governor Denney and Governor Robert P. Robinson, a Wilmington banker who was elected in 1924, Townsend regularly attended national governor's conferences.

As a natural politician, Townsend effortlessly found himself a target for news photographer's cameras without even trying to do so when pictures were being taken for the rotogravure sections of the Sunday papers. One finds him standing in a complete coal miner's outfit, including the obligatory lantern on his helmet, at a 1923 governors' conference at White Sulphur Springs, West

Virginia, looking perfectly comfortable and at ease. That set of photos found its way into the *New York Times*, which was itself a news-making event in Delaware. His old friend Everett Johnson wrote of it in his *Newark Post* in this way:

Former Governor Townsend
(New York Times photo).

> It is a compliment to Delaware's former Governor when we say he makes a very husky, goodlooking, non-striking miner–yet the coal supply of his friends is about as low as usual. He looks perfectly natural in overalls and jumper–just as natural as he used to in days gone, with a team of oxen or mules, with him wielding a bob-crack whip. He can drive a six-mule team without leads, and crack a fly off the ear of the head lead. He *looks* as natural in a miner's suit as he used to at the buck-end of a cross-cut saw down in Sussex pines. He looks as natural as he used to Sunday afternoon with a dainty bay pacing mare, known in Sussex as a "wracker," and a red running-geared, side-bar buggy. He looks just as natural as he used to at the strong end of a saw long just after the whistle blew. He looks as natural as he does buying strawberries, telephoning instead of writing, at his business desk. He looks like the same John Townsend that was the Governor of Delaware for four years, with a personal acquaintance and friend in every school district. It is the same John Townsend, because no matter where he is or how he is dressed or what his job is, he never forgets that his first name is John and that title given him "Way down Yan" is the one he likes best. "Mister," "His Excellency," or "Governor" are all representative of responsibilities to him, but none more serious than John.

Johnson was fully aware, of course, that he was promoting a bit of a political legend, but it was a good legend with more truth than most. There were then many New Castle Countians who were fresh arrivals from "Way down Yan" in Sussex County themselves. Between about 1900 and the Great Depression large numbers of young Sussex County natives moved north in search of high-paying jobs. Most still felt a great love of home and many *Newark Post* readers were very receptive to the kinds of images Johnson was calling up. It was perfectly clear that he was patting a friend of his on the back, but former Governor Townsend was widely perceived as a friend of everyone else's as well. By 1923, it was quite clear to most people that John was not the kind of politician who spends most of his time building a carefully planned image, making sure he gets every little touch just right. His hard work and brave stands for unpopular causes showed that. The former governor was a natural newsmaker without even trying.

In 1924, he attended a governor's conference in Jacksonville, Florida. In 1925, he joined newly elected Delaware Governor Robert P. Robinson at the 17th Annual National Governor's Conference at Maine's famed Poland Spring House. While Robinson stood dour and governor-like amongst others of the same type, Townsend stands with a big smile and Governor Al Smith's arm draped around his shoulder companionably. The charismatic John had a way of relating to the public as the same dynamic public figure he was as governor.

All of this was slowly propelling him in a certain direction politically, quietly and almost inevitably, with such ease that he hardly realized it himself. He was moving toward the U.S. Senate in a much more direct and natural way even than his old friend and ally, Coleman du Pont, had done. du Pont had been having serious trouble with his throat for fifteen years by 1927 and it was known to most people who knew him well that he had cancer. He had no real business going into the Senate campaign in 1924, but it was an effort he felt that he had to make to achieve vindication. In 1927, his fragile health took a further turn for the worse. He was operated on and his larnyx and vocal cords were removed. He was fitted with one of the first artificial larynxes ever made. It was a device built by Western Electric Company to enable someone without the proper equipment to talk. His recovery was never complete and through 1928 he slowly grew worse.

As the nominating conventions neared, du Pont and several other Republican Party leaders began urging Townsend to run for the U.S. Senate. Under the rotation system then honored by both parties, it was New Castle County's turn to have the Republican gubernatorial nomination and Sussex County's turn to have the senatorial nomination. In later years John always liked to tell people how he had been drafted by the convention and nominated without even being there. He gave the clear impression that he would just as soon not have had it, but that he had been pushed into it. That, of course, was the proper stance for a politician of his time to take. It was thought crass to hunger too avidly for a high governmental position. One wished to be a bit statesmanlike, aloof from the back room deals and horse-trading of the nominating process.

At the time it was still considered *de rigueur* for presidential candidates to refrain from attending the national party conventions. The prescribed technique was for them to remain at home, leaving the whole thing up to campaign managers on the scene, and, of course, to Western Union. The successful nominee was meant to wait at home, pretending not to know the outcome, until an elder statesman of the party, delegated by the convention, delivered the news in person. Then the candidate, making attractively modest protestations of unworthiness and gratitude to his fellow party members for the honor they had done him, would launch extemporaneously as it were into an acceptance speech he had been memorizing for weeks. Franklin D. Roosevelt electrified the nation in 1932 by brashly and boldly boarding a plane and flying to Chicago after his nomination to deliver his acceptance speech in person to the Democratic National Convention. John's unannounced candidacy should be seen against this background.

Another unannounced candidate for the job, also from Sussex County, was Ruby R. Vale of Milford. Vale was born and raised a Pennsylvanian and was a prominent Philadelphia lawyer. Oddly enough, he had made his principal residence in Milford for more than twenty years, commuting back and forth to his Philadelphia office. While he never seems to have cared to practice law in Delaware, he loved the state. Not only was Vale a Philadelphia lawyer, but he was a Pennsylvania legal scholar of the first order. He had written several books that had become standard texts in Pennslyvania law schools. Vale had been active in Delaware politics for about fifteen years. In the manner of all lawyer-politicians he was a regular presence around Dover when the General Assembly was in session, offering advice and building useful connections.

One reason Vale had trouble generating enough enthusiasm for his candidacy among local Republican leaders was that he seemed, inevitably, to be compared to J. Edward Addicks because of his Pennsylvania background. The two men had almost nothing in common, except that both were wealthy outsiders who sought to become U.S. senator from Delaware. Vale was allied with Milford state senator I. Dolphus Short, a frequent foe of Townsend's in past years. Vale was also a sometime associate of the Allees, a connection that could only make him seem even more Addicks-like in the eyes of the former members of the Regular Republican faction.

John took off shortly before the convention on a business trip to Florida. His nomination was by no means assured at the time of his departure, but the unofficial word was that things seemed to be leaning his way. By this time, Paul had become one of his father's chief political operatives and he was working behind the scenes on the nomination, as were John's other friends.

Another interesting factor in the situation was that the Republican leadership wished to bring about the nomination of C. Douglass Buck, chief engineer of the state highway department, for governor. Buck was Coleman du Pont's son-in-law. Coleman feared that this would cause the voters to reject Buck at the polls, but he was finally convinced otherwise. He had resolved by this time to resign from the Senate because of his health, but he carefully refrained from making this knowledge public so as not to influence the campaign. Coleman strongly supported Townsend's candidacy for the Senate. He did not resign until Townsend had been elected over Thomas F. Bayard. It is tempting to speculate under the circumstances as to whether, if Townsend had lost the election, he would have been appointed to fill out the two years remaining in du Pont's term.

In his political memoir, *Delaware Politics, 1904-1954,* Hastings recalled that things were uncertain up to the last minute, saying that "on the day of the Convention nobody knew who was to be nominated for United States Senate," and adding:

> The situation in Sussex County was such that there wasn't a delegate who was prepared to nominate either Townsend or Vale. When the chairman called for the nomination for that high office it was Dr. Samuel G. Elbert, a prominent colored doctor in Wilmington, and a delegate from Wilmington, who nominated Governor Townsend for that office. My recollection is that no other nominations were made and Townsend was selected.

As had frequently been the case in the past, leaders from other parts of the state had to head off opposition to Townsend from men like Dolphus Short in his own county who still inwardly resented his progressive actions as governor. It is worth noting, however, that by 1928 that old resentment was so slight that the Vale-Townsend rivalry for the nomination did not even become public. John's old enemies got behind his nomination even if they were not enthuasiastic supporters. Their vows of ten years before that the governor who had the gall to go against them was politically dead proved in the end to be just so much hot air.

John now returned from his trip, graciously accepted the nomination, and began preparing for the business of running against Senator Bayard. His campaign was an extremely traditional one. He aligned himself closely with the 1928 Republican national platform and with the presidential nominee, Herbert Hoover, both of which were logical things to do in Delaware in 1928. While Hoover had his problems within the Republican Party, specifically with Mid-western farmers and with the remnants of the old Progressive-populist bloc in the same area, those problems were as nothing to those faced by his Democratic opponent, Governor Alfred E. Smith of New York, the "Happy Warrior" whose nomination at the Democratic convention in Houston had alienated a large part of the traditionally Democratic South and West. Not only was Smith a big-city politician with big-city ways and speech in an overwhelmingly rural country, but he was a leading "Wet" while much of the South was strong in its prohibitionist sentiments. Smith's greatest difficulty in appealing to many Southern voters was the fact that he was a Roman Catholic. Many Americans were absolutely convinced that, if elected, Smith would take his orders directly from the pope. While this was one of the more absurd fears ever to influence the American electorate, in 1928 it was a very real factor in the campaign. (After Smith's defeat the humorist Will Rogers coined the fictitious telegram, "Dear Pope, Unpack. Signed, Al.")

The Roman Catholic factor played little part in the Delaware presidential race. Roman Catholics had been a very large part of the electorate for more than half a century in both New Castle and Kent Counties and anti-Catholic sentiment had long since run its course in most parts of Delaware. The casual observer might have expected Smith to do better in the state than he actually did, however, because his campaign manager was a Delawarean. John J. Raskob, himself an eminent Catholic layman, was heading Smith's campaign and had also been named Democratic National Chairman.

Raskob's climb to national prominence was another Horatio Alger tale of humble origins and hard work. He had risen from a lowly position of stenographer to Pierre S. du Pont while in his twenties to that of treasurer of the DuPont Company and member of its board at age thirty-five. Raskob is the man who convinced the du Pont family and the company board to make its major investment in General Motors, which added immeasurably to their wealth. When he and Pierre du Pont were actively managing the automobile company, Raskob had come up with the idea of selling cars on the installment plan, which evolved into the General Motors Acceptance Corporation (GMAC) and led directly to the position of preeminence that GM still enjoys.

Raskob was also a major figure on Wall Street by the late 1920s and one of the leading voices of the great Bull Market of 1927 and 1928. As a leading symbol of Wall Street he was unappreciated by many traditional Democrats, some of whom coined the slogan heard during the Smith-Hoover Campaign of "Rum, Romanism, and Raskob." In view of Raskob's local prominence in Delaware it is somewhat surprising that his state was not more receptive to Smith, but Delaware wanted no part of Smith.

The Prohibition question was considerably more important in Delaware than any worries over Smith's religious faith. By 1928 it was clear that the Prohibition Amendment and the federal law designed to implement it, the Volstead Act, had been less than successful and that in fact consumption of alcohol had increased among much of the population. The Delaware Bay was one of the more desirable spots along the coast for illegal shipments of contraband whiskey to enter the U.S. because of its sparsely populated bay hamlets and because the geography of the bay enabled the sleek, fast "rum-runners" that off-loaded the booze from ships beyond the three-mile limit to slip into shore unseen.

Another popular area was the Chesapeake Bay side of the Delmarva Peninsula. While it was in some ways superior as an access point because of all the rivers and creeks and hidden harbors, it was farther from the ocean and therefore somewhat more dangerous.

In Delaware some surprisingly prominent citizens were involved in the whiskey business during the 1920s. It was hard even for once-avid prohibitionists to escape the fact that the amendment was not having the intended effect. As a result, John had modified his views to a point *Vanity Fair* magazine would describe two years later as "Demi-Dry," meaning that while he felt the Prohibition Amendment should be preserved, he thought the government's stance needed some changes. He said in speeches and interviews that he favored the Volstead Act in principle. Bayard was keeping rather quiet on the subject, seeking to avoid being harmed politically by Al Smith's belief in repeal of Prohibition.

The 1928 campaign was one of the first in which radio was widely used as a political tool in Delaware. The Republican State Central Committee had regular radio programs every night of the week during October and the first days of November. Different Republican leaders spoke every night. When his turn came John devoted most of his talk to the issues of the national campaign and said very little about Bayard personally. The lack of personal attacks characterized the campaign. The Republicans knew that Bayard was personally popular, though not, they believed, as popular as Townsend. John lived by the credo that personal attacks on one's opponents generally did more harm to one's own campaign than to the subject of the attack, and he ran all of his campaigns that way. Besides, Bayard was already stuck with a national ticket that no Delaware Democrat could have felt comfortable with.

One Townsend speech from the campaign has survived among John's papers. It is interesting not so much for the document itself, which is about what one would expect in a campaign speech in 1928, but for the handwritten notations John added to it. It was evidently written for him by a staff member of the G.O.P. state committee. In the line that read, "Our senior Senator has said there is no prosperity," John crossed out the word "senior" and wrote in "Democratic." Then in the margin he wrote, "The audience might think of Coleman du Pont (if the word "senior" were left to stand). Most of them don't know Bayard exists." He changed another section that read:

> In the continuance of this policy [protective tariffs] of the Republican Party, our women voters have a vital interest, for they are always on the side of industry and prosperity. They may not fully understand the issues that lead up to it, but as the purchasing agents of the American home, they know the necessity of a systematic income . .

to read:

> In the continuance of this policy of the Republican Party, our women voters have a vital interest, for the maintenance of the health and welfare and happiness of family and of community depends upon sound industrial growth and prosperity. As the purchasing agents of the American home, they know the necessity of a systematic income.

Always sensitive to women's rights, he had carefully given women a great deal more credit for intelligence and political judgement than the speechwriter did. In another demonstration of his knack for understanding how his listeners felt about things, Townsend changed another line dealing with Al Smith from this:

> It is not reasonable to suppose that the farmer can expect anything from a New York politician whose birth, environment and training make him the representative of the consumer rather than the producer.

to this:

> It is not reasonable to suppose that the farmer can expect anything vital from the Democratic candidate for President, who by birth, environment and training is wholly a big city product, the representative of the consumer rather than the producer.

And in the margin John had written in parenthesis, "Theodore Roosevelt was a 'New York politician'." John did not particularly like giving formal speeches, but when he did he generally had a very precise idea not only of what he wished to say but of how his remarks would be received.

On November 1, the Wilmington *Every Evening* reported that Townsend had outspent Bayard by nearly two to one–Bayard reported total campaign expenditures of $4,000 while Townsend's anounted to $7,700. Of these totals, Bayard had raised $80 in outside contributions while Townsend financed his own campaign with no outside contributions at all. In the same article it was noted that Representative Robert G. Houston, running for his third term in Congress, had received contributions of $2,000 of which $981 had been expended. Even supposing that a 1928 dollar would be worth ten 1980 dollars, which is overstating the onrush of inflation considerably, Townsend, Bayard, and Houston spent only one-fifth or less of what candidates for the same offices spend today.

Also, none of the candidates had large campaign staffs. While they may have had someone who filled the role of campaign manager, most of the work of the campaign was done by the candidate or by the state party organization.

The bulk of John's $7,700 was spent on newspaper advertising and the printing of small posters that were tacked to walls, trees, and roadside telephone poles throughout the state. Most of the ads were similar to one that appeared in the *Sunday Star*'s issue of October 21. It had a large picture of the candidate and the headline, "To Vote for Townsend is as Important as to Vote for Hoover–No Republican who wishes to Uphold the Hands of a Republican President can do Aught but Vote the Whole Republican Ticket." At the bottom of the page were reprinted speeches by Senator Jesse H. Metcalf, Chairman of the U.S. Republican Senatorial Campaign Committee, extolling John's virtues as a candidate, and by Daniel O. Hastings criticizing Bayard's evasion on the prohibition issue and stressing that both Townsend and Hoover were for Prohibition in principle.

Election Day, 1928, was on Tuesday, Nov. 6. In its November 4 issue, the *Sunday Star* predicted that Hoover would sweep Delaware by 17,000 votes. Since Townsend was running against the most popular candidate on the Democratic ticket he was not expected to do as well, but he was expected to win. It was predicted that Bayard would carry Kent County, the traditional Democratic stronghold, by 500 votes, while Townsend would come out of Wilmington with a plurality of 5,000. He would carry rural New Castle County by 2,300 and Sussex by 1,600. All of this, the *Star* editors believed, would give Townsend an 8,400 vote margin. The Socialist Party and the Worker Party (communist) were also running tickets, but they had no candidates for U.S. senator.

The *Sunday Star* was correct that Hoover would sweep Delaware, but the sweep turned into a Republican landslide– possibly the biggest Republican victory in Delaware history. Hoover beat Smith in Delaware by more than 31,000 votes out of the roughly 96,000 votes cast. In 1924, Coolidge had carried the state by only 19,000 votes. It was so bad for Smith that he was even trounced thoroughly in J.J. Raskob's home election district in Claymont, 813 votes for Hoover to 145 for Smith.

John defeated Bayard by a vote of 63,725 to 40,828, beating him by over 700 votes in Kent, the one county Bayard was expected to carry, and by far larger pluralities in Sussex and New Castle. Buck, Houston . . . the entire Republican ticket was swept into office. The election was, in fact, the high water mark of Republican strength in Delaware. With the coming of the Great Depression in 1929 and 1930, the party never did as well again.

Right in the midst of all the excitement of the campaign John and several of his friends were involved in one of the funniest official functions of his years in public life–the Indian River Inlet Commission. The commission was appointed during the 1928 session of the General Assembly by Governor Robinson for the purpose of devising a method to reopen the Indian River Inlet. At that time the inlet had been closed completely for several years by shifting sandbars. The old Broadkill Inlet north of Lewes and the Chincoteague Inlet at the southern end of Assateague Island, Virginia, were the only links between the ocean and Sussex County's inland bays (the Ocean City, Maryland, inlet was a product of the great 1933 hurricane, while Lewes's Roosevelt Inlet was not constructed until 1937). Indian River Inlet's closing had effectively killed commercial fishing out of Indian River and had thus harmed a reasonably important local industry. The inlet commission was given the woefully inadequate amount of $40,000 with which to bring about a solution to the problem. In addition to John himself, the commission consisted of his close friend William J. P. White of Millsboro and P.D. Lingo of the Long Neck area. R.D. Montgomery was assigned to the commission as its engineer.

After considerable discussion as to how they should proceed, the commissioners and Montgomery finally decided to look into the possibility of dredging and blasting the sand out to form an inlet. Even in 1928, $40,000 would have been only a drop in the bucket toward the cost of getting excavation equipment in to dig the inlet. A Baltimore firm was hired to do some dredging at the ends of the channel, which ate up the whole $40,000. John was able to prevail upon the DuPont Company to donate 2,200 pounds of dynamite and the services of Mr. John S. Koester of the company's technical division, who set about planning the best way to do the job of linking the newly-dredged channel with the ocean.

Koester finally got a large quantity of stovepipe and put it together into 10 and 15 foot sections. These he had buried in two rows, 6 feet apart, for a distance of about 200 feet across the area where the sand had filled in the old inlet (about a quarter of a mile north of the present Indian River Inlet). Forty pounds of dynamite was placed in each section of stovepipe. The blast was originally scheduled for Thursday, November 1, but it had to be cancelled because of high winds that day. It took place instead on Saturday, the third. It could not have failed to occur to the senatorial candidate that such a public and progressive event three days before Election

Day could not hurt his campaign, and Saturday was a better day to have it anyway, because more people could come. As it turned out the blast attracted a crowd of hundreds of people. At the time only the crudest of sand roads led to the inlet from north and south and the crowds came up and down the beach in all manner of conveyances from automobiles to Deerborn wagons. All sorts of dignitaries and local politicians turned out as well. Robert G. Houston and other leading candidates were there.

It was only fitting that John, as chairman of the inlet commission, should throw the switch to set off the explosion. At four o'clock on Saturday afternoon, November 3, 1928, when the tide was just right, he did so. What was almost certainly the grandest explosion in the history of Sussex County thereupon erupted in what one Wilmington paper called "a volcanic blast of sand." The 2,200 pounds of dynamite threw up vast amounts of sand 150 feet in the air on both sides of the intended channel. Almost instantly the impounded waters of the bay began running out into the ocean through the opening. The sand was piled up 16 feet high on either side of the big ditch that had been blown open. Soon the channel was 6 feet deep and 60 feet wide. The explosion was featured in all the papers the next day. It had been a splendid event enjoyed by all who witnessed it. Politically, it was a perfect ending to John's senatorial campaign.

The only problem was that in the end it did not work as planned. The dynamite blew out the sand all right and the channel was reopened for several days. Then it started filling in with sand again and by the end of the winter the explosion might never have occurred. At first everyone was a little embarrassed by the whole incident. A month or so after the blast, the *Sunday Star* carried this somewhat muddled explanation: "the hole made by the blast was so deep that it tapped a well of quicksand under the solid sand surface and this welled up and blocked the passage of the water from flowing out into the ocean as expected."

Eventually John and Will White were able to take it philosophically, so philosophically in fact that they laughed over it for the rest of their lives. After all, the legislature had only given them $40,000 with which to perform a multimillion dollar piece of work and they had done the best they could with the resources they had. The inlet became a priority with John after he entered the Senate and by 1934 the federal government had opened a new inlet some distance south of the old one and made it permanent with bulkheads. And besides, the 2,200 pounds of dynamite made the biggest and best explosion any of them had ever seen.

Part VIII:

The Early Senate Years

21. Freshman Senator

WILMINGTON, Feb. 27 (1929). –On Monday when America elevates to the Presidency a man whose first national renown came during the World War, this historic little State sends to Washington a man who during those same turbulent days was its war Governor.

Herbert Hoover and U.S. Senator-elect John G. Townsend, of Selbyville, have much in common. Both were born on a farm. One is the son of a blacksmith, the other of a mechanic. Neither is a great orator. Both write the important things they want to say, and, as Hoover is known as a 'doer' rather than a talker, so also does John G. Townsend's record of accomplishment speak louder than his utterances.

"The Strawberry King," they call him down Selbyville way, and along the Eastern Shore of Maryland, and he chuckles when he hears it. Even today, as he was about to take a train for Washington to prepare for his senatorial duties, he spent five minutes at a telephone in the Hotel du Pont, arranging to transfer from one storage point to another several thousand bushels of apples.

He is accustomed to being on time. He had an appointment at 10 A. M. Ten minutes later, the person with whom he was to talk not having arrived, the Senator was having him paged. A bell boy led the visitor, who arrived at that instant, to a big man with a curley wealth of hair almost entirely gray. The slight frown he wore could not erase the geniality in his round face.

"You came by train," he chided, his blue eyes atwinkle behind his spectacles. And not another word, then, about the tardiness.

"Did you know my son, Preston C., was elected president of the freshman class this year in Delaware College?" he asked. And then, calling to a rugged young man who sat not far away, he said: "This is Paul, another son. Paul is going to be my Secretary in the Senate."

A farmer himself, he feels deeply the need for farm relief and hopes, he said, that this subject will be one of the first to engross the new senate and President Hoover.

Governor Townsend never sought an office. He was on vacation when he won the Republican nomination for the Senate. So it was with all his earlier offices.

"Strange," he said, "I never really had any ambition to hold public office."

(Philadelphia *Bulletin*)

When John arrived in Washington on the afternoon of Wednesday, February 27, he and his small entourage of family members established themselves at the old Willard Hotel, still one of the city's leading hostelries. He was accompanied by Lyla, who would be his hostess in Washington, and by Paul, who as secretary would at least theoretically manage the small office staff. This job was really a combination of administrative assistant and chief political operative. Not only was Paul not expected to sit around taking dictation from his father, but he was not even expected to spend all his time at his new duties. He would still, in the customary Townsend fashion, attend to numerous other responsibilities, including the road-building company.* He was also expected to be

---

* *When Paul moved to Washington in 1929 to serve as his father's U.S. Senate secretary he also found the time to get into road work there. Through the early 1930s, Paul's company put modern hard surfaces on many famed Washington roadways including Bladensburg Road and New York Avenue. After going to Washington, Paul also got heavily involved in District of Columbia real estate. This led to an interest in the construction of housing in the district. Thus, the family highway construction company expanded from road-building into the construction of some of Washington's earliest high-rise apartment buildings.*

his father's liaison with Delaware during the periods when John was in Washington.

John had also prevailed upon Mrs. Louise Johnson, widow of his old friend, Everett Johnson, to become a member of his staff. At that time her secretarial skills were still minimal. She enrolled in night school after her arrival in Washington to learn typing and shorthand. Despite this lack of office experience she did have several qualities the Senator found invaluable, most important of which were her

U. S. Senator John G. Townsend, Jr.
as he appeared shortly after
taking office in 1929
(Lyla T. Savoy collection).

considerable intelligence and her absolute trustworthiness. She was a reasonably accomplished writer. As such she could and did compose many of his letters and speeches for him. She also had a wide circle of acquaintances in Delaware and was able to shepherd constituents in need of help around the federal bureaucracy.

In 1929, the president-elect was still inaugurated in March and new senators were sworn in at the same time. This custom, which was to change in 1937, had been the practice since the dawn of the Republic. Less than a month after John defeated Senator Bayard in November, Delaware's other U.S. senator, T. Coleman du Pont, was at last forced to resign from the U.S. Senate because of his worsening illness. Later in December, Governor Robinson appointed Judge Daniel

O. Hastings to serve the two years remaining in du Pont's term. This sequence of events meant that at the moment Senator Bayard's term officially ended and John was sworn in as U.S. senator he became Delaware's junior senator and Hastings its senior senator.

Louise Johnson arrived in Washington several days before Inauguration Day, March 4, and moved into a small residential hotel for women. She remembered that the big day was dreary and cold. She went down to see the ceremonies and inaugural parade outfitted with her heaviest coat, a woolen blanket, and a stack of old newspapers that she used to line her coat as extra insulation. Later in the evening, she recalled in her memoirs:

> Senator Townsend called at the hotel to ask me to meet him at his office the next day to greet the others who would be on his staff. He told me that he had seen Senator Bayard. As was often Senator Townsend's custom, he had asked Senator Bayard whether there wasn't something he could do for him. Senator Bayard said quickly, "Yes, you may. There is a Georgetown girl here, Olive Hurley, who needs a job. I hope you will take care of her."
>
> Of course, usually a new Senator brought a staff from his own party and State, and Senator Bayard knew that, but Senator Townsend knew Olive and she was placed an his staff. She was an efficient worker and a loyal one.

Once again John had displayed his talent for picking his people well. Both Olive Hurley aud Louise Johnson remained with him throughout his twelve years in the Senate, and both proved themselves "loyal and efficient." Olive had the further advantage of already being well-versed in the ways of Washington, having worked on Senator Bayard's staff. She was able to teach the others much in those first months in Washington about how a senatorial staff functioned.

The new senator's "suite of offices" in the Old Senate Office Building consisted of exactly two rooms. John shared the smaller but fancier of the two with Paul–fancier because it had a fireplace with a large, ornate mantelpiece. It was furnished with two desks, several chairs, and a very large, comfortable sofa. Olive and Louise shared the other room, which had two desks, chairs, and a large table. The office's appointments also included several filing cabinets, one or two closets, and little else.

The only other member of the staff was not really a staffer in the fullest sense of the word. This was a young man hired under what was known as "the senator's patronage" to perform any of a variety of jobs from elevator operator in the Senate office building to security guard. The person was also expected to help out when needed around the senator's office on an irregular basis. This job generally went to a young man attending college or law school at night in Washington while working during the day to pay college expenses. The first of a series of young Delawareans to hold the position was Wolcott Gum of Frankford. Others during Senator Townsend's years in Washington were Armel Long of Sussex and a young Kent Countian, J. Caleb Boggs of Cheswold.

As the new office became operational, Louise Johnson began to learn John's style. She had already known the man behind the "Strawberry King" image for many years, but now she came to know him in a new way. She found him a decent, no-nonsense boss:

> Senator Townsend never called us clerks, which was the way we were rated in the Disbursing Office where we were paid twice a month; he always introduced us as his secretaries. Salaries for Senators were then $10,000 or $10,500, as I remember. In our office the Secretary

[Paul] was paid $4,250; I received $2,400; Olive, $2,250; Wolcott, $1,800.

Senator Townsend was an early riser–five o'clock in Delaware, perhaps six in Washington. During his second term he lived at the Shoreham Hotel, where he had become well acquainted and fond of the two Senators from Virginia, Carter Glass and Byrd. He was always welcome at their breakfast table, if he could wait that long, but he was a very active man and would usually walk the four miles to the Capitol and had breakfast in one of their dining rooms. He would always find a buddy there.

By the time I reached our office at eight o'clock he would already have opened all his mail and left the part I could answer on my desk. I never received dictation from him. He would stop at my desk long enough to give me the gist of an answer to one person, or he might say, "You know how I feel about this letter."

At other times Senator Townsend would write a few words, never more than a sentence or two, on the bottom of a letter he'd received summarizing what he wanted the reply to express and one or the other of the secretaries would draft a letter for his signature.

When he went there in 1929, the U.S. Senate was still highly traditional and based on a code of courtly behavior that had descended little diluted from the days of the Founding Fathers. Numerous elderly senators had first entered public life in the administrations of Cleveland, Harrison, or McKinley. Old Oliver Wendell Holmes Jr, who had served as a Union captain in the Civil War, still presided as the liberal conscience of the U.S. Supreme Court across the way. The average United States senator of 1929 was older and had less formal education than his counterpart of half a century later. He often had a broader experience of life. He was less beholden to "special interests" since in all likelihood he had financed his own campaign (without having had to go into debt to do it). He was much less interested in how his public personality was perceived by "the media" (a term that had yet to be devised). He tended more toward the small-town banker-lawyer-father figure in appearance, with wire-rimmed spectacles or *pince nez*, formal vested suits, pocket watch, high-laced shoes, and, in summer, white linen suits and Panama hats. He was much more likely to smoke or chew (every senator still received his brass cuspidor as one of the "perks" of office; another was a steamer trunk). Few senators of the day bore much resemblance to Hollywood movie stars. None worried about how they sounded on the radio, which was in its infancy as a medium of political reportage. Television had been invented in a laboratory the year before but almost no one had heard of it.

While there were a goodly number of prima donnas and grandstanders among the senators, there were probably fewer then than today, in the age of the television sound bite. In 1929, party allegiance was a factor of much greater importance than it has since become. While rugged individualists such as Senator George Norris, the old Republican populist of Nebraska, were respected, party allegiance on important issues was also highly valued. Nor were senators as likely to seek the presidency. The only U.S. senator in nearly two generations to have been elected president was Warren G. Harding in 1920, and one hardly wished to follow in his footsteps. Service in the Senate was not perceived as a logical steppingstone in one's quest for the presidency; it was an end in itself. Those who had arrived there felt as free as they ever would in their political careers to stand up for their own principles. Few felt any compelling need to go racing off after every will'o-the-wisp of public opinion. The Senate, in those years just before the Great Depression, was still largely in the possession of classic American conservatives. Senator Townsend tended to stand with this group. For all his Progressive accomplishments in Delaware, he was still very much a conservative both fiscally and in matters of diplomacy. Nor, despite his efforts as governor to bring about modern public school and highway systems, was he in any way a believer in big government. Senator Townsend found certain practices in the Senate very much to his liking. Louise Johnson remembered:

> [He] was happy to learn that one of the traditional courtesies observed by new senators was to call on those already in office. That was just what he would like to do and, while doing that, he would manage to greet each Senator's staff. He was soon good friends with the men who ran the electric subway car that took us from the basement of the Senate Office Building to the Capitol. He would know about their families, too. It was natural to him. He was just interested in the people around him.
>
> Senator Townsend had one quality which I always noticed: he did not talk much, almost never, about himself or his family, but he was a natural good listener. If anyone were talking to him, he was more apt to show interest by asking questions than to make suggestions. That attitude gave the other person the feeling that he was being understood and appreciated. He was welcome in any group and learned as he listened.
>
> Writing this brings to mind another attribute of the man. He was silent when in trouble; no talking it over. In fact, although he was proud of his children, he never boasted of them or of anything they did, but his face would glow when they were spoken of approvingly.

For a freshman senator from a small state, Senator Townsend did surprisingly well on committee assignments. A possible explanation for this is the eagerness and geniality with which he went about making himself known to everyone else, no matter how insignificant, in any way connected to the U.S. Senate. Whatever the reason, he was assigned to the Agriculture, Appropriations, Banking and Currency, Claims, and Audit and Control Committees. Most subcommittees did not become a regular feature of Senate life until several years later. It was necessary, therefore, for each senator to be relatively well versed in the entire business of every committee to which he was assigned.

The Agriculture Committee was, of course, a natural assignment for one of John's interests and background. It was here that he made his first real mark in the Senate and he felt very comfortable on that committee throughout his years in Washington. Appropriations was an important assignment for a new man. It had the advantage of providing him with an overview of the workings of the entire federal government that it would have been difficult to have gotten any other way.

According to Louise Johnson, Townsend was the only member of the Claims Committee without a law degree. This committee's work consisted of appraising the claims of citizens and companies against the federal government:

> There was an able Secretary in the Claims Committee office at all times who had been there for years. He collected material so that he could answer questions from the members while they were in session. While we were there those subjects ranged from a claim for the destruction of an island the claimant had owned down to a smaller one made by a veteran who had received a recurrent injury in his forehead from following a direction to use some instruments in the Veterans' Hospital . . .
>
> The work on the Claims Committee required research and condensing the material read. I learned that work when I was asked by Senator Townsend to check on the case of the veteran with the sore on his forehead. The Library of Congress finally found a medical book for us that contained a description of such an accident. The man in question received a good sum for what he had been made to suffer. These claims went to the President for approval and our office had only one of our reports vetoed, and that during President Roosevelt's second term.

For several years during the Hoover Administration Senator Townsend chaired the Audit and Control subcommittee. He later served as a member of it when the Democrats were in control of the Senate. This was, by all measures, one of the more unenviable jobs in the place since it involved ruling on the legitimacy of expenses incurred by senators in the course of travels on fact-finding tours. It was a delicate task but one that John managed with considerable skill. The fact that he did not try to use this job as a springboard to power served to further endear him to his colleagues.

By far the most important of his committee assignments, however, was Banking and Currency. At the outset of his Senate career neither he nor anyone else in America realized just how crucial the work of this committee would become in the next few years. A ranking Democrat on the committee was the venerable Carter Glass of Virginia. He had served in Congress almost steadily since the turn of the century except for somewhat more than a year's service as secretary of the treasury at the end of the Wilson administration. He had also been the architect of the Federal Reserve System. Though the committee had a Republican chairman until 1933, Glass was its dominant member.* He and John quickly became the best of friends. Glass was an old Virginia aristocrat whose sister was president of Sweet Briar College. He had a deep appreciation for men with simple values and strong integrity. Though he was known for his irascable nature and his outspoken Southern

---

* *A story indicative of Senator Glass's power during this period is one told by a man who was travelling south from Washington on a passenger train. A short distance from Richmond, the train stopped and began backing up onto a siding. It continued moving in reverse for several miles. The man asked the conductor what was going on. He was told that Senator Glass's private car was attached to the rear of the train. He had his own siding built from the main line to his Virginia estate, where there was a small, private station. When he and his railroad car had been safely deposited at his home, the train continued on its way.*

Democrat partisanship, he and the banker-farmer-businessman from Sussex County, Delaware, hit it off from the start. Townsend quickly became valuable, not only to the committee but to the Senate as a whole, in the area of banking legislation because he was the only member who was actually a small-town banker. He was able to present a point of view entirely apart from the great apparatus of Wall Street, of J.P. Morgan and Company, the Chase Manhattan Bank, and all the rest. John also built a warm friendship with another member of the Banking and Currency Committee, Frederic C. Walcott of Connecticut, also a freshman Republican. Before the end of John's first term these three friends were to produce, working quietly and behind the scenes, some of the mechanisms claimed first by Hoover and later by Roosevelt that helped to pull American banking through the tragedy of the Great Depression.

John set about the task of learning his new duties as a senator with much the same style he had used in his other enterprises: long hours, attention to detail, careful listening, many thoughtful questions, and no nonsense. Almost from the outset Townsend became a favorite with the press because of his picturesque "strawberry kingship," his humble beginnings, his friendliness, and his sense of humor. He thus became increasingly a fixture of newspaper pages during the 1930s showing how he could peel an apple in one motion, demonstrating that he could still handle a telegraph key, having his handwriting analyzed for an article on senatorial penmanship, and so on. All of this tended to obscure the fact that he worked very hard at his job.

He prided himself on his record of attendance during Senate sessions when many of his more famous colleagues showed up on the floor only for important votes or newsworthy sessions. He could often attend only part of a committee session since several different committees on which he served met at the same time. Much of the work of the Senate is of a routine dullness. Washington has always had an ample supply of senators who choose to concern themselves primarily with furthering higher political aspirations, travelling around the country on speaking engagements, junketeering to foreign cities, or socializing with high-ranking constituents–doing anything to keep from having to sit through what they see as tedium, the endless hours of humdrum Senate business. This was what staffs were for. Their own time was more valuable. The senators whose names are household words are often among this group, though not always.

Those senators who take a different view of their duties, who take the trouble to keep themselves informed on all the business of the Senate, who sit through the boring sessions, who take the time to learn the ropes and to master the sometimes arcane rules, generally wield the real power. If they become famous at all it is as committee chairmen, as whips, caucus leaders, and the like. It is these men who make up the backbone of the Senate. The division between Republican and Democrat, like that between liberal and conservative, has much to do with the formation of friendships and alliances. Yet this division between the workers and the "glamour boys" is probably more important to that process. John was soon pegged as being a worker and this eased his entry into the Senate's inner circle.

His first opportunity for major achievement came nearly a year after his arrival in Washington. It came, appropriately, in the area of agriculture and grew directly out of his background as a cultivator of fruits and berries. He had long been friendly with Orlando Harrison of Harrison's Nurseries in Berlin. A younger Selbyville friend, Clayton Bunting, was also a nurseryman. He specialized in the sale of strawberry and other fruit plants through the mail, and his firm was becoming one of the nation's largest in this specialty area. Senator Townsend was thus in an excellent position to realize the need for what became known as his "Plant Patent Act." Until its passage by Congress in May of 1930, those who developed new plant varieties had no way of controlling or profiting from the use of their invention. They could, and frequently did, sell a small number of a new variety at very high prices, but beyond that first round of sales they had no control whatsoever. If the new variety proved to be an improvement, a buyer was perfectly free to reproduce the inventor's plant and begin selling it himself.

The drawbacks of this situation received some publicity shortly before passage of the Plant Patent Act when the famed botanist Luther Burbank died. Burbank left his widow in very modest circumstances. It was widely known that his work in the development of new plant varieties had revolutionized the cultivation of such crops as peanuts and citrus fruits. Yet Burbank received none of the immense profits his inventions had generated for growers across the country. At the same time inventors of more tangible items were growing rich. The preeminent example was Thomas Alva Edison, who now in his old age was worth millions of dollars as the well-deserved result of his work. Mrs. Burbank told the press that her husband had never wanted to get rich off his plant varieties, but still the slight rankled many, Edison included.

Patenting new plant varieties was a complicated undertaking. In the first place, it was no mean feat to prove that a plant was a new variety and not simply a minor variation on an existing strain. In instances where color was a factor, it was necessary for applicants to submit detailed paintings of their inventions since color photography was not yet reliable enough. The new bill, which was signed into law by President Hoover on May 23, 1930, directed the Department of

Agriculture to assist the Patent Office by making the determination as to what was and what was not a new plant variety.

The support for Townsend's bill was immediate and widespread. Among the numerous letters of support and thanks he received from around the country was one from Thomas Edison himself. The first plant patented under the Plant Patent Act was a type of climbing rose called the "New Dawn" Rose by its inventor, a New Jersey nurseryman named Henry F. Rosenberg. Rosenberg, according to one news account, chose the name "New Dawn" to symbolize a "new era in rose propagation."

Only seven plants were patented during the first two years the Plant Patent Act was in effect, though many more were being assessed by the Patent Office. Among them was a new variety of peach tree that yielded only large peaches. The nineteenth patent was issued in 1933 to Harold Ickes, Roosevelt's new interior secretary. In the seventy years since the law was enacted, thousands of other plant varieties have been patented. The process is now a standard part of Patent Office responsibility, but in 1930 some officials of the office were certain it would never work. It is a bit ironic that while Senator Townsend was concerned with many matters of far greater immediate importance during his twelve years in the Senate, his Plant Patent Act is one of his few Senate accomplishments still of vital importance in daily life.

22. The Crash

Eight months after John entered the U.S. Senate, the three-year-old speculative frenzy gripping Wall Street, which had propelled stock prices higher and higher, far beyond true values, came to a sudden, sickeningly abrupt end. Historian Samuel Eliot Morrison summed up the popular view of the bull market of the late 1920s as "the greatest orgy of speculation and over-optimism since the South Sea Bubble of 1720." Some observers had been expecting it for years. On September 5, 1929, Boston economist Roger W. Babson wrote, "There is a crash coming and it may be a terrific one." Babson predicted a decline of as much as sixty to eighty points in the Dow-Jones Index but most people greeted his fears with derision. The young "lone wolf" financier Joseph P. Kennedy had concluded by late 1928 that the boom could not last much longer. He had quietly withdrawn from the market, liquidating his holdings and waiting for the downward adjustment he was certain was coming.

When the crash finally did arrive on Thursday, October 24, 1929, many refused to believe it, even as speculators hastened to sell amidst a growing panic. The initial slump lasted only a few weeks; then, for a short time, the market paused and seemed to regain its equilibrium. Such august and respected figures as John D. Rockefeller Sr. and J.P. Morgan were quoted widely with optimistic comments like "business is fundamentally sound." But a slow, steadily downward slide commenced leading America inexorably into the Great Depression.

President Hoover was not surprised. He had been fearful of just such a disaster as early as 1926 when, as Coolidge's secretary of commerce, he had decried the "fever of speculation" sweeping the country. At the time Hoover had found himself a voice in the wilderness. Thereafter he found it expedient to refrain from public pronouncements of his views, to go along with the unbounded (though dour) optimism of President Coolidge and his staunchly traditional treasury secretary, Andrew Mellon. In light of Hoover's early fears and warnings and his true concern for those who were hurt by the Great Depression, it is all the more tragic that many Americans blamed him for it.

In examining the period from a remove of seventy years, it is tempting to conclude that if Hoover had taken decisive action in response to the dire events of 1929 and 1930, it might just have been possible for him to save the nation from the worst ravages of the disaster that ensued, presuming, of course, that he could have gotten Congress to go along with him. Matters were not so clear at the time. Hoover and the Congress did apply the most widely accepted methods of dealing with such periodic economic slumps. These steps were based on past experience, but the severity of the present crisis was unprecedented. As measures were tried and failed, new ones were tried in their turn. It is quite likely that, had Franklin D. Roosevelt been president in 1929, his initial remedies would have been no more successful than those used by Hoover. Roosevelt had the luxury of applying radical new approaches after he took office in 1933, only because the accepted wisdom already had been applied and found lacking. Even then it took the onslaught of World War II in 1939 and 1940, with its enormous demand for manpower and manufactured goods, to bring on the full economic recovery for which F.D.R. and the Democrats had long since taken credit.

For John, the depression began early and in a very personal way when he received an unexpected visit to his Washington office from his fellow townsman Edward Baker, cashier of the Selbyville National Bank (and later state treasurer). The National Bank, known in the early days as "the McCabe Bank," had been the Baltimore Trust Company's main competitor since Baltimore Trust opened its doors in 1903. The two institutions had sat cater-cornered across the town's main intersection for more than twenty-five years. Now, the Senator learned from his visitor, the National Bank was in serious trouble. As Senator Townsend recalled the incident in later years:

> He asked me if I wanted to take over that bank. He said that someone was going to have to do it . . . I went home and got together with the bankers of the county and returned to Washington to talk it over with Herbert Hoover.

As an active member of the Banking and Currency Committee, John had had an opportunity to deepen his slight acquaintance with Hoover, whom he had met some ten years earlier. He had already been a dinner guest at the White House several times since his arrival in Washington, and the two men had become friendly. Thus developed the situation in which a small-town banker from southern Delaware, faced with the need to make a difficult decision, could obtain the most exclusive advice in the nation.

> There was then a number of weak banks over the country. He [Hoover] said he thought it would be a tragic thing to let a bank in our midst close, that it could not help but hurt the other banks. We looked over the securities held by the National Bank and talked them over with men from other banks in the county. It seemed we would lose

about $40,000. They agreed to help and all did except one. I agreed to put in $15,000 for myself and the same for our bank. I told Ed Baker I would take his bank over and we did so. One night soon thereafter we moved over. [We] employed their own help. No depositor of that bank lost, but the other banks and I lost as did the Baltimore Trust Company. We sold the almost worthless securities and absorbed the losses.

Bank failures were not anything new. More than 400 banks failed in the United States in 1929, before the crash. A similar number had failed every year through the 1920s. Many more came close to the edge but were somehow saved in time. The depression caused many more banks than normal to be overcome by a combination of poor management, bad loans, and investment in speculative securities. Between 1930 and 1933, there were more than 5,000 bank failures across the nation. Nor, during these early years of the depression, were there any government mechanisms to assist struggling financial institutions, like the Reconstruction Finance Corporation, begun by Hoover in 1931, and the Federal Deposit Insurance Corporation, established by the Roosevelt administration several years later. In 1929 coping with economic hardships was still a private endeavor. The leaders of the industry had begun their careers in the days when a J.P. Morgan could step in singlehandedly and avert a financial panic by a few well-timed steps to use private funds to shore up a sagging market.

The near failure of the Selbyville National Bank was typical of the problems faced by small-town banks. It was apparently caused when some of the bank's largest customers, facing major losses in stock and property values, defaulted on their loans. The bank, reeling from its own investment in shaky securities, did not have the necessary reserves to absorb the loss. It was only later, during the New Deal, that Senator Carter Glass succeeded in getting legislation through Congress severely restricting the ability of banks to invest in the securities market. Edward Baker showed unusual ability in minimizing the Selbyville National Bank's losses. Most bankers facing similar situations held on too long, hoping for a recovery. Their inability to take a realistic view of the situation until it was too late was a major factor in the thousands of bank failures. Baker had saved the deposits of his customers by admitting the worst and doing what had to be done, though it must have been painful to place the fate of his institution in the hands of his old-time rival. It is almost certain that if the situation had occurred even six months later, nothing could have saved the bank's depositors from substantial losses.

As it turned out, Delaware weathered the Great Depression without a single bank failure, the only state to do so. Most of the state's smaller banks had been exceedingly conservative in their practices, even during the booming pre-1929 economy. Many individual Delaware investors were not so lucky and were wiped out by the crash and its aftermath. Most of these were in New Castle County. In southern Delaware most people of wealth tended to have their capital invested in more tangible things like land, manufacturing facilities, and machinery, all tied to the agricultural economy of the area. If they did have investments in securities, it was generally money they could afford to lose. This was especially true of John Townsend, who lost little in the depression beyond the $15,000 he put into saving the Selbyville National Bank.

Even though Senator Townsend's own financial problems were minimal, as a Republican in Congress he had more than enough to worry about. He and his fellow members of the Banking and Currency

Committee were among the most active of all senators in working to find some answer to the growing number of bank failures. The effects of the stock market crash were heightened by a slowdown in business activity that had already begun six months earlier. A serious weakness of the economy in 1929 and 1930 was that most recent business expansion was the result of the production of high-priced consumer goods. This business quickly succumbed to the cash shortage among higher-income consumers after the stock market crash. As sales of homes, automobiles, large appliances, and luxury items declined, unemployment multiplied. Bank deposits declined, creating severe liquidity problems.

The complex problems besetting the American economy were further intensified by an existing slump in the agricultural economy in the American West and by a worldwide economic downturn, with falling commodities prices, increasing unemployment and a growing likelihood of default on the massive war debts that most European nations still owed to the United States. Many countries, including the United States, sought to insulate their own economies by raising tariffs on imports and instituting other protectionist measures. These steps only hindered world trade further and worsened the crisis. Though few were prepared to admit it, even in 1930 the world economy was largely interdependent and no major economic power could take unilateral steps without affecting the whole. The United States, still feeling its way as a world power, had been among the most protectionist nations for decades. The Great Depression showed the pitfalls of this policy, that had already had the effect of weakening the nation's economic underpinnings, thus helping to turn what might have been merely another periodic slump into the greatest economic crash in American history.

President Hoover took such measures to aid the economy as speeding up public works projects that had already been scheduled and halting foreign immigration to slow the growth of unemployment. He offered government assistance in coordinating various relief efforts, but he still insisted that those efforts be funded from private sources. One national campaign in the winter of 1929 and 1930 to raise private contributions for this effort netted a paltry $15 million, much to Hoover's consternation. As meagre as these steps now seem, they represented what most felt was a reasonable attempt to deal with the situation. As evidence of this fact, the Republican incumbents running in the off-year election of 1930 did quite well, managing to retain narrow control in both houses of Congress. In Delaware, Senator Daniel O. Hastings was elected to a full term in his own right and Congressman Robert G. Houston was reelected handily. The political fallout still lay in the future.

Members of the House and Senate knew just how bad things were becoming. The problem was that they could not agree among themselves how best to deal with the economy. Many Democrats and farm-bloc Westerners favored an increased public works program to provide jobs for the unemployed funded by heavier income taxes on the wealthy. Yet nearly everyone, Democrats, Republicans, and President Hoover alike, still saw a balanced federal budget as a necessary prerequisite to any recovery.

Many Republican conservatives thought that the government should do as little as possible. They believed that the economy should be left alone to sort itself out. This view was typified by Secretary Mellon who stated, "People will work harder, live a more moral life. Values will be adjusted, and enterprising people will pick up the wrecks from less competent people." Others of Mellon's class, who were themselves hardly conscious of the depression, expressed the hope that the disaster would kill off the unions and return the nation to the lost days of yore when a dollar a day was a reasonable wage for a working man. Hoover certainly did not see things Mellon's way, but he still opposed direct government intervention into the economy. As Samuel Eliot Morrison wrote:

> President Hoover did his best according to his lights, and he had a warm heart which responded to the suffering. But he was restrained from taking any bold, imaginative steps by wrong estimates of the situation and by his laissez-faire philosophy, which taught him that nature would cure all, whilst government intervention might ruin all. At his elbow was Andrew Mellon . . . whose one idea was to keep hands off and let the slump liquidate itself.

Nearly everything in Senator Townsend's experience led him to a position similar to Hoover's, a fact that brought the two men closer together through 1930 and 1931. Not only was John a free-enterprise capitalist, but he came from a state where in fact the private sector had done a remarkably fine job of public assistance over the years. Nor were the efforts of the du Ponts and others just a thing of the past. In 1929, Alfred I. du Pont instituted his own pension fund for needy older Delawareans, mailing out well over 1,000 monthly checks by 1930. With this kind of private effort going on at home it is hardly surprising that John agreed with Hoover's view that the private sector was the proper source of relief funds. He did feel that it was acceptable for government to operate the programs financed with those private moneys. The entire history of modern social services in Delaware had been based on that principle.

Most men of Hoover's and Townsend's age had come to

maturity during the depression of 1893-1897 that, in terms of the human misery it caused, was arguably as bad or worse than the Great Depression. During the 1893 "panic" it had been left entirely to private charitable groups to deal with the social problems resulting from the economic ones. In this sense, Hoover's willingness for government to coordinate the private effort, much the same sort of role performed by his famed Belgian Relief during World War I, was a distinct step forward. In the eyes of many struggling Americans of the 1930s, however, it was not a big enough step.

By 1931, the very mention of Hoover's name at many public gatherings was enough to bring forth a chorus of hisses. Derogatory rumors about his early business career popped up and circulated around the country. Hundreds and thousands of unemployed men congregated on the edges of U.S. cities in impromptu communities of rude shanties and huts made of bits of scrap metal, cardboard, and lumber. These quickly came to be known as "Hoovervilles." An empty pocket pulled inside out was called a "Hoover Flag." Through it all Hoover worked diligently to bring relief to the nation. Several of his initiatives, such as the Reconstruction Finance Corporation, did prove effective and were later picked up the Roosevelt administration and absorbed into the New Deal.

In August 1931, Hoover invited Senator Townsend and his daughter, Lyla, to spend a weekend at Rapidan, his camp in Virginia's Blue Ridge Mountains in an area that later became part of Shenandoah National Park. It was the first of several such weekends the Senator spent there. For the gentlemen in the party it was to be largely a work weekend devoted to formulating a plan for a national unemployment relief program. Among those in attendance were Agriculture Secretary Arthur M. Hyde of Missouri and Representative Will R. Wood of Indiana, chairman of the House Appropriations Committee. Also present was Walter S. Gifford of New York, president of the American Telephone and Telegraph Co., whom Hoover had chosen to head the new relief effort. The guests also included two publishers of major daily newspapers in the northeast and members of the presidential staff. The trip was memorable in other ways as well. According to a *Washington Star* account of the weekend:

> The Presidential party rode in the rain all the way to the camp. For a short way out of Washington it was merely a disagreeable drizzle, then it turned into a driving downpour, continuing thus until evening. So severe was the rain that the President had to abandon his usual route to the camp, which leads over about twenty miles of country dirt road, and go a longer way over hard-surfaced highways.
>
> Ditches on each side of the highway ran red with muddy water and streams were swollen to capacity . . . The President early in the summer summoned department heads to plan economies in the Federal establishment in a general plan for retrenchment during the times of Great Depression . . .
>
> Significant of the President's movement toward a relief plan . . . was a message given out at the camp as having been received from Governor Rolph of California. The message struck the keynote of the Hoover program in that Governor Rolph pledged his State "to care for its own unemployed," thereby acknowledging local responsibility for relief, which President Hoover has said from the start must follow if any plan is to succeed.

In this informal setting Hoover could relax and be a genial host. He was a fanatic fly fisherman and had carefully chosen the location of his mountain camp for the trout stream that ran past it. In the atmosphere of rustic buildings, hunting dogs, forest walks, and fishing, Hoover could escape for a few moments from the nearly constant stress of his office. It was difficult for the president to charm people in large public gatherings in the way that Roosevelt was later so skilled at doing. Such weekends were one way of maintaining friendly contacts with congressional leaders and others upon whom he depended.

A much more typical experience was Senator Townsend's presence several months later at a major White House conference called by Hoover to publicize his latest recovery plan. In attendance were more than thirty leaders of both houses of Congress and both major parties, Secretary Mellon, and various other luminaries. Hoover's remarks are a good reflection of his belief that both the world situation and the public psychology were of crucial importance to the nation's economy:

> The prolongation of the Great Depression by the succession of events in Europe, affecting as they have both commodity and security prices, has produced in some localities in the United States an apprehension wholly unjustified in view of the thousand-fold resources we have for meeting any demand. Foolish alarm in these sections has been accompanied by wholly unjustifiable withdrawal of currency from the banks.
> Such action results in limiting the ability of the banks in these localities to extend credit to businessmen and farmers for the normal conduct of business, but beyond this to be prepared to meet the possibility of unreasoning demands of depositors the banks are compelled to place their assets in liquid form by sales of securities and restriction of credit so as to enable them to meet unnecessary and unjustifiable drains . . .

All of this was true enough. The problem was that such views were almost incomprehensible to the average man. Roosevelt could sum up the same complex sentiments in a few well-chosen words: "Let me assert my firm belief that the only thing we have to fear is fear itself–nameless, unreasoning, unjustified terror . . ."

Though Townsend continued until the end to support Hoover, he was politician enough to know that the president was losing the battle. Early in February 1932, a full nine months before the election, California Senator Hiram Johnson, a Republican Progressive, said, "There is not a single soul thus far I've met, stand-pat, Progressive or otherwise, who believes Hoover can be elected." For all Hoover's brilliance, for all his extensive knowledge of economic theory, for all his concern for the common man, he could not find an effective strategy to deal with the depression. He was not a politician and he found the necessity to deal with those who were extremely difficult. Most close observers thought the problem was Hoover's air of defeatism, his complete pessimism as the economy worsened. While certainly understandable enough, this view proved fatal to his acceptance by the people. The impression he conveyed to many was aptly put by the sculptor Gutzon Borglum, who said, "if you put a rose in Hoover's hand it would wilt."

Easily the worst public relations blunder of Hoover's presidency (and one of the worst of any American administration) was his harsh treatment of the former American Expeditionary Force soldiers known as "The Bonus Army." This group consisted of hundreds of veterans from around the country who had fallen on hard times. Out-of-work, down-at-the-heels, homeless, and broke, these men descended on Washington in the spring and summer of 1932 to plead for a speed-up of the veterans' bonuses that Congress had promised to pay World

War I veterans in the year 1945. Calling themselves the "Bonus Army," they established a shantytown on the Anacostia Flats just outside the city, eventually spilling over into several unused government buildings on the further reaches of Pennsylvania Avenue. Congress ultimately rejected their petition, but many veterans with nothing and nowhere to go stayed on in Washington, more hopeless and desperate than before. The Bonus Army was too dispirited to be dangerous and city authorities were coping with them successfully by using a kind and understanding approach. Many Congressmen went down to the flats to visit the men and talk over their problems–there is one newspaper photograph in the Townsend family scrapbooks of John, Senator Walcott, and a reporter on one such jaunt. As the "Army" stayed on and on through the summer, Hoover seemed to lose his sense of proportion. He allowed himself to be talked into believing that the veterans represented the imminent danger of a Communist revolt. He ordered the White House placed under military guard and the streets around it cleared, thereby heightening the public perception of him as being increasingly isolated, under seige by the unkempt masses. Next, Hoover called out the military under the command of Army Chief of Staff Douglas MacArthur. Ably assisted by his efficient aide, Major Dwight D. Eisenhower, MacArthur carried out his assignment with a thoroughness most Americans found repugnant, using drawn sabers, tanks, and armed soldiers to force the unarmed veterans from their pathetic abodes.

In spite of President Hoover's troubled administration, some of his policies were having a positive impact on the economy in late 1931 and 1932. Following one conference Senator Townsend attended at the White House in the fall of 1931, the president unveiled a set of initiatives designed to shore up sagging banks and to strengthen the European economy, the problems of which were making the American depression much worse. The most important result of this package of legislation was the Reconstruction Finance Corporation, signed into law by the president in January 1932. The RFC lent money to banks, railroads, industry, agricultural agencies, and commercial enterprises. This kept many banks from failing as the depression bottomed out in the winter of 1932-1933, and helped to slow the overall decline, but it did little to start the country on the road to recovery.

Even so, other Hoover measures seemed to be having that effect during the summer of 1932 when, for a brief time, the stock market appeared to be rebounding and employment picked up slightly. The hoped-for recovery was fleeting. By the early winter of 1933, after Hoover's defeat in the November elections but before the new Roosevelt administration took office in March, the country was in a state of deep economic crisis once more. Nearly three-quarters of all banks across the country were closed by executive order of state governors who were fearful of mass runs by frantic depositors hoping to withdraw their funds. Had this been allowed to occur, it would have led to the almost complete collapse of the nation's banks. In later years Hoover claimed that the economy had begun its comeback in the summer of 1932 and that the 1933 crisis was caused by public uncertainty over what Roosevelt would do. One cannot conclusively prove or disprove this allegation, but it appears highly dubious. Would Hoover's programs eventually have restored the economy to health? Who knows? John thought that they would, but many of his friends, including Pierre du Pont and his brothers, held the opposite view.

23 - Taking On Wall Street

Perhaps the most interesting experience of Senator Townsend's service during the depression was his service as a member of what came to be known as "the Pecora Committee." This investigative body was created as a subcommittee of the Banking and Currency Committee in the spring of 1932, prompted by the widespread belief that the depression had been caused by the excesses of "Big Business" in general and by unethical and illegal stock manipulations by Wall Street financiers in particular. The investigation was formally requested by Senator Frederic Walcott, one of John's best friends in the Senate and a frequent Hoover administration spokesman. This was a sign that President Hoover, himself a believer in the prevailing low view of Wall Street, wanted to get to the bottom of the mess. No doubt he also wished to deflect some of the public rage against himself as the 1932 campaign commenced. South Dakota Senator Peter Norbeck, then chairman of the Banking and Currency Committee, acted on Walcott's request, establishing a subcommittee to spearhead the investigation. In view of its importance, Norbeck named himself chairman of it. He appointed two other Republican senators and two Democrats to the subcommittee. The Republicans were Senator Couzens of Michigan and Senator Townsend. Conservative Democrats Carter Glass and Duncan U. Fletcher, the ranking Democrats on the Banking and Currency Committee, were also appointed. Fletcher, an elderly gentleman of the old Senate type, had represented Florida in that body since 1909. A small investigative staff was hired and, toward the end of April 1932, the investigation got underway.

During the first year the committee turned up relatively few irregularities. Such prominent Wall Street figures as New York Stock Exchange President Richard Whitney appeared before the subcommittee to give testimony. He acted much aggrieved by the

Reformers: *Senator Townsend, left, is seen with Senate Finance Committee Chairman Carter Glass of Virginia and Senator Peter Norbeck of South Dakota as they hear witnesses on one of the committee's banking reform measures. The bankers testifying before them, Glass asserted, "learned their testimony at a 'night school'" and were repeating it "parrot-like" (Townsend family scrapbooks).*

inconvenience, and his remarks were considerably less than candid.* Whitney, a former Morgan partner who now headed his own brokerage firm, noted in particular that President Hoover's fears of widespread "selling short" and "bear attacks" in the market were groundless. "Selling short" is the practice of committing oneself to selling stock one does not yet own at a certain price in the belief that one will be able to purchase the stock at a lower price before the date of delivery. "Bear attacks" or "selling the bear" are efforts to profit by

---

* *Some years later it was learned that not only had Whitney been lying to the committee but, at the time of his appearance, he was engaged in the systematic embezzlement of his clients' funds and various types of stock fraud, and had been since before the crash. Having found his summons to appear before the committee offensive, Whitney was to face the further indignity of a federal prison cell.*

running a good stock into the dirt. Both are methods of profiting from a declining market at the expense of less knowledgeable investors.

The hearings were suspended temporarily in the late summer and fall during the election campaigns, but resumed full force in January of 1933 under a fiesty Italian-American judge named Ferdinand Pecora, who was hired as committee counsel. A no-nonsense man of the highest moral standards, Pecora set out to question the best-known names on Wall Street–J.P. Morgan, Clarence Dillon, Winthrop Aldrich, James Forrestal, and others. A number of these one-time "high priests of finance" admitted under Pecora's persistent questioning that they had rigged "pools" routinely. The use of a stock pool involved several financiers getting together and pooling their resources to buy a large block of stock of some particular company in the name of one person or brokerage firm. They would then begin buying and selling the stock among themselves, thus creating the appearance that the stock was becoming a hot property and attracting new buyers. This would have the effect of raising its price and luring unwitting investors, hopeful of getting in early on a developing wonder stock. When the price of the stock reached an agreed-upon level, the members of the pool sold out, dumping their stock on the market, reaping their profits and backing off, leaving the suckers who had followed their lead holding grossly overvalued stocks. Another favored procedure was pegging bond prices artificially high and taking fantastic profits from unknowing investors.

It was also learned that J.P. Morgan, head of the nation's most prominent banking firm, had paid no income taxes at all in 1930, 1931, or 1932, despite his seven-figure income. In 1931 and 1932, few, if any, of his twenty partners had paid any, either. Nor had George Washington Hill of the American Tobacco Company, or Albert H.

Wiggin, president of the Chase National Bank, who admitted to selling his own bank stock short. The committee was also told that when officers of New York's First National City Bank faced financial ruin during the crash because they could not cover their investments, the bank gave them interest-free loans, while selling out its own customers.

The "Pecora Committee," as it was called in the press, was attracting national attention as millions waited to see what the next day's hearings would turn up. Edwin C. Hill, a "Famous Reporter and Radio News Broadcaster," wrote in his column in the *Washington Times* a description of the scene as experienced by Senator Townsend and the other participants:

> J.P. Morgan, colossus of international finance, with $250,000,000 in his wallet, even in this flattened world, makes his way, as this is written, to resume his sensational testimony before a divided and wrangling Senate Committee on Banking. If the course of this fair May day is as pyrotechnic as the first day Mr. Morgan smiled and joked his way through a hurricane of testimony, they'll have to call out the Regular Army to herd back the crowds from the committee door.
>
> . . . the hunt is on, full cry. The hounds are baying on the trail, but the bear they are after (or bull, if you like) trots ahead, placidly, even good-humoredly and still a bit ahead of the hue and cry. It's drama with a capital D. It has been since the moment the hearing began.
>
> A long, high-ceilinged room, whose gray-green walls are relieved by flat, glistening marble pillars, is the scene of the first day of the most arresting hearing in many years. Half the room (the rear half) is occupied by the seated crowd, folds with enough pull to get through the crowds and rest their bones upon the close-set chairs. The other half is taken up with three long mahogany tables, for Senate Committee, counsel, and the gentlemen of the press.

The "Pecora Committee" in action, 1932:

Morgan Inquiry: *This photo, reproduced from a newspaper clipping in the Townsend family scrapbooks, give a sense of the scene that unfolded when the Van Sweringen brothers, Cleveland railroad magnates, appeared before the committee to testify about how a loan from J. P. Morgan helped them build their railroad empire. Standing, left to right, G.P. Van Sweringen, J. P. Morgan and M. J. Van Sweringen. Seated, left to right, Senators Townsend, Goldsborough of Maryland and Chairman Fletcher of Florida, and committee counsel Ferdinand Pecora (Associated Press photo).*

Off in the blue from wide open French doors, leading to a balcony, the great dome of the Capital looms majestically in the bright sunshine, rising from a sea of tree tops. Over in the corner a dozen motion picture cameras are loaded and leveled, ready for the appearance of the greatest banker in the world . . . Finally, after lo, these many years, they have at their mercy the magnificent Morgan, or soon will have.

. . . The Morgan entourage appears in the rear door of the committee room, headed by John W. Davis, candidate for President on the Democratic ticket in the almost forgotten year of 1924. White-haired, pink-cheeked, well-nigh ecclesiastical, Mr. Davis appears on the threshold and spreads a keen glance over the buzzing, weltering crowd.

There is no smile on the Davis face for it is plain to be seen that every fiber of his being revolts at the spectacle of his friend and employer being dragged into the limelight to make sport for the populace.

On the following day, this "public spectacle" was heightened still further when a young female circus midget, seeing a chance at immortality, leaped into Morgan's lap as scores of cameramen snapped her picture. Morgan wore the same bemused smile with which he gazed upon the entire hearing. After this interruption, when he and his party of eminent attorneys and partners were seated, the senators came in. By now the full Banking and Currency Committee was attending the hearings, drawn by the glare of publicity (though John and the other members of the subcommittee still did most of the behind-the-scenes work with Pecora and his staff). The senators passed the great financier on their way to their seats:

> they approach Mr. Morgan for a nod and a handshake. Some of them act as if they hope the cameramen won't catch them in the sin of actually shaking hands with a Morgan–the Morgan–for statesmen from extremely rural constituencies are sensitive about public contact with the rich.
>
> Others, however, like McAdoo of California, Carter Glass of Virginia, and Couzens of Michigan, step right up and smile, and wring Mr. Morgan's hand, and utter the usual pleasant platitudes. They are the members of the committee who really know something about banking, although one may include Senator Townsend of Delaware, who happens to be a banker himself.

Later in the month when some committee members wanted to call a halt to the proceedings for the summer, Senator Townsend made a motion to carry them through to their conclusion. Speaking to a reporter several days later, he noted that he "hardly had a right to complain about the heat":

> But I think it is better that the investigation be carried on now. As no one had any idea what would develop, I believe it would have resulted in a great deal of uncertainty to put the hearings over until fall. This uncertainty might have had adverse effects.

The Senator spoke of the revelations of the hearings and of his efforts to close such loopholes in the tax laws as those which enabled Morgan to skip paying income taxes for three years.

Pecora summed up the results of the hearings in a 1939 book, *Wall Street Under Oath*. He wrote that the stock exchange "was in reality neither more nor less than a glorified gambling casino where the odds were weighted heavily against the eager outsiders."

Not much could be done by the Senate to stop the casino quality of stock dealings but they set out immediately to even out the odds. Two areas in which Senator Townsend was especially active were the redesign of the nation's banking laws and a new set of regulations governing the actions of the stock exchange (which ultimately resulted in the creation of the Securities and Exchange Commission).

Large investment banks and Wall Street financiers had totally discredited themselves in the eyes of most Americans as a result of the committee hearings and other events that occurred at about the same time. In one celebrated case, Ivar Kreuger, the "Swedish Match King" who had won international fame for having put together a business empire worth hundreds of millions of dollars, committed suicide in his Paris apartment in March 1932. Within a month the world was shocked to learn that Kreuger had, in fact, been a swindler

Government consolidation: *Among Senator Townsend's Senate duties was service on a committee convened by his friend, Senator Harry Flood Byrd of Virginia, to explore the idea of consolidating a number of government agencies into one, presumably more efficient, unit. Seated left to right in this photo, from a newspaper clipping in the Townsend family scrapbooks, are Senators Mahoney of Wyoming, Townsend of Delaware, Byrd of Virginia, Robinson of Arkansas and McNary of Oregon (Associated Press photo).*

and forger who had fabricated $100,000,000 in bogus bonds for use as collateral in acquiring massive loans from American banks.

Then, while the financial world was still reeling from this revelation, utility magnate Samuel Insull, a self-made multimillionaire said to have done for the structure of power companies what Thomas A. Edison did for the the electric lightbulb, shocked the country by resigning from his chairmanship of sixty-five utitily companies, his directorship of eighty-five more firms, and his control over a dozen utility holding companies spreading across thirty-two states. He then left on an extended trip to Europe. Within weeks his empire began collapsing like a house of cards.

All in all, 1932 and 1933 were two of the most disastrous years on record for the financial world. Senator Glass summed up the prevailing view in a quip to Townsend and other friends on the committee (which also reflected the rather casual racism of his time and place): "One banker in my state attempted to marry a white woman and they lynched him."

Invaluable Assistant: *Mrs. Louise Staton Johnson is shown on the grounds of the U.S. Capitol in Washington, D.C. during the 1930s. She served as Senator Townsend's primary clerk and office manager throughout his years in the Senate. She was also a frequent speech writer, tour guide and friend (courtesy of Judith M. Pfeiffer and Robert C. Barnes).*

24. The New Deal

The 1932 election outcome was no great surprise to John, although as a friend and supporter of President Hoover he had hoped for a different result. One thing surprising to some commentators was that the outcome was not a mandate for revolutionary change. Roosevelt's victory was substantial–some 55 percent of the popular vote and an electoral vote landslide, but the conservative position was by no means totally repudiated. It was later popular to speculate that Roosevelt saved America from revolution, but that was highly dubious. The people were less revolutionary than disillusioned and dispirited. While Americans did turn to violence in a few cases, such as the uprisings of debt-weary farmers in the West in the face of the widespread foreclosures of their farm mortgages, these instances were not widespread. As the Great Depression neared its bottom people were more pathetic than threatening. In a year when Communists had an opportunity to do as well in America as at any time in the nation's history, the best their presidential candidate William Z. Foster could do was 120,000 votes. The considerably more respectable Socialists, whose candidate, Norman Thomas, was making the first of six runs for the presidency, did better than that, but their showing was far below those of such past elections as 1912 and 1920. One interesting sidelight on the election was that the Farmer-Labor candidate was old Jacob S. Coxey who had led "Coxey's Army" of unemployed men on Washington during the 1893 depression. Coxey, now mayor of Massilon, Ohio, and in his late seventies, did not even do as well as the Communist candidate, but it was somehow comforting that he was still fighting his fight after all those years.

Delawareans seemed more concerned with the local picture than with the national. Delaware was one of the few states outside New England to go for Hoover. Neither U.S. senator was up for reelection, which freed Senator Hastings to serve as Hoover's deputy campaign manager for the East. Congressman Houston was the subject of a party squabble over Prohibition in Sussex County and failed to win renomination to a fifth term in Congress. The Republican candidate, Reuben Satterthwaite Jr., lost to Democrat Wilbur L. Adams of Wilmington. The overall results were mixed, but there was no Democratic landslide and that in itself was remarkable in America in 1932. Even so there were signs that Delaware's solid Republicanism was unravelling a bit. It was worth remembering that the G.O.P. had come in on the heels of the 1893 depression.

One unusual feature of the 1932 election was that Pierre, Irénée and Lammot du Pont supported Roosevelt. Though the New Yorker had hardly been the choice of John J. Raskob's wing of the Democratic Party, he was able through carefully-worded speeches favoring decentralization and government economy to hold these conservative, big-business Democrats in line until the election. Lammot was a registered Democrat. Irénée and Pierre tended to be independents but for the moment they, too, were Democrats. Roosevelt had talked of the need for balancing the budget during the campaign (a feature of his program that was shortlived to say the least) and otherwise appealed to conservatives. When the full import of the New Deal was understood, the du Ponts and Raskob and many others left him, but by then he was solidly entrenched in power.

The 1932 election had in some ways enhanced the standing of Senators Townsend and Hastings. So many senior Republican senators had been voted out of office that they were much higher up in seniority. One piece by Robert N. Lynn, the *Every Evening*'s Washington correspondent, addressed this development. It was headlined "2 Del. Senators May Develop into National Leaders . . . Hastings and Townsend in Line for Posts Vacated by Old Guard." Lynn pointed out that Hastings was the more politically active of the two during the Hoover administration and predicted that he would advance in Senate leadership, and added, almost as an afterthought: "Senator Townsend likewise will have the opportunity to increase his prestige and influence. He is not as politically-minded as his aggressive colleague, however."

Hastings had made a name for himself as a leading administration spokesman in the Senate, as a kind of political gunslinger. It was a reputation he was to enhance greatly when he went on the attack against the New Deal. John, on the other hand, had become well known and very much appreciated within Congress itself as a "Senator's Senator," as a man who worked hard and quietly to get the job done. His "prestige and influence" were quieter and less showy than those of Hastings, but in the end Senator Townsend made more difference. It was also noted with interest that both senators were transplanted natives of Maryland's lower Eastern Shore –Townsend from Worcester, Hastings from Somerset.

The amendment moving the date of inauguration day up from March 4 to January was not finally ratified until February of 1933. This meant that the provisions of the amendment would not take effect until the inauguration of the winner of the 1936 election. Thus, Roosevelt's inauguration did not take place until March 4, 1933, four months after the election. As a member of the Senate, John was present at the ceremony and heard the new President give his classic "The only thing we have to fear is fear itself . . ." speech and liked it. He told a reporter later that he was hopeful the new administration would prove effective in dealing with the problems of the country, and that he planned to cooperate when he could, especially in the area of banking legislation.

At this time the Pecora Committee was still gearing up for its most stunning revelations and there was much work to be done in the area of banking and securities. While Paul, Louise Johnson, and Olive Hurley ran the office and attended to the needs of constituents, John was spending the great bulk of his time on these problems. A few days after the inauguration he, Glass, Walcott, and committee member William Gibbs McAdoo went around to the White House to meet the new president and talk over their work on the committee. McAdoo, President Wilson's son-in-law and a former cabinet member, was now a senator from California, where he was the leading spokesman for the William Randolph Hearst wing of the Democratic Party. He had cooperated halfheartedly in Roosevelt's nomination but was not a close ally. Roosevelt had offered Glass the position of treasury secretary but Glass turned him down, not believing that Roosevelt was truly committed to balancing the budget as he had said he was during the campaign. As it turned out, events proved Glass right even though Roosevelt still declared himself publicly to be in favor of balancing the budget in March 1933.

Banking and securities legislation were the two notable areas in which Senator Townsend started out in agreement with Roosevelt, with minor differences of opinion. Virtually the first act of Roosevelt's presidency was the declaration of a bank holiday, closing down all the

A Visit with F.D.R. – *Senators Frederic Walcott (R., Connecticut), William G. McAdoo (D., California), Carter Glass (D., Virginia) and John G. Townsend, Jr. (R., Delaware) were pictured in a May, 1933,* New York Herald Tribune *Sunday rotogravure section as they emerged from a meeting at the White House with the recently inaugurated President Franklin D. Roosevelt (Townsend family scrapbooks).*

nation's banks to give them a chance to get back on their feet in the face of panic runs by customers in the weeks before his inauguration. In the spring and early summer the Banking and Currency Committee put together the final form of the bill which came to be known as the Glass-Steagall Banking Bill (an earlier bill of the same name had been passed the year before under Hoover, establishing the Reconstruction Finance Corporation, among other things). With the Pecora hearings pointing up the need for major reforms, the bill was passed easily by the Senate two days after the hearings ended. One feature all supported was the separation of investment from commercial banking. It had been excesses in the investment end of banking that ran many banks out of business during the depression.

A much more important element of the bill, and one in which Senator Townsend was personally very instrumental, was the Federal Deposit Insurance Corporation. It had been the creation of the "small bank" faction of Congress, led in the Senate by John and Senator Arthur H. Vandenberg of Michigan and in the House by Congressman Henry Steagall of Alabama, chairman of the House Banking Committee. Many large bankers frowned on the idea as did Senator Glass and President Roosevelt. His more conservative advisers such as Dean Acheson, then an under secretary of the treasury, were dead-set against it. But the F.D.I.C. was a measure that grew directly out of the needs of small-town America and it passed Congress easily. The F.D.I.C. turned out to be a brilliant success. Fewer banks went out of business in the seven years remaining of the 1930s than in any single year of the 1920s. The administration promptly took credit for it.

In the incredible burst of energy known as "The Hundred Days," during which the first phase of the New Deal was enacted, it was difficult for John and every other Republican in Congress to maintain any sort of equilibrium. Senator Townsend found much of Roosevelt's program flawed and thought it dangerous. In the two areas in which he had the most expertise, banking and currency and agriculture, he gave the president mixed reviews. He supported him on most early banking and securities legislation and voted against him on such New Deal measures as the Agricultural Adjustment Act.

In general he opposed the New Deal because he saw it as creating an opportunity for many of the abuses of big government that have in fact occurred in recent decades. He also feared the creation of massive government deficits. Yet he was more responsible in his opposition than some senators. He tried to weigh bills on their merits, though this was often hard to do in the midst of the incredible barrage of legislation Roosevelt aimed at Congress during 1933 and 1934. Hastings became almost a professional "aginner," a leading anti-New Deal orator in the Senate, levelling charges at every administration action. Sometimes they were well founded, sometimes less so, but a steady stream of anti-Roosevelt rhetoric issued forth. A book of his speeches was printed in time for the 1936 elections.

This kind of rigid opposition obscured the odd fact that, but for Hoover's firm faith in the balanced budget (a faith he might well have abandoned in a second term, just as Roosevelt abandoned his), he and F.D.R. were not all that dissimilar. Their major differences were of style, not of substance. Roosevelt was a master politician and salesman for his programs. Hoover was not. But no less an authority than Rexford Guy Tugwell, a member of Roosevelt's "Brain Trust" and later an assistant secretary of agriculture, had this to say of F.D.R.:

> He seems heroic to those who measure him by his predecessor, but that is because they cannot accept his amazing resemblance to Hoover–under a contrasting mask. They do not realize that both saw the same light and followed it. Hoover had wanted–and had said clearly enough that he wanted–nearly all the changes now brought under the New Deal label.

On a more personal level, Senator Townsend came into touch with the depression on an almost daily basis. Washington, as the only source of hope for many victims, seemed to draw hordes of people through 1932 and 1933, looking for work, for help, for anything. As

Louise Johnson remembered those days:

> the park benches were filled all day with slouching, unemployed people. The Capitol halls were lined with waiting people, who were coming from everywhere, it seemed, to find relief.
>
> The newspapers were asking each person to do his or her bit to relieve the situation. I decided to pick one of the names of those in need who lived near the Capitol. I found a mother and father with small children who were not far away. It happened that Senator Townsend offered to take me home that day at the close of business. I replied that I was going only a few blocks, but would gladly ride that far.
>
> When I asked the driver to stop, Senator asked why I was going there–it was one of those very poor districts near the Capitol. When I told him, he reached into his pocket and handed me a sizeable bill. I am sure that wasn't the first time he and other senators had done that; he even paid a month's rent for a family of six awaiting him one morning at the office, and I am sure they had never been in Delaware.
>
> When I called on the family near the Capitol, I found a man and his wife with four children in one large room. The only room. In the hall, outside the one door, was a sink–the only water, except in an adjoining toilet. In the room there was a small stove.
>
> I gave them the money and told them a senator had sent it, but I did not tell them his name. Then I stopped at a corner store and spent my little offering for them. But we were constantly aware of the seriousness of this depression, and such gifts seemed so temporary.
>
> . . . Our office was opposite that of Senator [Robert F.] Wagner of New York. There were more than twice as many on his staff as on ours, and his secretary directed all of them. In addition to supervision of those at desks, she greeted visitors and she tried, if possible, to save some time to talk things over with Senator Wagner before noon, when the Senate usually assembled.

During the Depression, she had to ask for more chairs to be placed along the hall near their door because the front office filled so rapidly. People would be waiting when she arrived in the morning. The Senator had to find a hide-away spot in which to work on important matters before seeing them.

We were in a three-room office by that time. During one morning my door opened and a frantic woman entered and closed the door. "I must get away! I wish everyone in the world was dead!" I knew she did not mean that; she was worn out and saw no respite. It was Senator Wagner's secretary!

25. The Farmer-politician

In Delaware the depression was felt more acutely in the northern end of the state where the large industrial plants were located. Thousands were unemployed and private relief agencies were having a difficult time coping with the need. Yet, through most of the length of Delaware people were more fortunate than in many other parts of America. Part of the reason why was the battle John Townsend had fought as a young man. In the 1893 recession, southern Delaware had been in poor condition, its farmers reduced to near subsistence level. During the Great Depression years the sons of those men could freely move their crops to nearby cities, whose residents had to eat, no matter how bad the economy. The modern highways of the 1920s and 1930s were a vast improvement over the corrupt railroads of a generation before.

It has been said that a farm is a much better place to weather an economic depression than a city because, although you may have no money, you will not starve. Beyond that basic fact of rural life, southern Delaware was saved from the worst ravages of the Great Depression by something altogether new–the "Delmarva Broiler." The commercial broiler was a new agricultural product that reached large-scale development just as the depression was spreading across America. This new way of marketing poultry had been the brainchild of a woman from the Cedar Neck section of Baltimore Hundred near Ocean View. Her name was Cecile Steele and she was the wife of a U.S. Coast Guardsman named Wilmer Steele, who was stationed at the Bethany Beach Life-saving Station. In those days, the Coast Guard tried wherever possible to staff such outlying stations with local men so as to keep the station crews as content as possible. So it was that Steele, from a local family, was both a farmer and a Coast Guardsman.

One of the more important sideline businesses of southern Delaware's agricultural economy during the turn-of-the-century period was producing eggs for market. The egg business was somewhat unusual in that, particularly in the early days, it was carried on mainly by farm wives, each with her flock of laying hens and two or three prize roosters. Though the amount of income from the market egg business was not great, it added up over time. Some of the older residents of Delmarva can recall all sorts of wonders that were performed around the place with "mother's egg money." By the early 1920s the market egg business had grown to the point where there were now some moderately-sized commercial operations as well as a small supporting economy of hatcheries, poultry feed suppliers, and the like. The area even took part in annual competitive egg-laying contests in which the eggs were weighed for size and other desirable qualities. One local poultryman, a transplanted Englishman named A.C. Jones who had settled in Georgetown, won a national contest and became very well to do as a result. People from all over the country wrote him in search of eggs from his prize hen. According to some reports the poor hen produced a truly extraordinary number of eggs thereafter.

Egg producers generally hatched out some eggs in the late winter and early spring to create a new supply of hens to keep their flocks going. The males produced by this process, known as "cockerels," were not highly valued and were considered a byproduct since most people ordered their roosters from special breeding stock. The cockerels were sold to poultry vendors in nearby cities, who in turn sold them to their customers as "broilers," a highly prized summer delicacy. Poultry was still only an occasional meat for most people and was not in continuous demand except among certain groups. The best customers were members of the large Jewish communities of Philadelphia, New York, and other cities. Rabbis went to the poultry shops and ritually slaughtered the birds in the approved kosher fashion. Most of these chickens were Barred Rocks, Rhode Island Reds, and Plymouth Rocks. Though customers had their individual preferences, the Barred Rocks were generally the most highly prized.

Early in 1923, it occurred to Mrs. Steele that if she could raise a flock of cockerels and have them ready for market before most other people in the area had their cockerels ready, she could get top price for her flock and realize a tidy profit. She started out with 500 cockerel chicks, raised them, and sold them at a very good price. It was the first time on record that anyone had set out to raise a flock of broilers just for the sake of raising broilers and not as a sideline to the raising of laying hens. This worked so well that the next summer she got her husband to build her several more houses. She was finding that the market was expanding to take all the broilers she could produce. Within a few years she had a growing capacity of 25,000 chickens and Wilmer Steele had retired from his Coast Guard career to help take care of them.

None of this escaped the notice of the Steeles' neighbors, who promptly followed suit with broiler flocks of their own. By the late 1920s a new industry had been born in Sussex County and was spreading rapidly to surrounding counties. It was just entering its real development as a valuable commercial crop when the depression hit. By 1928, 500 growers in southern Delaware were producing a total of 1 million broilers. The following year the total doubled to 2 million.

The market egg business that had given rise to broilers was still very good and continued to exceed broiler production in terms of farm income until the early 1930s. By 1930, the combination of the two had become Delaware's most valuable agricultural crop. This worked out well for the state's farmers since some of their older crops were declining in value. Strawberries declined after 1923, the last year in which they were classified by the state as a "million-dollar crop." Apple production was losing some ground as well, though orchards were still an important part of overall farm income.

The broiler business grew during the early 1930s not so much in terms of larger numbers of growers but in the number of chickens each farmer raised. The number of poultry growers leveled off at about 500 for several years, but each of the 500 growers was growing more and more chickens. In 1930, the standard growing unit for commercial growers was 2,000 chickens. By 1935, a flock of 2,000 was considered a "mom and pop" operation that a couple could carry on in their spare time in the backyard while doing some other work as their main occupation. By 1940, a flock of 10,000 was a backyard operation. Wilmer and Cecile Steele had expanded their operation to an unheard-of 25,000 capacity in 1927, four years after they raised their first broiler flock. By 1935, they had a capacity of 200,000 chickens. Poultry production in Sussex County increased by 1 million chickens per year between 1930, when the state total production stood at 1 million birds, and 1935, when it stood at 6 million.

This rate of growth sounds phenomenal until one examines the figures for the next five years. The late 1930s were the start of the real boom in poultry production on the central Delmarva Peninsula. In those years, people who had led a hardscrabble existence all their lives grew rich almost overnight. Even those who did not grow rich were helped through the worst of the depression by the growth of the chicken business and the related economic activity this new industry spawned. As farmers expanded their broiler capacity, they sought loans at the small local banks. They purchased lumber and building materials from local lumber companies and hired carpenters to build poultry houses. They installed "Delco Plants" –gasoline-powered generators with banks of storage batteries–to provide electricity for pumping water to the chicken houses. Hatcheries that had started ten or fifteen years before to supply laying hens for market egg production shifted over to the more lucrative production of chicks for broiler flocks. New hatcheries were being established. The same process brought many new feed companies into existence and enabled older ones to expand. By the mid-1930s thousands of cars of poultry feed were being brought into southern Delaware every year. Truck sales were brisk as feed companies, poultry growers, and buyers purchased vehicles for use in various phases of the business. In the early 1930s it was still necessary to send chickens to nearby cities to be killed and dressed. Sussex County's first dressing plant was not opened until 1938. The poultry business was rapidly dominating the entire local economy just as strawberries had done a generation earlier.

John was well aware of how important the new industry was. As a banker he could hardly miss its economic impact. As a member of Congress during the depth of the depression he could not help contrasting favorably the conditions at home with those in much of the rest of America. However, he was not yet ready to venture into poultry himself because he had not had time to study it properly. He still saw himself as an orchardist first and foremost, and then as a canner and packer of fruits and vegetables. He was becoming nationally known for his Sussex County orchards–and for being among the leading exporters of American apples to other parts of the world. One feature article in the *Sunday Star* in January of 1934 presents an excellent picutre of what the Townsend orchards were like:

> Senator Townsend is one of the three largest apple growers in the world. Scattered all over the lower end of Sussex County are the far-reaching orchards which in spring paint the landscape into scenes of bewildering loveliness . .

. The largest and most interesting . . . both in beauty and development, is the one near Bridgeville. It contains a thousand acres, a mile and a half long by a mile and a quarter square, now celebrating its tenth year.

TREK TO VIEW BLOSSOMS

Early in the spring, these acres of gorgeous apple blossoms attract nature lovers from everywhere. Thousands upon thousands of beautifully shaped trees, lovely in the delicate pink flush of bursting buds, are everywhere. In the bright days of early fall, when the work of the Great Husbandman has been accomplished through the summer, the scene has altered. The trees are bowed down under the weight of their luscious burden. As they wait patiently to be stripped of their load they are supported by great props, and even though twisted and bent they retain their beauty.

There are many varieties of apples, both early and late and all of them are found in abundance in the orchard. The early species which ripen in July and continue throughout the month, are the Yellow Transparent, Fourth of July, William's Early Red and the Early Ripe. The late varieties, coming the first of September and remaining through the frosts of October –frosts that color them even more vividly– are the Stayman Winesap, Jonathan, Old-Fashioned Winesap, Grimes Golden, Golden Delicious, Rome Beauty, Stark Delicious, Macintosh and King David. The apples of Senator Townsend go all over the world, to South America, to all European countries and even into Africa.

VILLAGE IN MINIATURE

This orchard with its sixty thousand apple trees is a little village in itself. Back from one of the many intersecting highways is a road, flanked on either side by sturdy trees, that leads to one of the large farm houses which is the home of the superintendent, T.W. Hansen, a delightful person . . .

Another large farm house and seven tenant houses complete the little community and far off, across the orchard, is the barracks, where the apple pickers are housed. Here the many Negroes, who have worked their way from one crop to another, all the way up the Peninsula, spend a few happy and prosperous weeks. Men and women are busy all through the orchard during the picking season with their bags strung about their necks to catch the apples as they drag their twenty-two foot ladders about so that they might reach the topmost limb. No tree is ever shaken and each apple is carefully picked to avoid bruising it . . .

EMPLOY MANY

Some 125 persons are given employment in this particular orchard and between forty and fifty others get the fruit ready for shipment at the packing house in Bridgeville. Many caterpillar tractors are used in drawing the apples out of the orchards, to the Reo Speed Wagons that take them into the packing house, where the most modern apple grader and equipment convinces buyers that they are getting the very finest pack.

. . . [in spring] Each Tree is given first from four to five pounds of bone meal. Then in a short time from four to five pounds of nitrate of soda is added and a little later the same amount of sulphate ammonia. All of the fertilizers and spraying materials are bought in bulk and a chemical plant is maintained in the orchard, where the mixing is done. Disc harrows are used in tilling and the entire orchard is gone over seven times. The first tilling is done in March and the work of cultivation is continued until late in June.

LET US SPRAY

In Late Winter spraying starts and lime sulphur is used. Then as the buds unfold, arsenic of lead is administered and finally a Bordeaux mixture, when the blossoms shed and the petal has fallen. In July a Bordeaux dust is used for insects and fungus and this is blown on the trees by seven liquid dusters, each having a capacity of three hundred gallons. This destroys the coddling moth and any fungus which may blemish the fruit.

A normal year's crop, close to one hundred percent, it is estimated that 200,000 bushels will be harvested. In a normal year this orchard's value would be placed at approxiately $300,000. An average of 3,500 bushels is the usual day's work and the perfect fruit is dumped from the picking bags into the fir crates which are piled on the waiting wagons and then taken to the main roads where the big trucks are loaded.

The inferior fruit is sold for cider and the perfect apples are shipped to cities all over the United States. Many are exported and still quantities are put in storage, some in local storage, but more in New York and Philadelphia, where they will be kept for sale in the winter.

When all the fruit has been picked and the cider apples disposed of, the decayed fruit that lies about under the trees is buried and destroyed by chloride of lime. After the entire crop has been harvested it is about time to start the winter work of pruning. All through the winter a force of sixty men is kept busy, getting the trees ready for spring time. The brush is pushed from under the trees by huge forks attached to the tractors, out into main roads, where fires are kept burning. One need not leave Delaware to see perfection in the growing of apples, for these orchards are unsurpassed in their beauty and in the quality of their fruit.

In 1931, John had sold part interest in this orchard to his Selbyville friend, Clayton Bunting, owner of Bunting's Nurseries. In 1934, a few months after the *Sunday Star* piece was written, local residents were somewhat surprised to see an eighty-five-foot-tall derrick going up in the middle of the orchard. Their surprise turned to astonishment when they learned that it was an oil well. . . a test well driven by a Cleveland, Ohio-based independent oil company that had quietly gone all over the countryside between Milford and Bridgeville buying up mineral rights for one dollar and a one-eighth share of whatever oil or gas was recovered. No one had expected it to amount to anything and George W. Spohn, Cleveland Petroleum Corporation's man on the scene, had

amassed 386 leases covering more than 40,000 acres of
northwestern Sussex County. After all, it was in the midst of the
depression and no one had anything to lose.

Suddenly, during the second week of May 1934, everything
seemed to change. One of Spohn's men walked into George Lord's
combination store-restaurant-gas station on the Bridgeville highway
with a soda pop bottle half-filled with "a dark, thick fluid," which he
said was crude oil. The word spread around the state and beyond
that oil had been found in the middle of Senator Townsend's orchard
and a subdued, but clearly detectable, hubbub of excitement began.
It was more noticeable outside the immediate neighborhood than
within it. None of the local farmers rushed out to try and work out
land deals. No one stopped working in the orchard to loiter around
the derrick. According to the papers, the boom was pretty much a
matter of Bridgeville townspeople coming into Lord's establishment
to examine the contents of the soda bottle and talking about how
nice it would be if the area turned out to be sitting on top of a major
oil field.

Spohn's drill was down six or seven hundred feet. He told
reporters he could go down to six thousand feet unless he hit granite
first, in which case he was finished. At a level of about two thousand
feet he did hit oil but the flow was sufficient to produce only about
three barrels a day. They tried another spot, but the derrick was
finally dismantled and that was the last anyone heard of oil wells in
Bridgeville. During the course of the excitement, however, someone
remembered that one David Levy of Wilmington had journeyed to
the Isle of Wight at the tip of Worcester County's St. Martin's Neck
some years earlier in search of a pool of oil said to have supplied
local Indians with an oily, medicinal substance in colonial days. Levy
also came up empty-handed. So central Delmarva never became

another Texas. The senator never said anything about it one way or the other for the record. He just kept on growing apples.

In the midst of the exacting work of the Banking and Currency Committee and his other Senate chores, John was living a full and busy social life from a large apartment at the Shoreham, one of the city's leading apartment hotels. Most members of Congress lived in such residential hotels instead of buying their own homes in the capital. Among the Townsends' Shoreham neighbors (Lyla lived with her father during most of his Washington years and served as his official hostess) were Senators Carter Glass, James Byrnes of South Carolina, Arthur Vandenberg, William G. McAdoo, Frederic Walcott, and, after 1933, Harry F. Byrd of Virginia and Royal S. Copeland, all of whom became close friends. Copeland, a New York Democrat, was also a medical doctor. Mrs. Copeland became one of Lyla Townsend's best Washington friends. McAdoo, an easterner turned California Democrat and onetime presidential contender, had served as President Wilson's secretary of the treasury before Glass took the post. He also later became Wilson's son-in-law.

Of this group, John's closest friends in the earliest years were Glass and Walcott, because of their service with him on Banking and Currency and on Appropriations. Later on, Harry Byrd entered the group. They often breakfasted together to discuss the upcoming day, but John tended to be an earlier riser than the rest. He was the impatient type and often set out on foot for the four-mile walk to the Capitol, where he would breakfast in one of the Senate dining rooms before arriving at his office well before eight o'clock. Vandenberg, another early riser, also went to the office early. His office was next door to Townsend's in the later 1930s and Louise Johnson recalled that she often heard Vandenberg in the office alone, before his staff arrived in the morning, typing away at the speeches he customarily wrote himself, using his dependable two-finger method.

This close relationship between the men often took them out of Washington together. Townsend would visit Vandenberg in Michigan and Walcott in Connecticut. He would stop to visit Byrnes on his way to Florida in the winter. He always spent time with Byrd at his Berryville, Virginia, home and all these senators visited him in Delaware. McAdoo became a frequent visitor to Rehoboth Beach in the summer. An aviation enthusiast, he always insisted on flying everywhere that he possibly could. He would arrange for a pilot to fly him over from Washington to Rehoboth in a small plane. More than once they had to land in some farmer's pasture when problems arose. John also called on his Republican senatorial friends to give speeches before Delaware Republican organizations. Walcott and Vandenberg in particular did many such political chores for him.

His social schedule, like that of most senators, was formidable. Without the help of his daughter he could not possibly have done as much entertaining as he did. In addition to the many small dinners for senators, government officials, and friends and family, she also assisted him in entertaining visiting delegations of Delawareans and showing them around the city. They also attended dinners, banquets, embassy receptions, and similar functions. During Hoover's years in the White House there were regular invitations to dinners there. When Roosevelt was president and Senator Townsend one of his frequent critics, John was still invited to the executive mansion for formal receptions but not for personal social evenings.

One problem with such entertaining before 1933 was the issue of alcoholic beverages. Alcohol was not served at official functions for obvious reasons but one was usually offered drinks at most private

SENATOR CARTER GLASS—DRY

SENATOR JOHN G. TOWNSEND, JR.—DEMI-DRY

SENATOR GEORGE NORRIS—DRY INCLINATIONS

SENATOR ARTHUR VANDENBERG—DRY

SENATOR ROBERT WAGNER—WET

Stance on Prohibition: *Senator Townsend was among those senators caricatured in a 1932* Vanity Fair *magazine illustration, accompanying an article by famed attorney Clarence Darrow, concerning their stance on repeal of the Prohibition Amendment to the U.S. Constitution. Senator Townsend was characterized as "Demi Dry" (illustration reproduced from clipping in Townsend family scrapbooks).*

parties. Senator Townsend refused to drink during Prohibition and he initially refused to allow Lyla to serve drinks to their guests. This led to an argument, which she ultimately won, though he still refused to drink himself until after repeal of the Prohibition Amendment in the spring of 1933.

By the late 1920s it was clear to most people, Townsend included, that Prohibition was not working out as planned. He took the middle ground and favored changes in the Volsted Act that enforced the amendment, but the trend was definitely moving toward repeal. In a 1932 article in *Vanity Fair* on the outlook for a repeal resolution in the Senate, written by none other than Clarence Darrow, Townsend was listed as a "Demi-dry" while others ranged from "dust dry" to "wringing wet." Representative Houston was the driest of the dry. His rigid and unyielding stance on the issue led to a party fight and the end of his Congressional career. When the repeal vote finally did come, shortly after Roosevelt's inauguration, Townsend voted against it, but he later accepted repeal to the point where he would take a social drink.

As a senator he was constantly asked to serve on boards, commissions, and councils and to join groups of all kinds. Most such invitations were routinely refused but he did accept a few. He served as a trustee of two private colleges, Goucher College in Baltimore and Washington College in Chestertown, and of the U.S. Naval Academy. He served as a member of the Mount Rushmore Commission, which worked with sculptor Gutzon Borglum on planning the monumental portraits of the presidents. He served as a member of the Delaware and Maryland Societies of Washington, which were social groups for natives of those states now living in the city. He served as a member of the Lewes Tercentenary Commission in 1931 and was active in the project that resulted in the building of the Zwaanendael Museum there. In 1938, he was likewise a member of the Delaware Valley Tercentenary

Yorktown Sesquicentennial: *In 1931, Senator Townsend served as a member of the Yorktown Sesquicentennial Commission in organizing the 150th anniversary observance of the decisive Revolutionary War battle. Pictured in the front row, above, left to right, are: Marshall Henri Pétain of France, President Herbert Hoover, Mrs. Hoover, General of the Armies John J. Pershing, and Senator Townsend (photo reproduced from a U.S. government commemorative volume).*

Commission commemorating the Swedish settlement of 1638.

One of the more interesting semiofficial duties of this type was the Yorktown Sesquicentennial Commission of 1931. Amidst a flurry of commemorative coins, stamps, and medals, every state participated in a massive celebration of the American Revolutionary War victory, which climaxed in a huge pageant at Yorktown in October of that year. The senator was detained in Washington and missed the banquet on the first night of the weekend festivities at Yorktown, so he asked Lyla to represent him. She did so and was there to see Governor Franklin D. Roosevelt of New York enter the hall with a huge entourage and great ceremony. When her father arrived the next day she warned, "Father,

The Townsend family home: as it appeared during John's years in the U.S. Senate. John had enclosed the porch on the south end of the house (at left in photo) and turned it into a sun parlor where the family was to spend much of their time. Following Senator Townsend's death, his family donated the home for use as a public library for Selbyville. The building continues to serve that purpose today (photo from Townsend family collection).

you'd better get home and mend your fences. Roosevelt's going to run just as sure as you live. He never would have come in with a fanfare like that if he weren't going to run–and if he runs, he's going to win."

Another development in the family's Washington life was Paul's marriage at Christmas 1931, to Miss Theodora Thomson of Philadelphia. The young couple set up housekeeping in the Washington suburbs. Paul still served part-time as his father's secretary and was an increasingly successful road builder and real estate developer in the city. He also had a growing reputation as a prominent gentleman-sportsman. Soon after coming to Washington, he had become a regular visitor to the trout-fishing camp of Lawrence Richey, President Hoover's secretary, in the foothills of Maryland's Catoctin Mountains, near the present-day site of Camp David. Paul enjoyed the sport so much that he later rented Richey's camp with its section of trout stream. A year or two later he bought his own property with a section of stream near Thurmont, Maryland. There he built his own camp which he called Otter Valley Run. Its small complex of buildings included sleeping cabins clustered around a central lodge. Paul established an informal organization in typical style consisting of a group of friends and acquaintances he called The Order of the Jungle Cock (so-named for the colorful neck hackle feathers used in hand-tied fishing flies). This group was dedicated to good sportsmanship and conservation and met at Otter Valley on spring weekends to enjoy what was soon considered one of the finest trout streams in the region. In 1934, Paul and Theo Townsend had the first of their four children, a son named Paul Jr. Later, two daughters and another son were born. Paul continued to be an extraordinarily active man as he entered his early thirties.

Preston had graduated from the University of Delaware in 1932 with a degree in agriculture. He was spending most of his time working at the orchard business at home in Sussex, though he did take a five and a half month leave of absence in 1936 for a round-the-world trip by steamship. In later years he said that he had learned more in those five and a half months than he had in four years of college. Julian was running the canneries and making a name for himself in local civic and political circles. He and Mildred (or "Mim," as she was known) had two children, young Jack Townsend and their daughter, Eleanor. He was also being mentioned as a possible gubernatorial candidate during the 1930s. The elder Jack Townsend functioned as both the banker of the family and its trouble-shooter. He got into a little of everything, filling in where he was needed in addition to overseeing the operations of the Baltimore Trust Company. Edith's husband, Jack Tubbs, and John's nephew, Covington Townsend, were the family's lumbermen, overseeing both the Selbyville Manufacturing Company and the Townsend Lumber Company of Laurel.

When John was at home during his Senate career, his schedule was much the same as it had always been. He was up very early and frequently went around to "Grandma Townsend's" for breakfast. Since 1928, he had employed a young couple, Harley and Evelyn Derrickson, to look after the home and keep the domestic routine running smoothly. The Derricksons lived in the rear wing of the big house. Evelyn cooked and kept house while Harley did odd jobs around the property and served frequently as John's driver. In most cases the senator drove himself back and forth to Washington, however. In her first years there, Evelyn cooked most of the family's meals on the huge, old woodburning cookstove in the kitchen.

Preston continued to live at home as a young bachelor and he and his father frequently had visitors from Washington and elsewhere. The main focal point of the home during the 1930s and thereafter was the large enclosed sun porch at the south end. A fire burned in its large brick fireplace on most cool evenings; it was only appropriate that applewood was burned almost exclusively. In earlier years, when Preston was a boy, it had been his job to keep the wood box filled, for which he received a dollar a week. That, he recalled, was his first paying job.

The senator also made his annual wintertime treks to Florida, often in the company of such close friends as William J.P. White and his wife, Georgina, of Millsboro. Later, after Will White's premature death in 1936, his son, Reese and his wife, Sarah, often accompanied John. In Florida, he generally stayed at the Columbus Hotel in Miami proper rather than across the bay in the increasingly fashionable Miami Beach. By the early 1930s, Senator Townsend was practically as well known in South Florida as he was in Delaware.

Part IX:

The Political Life

26. The Republicans Hang On

John remained very much involved with local Delaware politics throughout his years in the Senate, although at some remove. As the depression wore on, the Delaware G.O.P. succumbed to the same kind of malaise that afflicted Republicans everywhere in those dark days. In the 1932 election, the G.O.P. lost its grip on Delaware's lone congressional seat and a number of lesser offices. In 1934, the Democrats were gunning for John, who was up for reelection that year. The leading early contenders for the Democratic senatorial nomination were James M. Tunnell, the Georgetown attorney who had run against T. Coleman du Pont in 1924, and Judge Hugh M. Morris of Newark, another one-time Sussex County boy who had done well in northern Delaware. As time wore on, both men gradually thought better of running and bowed out, leaving the field open for Congressman Wilbur Adams, who had been elected to the lower house in 1932. Adams was something of a cipher in Congress. He had gone to Washington, voted straight down the line with Roosevelt for two years, and now sought to elevate himself to the Senate.

The national Democratic party was more concerned with defeating Senator Townsend than the state party was. He had practically as many Democratic friends at home as Republican and unseating him would be hard. The Democrats first tried offering him a fancy job. Since he had had such a large role in the design of the Federal Deposit Insurance Corporation in the spring of 1933, someone in the Roosevelt Administration offered him one of the three seats on the F.D.I.C.'s governing body. This group, which had just been established, was required to have one minority and two majority party members. The position paid better than his $10,000 senatorial salary, but he would have had to resign his Senate seat to take it and no one was greatly surprised when he turned it down.

White Tie: *Senator Townsend as he appeared in full dress in this Harris & Ewing portrait dating from the mid-1930s (courtesy of Judith M. Pfeiffer & Robert C. Barnes).*

The 1934 senatorial campaign in Delaware was mostly clean. As a measure of Townsend's popularity, Adams chose to run solely on the issues. The major area of contention was the New Deal, but Townsend was stronger here than someone like Delaware's other senator, Daniel Hastings, who was known as a virulent New Deal opponent. John had weighed Roosevelt's proposals carefully, voting for some things and against others. Moreover, he was identified in the public mind with efforts to control the Wall Street financiers. Delaware voters knew and trusted hin, even if most were a bit more receptive to Roosevelt's programs than he was. In those days before commercial television, with radio campaigning in its infancy, it was still possible to discuss complex issues and ideas quite thoroughly and receive in-depth coverage in the state's newspapers. Party platforms received closer scrutiny from the voters in many instances than the cursory glance that later became the rule. This was especially true when something as fundamental as the New Deal was being considered.

An extremely effective, even devastating, attack on Adams's strong support for the administration came in a speech by Senator Wallace A. White, Republican of Maine, at the Dover Armory a couple of days before the election. White pointed out that during the first half of 1934, Delawareans paid out $5.20 in taxes to the federal government for every federal dollar received in services. By comparison, Arkansas, home state of Senate Majority Leader Joseph Robinson, received $24.00 from the federal government for every dollar it paid in taxes. What's more, little Delaware paid six times more to the federal government in taxes than Arkansas did, yet received a tiny fraction of the total federal assistance. It could hardly be argued, therefore, that the New Deal was materially benefitting the average Delawarean.

Though both sides were reportedly confident of victory, the election turned into a Republican sweep. The entire state Republican ticket was elected. Three out of four Republican state senate candidates in New Castle County, two out of three in Kent, and three out of three in Sussex were elected. In both Sussex and New Castle Counties nearly the entire county Republican tickets were elected. Senator Townsend led the ticket, defeating Adams by 7,124 votes statewide. The result surprised even the Republicans, who were expecting things to be much worse, as, in fact, they were nationally. This was the first year since 1864 in which the party in power, in this case the Democrats, made substantial gains in an off-year election. The Republicans lost ten seats in the U.S. Senate, including that of John's friend, Frederic Walcott in Connecticut, and many more seats in the House. They lost many governors' races as well. One answer for the surprising Republican victory in Delaware was the state's relatively easy experience of the depression; another was the generally superior Republican state organization under the reigning state chairman, Colonel Edmund Mitchell of New Castle County. Townsend's own popularity was no small part of the G.O.P. success. Even those who wrote letters to the editor in support of Adams were usually careful to point that they had nothing against Townsend personally.

The new U.S. Senate was incredibly lopsided, with sixty-nine Democrats and only twenty-seven Republicans, several of whom, like Robert M. LaFollete Jr., were now calling themselves Progressives or Farmer-Laborites. John found himself a part of what the press was calling the Republican "Old Guard"–that is, the small remaining body of a dozen or so more or less traditional Republican conservatives. The rest of the G.O.P. delegation were one kind or another of liberal or Progressive (at least in their campaign rhetoric). A significant portion of the widely heralded Democratic strength was illusory, predicated upon the idea that the sixty-nine Democrats formed a monolithic voting bloc. Democratic cohesiveness was achieved with some major administration initiatives, but it was not a sure thing in any and all instances.

John's friends like Carter Glass, Harry Byrd, and other Southern Democrats were much closer in their thinking to the Old Guard Republicans than they were to the Roosevelt administration.

Roosevelt, the master strategist and pork-barrel politician, could usually think of some way of keeping them in line on those pieces of legislation he considered essential, but there were very notable exceptions to this rule. The best example came some years later during what was termed by the press Roosevelt's "court-packing scheme" of 1937, when the president's hopes of enlarging the U.S. Supreme Court were overwhelmingly rejected by congressional Democrats. Despite such occasional defeats of Roosevelt initiatives, however, it was abundantly clear by 1935 that the previously accepted political rules of the game, including those realities that had prevailed during John's first term in the Senate, had been permanently altered.

The senator's first action in the new Congress was the introduction of another of his periodic Equal Rights Amendments, this one entitled "the Lucretia Mott Amendment" in honor of a pioneer of the women's rights movement. His old friend from Delaware's women's suffrage fight, Mrs. Florence Bayard Hilles, was now national president of the National Woman's Party.* She launched a publicity campaign in Delaware to highlight Senator Townsend's latest effort, which brought him much favorable publicity–and some groans from old adversaries like the redoubtable Mrs. Mary Wilson Thompson. One editorialist noted that few Delawareans realized that women had not gotten equal rights under the Constitution when passage of the 19th Amendment extended voting rights to them. Nor, for that matter, did they know that Senator Townsend had been working for an equal rights amendment

---

*   *In another example of the often strange juxtapositions of Delaware politics, Mrs. Hilles was the sister of former U.S. Senator Thomas F. Bayard, the man Townsend had defeated in the election of 1928 to win his U.S. Senate seat. Her friendship with John predated this event, however, beginning during the great battle over the suffrage amendment in 1920.*

for years. Such was the level of public awareness in Delaware and elsewhere at the time that many people were not even aware that equal rights for women was an issue. John's efforts in this direction during his U.S. Senate career showed that his courageous stand for suffrage as governor was motivated by a deep-seated belief in the equality of women.

As for John's personal philosophy of government as he began his second term in an atmosphere of radical change, he summed it up nicely in an article he contributed to a special edition of the *Eastern Shore News*, the Berlin weekly newspaper. The article was written at the request of the student newspaper staff at Selbyville High School, which had been given an opportunity to produce a student edition of the weekly newspaper.*

"Why don't they make a law about it?" asks the irritated citizen. And, alas! More laws are made and his irritations are increased.

But thanks to a comparatively small body of men and women elected to the Congress, who sit, more or less patiently, through seemingly endless hours of committee work and debate, relatively few of the thousands of bills introduced pass the test of legislative deliberation.

In fact, although more than 3,000 amendments to the Constitution of the United States have been proposed, only 21 have been passed and ratified. During the last session of the Congress, there were introduced 15,101 bills, 733 resolutions, 522 joint resolutions, and 72 concurrent resolutions. Of this number there were enacted only 487 public laws, 53 public resolutions, and 436 private bills. It would seem that we have still a

---

* *Among the student journalists was Miss Rachel Morris who, some years later, would become Mrs. Preston C. Townsend*

national policy of prudence and discretion.

Yet in spite of this apparently conservative output
of the legislative mill, too many bills are passed–too many
laws are made. When one considers that this business
of lawmaking goes on year after year, one is convinced
that the volume is too great. . .

After all, the citizen is the Government and he
must pay the bill. He is taxed in so many indirect ways
that he is apt to be insensible to the fact that it is he
who supports the Government and not the Government
who supports him. If he should delude himself into
thinking that this is not true, his day of awakening will
come. And this is as it should be; for in no other way
may the proper restraint be maintained. . .

The first big battle of the 1935 session concerned an
administration work relief appropriations bill, which would authorize
the expenditure of just under $5 billion in aid to the unemployed.
At this time enormous numbers of people were on the government
payroll under the auspices of the various New Deal programs doing
almost every job imaginable from digging mosquito control ditches
through the marshes of Sussex County to painting murals in U.S.
post offices across the land. Townsend and most other "Old Guard"
senators believed that $2 billion could be cut from the proposed
legislation without destroying its effectiveness. As was all too usual
that year, they lost the fight, but not without making their point that
there was a difference between giving people enough to eat and
providing meaningful work on the one hand, and paying them
handsomely to perform nonessential work at a leisurely pace.

He won, or rather helped his friend Carter Glass to win, a
major victory on a new banking bill onto which the administration
and other senators tried to tack amendments calling for a variety
of liberal measures John and Glass opposed. One, for example,

would have turned the radio priest, Father Charles Coughlin's, plan for an all-powerful central bank into a reality. The administration hoped, basically, to get an amendment passed placing the Federal Reserve System under the total control of the White House and this above all else was opposed by Glass.

The Roosevelt effort to transfer control of banking to the federal government "is being followed with more anxiety than has been witnessed since the establishment of the Federal Reserve system in the first term of President Wilson" according to one reporter, who went on to say:

> Fortunately, as bankers see it, Senator Glass, chief patron of the reserve system, is at the head of the conservative forces now intent on thwarting efforts by the Administration to change radically the nation's banking structure. Standing sturdily with Glass is Townsend . . . [who] exercised an influence second only to that of Glass in causing modifications in the radical measure President Roosevelt initially proposed.
> Senator Glass, the scrapper and colorful personality, hit the headlines, but Senator Townsend, quiet and conciliatory, was the man who time after time composed differences in committee and kept the way open to agreement of a majority on the really vital amendments, according to eminent men who as experts in the field of banking sat in on executive sessions of the Senate committee, where the main fight took place.
> . . . the Delaware Senator, it should be said, made his own study of the bill. His role was not that of a subordinate carrying out suggestions of Senator Glass. In their different ways, both exerted preponderant influence with their colleagues . . .

They also exerted great influence on the Senate-House conference committee that met to work out a final version. The House had approved the administration bill virtually as written. When the two sides got together in the late summer of 1935 to work out a final version, it was little changed from the Townsend-Glass bill approved by the Senate.

However popular the Democrats had been with voters in most states in 1934, the depression was not much nearer to being over in most of the country and people were getting tired of waiting. Hundreds of thousands of them began heeding the cries of several radical demagogues with simplified and none-too-well-defined answers to the nation's problems. One unlikely and essentially well-meaning member of this group was Father Coughlin of Detroit, a Catholic priest with an easy, compelling speaking style who became a voice for millions of disaffected persons.

Another popular figure was a retired California physician, Dr. Francis E. Townsend, who came up with a scheme for old-age pensions that swept the nation before Roosevelt came forward with his own Social Security idea. While proposals to provide government-funded old-age pensions were nothing new, Dr. Townsend's plan was accepted eagerly by millions of Americans suffering from the ravages of the depression. Roosevelt's Social Security legislation of 1935 borrowed certain broad concepts from "The Townsend Plan" and was in part a response to it.

The Townsend Plan was not particularly bad thinking, except that Dr. Townsend was rather sketchy when it came to defining how it was to be financed. Few people let that detail stop them from expressing wild enthusiasm for it. This situation raised a problem for Senator Townsend, who was becoming increasingly well known around the country. Many of those who became enthusiastic supporters of the Townsend plan were convinced that he was its originator. In 1934 and early 1935 the senator received literally hundreds of letters from various unfortunate Americans commending him on his thoughtfulness and nearly as many more taking him to task for his rattle-brained scheme. But, as one news story pointed out, "he answers every letter and explains the writer has the wrong man."

The mistaken identity problem was all the more uncomfortable for John as Roosevelt's Social Security Act was introduced since he and Senator Hastings opposed it along with most other Republican senators. Once again, John's main objection was the cost and what he saw as long-range funding problems, concerns which have proven to be somewhat prophetic.

Hastings and Townsend opposed so much New Deal legislation during the session that a Wilmington *Journal-Every Evening* article predicting future opposition by the two senators to Roosevelt administration measures prompted this response from one reader:

TO THE EDITOR,

In Thursday's *Journal-Every Evening* I see a headline that reads: "Del. Group in Congress Will Hit New Deal." If you think that's news you can't be much of a newspaperman. But apparently you thought it was hot enough stuff to run near the top of the front page.

Any time you get a story that Senators Hastings and Townsend and Congressman Stewart are swimming with President Roosevelt in the White House pool or that they have decided to run on the Democratic ticket in the next campaign, that will be news. But why bother to tell your readers in big type something that everyone but an idiot knows anyway?

If you keep on palming off things like this as news on your front page it won't be long before nobody will be reading your paper. By the way, here's something that ought to be a hot tip for you to follow up that story with. I understand that President Roosevelt has let it be secretly understood that he may vote Democratic at the elections next year.

DISGUSTED READER

By far the most politically adroit, and therefore the most threatening, populist demagogue who arose during those years was former Louisiana Governor Huey P. "Kingfish" Long who then became that state's U.S. senator. The Kingfish was one of the true originals of American politics. He was a very real threat to the established order because he had a much better chance of rising to a position of national power and a much better idea of how to use power effectively when he got it. Huey might very well have been elected president in 1936 or 1940, with who knows what consequences, had he not been assassinated in a hallway of the Louisiana State Capitol at Baton Rouge on his return home from the 1935 Senate session.

The man upon whom Robert Penn Warren based his novel *All the King's Men,* Huey was a true political genius in the opinion of many knowledgeable observers. He was also brash, impetuous, arrogant, boyish, utterly brilliant and a born performer who had succeeded in creating a virtual dictatorship in his home state. He had quite blatantly arranged the election not only of the state's other U.S. senator but also of its governor. He openly ran Louisiana either from home or from his office in Washington. It was accepted as a fact by many politically knowledgeable observers that his Louisiana delegation had swung the deciding votes to Roosevelt at the 1932 Democratic National Convention, enabling F.D.R. to win the presidential nomination. Huey wasted no time after Roosevelt's

Tasting "Potlikker": *This artistically-enhanced newspaper photo appeared in a 1932* Washington Herald *article entitled "Senators Sample Long's Famous Potlikker Dish." Beginning "Potlikker yesterday became a national dish," the article went on to recount that Sen. Huey P. Long of Louisiana personally supervised the preparation of a large pot of the classic southern delicacy and then invited a dozen of his Senate colleagues (including John) to the Senate Dining Room to sample the dish. "At the table considerable discussion arose whether the corn pone, served with the potlikker, should be dunked or crumbled into the potlikker. The dunkers, championed by Long, won over the crumblers, championed by Senator Black of Alabama [Hugo Black, later a U.S. Supreme Court justice] In the photo above, Long shows Senators Fletcher of Florida and Townsend of Delaware how to dunk without burning a thumb (Townsend family scrapbooks).*

election in letting him know that he expected to be repaid for his assistance–this at a luncheon at Roosevelt's Hyde Park mansion at which the president-elect's aged mother, the imperious Sara Delano Roosevelt, was heard to ask loudly, "Who is that awful man talking to my son?" It was after this episode that Roosevelt told a visitor that Huey was one of the two most dangerous men in America (the other, he said, was General Douglas MacArthur). Needless to say, their friendly relationship was shortlived.

By 1935, Huey had built a national organization around his "Share the Wealth" and "Every Man a King" slogans and was building an ever-broadening grass roots power base with the clear intention of taking on Roosevelt. Long and Roosevelt were without a doubt the two most effective politicians of their day in America and it is by no means clear which was the more so. During his five years in the Senate before his death, Huey used the Senate floor as a stage for his carefully calculated displays of outrageous behavior. Much of it was good fun and utterly hilarious. He was a master of the filibuster and once carried on single-handedly for nearly twenty hours on the floor, reading old Louisiana recipes and other nonsense to keep an administration bill from passage.

Huey and Townsend hit it off in a very gingerly way. They were about as different as two men could be in politics and style but they both had country origins and enjoyed people, and they built a certain rapport. Senator Townsend was appointed to a Senate committee to investigate the 1932 election of Louisiana Senator Overton, a Long cohort, but withdrew from it because of the press of other duties without ever going to the state on committee business. In any case, Huey liked Senator Townsend enough to give him a walking stick, that the senator prized highly thereafter.

Huey became a favorite attraction with visitors to the Senate chamber. Visiting Delawareans would request to be taken to the visitors' gallery when Huey was speaking and his performances always drew a standing-room-only crowd of onlookers. Louise Johnson became something of a connoisseur of senatorial speaking styles from her frequent attendance as an escort for visitors. She noted of Huey that "he was a strolling speaker. He was supposed to make his speeches at or near his own seat, and always on his own side of the Senate chamber. But not Huey! He paraded that

Senate floor as if it belonged to him. On one occasion Marjorie [Mrs. Johnson's daughter] and I listened to four hours of one of his famous filibusters."

One Long filibuster ended the 1935 session of the U.S. Senate. Huey got the floor before the Senate had acted on the appropriations bills for most of the major legislation passed during the session, including Social Security. He went on and on and the show was so good that many representatives deserted their own chamber to come over and hear him. John was there and listened to the bitter end, that came when a disgusted Vice-President John Nance Garner, never one to brook much nonsense, smashed down his gavel and declared the Senate adjourned. Though no one knew it at the time, it was to be Huey's last performance.

While most senators were much more restrained than Huey Long, the Senate was full of characters. One of the more interesting was elderly, bearded Senator James Hamilton Lewis of Illinois, the majority whip and the Senate's most flowery speaker. He was known behind his back as "Jim Ham Lewis." His full head of hair was far more luxuriant than his beard, which was itself quite lush. Louise Johnson reported that the reason for the fine reddish hair in one so old was that Senator Lewis wore a wig, or rather several wigs.

> He wore not just one wig but many–a series of them which would change after the growth of the hair. When it was getting too long he would put on one that looked as if he had just been to the barber's; in a week or so, another of the same pinkish color but a bit longer, and so on.
> One day Senator "Jim Ham" Lewis disappeared. He had done that before, but on this occasion he did not return in due time. His staff had wondered where

Strawberry Feast: *Senator Townsend is shown in a mid-1930s magazine photo hosting his annual strawberry shortcake feast. With him at the table are Mrs. Frank Tallman, Delaware's Republican national committeewoman, and Senator Robert Taft of Ohio (Townsend family scrapbooks).*

he had gone. Finally, they called Mrs. Lewis, who knew no more than they did. The secretary said, "But there is a barrel of hams from Chicago here. What shall we do with them?"

Mrs. Lewis' reply was, "Divide them and take them home with you." Without explanation Senator Lewis returned from Africa one day.

Another of her favorite recollections involved Senator Ashurst of Arizona who was handsome and debonair and used his suave speaking style to demolish the positions of his colleagues without their fully appreciating the damage he had done. In one such instance, Ashurst's friend, Senator Hiram Bingham of

Connecticut, got up at the conclusion of Ashurst's graceful attack on him and responded, "Let me say that when I am chastised by the pulchritudinous Senator from Arizona, I feel that I have been massaged by a pearl."

One thing that endeared Senator Townsend even to those colleagues who disagreed with him was his sense of hospitality. Early in his Senate career he had gotten into the habit of hosting the entire Senate at annual dinners. First it was canvasback duck dinners in the Senate Dining Room with the ducks supplied by his sons from their hunting place down on Chincoteague Bay. Then in the early 1930s the Senator began treating his colleagues to baskets of Delaware apples. Most popular of all was his annual strawberry feast in June. The first year the strawberries were mistakenly sent to the White House, whose staff found themselves with forty-eight crates of unexpected ripe, luscious strawberries on their hands. The mistake was soon sorted out and they were sent on to the Senate Dining Room where shortcake and whipped cream were supplied to go along with them. The Senator treated not only the entire Senate, but pages, sergeants-at-arms, committee staffers, secretaries, elevator operators, custodians and everyone else in the place. His old sobriquet from gubernatorial days, "The Strawberry King," was resurrected and travelled with him from then on.

Senator Townsend was not the only member of Congress who provided a feast of local delicacies for his peers. Even Huey Long produced a regional treat. He introduced the Senate to potlikker, that standard of the rural South that is essentially the savory liquid left over after a mess of greens and fatback have been cooked up. He worked in the kitchen of the Senate Dining

Room with the head chef, showing him how to prepare the stuff, and then insisted that it be kept available on the menu thereafter. While various senators, including John, tried it and liked it, the reception for the Delaware strawberries was considerably more enthusiastic.

STRAWBERRY TIME

THIS PINK CHEEKED, FLAXEN HAIRED GENTLE MAN WHO IS PICTURED CHUCKING A LUSCIOUS STRAWBERRY UNDER THE CHIN IS **SENATOR JOHN G. TOWNSEND, JR.**, OF DELAWARE.

BECAUSE OF HIS FRUIT GROWING, AND PARTICU- LARLY HIS PRODUCTION OF DELAWARE BERRIES, HE IS KNOWN AS "**THE STRAWBERRY KING**."

BECAUSE OF HIS FLAXEN HAIR — TO THOSE WHO INDULGE IN FREE COINAGE OF NICKNAMES — HE IS CALLED THE SENATE'S 14 KARAT, 100% "STRAWBERRY BLONDE."
— Malone – Washington – '34.

(reproduced from the original in the Townsend family scrapbooks)

27. Life in the "Loyal Opposition"

Crowning the queen: In this photo from the Sunday New York Times rotogravure section for May 10, 1936, Senator Townsend is shown crowning the Apple Blossom Queen as her court looks on. The annual event was held in the heart of the Shenandoah Valley orchard domains of John's friend, Senator Harry Flood Byrd of Virginia (Townsend family scrapbooks) .

For the nation as a whole, the Great Depression reached its nadir in the winter of 1932–1933, but it did not bottom out for Republican political hopes until 1936, the year the dispirited party hovered on the brink of total failure. Party leaders were forced to face the sad truth that while many might be philosophically opposed to the dole, a great many more will stand in line for their share of the money and cast their votes for those who give it to them. By now the G.O.P. had tried every tactic conceivable to defeat the New Deal. Every new approach they tried seemed more prone to failure than the one that came before it. In 1936, they changed their plan of attack once more, adopting a stance of limited acquiesence to the concepts embodied in Roosevelt's New Deal "If you can't beat them, join them," in other words. This approach was even worse than outright opposition to Roosevelt.

Herbert Hoover was attempting through his continued dominance of the Republican National Committee to bring about his own renomination in hopes of winning vindication. In the end his candidacy was decisively rejected by the party rank and file, as were the electoral hopes of various other party luminaries who were acceptable to the wing of the party that represented the views of the Eastern business establishment. The crusty old renegade, Senator William Borah of Idaho, who had done more to hurt the party over the years than to help it, announced his candidacy. He railed and roared not only against Roosevelt but against Wall Street. He was opposed in many of the primaries by Frank Knox, an old Bull Moose supporter of Theodore Roosevelt and now publisher of the Chicago *Daily News*. The two men finally succeeded in killing each other off.

This left the field open to the candidacy of Kansas Governor Alfred M. Landon, a mild Progressive with a well-established independence from the Wall Street crowd. Landon ran a skillful campaign with the help of such able veterans as William Allen White, famed Roosevelt Progressive and publisher of the *Emporia Gazette*, a small Kansas daily with a large national following. John's Senate friend Arthur H. Vandenberg of Michigan also let it be known that he was available for a draft, but with Landon the clear front runner, he was never called on. When the party met at Cleveland in June they nominated Landon on the first ballot.

"Alf" Landon was an impressive candidate who in other circumstances might have won and gone on to a fine record of accomplishment in the White House, but 1936 was not his year.

The national political strategist:

Advising the candidate:
Senator Townsend (right) and his deputy G.O.P. Senatorial Campaign Committee Chairman, Senator Frederick Steiwer (Ore.), paid a visit to Gov. Alfred M. Landon in Topeka in the summer of 1936 to coordinate their campaign efforts. One Washington cartoonist was prompted by the visit to produce the sketch below.

(Both from Townsend family scrapbooks)

The caption for the cartoon at right read:

"Senator Townsend, of Delaware, was a recent visitor to Topeka. The Senator was very secretive about what he and Governor Landon discussed. Of course, they might have discussed party politics, or the Delaware Republican crop of voters of 1936. Maybe they discussed Delaware's big, little three electoral votes. After all, when three little votes jump over the fence from one side to the other it makes a difference of six counters–Malone"

He had been a Midwestern Progressive throughout his career, but while he believed the government was obliged to help needy citizens, he also believed in balanced budgets. His main criticism of the New Deal centered around the problem of deficit spending, that he believed would set the nation off on a round of runaway inflation. He had a simple, common-sense way about him–not dissimilar to his fellow Midwesterner, Harry S Truman. He was a creditable candidate but he did not offer a great enough contrast to F.D.R.

Shortly before the national convention, Senator Hastings surprised his fellow Republicans by announcing his intention of retiring from the Senate at the conclusion of his term to return to the full-time practice of law. He requested as well to be relieved of his duties as chairman of the Republican Senatorial Campaign Committee, that he had held since 1934. Though Hastings enjoyed the Senate and was doing an able job on the campaign committee, he seems to have become weary of being the Republican Party's leading "voice in the wilderness" against the New Deal. He was growing older and had never been wealthy. He felt the need to make the sort of money one could not make in politics if one was honest. He had no independent business interests to sustain him as Senator Townsend did. It was a decision most of his friends found hard to accept.

Senator and Mrs. Hastings went off on a trip to Palestine that summer in the company of Senator and Mrs. Copeland and another couple as guests of the Hearst Syndicate to examine the merits of the Zionist cause. While there, Hastings learned that the Republican State Convention had renominated him to the Senate. In his memoirs he recalled that "when I got home and found what had happened in the Republican Convention I concluded that the Republican Party was about to fall apart."*

In Delaware, matters were complicated further by another of the seemingly endless series of Republican schisms. Three leading Republicans who were angry at the regular state party organization for three different reasons had banded together to form the Independent Republican Party. These were J. Austin "Big Jim" Ellison of New Castle County, I. Dolphus Short of Milford, and former Congressman Robert G. Houston of Georgetown. Ellison, according to Hastings, was just contrary and difficult to deal with. Short fell out with the party after he had been deprived of the gubernatorial nomination in 1932 in what he thought was a violation of the old, unwritten county rotation rule. Congressman Houston had parted with the mainstream of the Delaware G.O.P. in 1932 over the issue of repeal of the Prohibition Amendment.

By 1932, the Republican party in Delaware fit into the same general category as Senator Townsend's portrayal in a *Vanity Fair* caricature, "demi-dry." They did not advocate repeal, but they did not man the barricades to oppose it either. Houston did man the barricades. He was a radical dry and had been unable to accept the gradual liberalization of the party on the issue. This was the source of his failure to win renomination to a fifth term in 1932. In the years that followed he drew farther and farther from the state party in his views until by 1936 he was ready to join forces with Ellison and Short to form the Independent Republican Party. Houston was the faction's candidate for the U.S. Senate.

Ellison ran for the House of Representatives against the Republican incumbent George Stewart and Seaford Democrat

---

*   *Daniel O. Hastings,* Delaware Politics, 1904-1954 *(privately printed, 1961).*

William F. Allen. Short ran against Republican gubernatorial nominee, Harry Cannon of Bridgeville, and former Wilmington Mayor Richard C. McMullen, the Democratic nominee. As their candidate for the U.S. Senate, the Democrats nominated James H. Hughes of Kent County, the man who had opposed John in the race for governor in 1916, to run against Houston and Hastings.

The brilliant Wilmington attorney John Biggs Jr. was elected Delaware's Democratic State Chairman in 1936, a development that was to have a significant positive impact on the Democratic state campaign. Biggs was the scion of a prominent Delaware family and was friendly with several members of the Roosevelt family. He was himself a published novelist and had briefly considered pursuing literature as a career during his years at Princeton. While in college, he had developed a close friendship with such literary figures as novelist F. Scott Fitzgerald and Edmund Wilson, the brilliant critic, scholar, and author.*

As state chairman during the 1936 campaign, Biggs ran one of the best-engineered state campaigns the Democratic party had ever seen. That fact combined with the Republican factional dispute and the onrushing tide of the Roosevelt campaign to produce the most dramatic Democratic victory in Delaware in forty years. Delaware elected its first Democratic governor since Ebe Tunnell had left office in 1901. Hughes soundly defeated Hastings and Houston. Their combined vote would not have been enough to

---

* Biggs, by now a federal judge, served as executor of Fitzgerald's estate after the latter's untimely death in 1940. Biggs's wise and careful nurturing of Fitzgerald's literary legacy is largely credited with bringing about the resurrection, during the 1950s and 1960s, of Fitzgerald's reputation as one of America's greatest twentieth century authors.

have put either Hastings or Houston over the top had either been running as the lone Republican candidate. Allen also soundly defeated Congressman Stewart and Ellison in the House race and Democrats did well in lesser offices.

In Delaware, 1936 was one of those watershed elections that marks the ends and beginnings of eras. What had ended was the period of solid Republican dominance that grew out of the resolution of the Addicks fight. Things were even worse for Republicans at the national level where Roosevelt was reelected by the greatest landslide in the nation's history. Landon carried only Maine and Vermont, even losing his home state.* Old Republican Senate leaders went down to defeat everywhere. Incredibly there were only sixteen Republican U.S. senators after the 1936 election, including two newcomers, H. Styles Bridges of New Hampshire and the young Henry Cabot Lodge of Massachusetts, grandson and namesake of the famed turn-of-the-century Senate leader of the same name.** Seven of the sixteen were Republican insurgents of one kind or another who had refused to support the national ticket, leaving only seven mainstream Republican veterans in the Senate. On the numbers alone, the Republican Party had not been in worse shape since the party was founded in 1856.

The New Dealers were ecstatic in their victory, believing that the time had arrived for even more drastic alterations in the nature

---

* *The old maxim of generations past, "As Maine goes, so goes the nation" gave way that year to "As Maine goes, so goes Vermont."*

** *This younger Henry Cabot Lodge went on to a distinguished career in the Senate before becoming Richard M. Nixon's vice-presidential running mate in the 1960 election. He was later appointed U.S. ambassador to South Vietnam by President John F. Kennedy.*

of American life than those that had occurred in the preceding four years. H.L. Mencken, the cynical sage of Baltimore, summed up the prevailing attitude in a letter to a friend: "Give your mind seriously to the question of the Second Coming."

Yet even with their ranks alarmingly decimated, the Republicans in Congress were not as bad off as it might first have seemed. The Democratic Party was very far from being a cohesive entity. Even Roosevelt, the much-touted master politician, had only succeeded in bridging temporarily the gap between the Democrats of the Northern industrial states and those of the rural South. The Southern Democrats had supported the president during the first phase of the New Deal when many of his programs were directly beneficial to farmers, but their ardor for his programs cooled considerably thereafter.

Even in the absence of his former conservative Republican colleagues, John Townsend could still count on the cooperation of the venerable Senator Glass, Harry Byrd and other Democratic Southerners. A few Northern Democratic senators such as Copeland of New York were also basically conservative in their outlook.

In February 1937, only a month after the start of the new session of Congress, an overconfident Roosevelt made a very fundamental error of political judgement, which drove his conservative foes within his own party into the welcoming arms of the Republicans. An important setback to his original New Deal legislation had been the conservative restraint imposed by the U.S. Supreme Court. The justices had declared several of the major New Deal programs unconstitutional, forcing the administration to scrap them and start over. Roosevelt decided after the landslide of

November 1936, to find a way to bring about a Supreme Court more inclined to be favorable to his program. After some deliberation he decided that the answer was to enlarge the court from nine members to a total of fifteen justices. Since several justices already tended to support the administration, the appointment of an additional six liberal justices would give him a majority. While all of this alone would have created problems enough, Roosevelt compounded his error first by failing to discuss his plans in advance with the Democratic congressional leadership and then by attempting to bury the Supreme Court provisions in the fine print of a larger bill designed to streamline the federal judicial process. This fooled no one and lost the president even more support since it was clear that he had attempted to slip the action past the Congress.

What quickly became known as Roosevelt's "court-packing scheme" created an immediate and lasting furor on Capitol Hill. Not only did the Southern Democrats raise a chorus of howls, charging that F.D.R. was trying to subvert the constitutional process, but many Western senators who had themselves been critical of past Supreme Court decisions opposed the president. When they saw the effect all this was having on the so-called Democratic majority, the Republicans wisely chose to keep quiet about the matter, making relatively innocuous public statements about it when they mentioned it at all, and allowing the Democrats to fight it out among themselves. They feared that a loud Republican attack on Roosevelt would serve to unite the Democrats in defense of their party leader.

Ex-President Hoover was reluctant to cooperate in the overall Republican strategy, however. He was as anxious as ever to undertake a frontal assault on the White House and could not see

that a more subtle approach might accomplish more in the end. Nor did many Republican voters understand why the party's congressional leaders were not taking a more aggressive stand. As the months wore on with no end to the fight among the Democrats, the Republican strategy had the desired effect.

Finally, by summertime, President Roosevelt was openly seeking to effect a compromise and had

Senator Townsend: *shown as he appeared during the mid-1930s, at the height of his power in the U.S. Senate (courtesy of Judith M. Pfeiffer & Robert C. Barnes).*

Senate Majority Leader Joseph Robinson working on a measure to increase the number of justices by two instead of six. This was not much more welcome to the by-now militant Senate than the original proposal had been, but they had not yet rejected it by the beginning of July 1937. Only a few days before the majority leader was to leave Washington for a visit to Senator Townsend in Ocean City, Maryland, where the two were planning a deep-sea fishing trip, Robinson suddenly dropped dead. With Robinson's unexpected passing, Roosevelt's last hopes for salvaging anything from his Supreme Court plan passed away as well. The coalition of Republicans and Democratic rebels solidified and resoundingly defeated the president.

The defeat of the court-packing scheme brought a whole new air into Congress. It had shown that the seemingly invincible Roosevelt could be defeated by concerted action if the issue was basic. It showed also that the 1936 Democratic victory had not been a victory for the New Deal at any expense. Having tested their power and been triumphant, albeit in a quiet way, the Republicans and the Southern Democrats moved forward during the session to thwart many of the President's plans. Some minor New Deal legislation was approved during the remainder of the session, but for all practical purposes the cutting edge of the New Deal had been permanently blunted.

Some Republicans were hopeful that the cooperation between congressional Republicans and conservative Democrats would lead to a realignment of political parties along conservative and liberal lines, thus making conservatives a potent electoral force as early as 1938. John and most of the party's other experienced congressional leaders knew this would not happen. Such a realignment overlooked the fact that the Democrats who worked most closely with the Republicans, such as Senator Glass, would lose their committee chairmanships and other powers if they broke completely with the Democratic Party. They realized that the best they could hope for was a loosely-structured cooperation on an issue-by-issue basis, built upon friendships and mutual concerns. This was precisely the milieu in which Senator Townsend was at his best.

In this way John entered the most effective phase of his Senate career, reaching the height of his political power just at the point at which his own party was to all outward appearances in its greatest decline. Only rarely had a Delaware senator achieved a comparable level of power in his respective party caucus in Congress. In good times, when some relative equality existed between the two parties, fair-weather senators from larger states came in for much of the power. In 1937 and 1938 any mainstream Republican in Congress had power, especially when he was also a man of great personal popularity among the Democrats as Townsend was.

He almost never spoke on the floor of the Senate or participated in floor debate. Although such public exposure would have brought him much press attention, it was simply not his style. He spoke only when he had to in the Senate. He enjoyed talking to groups of constituents at home in Delaware but he was no orator and he recognized that fact. He left the main debating chores in the 1937 session to Senator Vandenberg, the Senate Minority Leader, with whom he worked very closely on legislation. Other senators who led the Republican debates were Steiwer and McNary of Oregon. Steiwer, who was John's assistant on the Republican Senatorial Campaign Committee, was an able public speaker and enjoyed debate. McNary served as Minority Whip despite his public stance of less than enthusiastic support for the G.O.P. national ticket during his own reelection campaign in 1936. The party leadership knew that only through such survival tactics had he been successful in getting reelected and he was allowed to retain his leadership role.

Senator Townsend concentrated on committee work, the area in which he excelled, and on maintaining the extensive network of Senate friendships that were the key to his ability to get things done. He worked to maintain the fragile coalition that enabled the Senate Republicans to survive as a viable force. It was almost as if he were slowly luring and cajoling away many of Roosevelt's most valuable functionaries in the Senate, except it was never that sort of overt, conscious effort.

Glass and Byrd had long been his closest Senate friends. Neither man had ever been very enthusiastic about the New Deal in any case. But other friendships grew with senators like Byrnes of South Carolina, McAdoo of California, and Truman of Missouri, and with Vice-President John Nance Garner ("Cactus Jack"). These men felt much easier with Townsend than they did with the president and his liberal young New Deal functionaries. Their views, their constituencies were more like his. Their commonality of interests had more to do with the experience of rural, smalltown America than with Republican and Democrat.

Senator Hughes never got along as well with his fellow Democratic senators as John did. As a result the latter was generally better able to get things done for Delaware during a Democratic administration than Hughes was. Hughes got off on the wrong foot when the court fight erupted just as he was getting established in Washington. Taking the seemingly prudent course of going along with the president, Hughes was one of only two senators who held out to the bitter end in support of the court-packing scheme. His stand won him few friends within his own party.

In the summer of 1937, John first raised an issue with which he was to be vitally concerned for the remainder of his Senate career when he took aim at the administration's bizarre silver purchasing policies. By 1937, silver had been a potent political commodity in America for nearly two generations, dating from the time when such western states as Colorado and Montana had entered the Union. Western senators tended to be closely united in their support for the silver mining industry just as Southern senators later were for tobacco. Yet silver mining was a tiny and relatively unimportant segment of the nation's economy, employing perhaps five thousand people. Silver occurred in such abundance, moreover, that it could never claim to be the sort of precious metal gold was. Because of their extreme independence and their tendency toward populism, the "silver senators" often held the balance of power in the Senate. They wrung from this advantage every possible concession they could for the silver industry, especially when Democratic administrations were in power, since they tended to align themselves more readily with the Democrats.

The height of folly, as far as the federal government's silver purchase policies were concerned, came early in 1934 with the passage of the infamous Silver Purchase Act of 1934. The leader of the silver group, Senator Key Pittman of Nevada, had brought about a maneuver to get President Roosevelt to commit the government by executive order to purchase virtually the entire U.S. output of silver for a period of four years at 64.5 cents an ounce, more than 21 cents per ounce above the current free market price. According to one writer, silver miners "shot off revolvers in the streets of Leadville and danced with girls atop the bars of Tonopah" when they heard news of Roosevelt's order.*

Still not content, even after this concession, the silver senators went after still more. In January of 1934, Senator Burton K. Wheeler of Montana introduced a bill requiring the government to purchase another billion ounces of silver and to issue U.S. currency against it. This bill only narrowly missed passage in the form in which it was written. A much more subtle House version passed

---

*   *This discussion of the silver situation is drawn largely from William E. Leuchtenburg's* Franklin D. Roosevelt and the New Deal *(New York: Harper & Row, 1963), pp. 82–84*

because it provided for the sale of farm surpluses abroad in return for silver at a rate above the world price of silver. Roosevelt was adamantly opposed to the bill and tried everything in his power to defeat it, but it passed in a form that required the government to buy silver until it reached one-fourth of the nation's monetary reserve or until the world price of silver reached $1.29 an ounce (some three times the current price). The Treasury was to issue U.S. silver certificates to cover the cost. The idea was to create a false scarcity of silver worldwide, thus vastly inflating the price of the metal and in the process making silver speculators rich. A major problem was that the currencies of three nations, China, Mexico, and Peru, were then based on silver and the executive order and the later Silver Purchase Act threatened to wreak havoc with the economies of those nations.

This was the situation that John attacked during the 1937 session. He was the first senator to make a formal assault on the policy, befitting his status as the ranking Republican on the Senate Banking and Currency Committee. As one editorialist wrote of his attack, "Senator Townsend of Delaware rarely speaks from the Senate floor, but when he does he generally has something of importance to say." In his speech, John pointed out that President Roosevelt's proclamation of 1933 and the Silver Purchase Act of 1934 had failed to benefit the public with the exception of "Chinese and Japanese smugglers and speculators in silver [and] Mexican, Indian, South American and other foreign producers and hoarders of silver, holders of shares in producing companies, and speculators in silver the world over." He said that another supposed goal of the Silver Purchase Act had been "to do something for China," but that in reality what had been done was to force China "to close all its banks, suspend the silver standard, and suffer a drastic deflation, thereby crippling its purchasing power."

In an accompanying resolution, he called for a full investigation of the entire question of the government's silver purchase policies by the Banking and Currency Committee, making the interesting point that the total world production of silver for the calendar year 1934 was 215 million ounces, less than one-fifth the amount that the presidential proclamation and the subsequent Silver Purchase Act required the U.S. government to buy. He noted that "the present artificial stimulation of silver production . . . results in taking vast hoards of silver from the ground only to be reburied in the ground [it was stored underground at West Point and other depositories]." His resolution got nowhere in 1937. Senator Alben S. Barkley of Kentucky, then chairman of the Banking and Currency Committee, buried the measure in committee.

In 1938, he tried again, introducing measures to repeal the Silver Purchase Act of 1934 and to end the authority of the president and the secretary of the treasury to fix the weight of the silver dollar and to provide for unlimited coinage of silver. Again his resolutions failed, as they did for the remainder of his Senate years, but the issue proved more popular with knowledgeable bankers and financial journalists than with politicians. The Silver Purchase Act survived relatively intact until the Kennedy administration when it was finally repealed. By that time the silver lobby had benefitted from federal largesse to a point undreamed of by Southern peanut farmers, Southwestern oilmen and others who are generally perceived by the public to be perennial feasters at the government pork barrel. Yet few Americans really appreciated the nature of the government's handout to the silver industry.

Late in life as he looked back on his years in the U.S. Senate,

John often said that he saw his "silver bill" as his most important work in Congress even though it had been unsuccessful. Though his resolutions failed, they succeeded in defining the nature of the problem. One of the oddities of recent American domestic history is that most Americans today see the 1930s, 1940s, and 1950s, with their abundance of silver coinage, as having been some sort of an ideal time of monetary stability. In fact, as Senator Townsend and a few other voices in the wilderness tried to tell them, the reverse was more nearly true. They saw the abandonment of the gold standard by Roosevelt in 1933 as perhaps the beginning of the end for sound U.S. currency. What followed the Silver Purchase Act of 1934 was for John one of the greatest boondoggles of the age.

The off-year elections of 1938 furthered the trend that had developed during the court fight of early 1937. The campaign and the months leading up to it were especially busy ones for Senator Townsend. In the autumn of 1937, the nation had slipped once more into a serious economic slump before it had truly recovered from the depression. John saw that the policies of Franklin D. Roosevelt had not been much more successful than those of his Republican predecessor. As the ranking Republican on the Senate Banking and Currency Committee, he made his first open attack on the Roosevelt administration on the Senate floor. The direct impetus for his speech was Roosevelt's request for sweeping new economic powers with which to combat the latest setback in the economy. These new presidential powers were contained in the provisions of a government reorganization bill. In March 1938, as the Senate deliberated the measure, Townsend took to the floor. As reported in the New York *Herald Tribune*, the speech hit hard:

Five years ago today, American economy was wedded to a new philosophy. Perhaps I should say that a new economic philosophy was joined to reckless experiment, without regard to facts, experience or economic laws. Its own present to itself for its fifth anniversary is a log-jam of serious proportions. The offspring of this union with which all Americans, whether in the laboring class or in industry, have been presented is a sharp slump that promises to reach a depression of major importance from which all must suffer.

The senator said that the Roosevelt administration was simply using a "depression dodger" in referring to the latest slump as a

Taking on the New Deal: Wilmington Morning News *cartoonist Gee Tee Maxwell marked the occasion of John's attack on Roosevelt Administration policies with this 1938 cartoon (Townsend family scrapbooks).*

"recession." He charged that the statistics showed that "the slump in business since last October was sharper than that which followed the collapse in securities prices in 1929."

What is the situation today? Are we pulling out of the tailspin? The answer is no. The figures for January [1938] show some flattening out, some improvement even, in certain lines of activity, yet in February the downward trend was resumed. Today industrial production is well below 80 on the Federal Reserve Board index [as opposed to 147 the previous summer].

This is the situation as we find it today; we were promised a balanced budget—and in five years we saw the national debt increased by 15 billion dollars. We were then told that this mad expenditure would aid in recovery and that recovery had been achieved, and we see that the so-called recession of 1937 has been more acute in its first three months than was the depression of 1929 in its first three months.

I cannot too ardently urge that this body give thought to these facts when it considers legislation burdening industry, which must be relieved of its shackles and harassments if we are ever to recover from the depression. To listen to some of the recent administration spokesmen on such subjects as "monopoly" and prices, one might be led to the conclusion that government policies have had nothing to do with this depression, that this business collapse has been a case of Big Business knavery.

In 1932, leaders of the present administration wouldn't concede, as was generally conceded, that the American depression was only a part of a much broader and unprecedented world depression. They maintained that the earlier administration was responsible for it. And in 1936, they claimed credit for recovery. This time there can be no doubt of the responsibility. There is certainly no doubt that the depression of 1937-1938, and who knows how much longer, bears the indeible mark, "Made in America."

A month after his speech, Senator Townsend was a guest for dinner at the White House—along with ninety others of both parties to be sure, but the fact that he was invited at all says much for the spirit of decency that underlaid the relations between the various branches of government. John was a member of the opposition and a leader in helping to set its economic and fiscal policy. As such it was understood by most people on both sides that when he took the Roosevelt administration publicly to task, he was only doing his job and there was nothing personal involved in his attack.

With his speech, he had set the keynote for the 1938 campaign and he set about pursuing a hoped-for victory energetically, criss-crossing the country by train through the spring and summer, helping to organize senatorial campaigns, attending state party conventions, dispensing tactical advice and doling out committee funds carefully in races where Republicans looked like good bets. He told reporters he hoped to win ten new

Once a telegrapher...
Senator Townsend demonstrated to reporters one day in the late 1930s that he could still handle a telegraph key nearly half a century after he began his telegraphy career with the railroad (newspaper clipping from Townsend scrapbooks).

Senate seats in the campaign and said that the party planned to "turn on the steam" in twelve states: Oregon, Iowa, Kansas, South Dakota, Ohio, Illinois, Indiana, Kentucky, California, New Hampshire, New Jersey, and Maryland. He was also hoping for a Republican gain of eighty seats in the House of Representatives. To accomplish all this, the Republicans had set a budget of $175,000 for the Senate races and $500,000 for the House.

In June, Senator Townsend lost one of his closest Senate friends with the death of New York Senator Royal S. Copeland, whose family had also been close to his own family over the years. John was one of those appointed by Vice-President Garner to attend the funeral on behalf of the Senate. At sixty-seven, he was finding that many of his old friends and colleagues were passing from the scene.

At home in Delaware, where he was able to spend some time during the early summer worrying more about apples and strawberries than about votes, he had

Heavy, heavy hangs over thy head . . .
read the caption from a 1938 Associated Press photo showing Sen. Robert A. Taft and Agriculture Secretary Henry Wallace shaking hands at a Senate banking subcommittee meeting over the head of Senator Townsend (Townsend family scrapbooks).

things relatively easy that year with no senatorial or gubernatorial races to worry about. The Republican candidate for Congress was his old friend, George S. Williams of Millsboro, a onetime partner of Will White's in the lumber and basket business and another of the seemingly endless supply of Baltimore Hundred natives active in Delaware politics in those years. John held his usual dinner for state Republican leaders and committee members at the old Belhaven Hotel in Rehoboth Beach, an event which he had started upon his election to the Senate in 1928 and that now had become a high point of the political season.

He also interested himself in the continuing work to stabilize the Indian River Inlet, for which he had finally succeeded in winning federal funding the previous year. Another public works project he was following closely was the construction of a new post office for the town of Selbyville. The town was unusual in being one of the smallest towns in the United States to rate a second-class post office. Selbyville had won this distinction because of the huge volume of mail-order business resulting from its status as home to Bunting's Nurseries, owned by John's old friend and sometime orchard partner (and Republican state senator) Coleman Bunting. Bunting's company had grown into one of the nation's largest wholesale and retail mail-order nurseries, even supplying certain plants to Sears & Roebuck's catalogue customers.

By the end of July, John was turning once more to national politics. In August, he traveled to Washington, Indiana, for a mammoth gathering of G.O.P. leaders from across the nation. The meeting took place at a curious event known as "The Cornfield Conference," held at the large farm of Homer E. Capehart, vice-president of the Wurlitzer Organ Company and a leading financial backer of the national Republican Party. Capehart set up 38 circus tents and 4 huge field kitchens manned by a staff of 350 waiters. He also provided parking for 20,000 cars to handle an expected crowd of 50,000. In addition to being lots of fun, the Cornfield Conference gave the Republican hierarchy an opportunity to engage in an extended strategy session. The chairman of the Republican National Committee, Congressman Joseph W. Martin, chairman of the Republican Congressional Campaign Committee, and the state chairmen of most midwestern and far western state G.O.P. committees were also in attendance.

From the Cornfield Conference, John moved on to the Illinois State Republican Convention in Peoria and then across the western United States to Oregon. At every stop he met with local Republican leaders and U.S. senatorial candidates, outlining the party's plan of attack. He was back home in time to present the keynote speech at the Delaware Republican Convention in Dover on September 14. Of that speech, the *Sussex Countian*'s political columnist "Ispet" (who, one suspects, was probably old Congressman Houston himself), wrote in advance:

> I want to hear the keynote speech of our own John G. Townsend, Jr. John G. will doubtless bombard the "New Deal." John will be interesting. He is always more interesting than instructive, so I will be interested in hearing what John may say against the New Deal, and still more interested in what John may offer that will prove more attractive to the voters of Delaware and of the nation than this "New Deal."

"Ispet" went on to observe that Republican leaders would never defeat Roosevelt and the New Deal until they figured out something more tempting to the voters. He spoke of Senator McAdoo's decisive defeat in a California senatorial primary to a candidate who had worked the Dr. Francis Townsend old-age pension plan into a new form and noted that no one who had ever proposed such a plan had ever been defeated at the polls. He ended with the observation that:

> I have been trying for a long time to figure out just what this "New Deal" is and I have come to the conclusion that it is nothing more or less than the Townsend Plan administered in a number of different and diversified activities. It is an indirect system or series of systems of getting public money into the hands of the masses that has its influence at the polls.

The 1938 election that followed proved to be the first decisive defeat for the New Deal and a personal triumph for John, who picked up seven of the ten Senate seats and seventy-one of the eighty House seats he that he wanted. Among the victors was Delaware's Republican congressional candidate, George Williams. Even more encouraging was the fact that many anti-Roosevelt Democrats had successfully overcome efforts by the president to keep them from being renominated and had gone on to win reelection. Their victories created the opportunity for what party leaders hoped would become an even more effective coalition of Republicans and anti-New Deal Democrats to set the stage for a Republican victory in 1940.

28.   The Election of 1940

The German attack on Poland in the first week of September 1939 brought an immediate and lasting shift in emphasis from domestic politics to foreign affairs and public concerns with defense. The entire thrust of most congressmen and a large part of the American public had been inward. People were concerned with the economy, with recovery from the depression, with Hollywood romances, baseball, fashion—with all the minutiae and provincial concerns of American life. The Republicans were honing their blades for slashing attacks on the increasingly vulnerable Roosevelt administration and its failure to "normalize" the economy. Most knowledgeable observers expected F.D.R. to seek an unprecedented third term and the G.O.P. intended to demolish him on the matter of the economy.

In the two years between 1938 and 1940, much of John's energy was spent on matters of concern to his constituents, more so than had been true of the early New Deal years when so much of his time had gone into broad national concerns. He was now working for such things as the continuation of the Civilian Conservation Corps (CCC) camps in coastal Kent and Sussex Counties. The C.C.C. boys under the leadership of Colonel Wilbur S. Corkran had been working in Delaware's coastal marshes on mosquito control projects for several years.* Now, with much work still to be done, the federal

---

* *Colonel Corkran was also beginning his efforts during these years to develop the Rehoboth Beach area's most exclusive subdivision, Henlopen Acres. His mosquito control efforts had been assisted greatly by a powerful ally in the person of Mary Wilson Thompson, John's old nemesis from the woman's suffrage battle. A longtime summer resident of the Pines area of*

(continued on next page)

Capital Cleanup
Adjournment Day

(International)
U. S. Senator John G. Townsend of Delaware clears the decks to get a flying start in the event of Congressional adjournment at midnight, as scheduled.

Cleaning House: *Senator Townsend is shown in this newspaper photo cleaning out his desk as the end of the 1938 session nears (reproduced from a 1938 Washington newspaper clipping in the Townsend family scrapbooks).*

government was preparing to cut the funding. Senator Townsend saw this as a case where the government was trying to stop those aspects of the New Deal that had, in fact, done the public some good while continuing many, such as the silver purchase policy, which actually hurt the people. Working on such matters of local concern was, of course, sound politics for a senator who was up for reelection.

He had recently been reappointed chairman of the Republican

(continued from previous page)
Rehoboth, Mrs. Thompson now devoted her considerable lobbying skills to making sure area marshes were crisscrossed with networks of mosquito control ditches. One Sussex County native who spent considerable time in the resort during those years recalls that the erstwhile grande dame was now known to area youth as "the mosquito lady."

Senatorial Campaign Committee by Senate Minority Leader Charles McNary, who said that Senator Townsend had been extraordinarily successful in his four years in the job. His acceptance of the post for the 1940 election campaign was unusual. Most senatorial campaign committee chairmen resigned from the position when they, themselves, were candidates for reelection in order to devote full time to their own campaigns. John's decision to continue in the chairmanship was partly the result of pressure from friends and associates at the national level. They hated to lose a chairman with his experience and success record in a year when important Republican gains seemed assured if only the right kind of campaign could be put together. It is fair to say that, in 1940, no one in the United States knew more about the mechanics of a successful senatorial campaign than John Townsend did. And so he stayed in the job. In the process he did a favor for the Republican Party that turned out to be one of the costliest favors of his life.

Most Americans in the first two or three months of 1940 thought little about the war in Europe or the Japanese incursions into China and Manchuria. Their focus for several years had been directed at domestic affairs, though the Polish disaster in the fall and the subsequent Russian attack on Finland (and the Finns' valiant defense) were frequent topics of conversation during the winter. All through the growing tension in Europe a large segment of the American public had taken the attitude that what happened in Europe had little or nothing to do with the United States, that if we remained at home on our side of the Atlantic we could avoid becoming embroiled in another war. Such respected leaders of the pre-World War I period as President Theodore Roosevelt and Senator Henry Cabot Lodge of Massachusetts had believed in standing up for

American interests abroad either diplomatically or militarily, depending on the circumstances, and a significant group of Republicans felt the same way now, as war broke out anew in Europe. Many others took a different view. The Republican Party, had, through most of its history, been strongly nationalistic without being precisely isolationist. The isolationist philosophy grew more widespread in the early 1920s as a backlash to World War I. Yet even such early isolationists as Republican Senator Hiram Johnson of California had held that America must maintain a strong defense establishment. Johnson had fought mightily against the dismantling of the American fleet in the late 1920s and early 1930s. His isolationism had taken the form of a belief that America could protect her own interests without having to become entangled in the kinds of grand alliances and collective security arrangements that had led to World War I.

During the early 1930s, Senator Gerald Nye, a North Dakota Democrat, had evolved a new form of isolationism with strongly pacifist overtones that was based on an extremely simplistic and erroneous view of the munitions industry. Nye believed that the great munitions makers, among whom Delaware's du Ponts figured prominently, had largely fomented World War I for their own selfish financial interests. This view was an extension of Nye's old-fashioned Western radicalism with its strong suspicion of Eastern capitalists. He used his chairmanship of a Senate committee to launch a series of spectacular hearings aimed at proving that the du Ponts and others had propelled the nation into the war in order to reap vast profits. Nye's charges were nonsense but, coming as they did just after the worst of the depression years, they struck a responsive chord with the American people, who were in a mood to believe in conspiracies and to search out scapegoats. Senator Townsend had to endure the charade of Pierre, Lammot and Irénée du Pont sitting for hours and days in Senate hearing rooms defending their family interests against the Nye Committee, New Dealers, and many of John's fellow Republicans. President Roosevelt allowed Nye to rattle on unchallenged, although he knew it was all nonsense, because it suited his political ends at the time. Even though Nye's belief in the evil "merchants of death" and in the desirability of further dismantling the American "war machine" were classic tenets of socialism, both parties quickly leaped on Nye's bandwagon. The hearings resulted in the passage of a series of neutrality laws in 1935, 1936 and 1937. These measures were designed to keep American businessmen from being in a position to profit from foreign wars and to keep American ships off the high seas in wartime to avoid the kinds of provocations that led to U.S. involvement in World War I. The strong Republican support for these laws was especially surprising in view of the substantial number of international businessmen making up one important wing of the party. But all stood more or less idly by while the party rank and file embraced Nye's cranky pacifism.

John confined himself to domestic affairs whenever possible, leaving the management of foreign relations to others. He more or less flowed with the tide of isolationism, making no effort to swim against it although he was far from extreme on the issue. While some of his speeches in 1937 and 1938 touch upon isolationism, he stopped far short of the radical positions taken by some of his colleagues. As events in Europe became more dangerous in 1938 and 1939, Roosevelt quietly distanced himself from Nye and everything he stood for, taking many Democrats with him.

A very vocal segment of the Republican party continued to

The British Ambassador
has received Their Britannic Majesties' commands
to invite ___ Senator John G. Townsend. jr. ___

to a Garden Party at the Embassy
on Thursday, the 8th June 1939

The reply should be addressed to the
Social Secretary, British Embassy

Garden Party: *One of the social highlights of Senator Townsend's years in Washington was the visit of the king and queen of England just before the outbreak of war in Europe. John was among those who had the honor of meeting the royal visitors at a British embassy garden party (Townsend family scrapbooks).*

speak out against any and all American involvement even as most G.O.P. leaders spent their time attacking Roosevelt and the New Deal on domestic economic issues. By the outbreak of the war in 1939, it had almost reached the point where the Republican Party was perceived by the public as the party of isolationism. While this was far from the truth, the failure of the party leadership to counter this idea was a major miscalculation. It was natural enough that they should be far more concerned with pursuing their attack on the New Deal, which was now being shown to have serious shortcomings. The G.O.P. had, after all, been on the ropes for five years and now they seemed to be coming back strongly. Roosevelt was by now calling for a "quarantine" of aggressor nations and similar measures beneficial to the Allies. As the European situation worsened he asked Congress to suspend the arms embargo enacted several years before, which would have banned the sale of weapons and armaments to either side in the event of a war. When the German attack on

Poland and the outbreak of war did come in September 1939, he called a special session of Congress and managed to secure a repeal of the embargo. Roosevelt, who had encouraged the pacifist direction of the Nye Committee in 1935 and 1936, now pressed for America to become the "arsenal of democracy."

This was the period of such organizations as "America First," which still strongly resisted American involvement. Some Republican leaders saw that America would be drawn into the war eventually and agreed with Roosevelt's actions on behalf of the allies, but by and large the party still failed to embrace any sort of bipartisan position in support of England and France. Typical of the confusion of the times was the fact that Charles Lindbergh, the famed aviator, was a leader of the "America First" movement even as his mother-in-law, Mrs. Dwight Morrow, led the crusade for American entry on the side of Britain. The Republicans were fighting a losing battle to keep America's interest focused on the economy and the New Deal. They sensed that Roosevelt was vulnerable if only they could get the voters to ask tough questions.

Events did not cooperate. Roosevelt skillfully used the war to create an image of the embattled national leader in times of crisis, far too burdened with affairs of state to concern himself with petty political bickering. Variations of this strategy have been used by every incumbent president in wartime but F.D.R. used it with consummate artistry. Many Republicans suspected, with some justification, that Roosevelt was seeking to propel the nation into the war despite his frequent protestations to the contrary ("I will not send our boys to fight on foreign shores," etc.).

Roosevelt may have been unbeatable in 1940 in any case, but by allowing the president to preempt the "leader of the free world" position the G.O.P. had a hand in its own defeat. As the Republican

Party went about the task of choosing a candidate for president in the winter and spring of 1939 and 1940, few clear choices stood out. At first the party was still looking for a candidate who could effectively lead the attack on the New Deal, even as such canny leaders as Governor Landon warned that foreign affairs was the arena in which the campaign would be fought. One emerging front-runner was Thomas E. Dewey of New York, Manhattan district attorney. As Republican candidate for the New York governorship in 1938, Dewey had impressed the party with his style even though he lost the election to Herbert Lehman. Another possibility being much discussed in party circles was Ohio Senator Robert A. Taft, son of the late president and chief justice and, after his 1938 election to the Senate, the most eloquent foe of the New Deal.

Both Dewey and Taft directed their attack at Roosevelt's domestic program that winter and spring. Both refrained from taking any position on international events in hopes of avoiding the touchy issue of isolationism versus foreign involvement. An indication that Republican leaders were none too enthusiastic about either man was the profusion of favorite son candidates cluttering up the race. Among them were McNary of Oregon, Vandenberg of Michigan, Rep. Joe Martin of Massachusetts, and others. The Delaware G.O.P. tried to talk up a candidacy for Senator Townsend but he quickly quashed the idea. Herbert Hoover was hovering around the edges of the race, quietly letting it be known that he was still available if needed.

In launching his blitzkrieg across France and the Low Countries and into Denmark and Norway Adolf Hitler effectively aided President Roosevelt's as-yet unannounced bid for a third term. The impact of these developments on the American public was immediate and profound. Most Republicans quickly realized that

American neutrality was probably too much to hope for, though they still favored careful and understated support for the Allies. With the onrush of events in Europe in May and June the candidacies of Taft and Dewey fell by the wayside, seeming almost insignificant in the gravity of the moment. The last thing anyone wanted to hear about as the British carried out their heroic rescue of the British Expeditionary Force at Dunkirk and the Germans entered Paris was an attack on Franklin D. Roosevelt's domestic policies.

In the last few months before the Republican National Convention in June the party grassroots produced a compelling but highly unlikely candidate in the person of Wendell Willkie, an Indiana native and well-known power company executive who had been a Democrat until 1936. Willkie had risen to national prominence during his attack on Roosevelt's Tennessee Valley Authority proposal a year or two before. He now emerged as an alternative to the more conventional Republican candidates. His major appeal was that he was a dynamic man among a field of boring candidates although his actual positions on the issues appeared little different from Roosevelt's. Party leaders quickly realized this fact but, having no better candidates in the wings, they were hardly in a position to quibble.

The party rank and file were quite taken with Willkie. People who had never before been involved in politics joined Willkie clubs and began volunteering to work on his campaign. Willkie was picked up by the press and radio and made the center of attention. National party leaders remained unenthusiastic. Though John said nothing publicly, he generally favored Robert Taft. The leaders had no intention of nominating a man who had been a Republican for less than four years. To make matters worse, Willkie had the distressing habit of talking about "you Republicans" in his speeches. Even though he was the archetypical outsider, as the June convention neared his momentum grew. Now some professionals were joining his campaign, having picked him as a winner. Among them was Joe Martin, John's counterpart on the Republican Congressional Campaign Committee.

Roosevelt kept the Republicans constantly off balance as well.* As a means of furthering his effort to become the national war leader he began casting about for some prominent Republicans to enter his cabinet as a way of forming a coalition government, or at any rate as a way of being able to call his administration a coalition government. He had approached Landon but Landon turned him down, agreeing to join the cabinet only if Roosevelt would refrain from seeking a third term. He now turned to two other leading Republican internationalists with better results: Frank Knox and Henry L. Stimson. Stimson in particular had been a cabinet official under several administrations. He had served as Taft's secretary of war and as Hoover's secretary of state. He now agreed to join the Roosevelt administration as secretary of war. Knox became Secretary of the Navy. The decision of Knox and Stimson to join the cabinet was clearly the result of foot-dragging by the isolationist wing of the Republican Party. It was also a major setback, coming just as France was falling to the Germans and only a few weeks before the national Republican convention. Landon and other middle-of-the-roaders had been working for a platform position favoring strong national defense and all possible aid to the Allies short of outright involvement in hostilities. This position seemed to

---

* *John G. Townsend Jr. left no recorded observations on Franklin D. Roosevelt the politician. His opposition to many of F.D.R.'s economic programs is well known, but his professional assessment of F.D.R. the political strategist and innovator would have been revealing.*

be winning acceptance until Roosevelt announced the Knox and Stimson appointments. These developments so infuriated the still-powerful isolationists that they made the party platform more non-interventionist and critical of Roosevelt's pro-Britain views than before.

John was, like Landon, a middle-of-the-roader. He sincerely believed that it was possible to support England without actually joining the conflict. A few weeks after the convention he was quoted by a Portland newspaper during a trip to Oregon on his views on Roosevelt's "Lend-Lease" proposal:

> The senator is fearful that sale of 50 destroyers to England means "We're in." Speaking slowly, he said he feels that this step would be the big push to send the United States into a war from which it should shy. He said he does not know whether congress can stop the sale. He said he is not a lawyer and he doesn't understand the fine points. He said Attorney General Jackson has held that congress need not approve the sale but he feels that congress ought to have something to say about it. On conscription he said he "feels that if the nation cannot raise an army by voluntary enlistment, then some form of selective service is necessary and should be set up."

Senator Townsend left most of the debate to others that spring as he made one last attempt to see his silver bill successfully through Congress. The U.S. government now had gold bullion reserves of some $18 billion, based on foreign gold purchases at $35.00 per ounce, and enormous silver stockpiles being stored at various points around the country. In addition to the silver needed for U.S. Treasury purposes for coinage, another one and a half billion ounces of the metal were in storage. Just the cost of keeping the metal amounted to something like $100,000 a day (in 1940 dollars). John was at last beginning to build appreciable support for his position but it was still largely his own personal crusade.

Much of his new support came during the winter of 1939-1940 when the Russian army attacked Finland. The U.S. government and most Americans were outspoken in their support for the Finns. Senator Townsend pointed out that the U.S. was doing far more to support the Russian war effort than we were the Finns because the government was purchasing virtually the entire annual output of Russian gold at inflated prices. Russia was then far and away the largest producer of gold bullion in the world and was selling gold to America as fast as it could be mined. The profits were used to prosecute the war against the Finns. While similar absurdities had characterized the government's foreign purchases of gold and silver from the beginning, the public had not been interested enough in world events earlier to realize it. The Finnish-Russian conflict finally brought Townsend's message home to his fellow congressmen.

In the spring his latest bill barring foreign purchases of gold and silver passed the U.S. Senate over the opposition of both the administration and the Senate Majority Leader, Alben S. Barkley. John turned his attention to the House. He argued that if the U.S. government wished to spend its money on foreign metals, it should be purchasing those metals which would be both in short supply and essential to the war effort if the war intensified. This bit of wisdom was ignored by the government which, less than two years later, was forced to adopt strict rationing or to find substitutes for many metals. To improve the bill's chances in the House, John urged the compromise position: if the federal government insisted on a government handout to the mining interests, the least it could do was to stop buying foreign gold and silver and confine its largesse to American mining con-cerns. The House, more dependent on administration support and patronage, defeated the bill by a narrow margin. Senator Townsend did succeed, however, in having his views inserted as a separate plank in the 1940 Republican Platform.

At the national convention in Philadelphia in June (the first one ever to be televised) Dewey quickly lost the narrow

John G. Townsend Jr.
as he appeared in 1940
(Lyla T. Savoy collection).

lead that he had carried into the convention. Such leaders as Townsend and Landon tried to swing support to Taft, but failed to overcome what had by now become the virtually unstoppable Willkie tide. Willkie won the nomination on the sixth ballot. Senator McNary of Oregon was nominated as his running mate. Joe Martin, who had thrown his support to Willkie earlier than most national leaders, emerged from the convention as the new Republican National Chairman. Being a good party man, Senator Townsend announced his strong support for the Willkie-McNary Ticket, but he and most other Republican professionals left Philadelphia with a decidedly uneasy feeling.

John was not entirely easy about his own reelection campaign either. Earlier there had been much talk about Democratic Governor Richard McMullen running against him for the Senate. He had even introduced the governor, on one of McMullen's trips to Washington that spring, to his colleagues in the Senate, informing them jovially that McMullen would be taking his place there the following year. Instead the Democrats nominated John's old Sussex County adversary from past elections, James M. Tunnell Sr. Tunnell was a more formidable opponent than McMullen in several respects. McMullen had entered politics somewhat late in life and still had not developed the

James Miller Tunnell Sr. as he appeared about 1929 (reproduced from W. L. Bevan's History of Delaware Past and Present).

avid hunger for victory that characterizes a true politician. Tunnell had been active in every Democratic campaign since the turn of the century. What's more, he had a strong interest in becoming U.S. senator. He had run against T. Coleman du Pont in 1924 and lost. He was well aware this was probably his last opportunity. He had been Delaware's Democratic National Committeeman for several years and had a well-established network of friends among the national Democratic leadership, much as Townsend did among the Republicans.

Coming from the same neighborhood as John, Tunnell also cut into Senator Townsend's traditional Sussex County power base. Although Tunnell had resided in Georgetown for many years, he kept his southeastern Sussex County ties and was a frequent speaker summer. Like Townsend he had links to banking and farming.

Tunnell also knew that John was vulnerable because of his past opposition to the New Deal. For the first time in more than a generation Delaware had gone heavily Democratic in 1936. Although the Republicans had won back some strength in 1938, it was clear that this would not be enough to overcome a strong Roosevelt bid for a third term if the Republicans were saddled, as was now becoming apparent, with a weak presidential candidate.

Another thing that both Townsend and Tunnell knew was that precedent was against John. No Delaware U.S. senator of the twentieth century had served a third term. Though oldtime Democratic Senators Eli Saulsbury and George Gray had managed this feat in the days of near total Democratic control after the Civil War, they had done so when senators were still elected by the General Assembly. The chances of John pulling off a similar feat were none too good in any case. In light of Wendell Willkie's candidacy and the worsening events in Europe, they were remote. Most Delawareans liked Townsend personally and were proud of his obvious national prominence, but they were buying the Democratic view that the country needed Roosevelt to pilot the ship of state through dangerous waters.

Republicans in general were captive that summer to the dire headlines emanating from Europe. That was the summer of the Fall of France, of Dunkirk. The Battle of Britain was at its height during the fall campaign. To many Americans, Roosevelt was coming to seem like an essential part of the war effort . To make matters worse, Willkie's campaign had serious problems of its own, quite apart from the war news. He was not a trained speaker and he quickly wore out his vocal cords during the first weeks of the campaign. His voice never fully recovered until after the election, meaning that most of his speeches were delivered in a hoarse whisper. While he made full use of radio in seeking to overcome this disadvantage, his live speeches were almost uniformly disasterous. John S. Spruance Jr. wrote in the Wilmington *Sunday Star* of November 3, 1940, of Willkie's appearance a few days earlier in Rodney Square. The crowd was overwhelmingly Republican and overwhelmingly favorable. Even so, Spruance wrote:

> any listener could tell what seven weeks of whirlwind campaigning had done to his vocal cords. From that point on most of the speech was a confused blur in my ears . . . circulating among the crowd in the square and on Market Street behind the statue I noticed that the attention of many persons had wandered. In such a situation the attention is bound to wander. When the speaker did make a point that drew grandstand cheers, some persons near the statue would address the sheepish inquiry to others: "What was that one? I didn't get it."

Spruance noted in contrast that John G. Townsend Jr., who introduced Willkie that day, had rarely spoken better in his career. Townsend, he said, never claimed to be a speaker but he at least could be clearly understood and generally had something to say.

Willkie was not doing all that well even when he could be understood. His approach to the campaign was poorly conceived in the sense that he persisted in attacking positions taken by congressional Republican leaders on the New Deal and foreign affairs, alienating many of them at a time when the Republicans needed every bit of unity they could muster. The in-fighting that resulted confused Republican voters and helped the Democrats. Willkie also failed to distinguish his own views clearly from those of Roosevelt.

G.O.P. presidential candidate arrives: *1940 Republican nominee Wendell L. Willkie (center) arrives in Washington, D.C., to begin his campaign. Among those meeting him at National Airport are, left to right: Senator Thomas, Idaho, Senator Bridges, New Hampshire, Senator Townsend, Delaware and Rep. J. William Ditter of Pennsylvania,* Washington Star, *July 3, 1940 (clipping from Townsend family scrapbooks).*

As the party leadership had feared, his positions were seen by many undecided voters as being only a watered-down version of F.D.R.'s own ideas.

Republicans spent much of their time during the campaign attacking Roosevelt's unprecedented third-term candidacy. While this was an obvious point of attack it also hurt John's senatorial campaign in Delaware. If the Republicans are so opposed to third terms, state Democratic leaders asked loudly, why are they asking the voters of Delaware to send John G. Townsend Jr. back to the Senate for a third term? While anyone with any realistic understanding of the American governmental system knows that one cannot fairly equate the Presidency with service in the U.S. Senate, the Democrats' question could not easily be answered. Placed on the defensive by this bit of "blue smoke and mirrors," John found it that much more difficult to run an aggressive, positive campaign.

The Democrats also printed bold advertisements charging that Townsend had a record of solid opposition to New Deal measures, to pro-labor legislation, to everything that helped the small people and that, moreover, he had voted against essential defense funding bills. The ads contained what were meant to be well-documented excerpts from the *Congressional Record* to substantiate the charges. In fact, it was something like the old "Do you still beat your wife?" approach. If John had voted against a defense funding bill containing some outrageous rider and then, a week later, had voted for a piece of replacement legislation accomplishing the same thing, he was charged with having opposed the bill. It was the same throughout.

Townsend campaign workers were able to rebut the charges with evidence of their own, but the damage was done. Senator Townsend had again been placed on the defensive. Most voters never bothered to read more than the broad headlines and this was truer than ever in 1940. Those who took the trouble to inform themselves of the true facts of the situation were the same ones who would have voted for John in any case.

Another factor at work in the election, which was not adequately appreciated by the Republicans of Delaware until later, was that in the eight years between 1932 and 1940, the political balance of power in Delaware had undergone a fundamental shift. Gone were the days when one of two Republican factions could win enough votes to put its candidates over the top even with another set of Republican candidates and the Democrats to contend with. Gone were the days when the state's entire black population could be depended upon to vote as a solid block for the G.O.P. The Democrats were now in the majority. That John did as well as he did in 1940 was a testament to his personal popularity, not to did in 1940 was a testament to his personal popularity, not to Republican Party power among the electorate. Roosevelt spent most of the 1940 campaign almost ostentatiously refraining from taking part in traditional campaigning. He travelled around the country on a series of ostensibly nonpolitical fact-finding junkets to "assess the nation's defense readiness," making a dozen or so statesmanlike addresses in major cities along the way. The rest of the time he spent in the White House tending to weighty matters of state and strenuously avoiding creating the impression that he was running for president. As usual his tactics worked perfectly.

Willkie was personally well liked by many voters but he was simply unable to convince a majority of them that the nation would be better off with him in the White House. On the eve of the election local pollsters predicted that Roosevelt would sweep Delaware but they shied away from predicting a Townsend defeat, saying that John would squeak past Tunnell. As it turned out, they were right about Roosevelt and wrong about John. Roosevelt carried Delaware by 11,328 votes. Senator Townsend lost to James Tunnell by 4,208 votes. While John had done considerably better than Willkie, it was not enough. The only statewide Republican candidate to win was the popular Wilmington Mayor Walter W. Bacon, who was running for governor against Secretary of State Josiah Marvel Jr.

For the first time in his long political career John had been defeated. It was somehow ironic that he had done so much and gone so far in his long climb to prominence in the U.S. Senate only to lose in the end to another Baltimore Hundred boy.* But that also

---

* *The irony was carried a step further when, in 1946, Senator Tunnell lost his bid for reelection to the then-political unknown, John J. Williams of Millsboro. Williams was also a native of Baltimore Hundred. He had been born and*

(continued on next page)

the campaign, the unfair charges of voting against things that helped Delawareans, for instance, it had been clean. Neither candidate had besmirched the character of his opponent. John bore no ill will.

The loss probably came as no great surprise. It is a truism of politics that nearly all candidates are convinced in the days leading up to an election that they will win. Even so, as the campaign developed, with Willkie's weakness and the dire events in Europe distracting the public from the issues, with the Democratic charges about his voting record, John must have had an inkling that he was in trouble. He had seen what happened to Daniel Hastings in 1936. Above all, he was a realist.

Louise Johnson recalled that Senator Townsend did not come to his Washington office for a week after his defeat. Several days after the election, she wrote, Senator Harry Byrd came into the office, "just to talk about Senator Townsend." Byrd had told her: "You have no idea how much I love Senator Townsend. He seems like a brother to me. You may be surprised, too, to know that I contributed to his campaign in Delaware and that he contributed to mine in Virginia"

"Senator Byrd was a Democrat," she wrote in her memoirs, "but Senator Townsend knew that at that time only a Democrat would be elected in Virginia and he wanted Senator Byrd to be that Democrat."

(continued from previous page)
raised near the village of Bayard in the southeastern part of the hundred, moving to Millsboro as a young man. Thus, Delaware was represented in the U.S. Senate by Baltimore Hundred men steadily from 1929 until Williams' retirement from the Senate in 1971, forty-two years later.

29. Paul Townsend, Sportsman

During his first term in the Senate, John was briefly involved in an effort to secure federal funding for an inlet at Ocean City, Maryland. Local citizens wanted the inlet to run through the narrow spit of sand just south of the town as a way of opening up what they thought would be a fine natural harbor behind the town where the Big Assawoman Bay joined the Sinepuxent Bay. At the time Ocean City was technically situated on the north end of Assateague Island. The more than thirty mile length of Assateague had been cut by so many different natural inlets over the years, both south and north of Ocean City, that most people did not give much thought to living on the island. For decades before 1933, local fishermen had been without any dependable inlet. As a result they were forced to do their fishing in large, wooden surf boats that could be launched from the beach through the breakers after being hauled there on horse-drawn carts. Not only was this method laborious and dangerous but it severely limited the size of fishing vessels that could be used and, thus, the size of the catch. Townspeople felt that a permanent inlet would allow them, once and for all, to develop their fishery properly. An Ocean City inlet would also benefit the neighboring Sussex County coastal area, much of which would have access to it through Big Assawoman Bay.

The effort to obtain federal funds for the inlet project was not doing too well until the late summer of 1933, when it was aided greatly by, of all things, Mother Nature. This help came in the form of the infamous "Hurricane of '33" that hit in August of that year. The 1933 storm came up the east coast and then veered inland at Cape Hatteras, crossing eastern North Carolina and the Norfolk region before entering the Chesapeake Bay. Because of its eccentric course, it hit the central Delmarva Peninsula from the southwest, much as the equally notorious Hurricane Hazel was to do twenty years later.

Inland streams backed up. Tidal estuaries filled and inland bays flooded behind the coastal strand. Scores of old mill dams were washed out across the peninsula, sending what, until then, had been marginally profitable water-powered grist and saw milling into a permanent tailspin. As the old saying goes, "it's an ill wind that blows nobody good"; the hurricane also cut a new inlet at the south end of Ocean City in almost the exact location where the town fathers had hoped the federal government would build one. With this new natural inlet as a beginning, it was relatively simple for the Maryland congressional delegation and Senator Townsend to obtain enough federal aid to stabilize the new inlet and make it permanent.

By the summer of 1934, both commercial fishermen and sportsmen could enter and leave the town harbor at will and a whole new era of Ocean City history had begun. Even in the old surf boat days Ocean City fishermen had gotten far enough off shore to report sightings of great white marlin and sailfish leaping from the sea. The Gulf Stream passes Ocean City some fifty to sixty miles offshore and such typical Gulf Stream denizens were not unheard of in local waters, but they had never been fished, or even officially identified.

Various members of the Townsend clan were already regular summer visitors to Ocean City and had been for decades before the 1933 storm. Jack Townsend and Jack Tubbs and their families maintained summer homes there. Jack and Paul, the avid fishermen of the family, had been big-game fishing in the Gulf Stream waters of Florida for over a decade. They were well versed in the intricacies of the sport. They listened to the local fish stories of Ocean City oldtimers with interest and quietly considered the possibilities. In the summer of 1934, they bought a large motorboat, a somewhat awkward-handling converted schooner which they christened the *Jacpau*, and went fishing. The oldtimers had talked about the shoal twenty-five miles or so southeast of Ocean City, known locally as "the Jackspot." This, it was said, was the best area for the big fish beginning in mid- to late-July.

Jack and Paul brought in some nice-sized marlin, the first in the town's history. They were of the white variety, rather than of the larger blue marlin type. In the summer of 1935, the brothers went out again with some improved equipment and did even better. That year quite a few other local fishermen tried their luck and were also successful at landing the scrappy sport fish. In 1936, the Townsend brothers bought a new and better boat. With them and others spreading the word up and down the east coast, Ocean City was beginning to enjoy some renown as a marlin-fishing center.

Paul in particular had developed during the 1920s and 1930s into one of the finest American sportfishermen of his generation. He was held in high enough regard by his peers that he was chosen in 1937 and 1938 to represent the United States

Big-game fishing: *Three of the four Townsend brothers are shown after a Florida fishing trip in 1933. Preston stands at left. Seated from left to right are Jack, guide Bill Hatch, and Paul. Paul's wife, Theo, and Jack's wife, Daisy, stand at right (photo from Preston C. Townsend collection).*

on the U.S. Tuna Team in international competition in the waters off Nova Scotia. In 1938, he was the captain of the team, which included some of the most famous sportfishermen of the day. By the time his and Jack's Ocean City adventures began, he had already travelled to well-known big-game waters all over the world: Cuba, Bimini, the Pacific, and elsewhere. But he never–then or later– found another spot to compare with the thirty miles of coastal waters between Ocean City, Maryland, and Chincoteague Island, Virginia, in those years before World War II. It was the most incredible sort of fish story to have travelled around the globe in search of the perfect hot spot, only to find it twenty miles from home, but that is precisely what happened to Paul Townsend. A columnist for the *New York Times* wrote about Ocean City in 1937:

> Ocean City came into its own last year. Fishermen from Washington, Montauk, Florida and other eastern spots, attracted by the unprecedented marlin fishing off the Maryland port, began to try it . . . they left with sore muscles and the memory of well over a thousand glorious scraps with fighting marlin. No one knows accurately how many marlin were boated last summer at Ocean City. The nearest figure that can be reached is that more than a thousand either were killed or were released after a long, drawn-out scrap, testing fishermen and tackle to the limit.
>
> But there isn't any doubt that Ocean City and its unequalled marlin fishing today is the hottest saltwater angling spot in the United States. It is the one spot in this country where you can't miss on marlin. Sure, Cuba is good in the spring. Lower Mexico is fine, and Southern California is good. But there isn't a place like this in this country. No where has the record for marlin that Ocean City rolled up last summer.

The new boat that Jack and Paul bought in 1936 was a gorgeous thirty-eight-foot Elco Angler that had been the star of that winter's New York Boat Show. It was a fine fishing machine in which they could cruise for a hundred miles off the coast in search of great fish. They engaged the services of a couple of Paul's old Florida friends at various times to run the boat for them. One of the most respected people in this realm was Captain Bill Hatch of Miami, an old master of the sport of marlin fishing who had worked the waters of Florida, the Bahamas, and Cuba for years as a captain and guide. With his help and that of their local mate, Bill Rodney of Ocean City, they thoroughly explored the possibilities of the Maryland and Virginia coastal waters and traveled down to the rough waters of North Carolina's Outer Banks, which was then about as remote a place as one could find to fish on the east coast.

Having proven that white marlin existed off Ocean City in large numbers, Paul and Jack were convinced that somewhere in Maryland waters they would find blue marlin, the giant cousin of the white, which could range up to a thousand pounds. The brothers had cruised the waters off of Diamond Shoals Lightship below Cape Hatteras before the season hit at home in July and they had caught every type of large fish common to the Gulf Stream in southern waters –many barracuda, dolphin, bonito, small tuna and other fish, but no blue marlin. A Virginia big-game fisherman had caught a three hundred pound blue marlin off the Outer Banks in the summer of 1936, however, proving conclusively that they were there when the conditions were right.

The white marlin arrived in the vicinity of Ocean City by mid-July and the town's small port began humming with activity in June in preparation. Often in those summers of the late 1930s, John brought congressional friends over from Washington for the fishing. In late July of 1937, he hosted Senator Frederic Walcott, his Connecticut friend. The two set out with the boys and Bill Hatch on the new craft which had been christened *Jacpau II*. The day's total catch was three marlin with each senator catching one (a columnist wrote of Paul a few years later that "when you fished his boat he did his best to see that if any fish were taken that day your tackle brought them in."). Two days later Hatch and Mate Bill Rodney went out alone with Jack and Paul. Everything was perfect: just a bit stormy and rough, the water very warm just the way the marlin liked it . . . perfect! In less than five hours of fishing the Townsend brothers caught seven marlin. Hatch announced that they had just broken the world's record for the number of marlin caught in one day. He was an expert on the subject since the old record of five marlin was his, made a couple of years earlier during a memorable afternoon cruise off Bimini.

The kind of luck the Townsend brothers ran into during those prewar summers of marlin fishing off Ocean City had existed in all the other world hot spots for brief periods before those areas had become widely known. As Ocean City's reputation spread more and more through the ranks of big-game fishermen the same leveling off and decline would threaten the fishery. Paul was a student of game fish as well as being their frequent nemesis. He knew their habits and their biology. He knew the patterns and was all too familiar with the process of fishing a place out, having seen it happen in a number of other places over the years. He felt a personal sort of responsibility to try to minimize this decline in Ocean City since he and Jack had pioneered the sport there.

Paul and Jack began offering prizes to the boat captain who tagged and released the most marlin during the summer. The idea was to help the U.S. Bureau of Fisheries determine just how rapidly the marlin were being depleted and to promote the releasing of marlin. They were at the point in their development as sportsmen where the trophies that mattered to them were the ones they carried with them in their memories, not the ones they could hang on walls. Finally in the summer of 1940, they had a special plaque executed by one of the nation's top wildlife illustrators to award as the first price.

The 1939 season had been incredible with 1,300 marlin taken off Ocean City by party boats from all over the East. Word of what was happening was enough to lure even so distinguished an angler as President Roosevelt out of the White House and down to the Maryland resort for a day of marlin fishing, though not as a guest of the Townsends. On the biggest day of all, 171 marlin were taken by all the boats. That season and the year after, the year of the wildlife art "Townsend Award," marked an end of an era. Those seasons brought to a close the magnificent beginning years of Ocean City's marlin fishery, the years when Ocean City established its reputation as the "White Marlin Capital of the World." By the summer of 1941, the war had drawn too close to American waters to permit off-shore fishing in safety and all sportfishing was suspended until the conclusion of hostilities in 1945. The Townsend family, even more than most people, saw the 1939 and 1940 seasons as the end of a very special era: they were Paul Townsend's last summers.

Tragedy first struck the lives of Paul and his wife, Theo, and their family in the early spring of 1939. They had gone away from home for the day, leaving their five-year-old son, Paul Jr., and his two baby sisters at home with their nurse as they often did. Only a week earlier the little boy had been found walking along a rain gutter bordering the roof of the family home and had been gently coaxed down. High places and precarious perches held a dangerous fascination for the child, a manifestation, perhaps, of the adventurous spirit that was so much a part of his father's character. The family knew of this and were terrified by it, but in those days the profession of child psychology was still far in the future. Little could be done to protect the child from his dangerous fixation, except to keep a close eye on him. This the family tried to do, but even with vigilant parents and nanny, he could move quickly and quietly amidst the distractions of his two baby sisters.

At a little after five in the evening of the fine April day the

Paul Townsend: *a tribute to Paul attesting to his fishing skills by Washington cartoonist Jim Berryman dating from the late 1930s (Townsend family scrapbooks).*

nurse, who was momentarily busy with the younger children, had heard a cry and had run out to the flagstone terrace behind the Townsend's Washington home where she found young Paul lying on the stones in a crumpled heap. Later the family guessed that he had climbed a tree in the patio and gotten onto the roof of a one-story wing of the house. He had slipped and fallen to the stone surface twenty feet below. He was rushed to a nearby hospital but nothing could be done to save him. Twenty minutes later, he was pronounced dead of a fractured skull.

A year and a half later, on November 19, 1940, just a few days after his father's defeat in his reelection bid, Paul, Sr. was driving down to meet his brother, Jack, at their rented ducking camp on Chincoteague Bay below Snow Hill, Maryland. Paul was almost as attached to baseball as he was to marlin fishing and numbered many of America's best-known baseball players among his closest friends. He was especially close to Washington Senators Manager Stanley "Bucky" Harris and had planned to entertain him at the camp several days later. Paul and Jack were to meet there early to get everything in shape for the upcoming week's hunting and Paul was driving down alone from Washington in a heavy rainfall. As he drove along a dirt road six miles below Snow Hill, he entered a curve and took his eyes from the road for a moment to look ahead. The car hit a soft place and skidded out of control, turning over in a field. Several other motorists had witnessed the accident and they loaded Paul carefully into a truck, still conscious, and raced to Peninsula General Hospital in Salisbury where doctors quickly determined that he had a broken neck. He held on for nearly a week. He was sometimes able to talk to his wife and family and he fought hard for life but in the end this most competitive of men lost his struggle. During the last week of November he died at the age of thirty-seven.

Paul was the kind of man who had many close friends and legions of acquaintances. Like his father he had possessed a talent for friendship. The outpouring of grief was immediate and widespread. One of the most touching tributes was that of his friend, *New York Times* columnist Raymond R. Camp:

> Too many men, even those who are real sportsmen, are inclined to consider the boating or netting of a fish, or the dropping of the game, as the real object of their sport. Paul was never that way. To him sport was in the playing of the game, not the score. He released many more fish, including the big game giants of salt water and the scrappy trout of the streams, than he ever took.
>
> As long as men go to Nova Scotia for giant tuna, to Ocean City for white marlin, to Hatteras for waterfowl, Paul's name will be mentioned with respect. He was internationally known as a big-game angler, but if he could know the respect and admiration and sorrow with which his name is mentioned in the little places on the Maryland and North Carolina coasts he would say this meant more to him than any international fame . . .
>
> Most people, including many who call themselves friends of ours, don't care to have much to do with you if you're a nobody. They measure their esteem and affection for you by the size of your bank account and your willingness to do them favors . . .
> But Paul Townsend wasn't that way. Never did he ask favors although he granted many. He might have been welcomed at the White House or on Park Avenue, but yesterday there were tears in the eyes of the clubhouse boys at Griffith Stadium. They were his friends and meant as much to him as did his close friends among the so-called upper strata . . .
>
> Life gave him much and he gave the world as much and more. Because Paul Townsend was an old shoe who wore well in this sordid little universe. The clubhouse kids were crying yesterday. His was the design for living.

Thinking back on the tragedy more than forty years later, his younger brother, Preston, smiled wistfully and said, "Paul was really the best of us." November 1940 was indeed the end of a wonderful chapter in the lives of Senator Townsend and his family.

Part X:

The Elder Statesman

30. Just a Chicken Farmer

No one who knew John Townsend had to worry about him sitting at home, brooding over his lost Senate career and sinking into decrepit old age. While all of his enterprises were now being run by his sons and his managers, he still took an avid interest in everything down to the last detail. He just came back home and went back to work on his own ventures.

The election defeat did not mean the end of Townsend's Washington years by any means. He maintained an office there and remained active even after the end of his term on the Republican Senatorial Campaign Committee. In 1937, Lyla had married the prominent Washington attorney G. Prew Savoy. The couple had bought a large home in the city shortly before the end of John's Senate term and their location there, together with that of Paul's family, would have drawn him to the city often even without his continued political responsibilities. Paul's wife, Theo, had been pregnant with another baby at the time of her husband's death and in early 1941 she gave birth to a son, Peter Townsend.

Every time John had experienced a pause in his political career, he had been in the fortunate position of having some new business to turn his attention to. In 1903, at the end of his term as a state legislator, he had started the new bank. In 1921, he had the new road-building business and then the orchards. Now, in 1941, he had the chicken business. His youngest son, Preston (Pres), had been mainly responsible for propelling the family into the rapidly expanding Delmarva broiler industry in the mid-1930s. Julian was still concerned with the canneries and the fruit and vegetable crops. Jack handled the bank. John's son-in-law Jack Tubbs and his nephew Covington Townsend ran the lumber company. Paul, before his death, had been responsible for the road building work and for construction operations in and around Washington, D.C. After his graduation from the University of Delaware in 1932, Pres had become involved in managing the Townsend orchards at Millsboro, Delmar, and Bridgeville. With a degree in agriculture, he was well prepared for the work and proved to be both an able farmer and a successful businessman, although he was bothered by the constant uncertainty of orchard crops. An unexpected late frost or a new blight could almost destroy an entire season's crop overnight.

The senator and his sons had watched the growth of the poultry industry with keen interest, but, preoccupied with all their other enterprises, they had not become involved even in a small way until 1935. John was approached that year by a Millsboro farmer named Wilford Revel who wanted to enter into a partnership to build several chicken houses and begin raising broilers. Five years later, John estimated that he had 150 such partners, several of whom were members of his own family. He had had almost as many partners in 1935, so Revel's request was far from unusual. John agreed to put up the money if Revel would do the work, and they would share the profits.

The partnership worked so well that John and his family began to consider the broiler industry seriously. Among other things, Pres reminded his father, poultry had the distinct advantage of allowing several crops a year regardless of weather conditions. If you had problems with one flock of chickens, you could raise several more in the same house in the same year so that the year was not a total loss.

Thus began the family's transition into the poultry business. As had been the case in the past, they did not abandon strawberries or orchards. They just took on something new. By this time, strawberries were declining in importance on the peninsula. The coming of war in Europe harmed what had been a brisk international market in apples, causing some reverses in the orchards after 1939. That factor and the severe manpower shortage caused by America's entry into the war gave added incentive for the shift into the poultry industry. In 1938, John incorporated the family's new poultry operation as Townsend's, Inc. The new company's first hatchery was built at the family's Swan Creek Orchard near Millsboro the following year. This location became the center of the poultry operation even as the orchards continued there. In 1940, Townsend's, Inc., began growing their own flocks of broilers with hired growers while continuing the kind of partnership arrangements they had entered into with Wilford Revel five years before.

Another key step in the growth of the industry came that same year with the opening of Jack Udell's Eagle Poultry Company at Frankford, the region's first dressing plant. Similar plants opened in the next few years at Milford, Millsboro, Seaford, Selbyville, Lewes, and other towns. These local dressing plants gave Delmarva poultry companies additional control over market operations.

Most of the small hatcherymen in the area purchased their eggs from New England. The Townsends took another step in the expansion of their operations by acquiring breeding farms in Massachusetts and New Hampshire during the early 1940s. In the years after he left the Senate, John poured much of his creative energies into the poultry business as did Preston.

An article in the November 1945 issue of *Country Gentleman* magazine gave an account of that period: back in 1940, the article noted, a rumor was going around southern Delaware that Townsend's passion for doing the impossible was running away with his good sense. A neighbor decided to give him a lesson in the economics of the chicken business:

"About 15,000 broilers is all a good foreman can look after. Let him raise three batches a year and that's maybe 50,000 birds. Get about three-four good men like that working for you–if you can find that many the way labor is today–and that's all you can keep track of. That'll give you maybe 200,000 birds a year. Biggest producer in the state never raised more than 400,000. Yet I hear you been talking about raising a million. Is that right?"

"Make that three million," Townsend answered with a twinkle, "and it is right! Maybe after the war when I can get the materials I'll do better than that."

Raising broilers is fraught with risk. Few hired hands could be trusted with responsibility. But Townsend found the answer: profit sharing.

To keep down epidemics his chicken houses are widely scattered over numbers of farms. Each farm is run by a foreman. If a foreman is good enough to look after 30,000 birds, he gets that many to raise. Otherwise he may be put in charge of a unit of 15,000 birds or one of intermediate size. His salary varies with the number of birds he raises. And in addition he collects five per cent of the profits of his particular unit. The system has worked so well that wages have doubled since Townsend started and profits soared as production rose.

"I'm always hoping one of these fellows will want to go into business for himself," Townsend says. "I show them how they can make money. Their next logical step is to strike out for themselves. When they do, I'm always willing to back them or go partners with them. There's

Townsend's, Inc. *- In 1935, Senator Townsend and his youngest son, Preston, became deeply involved in the rapidly developing Delmarva poultry industry. The two are shown above in a photo accompanying a November, 1945,* Country Gentleman *article about the senator and his many partners, one of whom stands at left in the photo (Lyla T. Savoy collection).*

room for a lot more independent businessmen–each new one means more jobs for others–and that's what we're after in this country. Competition? I've never found it hurt me to help somebody else get started."

"The trouble with most fellows," Townsend ruminates in his quiet way, "is they don't have enough confidence. Most of them–young fellows particularly– need a pat on the back and somebody who'll say, "Go ahead! I know you've got what it takes. I'll take a chance on you any day!"

In 1941, Preston married Miss Rachel Morris of Selbyville, daughter of his father's banking colleague, Raymond Morris. The young couple established their home in John's huge old house on Main Street in Selbyville. At the time he had been living in the large front section of the house by himself. Harley and Evelyn Derrickson occupied the rear wing. Having the young people move in was a very welcome change and he enjoyed the extra companionship it provided.

John gradually readjusted to the quiet pattern of life in Sussex County, rising early and walking around to eat breakfast many mornings with his elderly stepmother, Ida Townsend. Well before seven o'clock he and Harley would be off together in one of the succession of large Cadillac sedans he favored, each in its turn bearing his distinctive Delaware license plate bearing the number "36." They would head up the du Pont Boulevard in whose construction he had played such a pivotal role and make their way to Millsboro and Swan Creek. Though he still drove himself occasionally, the family tended to discourage this practice as he got older. Good at so many things, he tended to be a bit absent-minded about driving.

He also had an almost proprietary feeling about the roads of his homeland, natural enough since he had had so much to do with getting most of them built. It was not uncommon for him to stop at the Millsboro post office to pick up the mail for Townsend's, Inc., on days when he drove himself, leaving the car stopped in the middle of the town's Main Street with the engine running and the door open. No one who knew him thought much about it. People could generally get around him all right, but it could be a shock for those who did not know him.

After reading his papers he would tend to the myriad details of business. He spent considerable time at the Georgetown office of J.G. Townsend, Jr. & Company and at the bank and lumber company in Selbyville. He also spent much of his time during the warmer months of the year riding the roads of southern Delaware and just looking at the land, at his fields and forests, at the efforts of his various partners and foremen.

This was the period of his life that gave rise to the classic Sussex County "John G. Townsend story" wherein the senator was riding along one day and happened to see a farm he admired. He rode up to the farmhouse, knocked on the door and, introducing himself to the farm wife, said, "Ma'am, I like this farm and I'd like to buy it. Can you tell me who owns it?" To which the startled response was, "Why, Senator! You do!"

Whether or not this actually happened is open to question, although several versions of the story survive. It is true that John owned so much land that he occasionally lost parcels for a year or two. Preston or Julian or someone in one of the offices would be going through the land books and suddenly realize that no taxes had been paid on a particular parcel for a year or two. Then they would have to go to the courthouse and make up the oversight.

By now Senator Townsend and his various companies owned in excess of 10,000 acres of land. The total was possibly nearer 20,000 acres, but in any case it was substantially more land than anyone else in Delaware owned at the time. It would be accurate to say that John "collected" land in the same way that people collect antiques or stamps except that he always had his eye on its agricultural value before anything else.*

---

*   *During the summer after Senator Townsend's death, this writer, then a high school student, had a summer job working as an assistant clerk in the law office of the firm settling the senator's estate. It is perhaps worthy of note that the law firm was none other than Tunnell & Raysor, formerly Tunnell & Tunnell, the founding partner of which was James M. Tunnell Sr.   I was assigned to the task of going through the county assessment office property card files and writing down every parcel of land Senator Townsend owned. Working at it steadily for two months, I returned to school in the fall with the task not quite completed. - RBC*

When he returned home to Selbyville in the evenings, he often took walks around the quiet streets of the town, stopping here and there to talk for a few minutes. Frequently at night he spent an hour or two on the telephone talking to friends around the country, catching up on the latest political news and other matters. On Sunday mornings he taught the adult ladies' Sunday School class at Salem United Methodist Church. This group consisted of twenty or thrity matrons who were mostly middle-aged or older. Many of them had known him well for thirty-five or forty years and it was a high point of the week for both the teacher and the students.

In the summers, John and various members of the family moved to the beach. By the early 1940s, Lyla and Prew Savoy and a number of other family members owned their own cottages at Rehoboth, which was by now well established as "the nation's summer capital" with elegant homes and hotels and such popular gathering spots as the Indian Beach Club just south of the resort. Rehoboth was the scene of most of Senator Townsend's large-scale entertaining both during and after his Senate years. He continued to hold annual dinners for Delaware Republicans at the Belhaven Hotel and there were other social events and house parties from time to time.

John retained his seat as chairman of the Republican Senatorial Campaign Committee and he still kept a Washington office for that reason. After his defeat in his 1940 bid for a third term, the U.S. Senate's Republican caucus voted to take the highly unusual step of continuing him in the post even though he was no longer a sitting senator. The action was unprecedented but it made very good sense from a tactical point of view. In the past senators had been forced to resign from the campaign committee just as they

Ballgame: *Ex-Senator Townsend and his friend, Senator Harry Byrd of Virginia, attend a Washington Senators baseball game during the 1940s (newspaper clipping from Townsend family scrapbooks).*

were reaching a point of maximum effectiveness in order to devote themselves to their own reelection campaigns–or else they stayed on the committee at personal political risk as John had done in 1940. By naming an ex-senator to the chairmanship, the Senate Republicans were able to get a person who could focus entirely on the job at hand without being diverted by competing demands.

Senator Townsend was also under serious consideration in 1942 for the position of Republican National Chairman, which was then being vacated by Congressman Joe Martin of Massachusetts. In the end, the job went to a Midwesterner, Harrison Spangler of Iowa. Even so, John was even more involved in national Republican politics after he left office than he had been as a U.S. senator. He also spent more time at it than he did at the operation of his business interests, which were already in the competent hands of his sons and his managers.

The Japanese attack on Pearl Harbor hit him very hard because he had never lost hope that the U.S. would be able to stay out of the war. Ironically, all the isolationist sentiment, and all the isolationist measures, had been aimed at avoiding provocations in Europe and in the Atlantic that might lure the country into the European conflict. Few had expected the attack to come from the Japanese, and in the Pacific. As far as the war was concerned, John put all partisan politics aside, at least for the time being. His own family was affected in the sense that most of his grandchildren served in one branch or another of the armed forces. Even his granddaughter, Eleanor Townsend, Julian's daughter, was serving in the Red Cross by war's end, serving in the Philippines.

John kept a close watch on the war, as did most American parents. He also kept abreast of things through his Senate friends and his wide circle of acquaintances in Washington. Many wartime events had a personal significance for him in the sense that he had known many of the major participants in Washington before the war. He had known General Douglas MacArthur socially, for example, and had been entertained several times by General Jonathan Wainwright, the man who had to surrender American forces in the Philippines to the Japanese in 1942.

The war also increased the hardships of doing business because of shortages and rationing of essential commodities. The family's new poultry operations expanded steadily throughout the conflict, however, as did the Delmarva poultry industry in general. The war also served to kill off the strawberry business once and for all, and to severely impede the apple business because of labor

Strategy session: *Sometime in the late 1940s,* Life *magazine featured a photo of Republican leaders holding an early morning strategy session in the hotel suite of Rep. Joe Martin, then G.O.P. national chairman. Former Senator Townsend is at right (clipping from Townsend family scrapbooks).*

shortages. Despite the shortages, John still found enough strawberries to treat his former colleagues in the Senate to the annual strawberry feasts for which he had become famous.

The federal government had imposed wage and price controls and instituted rationing by the spring and summer of 1942. Even though this activity was necessary to some extent, many Americans felt that federal officials were excessive in their demands for total civilian support for the war effort. Something of a backlash resulted and was reflected in the off-year election results in November 1942, the first wartime election. The Republicans experienced their greatest electoral victory since the 1920s, picking up ten seats in the Senate and forty-seven in the House. Neither John nor the other national leaders deluded themselves into thinking that anything they had done had brought about the victory. Hard feelings about wartime controls had helped greatly. Even more of a factor was the rather dramatic decline in Democratic voters since 1940, caused by the displacement of millions of Americans leaving their homes to work in defense plants in other areas. Many of these blue-collar workers were Democrats and most had not bothered to register to vote in their new locations.

Even as they enjoyed their victory, Republican leaders were having to face the sobering reality that G.O.P. strength had declined greatly since the beginning of the Roosevelt years. Nearly every large city in America now went Democratic routinely. Unions were strictly Democratic. The black vote had largely shifted its allegiance away from the G.O.P. The 1944 election in which F.D.R. ran for a fourth term against Thomas E. Dewey (now the governor of New York) was particularly frustrating in this regard. The Republicans had no issues on which to run except Roosevelt's poor health and they had to be careful about mentioning that. The Republicans were able to keep most of their 1942 gains in Congress but it was a humbling experience to lose for a fourth time to the party's old nemesis.

The 1944 election was very interesting for John because his old friend from Senate days, Harry S Truman of Missouri, was elected vice-president of the United States. Roosevelt's health had been noticeably failing for a year or more, though it was not as bad as his last photographs make it appear–he had lost fifteen pounds at the order of his doctors and this had given his face a sagging, gaunt appearance. Five months after election day, as he sat in his Warm

Father and son: Senator Townsend is shown with his son, Preston, in the offices of Townsend's, Inc., in a photograph dating from the late 1940s (Preston C. Townsend collection).

Springs, Georgia, home having his portrait painted, President Roosevelt was stricken with a massive cerebral hemorrhage. His death came as a terrific jolt to millions of Americans who had come to see him as being an almost permanent fixture in the office of the presidency. Harry S Truman was president.

31. The United Nations

Senator Townsend celebrated his seventy-fourth birthday several weeks after the war ended in Europe. He looked forward to the return of those of his grandchildren who were still away in the service overseas and other young friends who would be returning home from all over the world. At an age when many men have been long since retired, he was still nearly as active as ever in the family businesses and in politics. By now, however, he was more the "chairman emeritus" than the manager. His routine was still much the same as it had always been–an early start from Selbyville and off to Millsboro or to the cannery in Georgetown or to inspect some of the poultry farms with which he was spending more and more of his time.

He still devoted much time to politics. His business hours were mostly fun hours, roaming around, stopping to jaw with anyone and everyone he encountered, digging into new things everywhere he went. In politics he was still the thorough, vigilant professional. He was appointed once more chairman of the Republican Senatorial Campaign Committee, his fifth term since 1936. Politics is one of the few fields of which it may be said that one tends to get better and better as one gets older. Now, at seventy-four, John was at the top of his form as a national political strategist. He seems no longer to have been seriously interested in running for office himself. He had the luxury of devoting himself entirely to strategy, to managing the campaigns of others.

Senator Townsend's circle of friends and acquaintances was vast and legendary. He knew virtually every important leader of both parties across the nation, and not just in a social sense. He knew their ways, their talents and capacities, and frequently their ambitions. Like most people with a talent for friendship, he worked at it very hard. He kept his contacts up to date in his frequent travels and his even more frequent phone calls around the country. He remembered birthdays, attended testimonial dinners for old friends, and hosted convivial gatherings at home and in Washington.

At ease: This photo of Senator Townsend was taken during one of his annual winter visits to Florida. It dates from about the time of his U.N. appointment shortly before his seventy-fifth birthday (Lyla T. Savoy collection).

Among his close friends there were several categories. Closest of all were the old ones from home. Like many men well along in years with what might be called "a youthful outlook," he numbered among these local friends some who were young enough to be his children, people like Inga Tubbs, the postmistress of the Selbyville post office who lived across the street from him, and J. Reese White of Millsboro, son of his deceased boyhood friend, Will White. His best friends from the Washington days were still Harry Byrd of Virginia and Frederic Walcott of Connecticut, the one still serving in the Senate and the other now president of the

American Wildlife Society. He also kept in close touch with such old friends and veterans of the Delaware political wars as Ruly and Walter Carpenter and Pierre and Irénée du Pont. His fine old Virginia friend and mentor, Carter Glass, died the year the war ended, well into his eighties, after more than four decades of public life.

No one who has been a member of the U.S. Senate ever entirely leaves it, even when one's term has ended. Retired or defeated senators often move into a sort of expanded congressional circle from which they continue to carry on a lively involvement in public life, in the decision-making process. Some become lobbyists, some lawyers. In John's case his involvement with the campaign committee kept him active. He still continued his strawberry feasts each year, though the strawberries were becoming a bit hard to find on the peninsula. If he did much thinking about his future as the war was ending in that spring of 1945, he probably saw himself helping to guide the G.O.P. through one or two more national campaigns and then coming home to Sussex for good. That is pretty much how things turned out, but fate had one more grand adventure for him first. In some ways it was the most remarkable of all. The "graduate of the University of Ebenezer" was about to become a founding father of the United Nations.

National leaders of all factions had been discussing the probable shape of the postwar world almost since the United States had entered the war. It had become clear to most that the U.S. could not avoid a role of active world leadership. The war years had been a time of great bipartisan effort in foreign affairs. Most former isolationists realized that some form of world organization was not only desirable but essential, a clear departure from the period after World War I when the American spirit had seemed to recoil from the shocking experience of the Great War, to fall back in upon itself. Those were the days when Congress had emphatically rejected all participation in the League of Nations that President Wilson had done so much to create in Paris.

Now the Axis had been totally defeated. The Russian hegemony in eastern Europe was not yet seen as the major threat it would soon reveal itself to be. The Chinese Nationalist government under Chiang Kai-shek was still wobbling along and world peace seemed attainable if an effective world organization could be devised to maintain it. The term "United Nations" had begun floating around during the war as a kind of fresh alternative to the more hackneyed "Allies." By 1943, it had taken on potent new meaning in a landmark paper by the New York lawyer and Republican foreign affairs spokesman John Foster Dulles calling for a postwar world organization. Many people were actively working for a "one world" government. In the conferences at Tehran and Yalta, then at the founding meeting of the United Nations Organization at San Francisco in the spring of 1945, and finally at a conference at the venerable Dumbarton Oaks estate in Washington, the U.N. had been transformed from a concept into a near reality. Though much of the hope that the U.S. and most other major powers placed in the U.N. was soon enough dashed, it was still alive, a driving force in world affairs, as the autumn of 1945 gave way to the terrible European winter of 1945-1946.

One of the last great holdouts in America against the U.N. concept had been John's old Senate colleague Arthur H. Vandenberg of Michigan, with whom he had worked so closely during his last four years in the Senate. Vandenberg was now the senior Republican on the Senate Foreign Relations Committee and one of the party's leading spokesmen on foreign affairs. He had experienced a dramatic change of heart one night in London on a 1944 fact-finding trip at the height of the V-1 blitz. Vandenberg and his British escort had been caught in an air raid. As he huddled in a shelter listening to the sound of German rocket bombs exploding in the battered streets of the ancient city he had had a sudden vision of the reality of world inter-dependence. "How," he had asked his companion, "can there be immunity or isolation when man can devise weapons like that?"

Before another year had passed Vandenberg's own country had unleashed a power far more terrifying over Hiroshima and Nagasaki. In late 1945, relatively few Americans understood the true ramifications of the atomic bomb, but many realized that the explosions had been the beginning of a new, far more dangerous age. Even as they turned hopefully toward the U.N. few Americans were living under the illusion that world peace had been achieved by the recent conflict or that it would be achieved through the new world organization. Still they thought the U.N. a first step toward some more rational order.

Now in the first postwar autumn, President Truman and the state department prepared for the first United Nations General Assembly and Security Council sessions to take place in London in January 1946. The naming of the American delegation was a matter of great importance and sensitivity. It was essential that the country be represented by a bipartisan group in order to avoid the sort of dissension that had toppled President Woodrow Wilson's League of Nations hopes in 1919. In choosing the delegation Truman was aided by Secretary of State James F. Byrnes, another old friend of Townsend's who had earlier served as senator from South Carolina, a U.S. Supreme Court justice, and as head of F.D.R.'s war mobilization effort.

The American team was to consist of five delegates and five alternates. Two delegates were automatic: Byrnes himself and former Secretary of State Edward R. Stettinius Jr., who was now serving as U.S. Representative on the U.N. Preparatory Commission in London. Stettinius, a former president of U.S. Steel though only in his forties, was Roosevelt's last secretary of state after the resignation of Cordell Hull and Truman's first secretary of state after F.D.R.'s death. He had been the primary American architect of the U.N. and was now appointed to serve as U.S. representative on the U.N. Security Council.

Other delegates were Senator Tom Connally of Texas, Vandenberg's Democratic opposite number, Vandenberg himself and Mrs. Eleanor Roosevelt. She was a surprise choice and one that drew immediate and broad criticism, though her detractors were restrained in view of her status as the late president's widow. It was felt that she was just a social do-gooder with little grasp of the art of diplomacy–it was felt at any rate by those who belittled women and did not know her personally.

Even so, Eleanor Roosevelt was quickly developing a constituency in America separate from the one she might be said to have inherited from her husband. She spoke out daily on national and international affairs in her syndicated newspaper column and in frequent public appearances. In opinion polls that year (and every year thereafter until her death in 1962) she was ranked as the most admired woman in the United States. She was particularly outspoken in her support for the U.N., the creation of which she saw as the greatest achievement of her husband's administration. As a symbol of her own commitment to the U.N. ideal she sought during the summer of 1945 to turn her family's Hyde Park estate over to the

U.N. as a site for a permanent headquarters. The offer was one of several that would be considered at the London conference.

The five alternate delegates–three Republicans and two Democrats–were Rep. Sol Bloom (D-N.Y.), chairman of the House Foreign Affairs Committee; Rep. Charles A. Eaton of New Jersey, ranking Republican on that committee; John Foster Dulles; Frank Walker, former postmaster general and former chairman of the Democratic National Committee; and John G. Townsend Jr. Of this group seven had been chosen from a list drafted by Byrnes's staff. Three had been picked personally by President Truman. His choices were Mrs. Roosevelt, Walker, and Townsend. All three came in for varying degrees of criticism. Townsend and Walker were found wanting by the liberal press because of their lack of foreign affairs experience. Mrs. Roosevelt was disparaged by the conservatives for the same reason. Yet Truman's appointment of all three can be defended quite easily in retrospect, particularly in the cases of Mrs. Roosevelt and Townsend.

The former First Lady of the United States went on to become what Truman himself called "The First Lady of the World." Townsend's appointment came as the result of his close friendship with the president, which had developed between 1935 and 1941, when Townsend was in his second term and Truman in his first as U.S. senator from Missouri. At the time Truman was considered by most to be none too impressive a figure. Still deeply in debt from his failed haberdashery business, an obligation he had refused to dodge by declaring bankruptcy, he came to Washington after years as a Missouri "county judge" (not an actual judicial position but, rather, equivalent to a county councilman or commissioner). In his early days in Washington Truman had been shunned by many members of his own party in the Senate because of his friendship with the recently convicted political boss of Kansas City, Tom Prendergast. Truman stood by Prendergast, stating repeatedly that the "Boss" had never asked him to do anything dishonest or dishonorable.

Townsend, who had begun his own career as a Union Republican in Delaware at a time when many prominent Republicans tried to imply that all Union Republicans were crooks, befriended Truman. Also, in those late New Deal days before the war, the two men found themselves frequently on the same side of the many issues, more "small town-big city" than Republican-Democrat. Truman had become familiar with Townsend's highly developed skills as a conciliator, had observed at close hand his ability to forge practical and pragmatic compromise between widely diverging interests. A primary objective of the delegate appointments was the achievement of a united American position on the U.N. Truman knew that Townsend was the perfect man to keep the peace among the congressional delegates. He already had plenty of foreign affairs experts in the delegation itself and in the staff of professional state department advisors accompanying the party. He needed someone well versed in politics and people.

Edward Stettinius, John Foster Dulles, and several others had been in London during the fall with the preparatory commission, planning for the January sessions. They had watched with growing concern and alarm as the Russians sought to subvert so many of the aims and goals of the Western allies. The Soviet foreign minister, Molotov, and the chief delegate, Andrei Vishinsky, proved adept at negotiating with the English foreign secretary, Sir Ernest Bevin of the newly elected Labor government. Bevin, former trade unionist, had a mercurial temper but felt guilty about his outbursts when they were over. Molotov would say something precisely calculated to send him off into transports of fury, after which the contrite Bevin would often give him what he had wanted all along. This and variations of the same procedure with others was the tactic the Russians used to deflect the attention of the delegates from issues they found not to their liking. Dulles in particular watched these goings-on with a growing sense of foreboding. The seeds of his strong anti-Soviet position of the 1950s were being sown in those London days. They would arrive at their full flowering in the Cold War when he would become the driving force of American foreign policy.

John had only a few weeks to prepare for his trip after receiving his call of invitation from Dean Acheson of the state department in early December. His children urged him to keep a journal of his experiences on the trip similar to the one he had kept during his western trip as governor. He agreed and his subsequent account of his experiences (that, when typed run to some twenty-six single-spaced legal-length pages) is a fascinating reference. Nor was he alone in recording the events of the conference. Many of the delegates and advisers kept journals, including Stettinius and Mrs. Roosevelt.

After several trips to Washington to arrange for his diplomatic passport and travel documents, he met a special train at Wilmington on December 30, 1945, which carried the delegation to New York to board the *Queen Elizabeth*. Jack, Preston and Julian had driven him up and he was met on the train by Lyla and Prew Savoy, who accompanied him to New York. In Manhattan the group was met by a fleet of twelve large black limousines complete with a motorcycle escort, which rushed them cross town to the dock. The *Queen Elizabeth* had, like the *Queen Mary* and most other large transatlantic liners, been used as a troop ship during the war and still wore its coat of battleship gray. Eleanor Roosevelt drove herself to the dock that evening in her small car and carried her own suitcase aboard. Just after five o'clock on the morning of New Year's Eve, the great vessel moved slowly away from the dock. By midafternoon it was well out in the river. Senator Townsend wrote:

> We began to move slowly out to sea. I ate a heavy breakfast and a heavy lunch and before dinner the ship began to reel and I decided after going to the table that dinner was not what I needed. I had met during the day all the delegates and alternates, including Mrs. R[oosevelt], and had begun to pick up some of the feelings among them. They said there was to be a New Year's Party at 12 o'clock but that did not appeal to me so I went to bed. My roommate was Mr. [Green] Hackworth from the State Department. He had been with the department since 1916. He is a very fine fellow.

Hackworth, an expert in international law, was a U.S. nominee to the newly reorganized World Court. Earlier in the day John had called on the Vandenbergs. Later he met with Stettinius to learn the details of his duties. On New Year's Day the delegates and staff held the first of the morning work sessions they were to continue throughout the voyage. Staff members brought the delegates up to date on the San Francisco conference and on all that had gone on since. After the first meeting Townsend wrote, "there are a great many things to straighten out yet. Walker and I sit together and I like him. Van [denburg] is looking for a place to raise H[ell]." And later in the voyage, "I have been checking up on rumors this A.M. Looks like things may get hot even before we get to London."

The delegation and the state department staff included many individuals who would emerge as pivotal figures in the American

Debarkation: *Senators Tom Connally and Arthur H. Vandenberg speak with U.N. Security Council Representative Edward Stettinius and Mrs. Eleanor Roosevelt on board ship as the American delegation prepared to sail (newspaper clipping from Townsend family scrapbooks).*

scene over the next two decades. Mrs. Roosevelt, obviously, and John Foster Dulles, but also among them was Adlai Stevenson, who retired from diplomacy to run for governor of Illinois in 1948 before mounting his two Presidential campaigns against Eisenhower and then ending his career as U.S. delegate to the U.N. Dr. Ralph Bunche, an African American, later became one of the most respected diplomats in the world. Abe Fortas, a Washington lawyer, was a presidential assistant to Truman and Lyndon B. Johnson and a Supreme Court justice under L.B.J.

Also present were Leo Pasvolsky, who had been principal assistant to Cordell Hull in the drafting of the U.N. Charter, and Alger Hiss, whose official role was that of "Principal Adviser" to the delegation. Hiss was then at the high point of his state department career, which was so abruptly ended a few years later by Whitaker Chambers and the infamous "Pumpkin Papers" scandal. At one of the preliminary conferences in the fall, as the various delegates were going over lists of likely candidates for U.N. secretary general, the Russians had mentioned Hiss as being someone who would be acceptable to them. Mrs. Roosevelt's journal mentions of Pasvolsky and Hiss that she found the first "a smooth article, but Hiss I am inclined to like." Her regard was shared by many in the delegation. She also wrote that she preferred the Vandenbergs to the Connallys, "but I don't like any of them much."

The ship docked in Southampton on Saturday, January fifth, at noon. The senator wrote that:

> [the] Lord Mayor was there to meet us. All moved up to meet him. Sol Bloom [was] mad because he was not asked first. He was [a] delegate to the San Francisco Conference and seems to resent being an alternate this time. Hope we can keep from blowing up but it looks pretty stormy now.

On the trip into London, the Senator rode with Senator and Mrs. Vandenberg,

> and what a ride! We were only two hours to London. Saw some nice herds of cows and sheep. No chicken farms. Arrived at hotel [at] 4:30... Have a nice room at Claridge Hotel...

Mrs. Roosevelt meanwhile was riding with Senator and Mrs. Connally. Connally kept asking, "Where is all this destruction I've heard so much about? Things look all right to me." Mrs. Roosevelt began pointing out signs of bomb damage, "but soon found he just wasn't interested."

When the party had settled into the hotel, Senator Townsend paid a short visit to "Senator V. and Senator C. and they were having a fit because they had rooms that cost $50.00 a day and they thought they had it to pay; so got them satisfied when they learned that S[tate] Department took care of that. Mrs. Connally ordered a bottle of sherry [and] it cost $13.00, so they thought that was a little much."

On Sunday morning, January Sixth, his first in London, he slept until ten o'clock. Then he got up and went to services at nearby St. Mark's Church, of which he said "no heat but fair congregation." In the afternoon he walked down to Piccadilly Circus, some distance from the hotel, and noticed for the first time evidence of the bombing of London during the war. The first formal delegation meeting was held on Monday morning. Alger Hiss announced the committee assignments.

Townsend found himself on what was known as "Committee 3," the humanitarian and social committee, as alternate to Mrs. Roosevelt. She later heard that she had gotten the Committee 3 assignment because the male delegates thought it would prove the most placid and least controversial. She and Townsend made some inquiries among members from other nations and came to the opposite conclusion. With such explosive issues as the repatriation of hundreds of thousands of refugees to countries many of them had no wish to return to, Committee 3 was to prove one of the most dramatic hot spots of the session.

At that first delegation meeting the discussion centered around the question of whether the group should present a united front to the press or whether each delegate should be free to express his or her own views openly. Senator Vandenberg had the most trouble accepting the limitation on his free statement of views, but he finally seemed to come around, or at least stopped arguing about it.

Shortly before the London Conference began, he had been angered at what he considered the ambiguous wording of a communiqué issued by the "Big Five" (U.S.A., U.S.S.R., Britain, France, and China) foreign ministers then meeting in Moscow. It called for the establishment of a U.N. Atomic Energy Control Commission. Vandenberg feared that under the terms of the communiqué the U.S. might be required to disclose atomic secrets before an agreement on adequate international controls had been reached. He threatened to resign from the U.N. delegation just before departure from New York, but remained when President Truman assured him no secrets would be released unless the controls were in place. Even so, Vandenberg had written a memorandum on the ship coming over which set forth his objections to the language of the Big Five communiqué. He released "confidential" copies of it to members of the press, giving one as well to Townsend. John wrote in his journal that he knew it would result in a public stink. Preparing a confidential memorandum and releasing it to the press are mutually exclusive undertakings, he observed.

After the first delegation meeting at which press relations had been argued out, Stettinius (the head of the delegation in the absence of Secretary Byrnes, who had not yet arrived) called a late afternoon press conference to present the unified view of the Americans on the work of upcoming U.N. sessions. He invited all alternates and delegates to attend, acting in ignorance of Vandenberg's maneuver with the confidential memorandum and thinking the senator had agreed to a united front. Stettinius was hoping to present a bi-partisan picture to the American and British papers.

Vandenberg's memorandum was front-page news in the

afternoon editions of newspapers on both sides of the Atlantic, the English papers coming out just before the Stettinius press conference was to start. Ten minutes before the conference, Foster Dulles informed Stettinius that he and Vandenberg would not attend. In fact the only delegates who did appear were Mrs. Roosevelt and Stettinius.

Senator Townsend also went and was a bit disgusted to learn that he was the only Republican there:

> Just as I predicted, the long article [on atomic energy] sent us by Vandenberg marked 'secret' was out in the N.Y. papers... He and Dulles were not going to attend the meeting. I could not back out then, so [I] had to go along. I was the only Republican there, which was very noticable. Had to make my first talk with only 10 minutes' notice. I said as the youngest member of the delegation, not in years possibly, but in service, I felt the hopes of the world were tied up in the success of this conference, and that we should work and pray to make this organization meeting lay the foundation for a permanent and lasting peace for the world.
> When I came out, Frank Walker said I was not the youngest member we were both born together [he and Townsend had been asked to serve in the American delegation on the same day]. My speech was last and closed the conference. About 120 newspaper men were there.

His remarks made headlines in most leading papers along with Vandenberg's conspicuous absence. After the conference broke up, Senator Vandenberg appeared outside and invited several reporters up to his room to hear his dissenting views. Mrs. Roosevelt was incensed by Vandenberg's behavior. She thought he was guilty of grandstanding over a matter that had already been resolved by Truman. "It seems to me pretty shoddy ... though I was in sympathy with parts of his memo. I think he is right that the language of the [Moscow communiqué] should be clear."

By contrast, Senator Townsend's performance after being put on the spot at the press conference impressed her. While John had skirted the issue of Vandenberg's objections, he was distinguished in her eyes as being more interested in the bipartisan nature of the U.N. conference than he was in party politics. This incident was the start of the friendship between them, that grew during the remainder of the London conference and lasted thereafter.

Secretary of State Byrnes's arrival had been delayed by his attendance at the foreign ministers' meeting in Moscow in December and a follow-up visit to the White House. He finally arrived the day after the Stettinius press conference. Senator Townsend went to his room to see him and suggested that he begin smoothing things over with Vandenberg and the Republicans as soon as possible. A good way to begin, Townsend said, would be for Byrnes to invite Senator and Mrs. Vandenberg to dinner the same evening in an apparently spontaneous gesture of good will. Byrnes did so and the Vandenbergs accepted.

With that matter out of the way, Townsend and Byrnes sat down to a discussion of U.N. affairs, American politics and other topics. During his chat with the secretary of state, John learned that Senator James M. Tunnell Sr., who had defeated him in the election of 1940, was loudly and publicly protesting John's appointment to the delegation. Tunnell was just beginning the last year of his Senate term and was preparing to run for a second term. He was infuriated by Townsend's appointment because he thought it meant that President Truman was trying to build up John to run against him even though he, Tunnell, had been a loyal administration senator.* Tunnell, who was on a fact-finding tour of American military installations around the world, "had made a statement in Europe somewhere that I had been appointed without their consulting him, and that he was definitely off the reservation from now on . . . too bad."

By this time John was nearing the age of seventy-five and it was obvious to most people that he would not be a candidate for anything in 1946, but Tunnell was worried. Truman apologized to him, but told Tunnell that he had wanted Townsend in the delegation for reasons that had nothing to do with politics.

Just as John left Byrnes's suite that afternoon, he spied the Vandenbergs coming down the hall and beat a hasty retreat around the corner, not wishing them to guess that he had had a hand in Byrnes's dinner invitation. Later he learned that his maneuver had worked. That evening he wrote "well, the dinner did the trick. Saw Van and he said he was in full accord now with the Secretary, so my efforts were very successful and the Conference looks much more harmonious."

Not knowing of John's hand in the matter, Mrs. Roosevelt had written in her journal the same evening, "all seems serene on the atomic bomb statement that stirred up such a rumpus with Senator Vandenberg. I am not sure the gentleman does not like a little newspaper publicity." On the whole Mrs. Roosevelt had a rather low opinion of the congressional type. "I am interested," she wrote,

---

* *The man eventually chosen by Delaware Republicans to oppose Tunnell in the 1946 election was a little-known, forty-six-year-old Millsboro feed dealer and businessman named John J. Williams, who said in later years that the major reason for his nomination was that no one else was especially eager to take Tunnell on. Williams was also a native of Baltimore Hundred who had grown up near the village of Bayard, where Louise Johnson met him on one of her first visits to Sussex with her husband Everett.*

"in the way all the legislators react. I think not having strong convictions they doubt their ability to defend a position which they may take, so they cannot decide on any position and go on arguing the pros and cons endlessly." She included Byrnes in this category as well, since he had been a senator.

Yet the "endless arguing" that so characterizes the American legislative process had certain advantages over the dramatic style of diplomacy. While congressmen are without doubt an unruly and contentious lot and while the deepest conviction of many of them is to get elected with the largest number of votes, they are sometimes able to achieve a position that is more nearly the reflection of the American people. In this instance they were working at determining America's proper role in world councils, a role they could sell to the American people.

At the Paris Peace Conference of 1919, President Wilson had conducted himself in the manner of a brilliant and idealistic statesman. He had made a whole generation of young American liberals (among whom had been F.D.R.) revere him. But he had come home and completely muffed the job of convincing Congress that it should support the League of Nations. Truman, a product of the legislative process himself, did not intend to make the same mistake and was willing to put up with a little nonsense from Vandenberg and others to avoid it. John, in a sense, was along as a referee.

The actual work of the U.N. sessions was typical of major diplomatic gatherings in that it consisted of relatively few substantive pieces of business, most of the details having been ironed out by professional diplomats before the meeting began. What was left were the touchy items of business the lower echelon officials had not been able to resolve: the election of a General Assembly president and a secretary general, the determination of which nations would sit on the Security Council, choice of a permanent site, and the initial committee deliberations on various troubling matters.

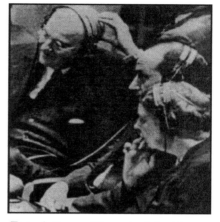

A backdrop to this conference was a growing controversy among Russia, Britain, and the U.S. over the continued Soviet occupation of northern Iran on the one hand and the British occupation of

Translation: *Alternate John Foster Dulles, staff member Adlai Stevenson and Mrs. Roosevelt listen to a translation of a speech during a U.N. General Assembly session (Townsend family scrapbooks).*

Greece on the other. The British held that they were in Greece at the request of the legitimate government while the Soviets had refused to end a wartime occupation of Iran they had originally shared with Britain. The issues were not resolved at the London conference, but they heightened the tension of that meeting.

The delegates and alternates were invited to all sessions of the General Assembly and those committee meetings that concerned them directly. Most delegates stayed away from all but the most important sessions both of the committees and of the General Assembly, preferring to let the state department staff attend to more mundane details. Mrs. Roosevelt, Senator Townsend, and Frank Walker were of the view that they should attend everything they possibly could, that this was why they had been sent to London. They came at times to feel like a delegation within a delegation and sat together through many boring hours of speechifying. In a journal entry for January 16, John recorded what it was like:

Left for the assembly at 10:15–three more speeches. If this don't get over soon will get the willies. Adjourned at 12:15. Came back at 3:00 to listen to four more speeches. First in French, then translated into English. One fellow spoke in Spanish, so his had to be translated in both French and English. Slow procedure . . . I see now why the [alternates] were sent over–to sit in the seats of the delegates to listen to all these dry speeches, but I have been a good soldier and listened to them all.

On Friday evening, January 18, he wrote:

I am having the newspaper boys that came over with us on the boat to dinner tonight, and have to go on radio. [Later] Went on radio at 5:15–World News. Gave Secretary [Byrnes] the best I could as I think his was a good speech and that he is doing a good job. He fails to delegate enough of his burden to others and I fear he will break under the terrific load. Listened to all the speeches. Same old faithful few–Mrs. R., Walker and myself. The Delegate from South Africa made the best speech of the day. Spoke for half an hour without a single note and then the interpreter gave it in French, and he only had a few notes. Very few. Most amazing I have ever seen.*

Selection of the member nations of the Security Council was carried out with relative ease but still it had its interesting moments. The English backed Canada for a position on the council, but most of the other British Commonwealth countries backed Australia. New Zealand was particularly adamant on the subject. When the vote was held Australia won, even though the U.S. had also backed

---

* *At this time the concurrent translating capacity the U.N. later developed had not yet evolved. The person gave the entire speech. Then it was delivered again in the various other languages required.*

Canada. Mrs. Roosevelt was struck by the startled glances the Russians gave this disagreement among the English-speaking nations: "They would feel such behaviour among their satellites showed weakness & it is going to take time to realize that when you are sure of fundamentals you can differ on non-essentials . . ."

The growing tension between East and West was translated into minor disputes on nearly every point in the proceedings. When the Belgian Foreign Minister Paul-Henri Spaak was elected president of the General Assembly over Norwegian Foreign Minister Trygve Lie, Lie was angered by what he thought was a desertion by the U.S. He told Townsend at a reception afterward that the Americans and English had "been off him" because they feared he would be influenced by the Russians as a Scandanavian socialist. This, he said, was ridiculous. He was especially incensed by Byrnes's statement of support earlier and his failure to come through. But Byrnes in fact had already thought of the possibility of putting Lie up as a compromise candidate for the far more influential office of secretary general. The Americans had earlier backed Lester B. Pearson for this job. Pearson was then the Canadian ambassador to the U.S. The Soviets would not accept him and the Americans would not accept someone from the East. Another would-be candidate was former U.S. Ambassador to Great Britain, John G. Winant.* Secretary Byrnes turned him down on the basis that no representative of a major power should hold the position. Winant did later win an appointment as U.S. representative to the U.N. Economic and Social Council.

---

* *Winant, a New Englander, was fascinated to learn that Senator Townsend owned poultry farms in his own state, Massachusetts. It turned out that Winant had just started a poultry operation himself and he pumped John for advice. The Senator invited him down to Sussex County to see things at first hand.*

With the election of Lie as secretary general the endless speechmaking of the General Assembly sessions gave way for some weeks to the even more protracted debates within various committees. Mrs. Roosevelt and Senator Townsend turned their attention to Committee 3. It was chaired by Sir Peter Fraser of New Zealand who, Mrs. Roosevelt noted, was absolutely fair in his duties. The major issue confronting the committee was the question of what to do with the hundreds of thousands of persons still occupying displaced persons camps in Europe and elsewhere. It was not simply a matter of sending them home to the countries from which they had come. In some cases, such as Latvia, Lithuania, and Estonia, their nations had been absorbed by the Soviet Union. In other instances, such as Eastern European countries like Poland and Czeckoslovakia, the countries remained but their systems of government had altered radically. Even more problematical were the thousands of persons from places like the Ukraine whose citizens had been so opposed to the harsh Soviet rule of their homeland that many had willingly fought for Germany against the Russians. As Mrs. Roosevelt wrote, "a new type of political refugee is appearing, people who have been against the present governments and who, if they stay home or go home, will probably be killed."

Mrs. Roosevelt and Townsend worked day after day trying to arrive at an acceptable solution to the problem. She wrote of having spent six hours one day working out agreement on twenty-five lines of a committee recommendation. Finally the agreement, which the Russians still opposed, was brought to a vote in committee and the U.S. position won. Later, in a full General Assembly session, Andrei Vishinsky, the leader of the Soviet delegation, prepared to fight the committee recommendation. As Mrs. Roosevelt recalled:

"The British had their representative ready to speak but I saw all the heads in our delegation come together because nobody was ready to speak except the woman in Committee 3 whom they had put there, thinking she would be harmless. Finally Mr. Dulles asked me to say a few words and I agreed to do so."*

Vishinsky was a formidible adversary in debate. Among the most skillful of Soviet diplomats, Vishinsky had been, Joseph P. Lash notes, ". . . the grand inquisitor, the relentless Stalinist prosecutor in the Moscow purge trials . . ." He was here ". . . arguing with the twentieth century embodiment of humanitarianism before a world jury."

"If Democracy had saints," Adlai Stevenson would later say, "Eleanor Roosevelt would be among the first canonized." Vishinsky summed up the Russian position that the solution to the refugee problem was a simple matter of repatriation. Those who did not wish to return to their own countries were simply traitors, collaborators "or worse and no consideration need be given them." Mrs. Roosevelt countered this position, noting that most of those who did not wish to return to their own countries took the position they did because of their fear of the Soviets. She scored a resounding victory in the exchange, which was perhaps the highest moment of drama in the entire U.N. session. The Soviet position was voted down. Afterwards, Townsend wrote in admiration, "She's a fighter!"

---

* *In his book on Mrs. Roosevelt's life after the death of her husband,* Eleanor– The Years Alone, *from which her views and journal entries quoted here are taken, Joseph P. Lash notes that Dulles and Vandenberg, at first so opposed to Mrs. Roosevelt's appointment, now spoke with amazement of her good judgement. "They really had not known her before, writing her off as an emotional, rattle-brained woman. 'One of the most solid members of the delegation they now agreed.'"*

32. European Travels

The most interesting aspect of Senator Townsend's travels was his experiences outside the formal committee and General Assembly sessions. The personalities he met and the places he went in London were far from commonplace, but his side trip to occupied Berlin was perhaps most interesting of all. He flew there in a military plane with John Foster Dulles during a slow period in the proceedings (this was prior to both the election of Trygve Lie to the secretary generalship and the Committee 3 deliberations). The men left London on a snowy morning–January 19, 1946:

> Up at six o'clock, packed my bag and over to Mr. Dulles' room for breakfast at 7:15. We then left the hotel at eight for the airport to get plane for Berlin. It had snowed during the night and frozen so the roads were a sheet of ice. Major of Philadelphia came along to take us with lady driver and we started out to drive thirty niles to airport. When we had gotten out about ten miles the car skidded and turned completely around and was heading for London. Fortunately we did not turn over and no one was coming to run into us but I must confess I was a little jittery on account of my experience last winter–or two years ago–when I turned over.*
>
> We took off at 10:15 for Berlin . . . the plane was very cold when we started off but soon warmed up. General Kenney sent along some sandwiches which we enjoyed on the plane. . . I rode in [the] pilot house quite some of the time over. Could see the country much better . . . Landed in

---

* *See note on following page.*

Berlin . . . [at] 3:15 Berlin time. Was met by General and several officers [and] the press of Germany. We were then taken in the General's car . . . to our place where we were to spend the night. Two soldiers with white caps on, in a jeep, led the way and kept all the traffic out of the way of our car. You might have thought we were Hitler come back.

Landed at our place and were shown to our rooms. Splendid place. We then went out to look around city until dark. Short time but long enough to see the terrible ruins. Most depressing sight I have ever seen. Everybody you see on the streets is carrying bags and bundles, mostly wood. Women and children and old men are the most people you see on the streets, all pulling little carts loaded with wood or pieces of furniture, moving. Houses all destroyed but they are fitting up one room and a cellar where they live. Did not see a smile. All the people poorly dressed and glum. Some pulling branches and others pulling whole cedar trees for wood . . . every little cart or wagon loaded with the most terrible looking rubbish.

The buildings are mostly destroyed but the rubbish is pretty well cleaned up... Berlin had 200,000 buildings and 40 per cent are totally destroyed; 20 per cent are only partially destroyed. They had 4,800,000 people before the war. Now [they] only have 3,000,000 and I could not see where that

---

*   ". . . when I turned over." He referred here to an incident in the winter of 1944, in which he had been involved in an accident while out touring poultry farms. An account of it led off an article about Senator Townsend that appeared in the November 1945 issue of* Country Gentleman *magazine and was later reprinted in* Readers' Digest: *"The road through the flat, South Delaware countryside was ice-slick and treacherous. A big sedan slewed sideways, hung over the road edge, then rolled over twice and lay on its side with two wheels spinning . . . it's occupant was J.G. Townsend, Jr . . . horrified neighbors pulled up at the scene, for J.G. at seventy-three was no youngster. Yet when Townsend hoisted his six-foot bulk through what was left of a door, he was grinning. He dusted off his pants, straightened his necktie. 'Mind helping me get her out of the ditch, folks? I want to take a look at four more of my chicken farms and get back to the office by noon!'" While there was obviously some poetic license used in this rendition, the basic facts were accurate. What the article did not say was that the accident had scared him badly.*

many could live. They have 900,000 in the whole of Germany in jail waiting trial as Nazi criminals and also 112,000 more taken to jail recently as members of organizations sympathetic to Nazis. Hopeless situation. We were invited to General [Lucius D.] Clay's for dinner at 7:30, so went over to his house.* There were Mr. Murphy and Mr. Angell, Mr. Dulles, General Clay and myself.**

The place where we stayed all night was taken over from the Minister of Education and his daughter is working in the kitchen for the Americans. The house where General Clay is, was taken over from a rich Nazi who had a wonderful wine cellar full of wine. He had three kinds of wine for dinner. Before we went to dinner [we] called on Mr. Murphy of the State Dept. He is the adviser to General Clay. Had a long conversation with him about the stand France was taking on the occupation situation and soon found he and Dulles were not in agreement on the issue. I was favorably impressed with Mr. Murphy. He was well informed on all the issues.

We then went back to our rooms and at 7:30 . . . went to dinner with General Clay. We talked quite a while before dinner and then went to dinner, and again discussed the many problems he had to face in working out the occupation with the Russians, British and the French—and I could see that he felt the French were the most unreasonable. He says we have told the world that we went through this war so that democratic principles should live and he thought we should do just that. After dinner we started all over again on this subject and he was very pronounced in his views. We talked until about eleven o'clock and I certainly learned more about this situation than I had ever known.

We then went to our house and...found that the U.S., British, Russian and French were all having a party together. The Russian girl was playing the piano and all the others were joining in the singing, so we went in and met everybody.

---

* *General Lucius D. Clay was the Chief of U.S. Occupation Forces in Germany.*

** *Robert D. Murphy was U.S. Ambassador to Germany. Angell was a member of Murphy's embassy staff.*

I stayed with them until about 12:30. It is this kind of fraternizing that will help us to know each other better and to gain the confidence we need. Then to bed, but I could not sleep after all the horrible destruction and depressed people I had seen . . . [I] decided the UNO must succeed and end all wars or the next war would destroy all civilization even without the atomic bomb. We left call for seven o'clock and were to go out and look over more of the destruction at eight o'clock . . .

Sunday, January 20th: We went to the Reichstag and to where Hitler's offices were. The Russians have this part of the city but the destruction is complete. All the works of art, literature, architecture, mosaics, floors, all destroyed. In fact, in this territory the destruction is 100 per cent. We then went to the airport, expecting to get off for London. Found we could not land there on account of fog, so went back and finally found we could get in at Paris, so we took off for Paris.* Arrived there at three o'clock. Army man met us. We then called up London to see if we could get through and finally they said the ceiling was too low and we would have to stay all night in Paris. This did not worry me as I had never been to Paris... As I drove around the streets there was the most amazing difference from Berlin. In fact, I noticed the great difference coming in on the plane. The houses all have red tile roofs on and in the sunshine looked wonderful in comparison to flying over Berlin where most of the roofs were off, and the people seemed so different. Plenty of life and children and young folks . . .

We were invited to dinner [by] Mr. Parsons, the son of the editorial writer and manager here of [the *International*] *Herald Tribune*, N.Y. They had plenty of champagne. When we went to dinner we had hard bread and white butter, and then we had pickled string beans and cheese and this, with a small piece of custard pie, was the dinner. Then it was that I saw what a desperate food situation existed here–no potatoes for five months, and practically everything rationed. Very

---

* *Mrs. Roosevelt was a bit skeptical. In her journal for that Sunday she wrote: "My buddy, Sen. Townsend, and Dulles went to Germany on Sat. a.m. and today I got a message they were grounded in Paris. The boys, no matter what their age, can't resist a good time."*

little coal. He had two fireplaces and had his wood brought in in double lengths and he then sawed it in the middle and made two sticks. Wood cost $50.00 per cord.

Stayed there until late in the evening. His wife is from California and went through the German occupation here. First she married a Frenchman. I don't know what happened to him but she married Parsons last June. She is a very smart girl. Several interesting people there. Gave me a lot of dope on the little countries. So we went home. I asked to be called at eight o'clock so we could go out to pay our respects to the Ambassador, Mr. [Jefferson] Caffrey.

Monday, January 21st: Up early. Had a nice breakfast, oranges, cornflakes and fresh eggs, bacon. The hotel is run by our army. Mr. Dulles and I went over to call on the Minister [Ambassador] and of course were too early for him as he had been up most of the night on account of [the] resignation of De Gaulle. Some of the people were saying there would be a revolution and some that the deputies would call De Gaulle back. Funny we should arrive just at the time of De Gaulle's resignation.

When we arrived at the Embassy I was surprised to be greeted by Mr. MacArthur, nephew of the General and son-in-law of Senator [Alben S.] Barkley. He was most kind to us and insisted that if I had to stay over I come to dinner with them, as his wife was so fond of me, but we expected to get away at 11 o'clock. Soon Minister McCaffrey [*sic*] came in and we had a nice chat with him. He looked and acted as if he was much worried and to me he seemed a little light. In fact, MacArthur looked and acted stronger than the chief.

. . . out to the airport, where they thought we would get away about one o'clock but when we arrived the ceiling was so low at Boxford end they would not clear us, so we waited around there for three hours and tried every way to get through, but no luck. So then we decided to go by train and boat, as they could not give us any hope for tomorrow. Went back to Embassy and they finally got our passports so we could get out of France, and we also found we could not get away until six o'clock next morning. The boy who MacArthur gave us to get our passports fixed up was from Delaware. His name was Jeb and he has two brothers who

are preachers and his father is also a preacher. He sure was
a nice boy and very helpful.

John had dinner with the MacArthurs after all, getting to meet their
small daughter and enjoying the simple evening with friends very much.
The following day he and Dulles made their way to Dieppe by train. They
caught a boat there for England and were back on British soil by late
afternoon, much the wiser for their four days on the Continent. While
Dulles was an experienced European traveler, this had been his first trip
back since the cessation of hostilities and so the jaunt had been educational
for him also.

One of the most fascinating aspects of Senator Townsend's U.N.
journal is the frequent observations he makes on the interesting people,
many of them world famous, he meets and talks to in his travels around
London.

Wednesday, January 30th: Go to the Port Authority
reception at six and then to Turkish at seven, and then back
here to hotel for 7:30 dinner with Mrs. R. She has more go
than I have and that is going some. They say I seemed to
come back from our trip in as good shape as the young fellows.
Went to the Port Authority to meet the Right Hon. Sir John
Anderson, M.P., and members of Port of London Authority.
It was held at Trinity Square. When we went we were
announced by a man all dressed in red, in a very loud voice.
We were then ushered up to the Lord Mayor. Stationed on
all the steps as we went up, three flights of steps, were men
all dressed in red with a large gold-looking ball on the sides of
their dress. Upon inquiry we were told these were all men
who had earned this distinction of wearing this medal by their
winning the matches which were held once a year and that
the money to buy these ... medals was left by a Baron in the
1500's ...

We left there and went to Turkish delegation, where
they were giving a reception. Met all the principal Turks and

then back to hotel where we went to dinner with Sir Alexander Livingstone. He is a crippled man, can't walk, and the way I met him–he was going up in the elevator in a wheel chair and in my usual way of speaking to everybody I said "How do you do. My name is Townsend, from U.S.A." And so he called Mrs. Connally, whom I suppose he had met before, and said he liked my face and wanted me to come to dinner. I suppose he had already invited them.

He gives these dinners and invites half Americans and half British, with the idea of cultivating better relations between the two peoples . . . He has been doing this every week since 1940 and has had over 200 of them now . . . He had 15 last night–Senator and Mrs. Connally, Senator and Mrs. Vandenberg, Judge Hutchinson from Texas who is here with the Palentine Commission, Mr. Adlai Stevenson with UNO and myself from US, and eight British including himself . . ."

Two days later, on Friday, February 1:

Had a nice chat with Vishinsky of Russia. He is a very fascinating fellow. He said Russia and the U.S. are the greatest countries and I said must not let anything create a misunderstanding, and he said that was right. He said Russia liked our wonderful productive capacity and great energy to do things. He's plenty smart. Has an interpreter, so got along with us . . . He is a great talker and when he left he used both hands to shake mine very warmly.

Monday, February Fourth: . . . Got dressed up for first time in tux and went to the Pilgrim's Dinner in honor of Mrs. R. at the Savoy Hotel.* Met a lot of the Lords and Sirs there. Mrs. R. is the only woman who has been so honored by the club and the club is 44 years old. It was a nice affair and very impressive. Of course, it was really for Franklin, whom they love very much over here as they think he was the one man who saved them, which is probably true.

---

*   *Joseph P. Lash writes, "The Pilgrim Society, dedicated to Anglo-American friendship, was one of the most prestigious in the realm."*

I sat at Table No. Two and at my table was Sir Campbell Stuart, Sir Ernest Fisk and the Lord Bishop of London. When I told the Bishop I went to his church, St. James, Sunday to hear him preach, he said, "I remember you. I picked you from the pulpit." My gray hair or broad face, I suppose. I had a very nice time with them and when they found out I was in the egg business (eggs being in very short supply in Britain) they said I should send them some eggs, which I shall try to do when I get home. Sir John Simon, Secretary of the Exchequer, was selected after Mrs. R.'s speech to introduce Mr. Frazier, who is chairman of our committee, and he took so long in introducing him that Sir Campbell turned to me and said, "Too long. You need not send him any eggs."

Upon his visit to the House of Commons with Senator and Mrs. Connally, Senator Townsend wrote:

Sir Howard greeted us and took us in to hear the Minister of Coal and Fuel discuss his bill to nationalize coal. He made a very good speech, a part of which I had heard at the Chamber of Commerce luncheon at the American Embassy. Just before he closed he came for us and insisted we go get a cup of tea . . . We then went to hear Anthony Eden and his speech was largely a criticism of the bill. The House of Lords is a large square room, with straight benches where 40 to 45 men sit, all side by side—the Conservatives on one side and the Laborites on the other and when the Speaker makes a point that they like, they all loudly say "here, here." Then when the point turns the other way they all say "no, no." I should think [this] very confusing to the speaker.

The seats are on both sides of this flat table and they sit with their feet up against the top of the table. In fact, when Mr. Shinwell was speaking there was one on each side of him with their feet against the table, so he was hemmed in on both sides. The Speaker has a little square tepee in which he sits, with a sort of scarf on his head, with his clerks in front of him with a twisted toupee on their heads and and long streamers in back. It was a very interesting sight . . . After Eden's speech an old man from Wales, and evidently a great friend of Lloyd George, spoke. He made the best speech of any of them in support of the bill. Was quite an orator and very logical. Reminded me very much of Key Pittman when he was in the Senate.

Wednesday, February Sixth: There was a good story at the Assembly today. The Russians always have a lot of plain clothes men to look after them, so they said Vishinsky had four plain clothes men with him at St. Paul's Church Sunday (at a special U.N. service) and Mrs. R. had only one—that was me. Ha.

On Saturday evening, February 9, the senator wrote about his trip to a reception hosted by the king and queen:

Went to King's reception at 9 o'clock and what a crowd. At about 10 the King and Queen were standing in a room adjoining the big reception hall—stood in line with the Queen Mother to receive. It was an immense crowd. All went in and spoke to them and I told them of meeting them in Washington and they said they remembered me. Guess that was nice thing to say. The Queen is still very pretty and very gracious. The Mother is a very stately looking woman. After all had gone in the third room for drinks and eats, a great many of us were asked to go back in the room to talk with them. The King was standing off to himself as was the Queen, and the Queen Mother and the two princesses [Princess Elizabeth, now Queen Elizabeth II, and Princess Margaret]. I talked with the Princesses and asked them when they were coming to the U.S. and they brightened up and said they hoped soon as they were sorry they could not accompany the King and Queen to U.S. on their last visit. They are real pretty. Also talked with the [Queen] Mother [Queen Mary, widow of King George V] She is a matter-of-fact somebody.

We milled around there until 11:30 and then Mr. and Mrs. Dulles and myself went to another party that we had promised to go to . . . Secretary General Lie [was] there and he promised to come down to see me when he got over to U.S. His wife seemed very anxious to come. She is a very domestic-looking and acting woman.

Another thread woven through the London trip was the senator's effort to help J. Reese White Jr. of Millsboro get home from Europe. White was the son of his close friends Reese and Sarah White. He was stationed in France in the army and was stuck there after the cessation of hostilities awaiting orders. The young man had called the senator at his London hotel on January 16. During the next several weeks John took his young friend to several sessions of the U.N. General Assembly. He took Reese to dinner and introduced him to various other Americans attached to the U.N. He contacted Reese's commanding general and even hired the young Sussex Countian as his secretary, paying him $50.00 to close the deal, but John was never was able to bring about the young man's release from active duty. When John left London for home on February 16, he still did not know where things stood with Reese, who had returned to his unit. Finally, John left Reese a letter, providing the name of a friendly contact at the American embassy: "Told my friend to take care of him and I would take care of him on any expense he had in getting him over on boat."

Nor were Senator Townsend and Reese White the only Sussex Countians in London during the United Nations session. On Sunday, January 28, Townsend had gone with Senator and Mrs. Connally out to an American military cemetery about thirty miles outside the city. After learning from the attendant that eight Delawareans were buried there, he had paid the man to place flowers on their graves. On his return to the hotel that evening,

the first fellow I ran into was Sen. Tunnell. His Committee had come in here today. They could not land in Paris. Went up to Senator Vandenberg's room and there was Senator [William] Knowland, so Jim Tunnell with the crew he had with him were all introduced to me and I invited them all to dinner, but they said they were going out to get some American food and asked me to go with them. But I could not go, so I had Senator Knowland [a California Republican] to dinner with me and he gave me the low-down on their trip. They are holding 3 short hearings here tomorrow and then going to Paris and from there home. Think to get home next Friday. [Jim Tunnell] did not say a word about my appointment. I went over the California situation with Knowland and he seems optimistic about his and Warren's chances.* Hope he is right but I don't think so. He and Warren will both have a hard fight both for nomination and election.

Not only is this passage revealing of Townsend, the Republican leader, consulting in London, of all places, with William Knowland about an election campaign in California, but it shows how small the world was even in 1945. Who should he run into in Claridge's Hotel but the man from Baltimore Hundred who had defeated him for the Senate in 1940 and who had protested his appointment to the U.N. delegation. The next day he reported:

> Senator Tunnell was in, but could not get him to have dinner with me, but had Sen. Knowland and Gen. who has charge of sending the war brides to the U.S., 50,000 of them. He ordered babies' cribs and 100,000 diapers. Also met Lt. General Merrill from Gen. McNarny's staff in Germany and he says he will help me out with Reese, so we will see what happens. Tunnell came back after dinner and stayed in the lobby with us for a while. He seems much better, not so nervous. Leaving tomorrow for Paris.

---

* *This passage refers to Senator Knowland's bid for reelection to the Senate and that of California Republican Earl Warren for governor. Warren later served as chief justice of the U.S. Supreme Court.*

The United Nations General Assembly adjourned on Saturday, February 16, the Russians still fighting and bickering to the end - a portent of the future. By then, Mrs. Roosevelt had left for Germany, though she would meet the delegation on its homeward journey at a stopover in Ireland. Frank Walker and his widowed daughter had left for France where the young woman wished to find her soldier-husband's grave. Then the Walkers were off to Rome for the ceremonies connected with the raising of Archbishop Spellman of New York to Cardinal. Senator Connally and his wife had left for further travels on the Continent. Connally was running for reelection and he told Townsend he had realized his campaign was going better with him in Europe being a statesman than it was when he was home, being a politician. Byrnes had left weeks before and Stettinius had been forced to go home because of poor health early in February. John G. Townsend Jr had stayed to the end. He was afflicted during his last week with an inflammation of the eyes–he said he looked like a losing fighter–and he was anxious to get home. After Ireland, where it began snowing, the flight took them to Goose Bay, Labrador, where it snowed some more and he wound up falling into a troubled sleep fully clothed in a spare hospital bed. At last they arrived in New York and a blare of press publicity. He made it just in time to the railroad station, arriving in Wilmington some thirty-six hours after leaving England. His last journal entry was:

> Never more tired in my life. Eyes sore. Can't sleep, so feel badly. Got a little supper and went to bed after talking to *Morning News* man for few minutes, which should have been deferred but was just plain given out.

33. A Distinguished Citizen of Delmarva

MY DAY: Southern Delaware is an Incredibly Rich Farm Section

By Eleanor Roosevelt
Thursday, June 16, 1946

NEW YORK, Wednesday–I am going again today to a drafting committee meeting of the United Nations Economic and Social Council. The council is trying very hard to finish its work before the end of June . . .

Yesterday my son and daughter-in-law, Elliott and Faye [actress Faye Emerson] and I went down to look at one of the most remarkable farming operations which I have ever had the pleasure of seeing. Of course, Southern Delaware, with its mixture of sandy soil and rich bottomland and its areas of woodland, is ideal farming country. The fields are broad and flat without stones. To a New Yorker it seemed an incredibly rich and easy land on which to farm. Over the whole area chickens were being raised in great numbers and every farm looked like a satisfactory and prosperous undertaking.

The extent and variety of enterprises on this particular project which we saw, are probably the reasons for the farm's great success. Perhaps if you had grown up with this operation it would not stagger you as it did me! The dairy farms were beautiful. The fields of peas and beans and other produce seemed endless. The peach orchards, we were told, produced very little this year because of a hot spell in February which brought out the blossoms too soon! The apple trees were not up to maximum either. I kept wishing that I could have seen these acres of fruit trees in bloom. Near us on the Hudson River, I know of no more beautiful sight than Mr. Henry Morgenthau, Jr.'s orchards in bloom in the spring. His land is hilly country, however, and you climb up and down to reach the various orchards. In Delaware all is level and where the new orchards are planted, rye grows almost to the tops of the little trees.

This particular undertaking is not just a one-man kingdom, but a family proposition. Sons and daughters, with their families, have an interest in land which is far-flung in the State of Delaware. Family holdings also include two chicken farms in Maine. The world is small and as we sat on the porch of a delightful house in a beach resort in the late afternoon, after having toured all day, a very pretty young woman commented that she remembered playing with my two younger sons at the Corning place in Albany and coming to the Executive Mansion for parties when they were all in their teens. Another charming girl told me that she had been at Connecticut State College when I had spoken there years ago. Since then she had served with the Red Cross in the Pacific and had seen the results of war in the Philippines. Altogether it was an interesting day. My son and daughter-in-law and I spent the time in our return train trip trying to determine what we could apply, from our new learning, to a very small farming project in New York State.

Eleanor Roosevelt in Sussex County. Indeed it was a small world! In the course of her visit, she had been entertained for lunch at Senator Townsend's old Selbyville home, where Evelyn and Harley Derrickson, the couple who had been with the senator since 1928, had put on a feast in the classic Townsend style with heaping plates of fried chicken, mashed potatoes and gravy, greens, biscuits, and homemade ice cream and cake for dessert. After lunch, Mrs. Roosevelt jumped right up from the table and strode out into the kitchen to shake Evelyn's hand and tell her how fine the meal had been. She was just as natural and nice in Selbyville as she had been in London and as she was everywhere. Mrs. Roosevelt's visit to Sussex and a similar visit Senator Townsend paid to her Hyde Park estate, her "very small farming project in New York State," soon afterward set off a flurry of speculation among the journalists and gossip columnists that a romance was developing between the seventy-five-year-old former senator and the sixty-fiveish former First Lady. Some reports even had it that they were about to marry. Both promptly denied the report. One Washington columnist, George Dixon, presented John's version of the friendship this way:

> I asked Mr. Townsend about this [the rumor]. He replied that it wasn't love; it was chickens. I must have looked bewildered because he added: "Mrs. Roosevelt is interested in raising chickens. I told her about some experiments I was making with hybrid hens and she wanted to observe the results."
>
> "Must be an engrossing hobby–I mean chicken raising." I said.
>
> "Hobby, my foot," erupted Mr. Townsend. "I raise three million broilers a year and one hundred thousand laying hens. I figure on averaging fifty thousand eggs a day this year."
>
> I wouldn't blame Mrs. Roosevelt if she pursued the romance. Think of the omelet she could make with just one day's output.

Though the alleged Townsend-Roosevelt romance had little substance, the rumor proved to be very persistent, explained, no doubt, by the fact that it was a rather nifty idea. What did exist between them was a friendship that grew out of their mutual respect, built during their six weeks together at the United Nations General Assembly in London. The friendship lasted until her death in 1962.

Through the late 1940s and early 1950s, Senator Townsend's life continued much the same way. His health was still quite good and he lived a full life, travelling widely still on business and for pleasure. Though many old faces he had known were passing away, many more

The Grand Old Man: *Still active in Republican party leadership, Senator Townsend is seen in New York City in 1952 with a delegation of Delawareans meeting General Dwight D. Eisenhower, the newly nominated G.O.P. presidential candidate. Among those pictured with Townsend and Eisenhower are (left to right) future Wilmington Mayor Harry G. Haskell Jr., Col. Herbert Barnes of New Castle County (between Haskell and Townsend), Earl Isaacs Sr. of Ellendale (next to Eisenhower) and, above Eisenhower, Henry Ridgely of Dover and Delaware congressional candidate Herbert Warburton (Townsend family collection).*

were still alive and healthy. The rhythm of his life remained much the same. Preston and Rachel Townsend lived with the senator in his huge old Selbyville home for several years after their marriage, sharing the establishment with him and with Evelyn and Harley, who had their own quarters in the rear of the house. Evelyn did most of the cooking, cleaning, and housekeeping. Harley acted primarily as the senator's driver, chauffeuring him around in his succession of large Cadillacs and entertaining the whole family with his wonderful sense of humor.* The Derricksons had no children of their own and used to dote on the

---

* *Harley and Preston Townsend both loved to hunt and would go out together most mornings during hunting season. Harley also had a passionate love for pork and pork products. As they would drive along, Preston recalled, laughing, Harley would tip his hat to all the hogs they passed.*

senator's grandchildren and great-grandchildren. The old traditional
family dinners and parties still continued.

The two major social occasions of John's year were Christmas
and his birthday. On both days the whole clan would gather from
wherever they happened to be and descend on the Selbyville home
for big dinners. One year at Christmas a crowd of thirty-seven family
members was on hand. Until her final illness and death in the mid-
1950s, Grandma Ida Townsend also held a big annual dinner a week
before the Christmas dinner at the senator's house. She would have
chicken, duck and country hams which she still took great pride in
curing herself just as she had done down on the farm at Bishops years
before. Then there were the turnip greens that she grew herself, timing
them carefully so they would be at their peak just at the right time.
For dessert there would be her special angel food cake. Both she
and Evelyn also specialized in baking "puffy" dumplings for these
holiday feasts. Though slippery dumplings are a more traditional Sussex
County dish, the Townsends always preferred the puffy kind. All the
in-laws and grandchildren and close friends would attend these affairs.
And interspersed during the holidays would be other big dinners at
Edith and Jack Tubbs's house or Mim and Jule Townsend's home on
North Bedford Street in Georgetown. Another Christmas tradition
that survived into the senator's last years was his practice of very
quietly carrying bags filled with groceries around to the homes of needy
residents of Selbyville.

In between holidays he still entertained often in a small way.
He had a more or less constant stream of visitors from near and far.
All were routinely invited to stay for lunch or dinner if their visit happened
to fall near a mealtime. Evelyn Derrickson had grown used to this sort
of thing and always seemed to be able to find enough to feed these

unexpected guests. Some visitors were more exalted than others, those like Mrs. Roosevelt and Senator Harry F. Byrd and his brother, Tom, who came over once to look at a new sprayer device Senator Townsend had acquired for his orchard. Others were local people. All were treated with the same hospitality.

As he had for years, the senator still loved to use the telephone. He had a phone sitting near his chair at the head of the dining room table. If he was eating and someone called, he would stop what he was doing and sit and talk at great length. Through the late 1940s and into the early 1950s much of this telephoning was devoted to national politics, in which he was still very heavily involved. In 1946 and again in 1948, he managed Republican Senate campaigns across the nation with his usual gusto and hard work.

During the 1948 campaign, the year Dewey ran against Truman, the senator accompanied Dewey and his host of managers and functionaries aboard the candidate's campaign train, tending to senatorial campaign duties along the way. One Washington columnist aboard the press section of the train wrote a humorous account of Senator Townsend's no-nonsense style of assisting in the various Senate races:

> ABOARD GOVERNOR DEWEY'S CAMPAIGN TRAIN (Sept. 28) Whenever this lint-picking scow pulls into a state where there is a serious senatorial contest, a whitehaired old gentleman lumbers off and proceeds to do some quiet but furious spadework.
>
> If you were among the station platform crowds you probably wouldn't be aware of the old gent unless you were a local big-shot politico. But the latter speedily feel his presence with the impact of a baseball bat across the whatsis. That's the old gent's business on this (ha-ha) "nonpartisan pilgrimage"; to bat, belabor, threaten, coax,

and cajole the politicos into stirring their stumps to elect Republican senators. This human cat-o'-nine-tails is former Senator John G. Townsend, of Delaware, a truculent 70-year-old who minces no words.* He is obsessed with the idea that it's even more important to elect a Republican majority to the Senate than to elect a G.O.P. President. So, while Thomas E. Dewey smiles, waves and orates, being the big attraction, ex-Sen. Townsend works unsung, on the politicos, painting horrid pictures of what will happen if they fall down on the senatorial angle. He looks as benevolent as an old Baptist circuit preacher, but, when he begins to lay down the law, even our so-called statesmen quail. He had a run-in just before this junket started with Sen. Arthur Vandenberg, of Michigan, from which the august Van is still shuddering. Ex-senator Townsend suggested to the great Vandenberg that he take the stump for G.O.P. candidates in doubtful states. Van demurred, implying that his statesman-like abilities were needed in Washington.

The elderly Mr. Townsend blew up.

"Listen, Van," he exploded, "I know you are now a great statesman, devoted to sitting up on that rostrum cogitating on the problems of the world. But if you don't get out and help elect some Republican senators you won't be allowed to remain sitting on that nice throne next year."

P.S. –Vandenberg agreed to go.

*   *   *

In Minnesota ex-Sen. Townsend found the G.O.P. big shots extremely cold to the reelection aspirations of Sen. Joseph H. Ball. Joe Ball has been as popular as the itch with the Minnesota Republican bosses since he endorsed F.D.R. in 1944, and they were giving him the snoot. "You dopes," barked Mr. Townsend, calling them to heel. "What're you trying to do? Elect a Democrat? Joe Ball may not be your idea of a sweetheart, but he's the only Republican you've got running for the Senate." P.P.S.–The bosses, who had been flirting mildly with the

---

* *Actually, at this time Senator Townsend was seventy-seven years old.*

Democratic senatorial candidate, Mayor Hubert Humphrey of Minneapolis, promised to end the dalliance and give their all for Ball.

*   *   *

When the Dewey special pulled into Des Moines, Mr. Townsend heard reports that Sen. George A. Wilson of Iowa had been skipping meetings he was scheduled to attend and breaking other political dates. "Listen, George," rebuked the G.O.P. Scourge, "They say you're sick. Well, you'd better get out and show them you're well. They might get the idea you're too sick to represent them in the Senate."

P.P.P.S.—Senator Wilson promised to quit date breaking.

George Dixon, *The Washington Scene*

Though somehow the person portrayed in Dixon's column sounds more like Dixon himself than Townsend, it is revealing of the duties of senatorial campaign committee chairmen, and of the rigors of the job. The senator was a vigorous man for being seventy-seven years old, but whistle-stop campaign tours are exhausting for men half that age. After 1948, he retired from the committee chairmanship, though he continued to serve on the campaign committee until he was in his mid-eighties.

Loyal churchman: Selbyville's Salem Methodist church was an important part of John's life. He is shown here in the late 1940s participating in the groundbreaking ceremonies for the church's new fellowship hall (courtesy of Salem U.M. Church).

Senator Townsend's later years were characterized by high amounts of energy and by adherance to routine, just as his whole life had been. He continued to go to one or another of the offices every day that he was home in Sussex, usually to Millsboro. He regularly attended state and national G.O.P. conventions. Even so, his level of involvement in the day-to-day concerns of political life was slowly lessening. He was winding down. In the 1940s and 1950s the poultry business was the newest of the family enterprises. Therefore, it took up most of his available time. He was always interested in what was new. In the mid-1940s, Townsend's, Inc., had become the nation's largest producer of poultry products. Though the company later lost that distinction, it remained among the largest poultry concerns. In 1948, Townsend's placed among the top contestants in the national "Chicken of Tomorrow" contest, which was sponsored by the A & P supermarket chain for the best-bred bird, based on a list of important factors. The object was to raise a "more meat" chicken with less feed.

In the early 1950s, Townsend's installed its first soybean processing plant at Senator Townsend's urging. With that development, having already built a rudimentary feed mill, the company achieved the first example in the poultry industry of what is known as "vertical integration," the capacity to control the poultry product not only from "egg to supermarket shelf" but to the point of cultivating the grain needed for poultry feed, harvesting it, storing it, and processing it.*

---

* _As early as 1945, Senator Townsend was quoted in the_ Country Gentleman _article about his life as saying that he hoped to open a chain of retail outlets in metropolitan areas to sell Townsend's products. Though this never came to pass during his lifetime, it would have been a logical next step in the vertical integration process. In the late 1970s, the latter-day Delmarva chicken magnate, Frank Perdue, became nationally known for his promotional abilities. In part, he was promoting the same ideas John had thirty-five years after he conceived of them._

In later years the senator had the luxury of being the adventurous one in the family. Having now given over day-to-day control of his enterprises to his sons and no longer needing to concern himself overmuch with the balance sheet, he was free to study new ideas and to launch new operations. He became the resident management consultant/philosopher. The businesses prospered under the leadership of the second generation as they had under the first. A new Baltimore Trust building was erected in Selbyville in the early 1950s, and another in Bridgeville. The Georgetown cannery was modernized and a frozen food plant erected. The family also built a branch of the Selbyville Manufacturing Company at Rehoboth Beach. The decade ended with the construction of a new poultry processing plant at Swan Creek, the largest and most modern of its kind in the world upon its completion.

As John's active involvement in political and public life waned, his "symbolic" involvement increased as he entered his eighties. He was invited to everything imaginable around the state. Whenever anyone had some important award to bestow or occasion to mark he was asked to do the honors. He awarded yachting trophies, cut ribbons, kissed babies. He even got to cut a birthday cake honoring the second anniversary of the Eastern Shore Poultry Grower's Exchange, a cooperative auction at Selbyville. These activities were not a chore for him. They kept him involved in the world of public life, kept him out and around and seeing people.

After another automobile accident in the early 1950s, the family prevailed on him to get someone to drive him regularly. He asked his old friend and employee, Clyde Smith, to take the job. Soon, the two were one of the regular fixtures of the local scene, Smith at the wheel and the senator on the front seat beside him, his knee often propped on the dashboard as they rode from farm to farm across the landscape of Sussex County.

Birthday: *The Selbyville Rotary Club organized a grand eighty-sixth birthday celebration in May 1957, to honor the town's favorite son. Among the dignitaries was Vice President Richard M. Nixon, shown at right looking on as Senator Townsend cuts his birthday cake. Earlier John posed on his front steps with his children. From left, above: John G. Townsend III, Mrs. Edith Townsend Tubbs, Preston C. Townsend, John, Julian Townsend, and Mrs. Lyla Townsend Savoy (both photos from the Lyla T. Savoy collection).*

Soon after his eighty fifth birthday in 1956, John was honored at the Delmarva Chicken Festival. The annual event, which moves from town to town around the peninsula, was held that year in Ocean City, where Senator Townsend was presented with the first "Delmarva Citizen of the Year" award in recognition of his lifelong crusade for Delmarva agricultural products "from the state house, through the halls of Congress and into the market places." The citation praised him for his many contributions "to the fine and gracious living of the area" and designated him the first "Distinguished Citizen of Delmarva."*

---

*   *Preston C. Townsend received the same award in 1983, marking the first time a father and a son have been its recipients.*

The following year the Selbyville Rotary Club organized a special eighty-sixth birthday party for him at the Salem Methodist Church hall, where a crowd of more than 200 people joined him for a dinner of fried chicken and strawberries. The group included a host of dignitaries, among them Vice-President Richard M. Nixon, attending as a personal representative of President Eisenhower. The vice-president read letters from Eisenhower and also from John's old friend, ex-President Herbert Hoover. Also in attendance was every living ex-governor of Delaware. His former Senate staff member, Cale Boggs, was also present in his capacity as Delaware's current governor.

After dinner the group moved over to the lawn of the Selbyville High School where they joined a huge crowd that had gathered there for a round of speeches by the array of eminent guests. Finally, the old senator got up to speak to his friends and neighbors. Wilmington *Morning News* reporter William P. Frank caught something of the moment:

> For the first time in his life he was speechless at the outset. He looked out at the throng of about 1,000 men, women and children–national, state, county and local leaders. Mr. Townsend gulped and said: "What's left for me to say except that I thank you all."
>
> He paused again and seemed to look out beyond the crowd toward the neat little town of Selbyville and the farm lands beyond and then said very humbly, "Delaware has been good to me."
>
> He would have loved to have sat down there, or just to go out among the people and shake hands in the Townsend manner that has never been equalled by any Delawarean for friendship and warmth.
>
> But the applauding birthday guests wanted to hear more from the man they were honoring . . . so he briefly recounted his public life, not boastingly but just to support his feeling that Delaware had been good to him. Then he

summed up what everyone knows to be true about John
G. Townsend: "I want to say that the most pleasure I get
in life is doing things for others."

He attended his last Republican National Convention in the
summer of 1960. On that occasion the assembled delegates honored
him with a standing ovation as the oldest one among them. He had
represented Delaware for the first time at the Chicago convention of
1904, where Theodore Roosevelt had been nominated to his first full
presidential term. This last time, his eighty-sixth birthday visitor, Richard
M. Nixon, was nominated to run against John F. Kennedy.

The old senator was slowing down now, but in some respects
his life was the same. He continued to go to the office most days until
his final illness. He still went to church, to occasional bank meetings,
and on trips to Dover or Wilmington. He still took an interest in politics.
He still stopped people with whom he was unfamiliar on the street to
introduce himself and find out all about them. Talking to him could be
quite an experience for newcomers who did not know who he was.
They could see Clyde Smith sitting in the background at the wheel of
the large Cadillac as this imposing, clearly prominent old gentleman
walked up and began questioning them about themselves, their relatives,
where they were from, and so on. Soon, of course, they found out
who he was, but the initial experience could be startling.

Perhaps his favorite activity of those last years was riding with
Clyde across his beloved Sussex County farmland and forest, finding
the same thrill in the soil and in the new fields of early summer, in the
sweep of corn rows off to the horizon that he had felt seventy-five
years before. In the end the land was what he came back to.

In the late winter of 1963-1964, Preston was clearing a large
tract of timber along the highway north of Millsboro for use as farmland.

The great stands of timber John had acquired back in the early days were slowly being converted to fields. Townsend's, Inc., had cleared a huge piece of land along the state road from Millsboro to Rehoboth a year or so before. Now they were clearing this tract. For a year or

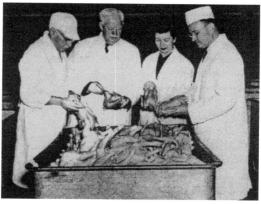

Still active: *Senator Townsend is seen above in a publicity photo at the new Townsend's poultry dressing plant in 1959 with two federal poultry inspectors and that year's National Chicken Cooking Champion (courtesy of the Delmarva Poultry Industry, Inc.).*

two more it would be called "the new ground."

The new ground. He had seen so much of it in his long life. He had seen much and lived much and in that early spring of 1964, he had grown old and very weary. In the first week of March, his health failed. He developed pneumonia and was sent to the University of Pennsylvania Hospital in Philadelphia. He fought it with all his remaining strength. At first he seemed to be holding his own, but in the first week of April complications arose. His old heart was wearing out from the struggle. On the eleventh of April, in the early morning, the heart that had been so large finally gave out.

His eldest daughter, Edith, was with him on that last morning of his life. She said later that in his final hours all his thoughts had been of the land, of the future of the land. His last words were about the newly cleared field. "The new ground," he had asked, "what are they doing with the new ground?" Then he was gone.

– MY CREED –

To live as gentle as I can;
To be, no matter where, a man;
To take what comes of good or ill,
And cling to faith and honor still;

To do my best, and let that stand,
The record of my brain and hand;
And then should failure come to me
Still work and hope for victory.

To have no secret place wherein
I stoop unseen to shame or sin;
To be the same when I'm alone
As when my every deed is known;

To live undaunted, unafraid
Of any step I have made;
To be without pretense or sham
Exactly what men think I am.

To leave some simple mark behind
To keep my having lived in mind;
If enmity to aught I show,
To be an honest, generous foe;

To play my little part, not whine
That greater honors are not mine.
This, I believe, is all I need,
For my philosophy and creed.

Edgar A.   Guest

(Reprinted from John G. Townsend Jr.'s
funeral program, Salem Methodist Church, 1964)

REFERENCE NOTES

Bibliographical Essay

PART ONE: ORIGINS

In this section of the book I have sought to paint a portrait of the St. Martin's District of northeastern Worcester County, Maryland, and the surrounding region as it existed in the last quarter of the nineteenth century when John G. Townsend Jr. grew up there. In addition I've attempted to place the Townsend family of Bishops into context by discussing their family origins.

A most useful reference work for anyone seeking to gain a sense of life in Worcester County during this period is *Worcester County–Maryland's Arcadia* by Reginald V. Truitt and Millard G. Les Callete (Snow Hill, MD: Worcester County Historical Society, 1977). This book, which was published as a bicentennial history of the county, contains a wealth of information about the area and its inhabitants. Much of the genealogical material concerning seventeenth and eighteenth century members of the Worcester County Townsend family contained in Clearing New Ground was derived from this source, as was much of the material about the towns, villages and personalities of the St. Martin's District.

Another valuable source for this section of the book is *The 1877 Atlases and Other Early Maps of the Eastern Shore of Maryland* (Salisbury, MD: Wicomico County Bicentennial Commission, 1976). It is basically a reprint of an 1877 atlas of all the Maryland Eastern Shore counties and their subdistricts, similar in style and format to D. G. Beers's 1868 *Atlas of the State of*

Delaware. As with Beers, the Eastern Shore Atlas maps are so detailed that one can clearly identify the homes of John G. Townsend Sr. and others who figure in this work, as well obtaining an understanding of the geographical relationships in St. Martin's.

Much of the 19th century Townsend family genealogical information used here was gleaned from the papers of John G. Townsend Jr. and from one or another of the biographical accounts of the family appearing in Wilson Bevan's *History of Delaware, Past and Present* (1929) and H. Clay Reed's *Delaware–A History of the First State* (1947). I should note here that both Bevan's and Reed's histories contain extensive biographical and genealogical sections, a sort of *Who's Who* of their respective eras in Delaware, which are very helpful. The families included in these sections paid for the privilege and presumably purchased copies of the finished work as a way of helping the publishers offset publication costs, but the information contained therein is very helpful to later historians.

Some genealogical information was drawn from interviews with Mrs. Edith Townsend Tubbs, Mrs. Lyla Townsend Savoy and Mr. Preston C. Townsend. Worcester County deed records housed at the courthouse in Snow Hill were useful in turning up information about the family's early real estate transactions. Other valuable sources were the *History of Sound Methodist Church*, compiled by the congregation and published in 1976, Dorothy W. Pepper's book, *The Folklore of Sussex County, Delaware* (Georgetown, DE: Sussex County Bicentennial Commission, 1976), and her marvelous unpublished (and frequently handwritten) historical notes about Selbyville and Baltimore Hundred.

I cannot stress too strongly how important Mrs. Pepper's assistance was in carrying out the research for this book. Mrs. Pepper, who was a contemporary of Preston Townsend, was born and raised in Selbyville and lived there all her life. She was the local historical repository and her home on Church Street was filled with her wonderful historical library, her voluminous notebooks and much memorabilia of a long and interesting life. She and her husband, Paul, spent more than half a century assembling historical notes and bits and pieces of information and they very kindly allowed me free use of it. Especially helpful were the recollections of David Long about the early timber industry, which she carefully preserved, and Mr. and Mrs. Pepper's matchless knowledge of the agricultural history of the area, a knowledge derived in no small part from the fact that they both lived that history, from strawberries through the poultry industry.

PART TWO: THE POLITICAL BACKGROUND

By far the most important source of information for this section on Delaware and Sussex County political history in the years before John G. Townsend's own political career began was an unpublished study of the Addicks Era in Delaware written by the late Dr. Harold B. Hancock in the late 1930s, a copy of which is available in the University of Delaware library. The work was prepared by him as a senior thesis when he was an undergraduate at Trinity College in Connecticut. It is, in my opinion, the finest study of turn-of-the-century Delaware political history available. Among other virtues, it is based in large part on oral history interviews with some men like former U.S. Senators J. Frank Allee and James Hughes who were politically active during the period and who have long since departed the scene. Dr. Hancock was able to catch them at just the right time, while their memories were still sharp but long after their active political careers were over.

Other useful sources in this section were Volume One of H. Clay Reed's three-volume *Delaware–A History of the First State*, which contains an excellent chapter on Delaware's political history from the end of the Civil War to 1914, also written by Harold

Hancock. Also useful here were John A. Munroe's 1979 *History of Delaware* (probably the best one-volume history of the state available), my own 1976 work, *The History of Sussex County*, and numerous newspaper sources.

Among those newspapers consulted are early issues of the Lewes weekly *The Delaware Pilot*, two Georgetown weekly, *The Union Republican* and the *Sussex Republican*, and *The Milford Chronicle* as well as various Dover newspapers. Assorted issues of these and other early newspapers are available on microfilm in the Delaware Public Archives in Dover. I also made use of the Wilmington papers, the *Morning News*, the *Every Evening*, the *Evening Journal* (and, after their merger, the *Journal-Every Evening*) and the *Sunday Star* from the microfilm collections of the University of Delaware and from the library of the Historical Society of Delaware. Once more, Mrs. Pepper's notes were of great importance as well.

PART THREE: REPRESENTATIVE TOWNSEND

I relied heavily in this section on Sussex and Worcester County deed, mortgage and incorporation records as well as on Dorothy Pepper's notes and on early newspaper records. The most useful of these were the old files of *The Delaware Pilot*, now on microfilm at the Delaware Public Archives, and the microfilmed files of the Wilmington *Morning News* at the University of Delaware library. The official House and Senate Journals for the General Assembly session in which John G. Townsend Jr. served, housed in the public archives, were most useful as were the various "Governor's Registers" for the period.

Also useful in this section of the book was George Kennan's article on Addicks, entitled *Holding Up A State*, published in the February 1903 issue of *The Outlook*. I was fortunate in being able to borrow an offprint of the article owned by Mrs. Mary Houston Robinson of Georgetown. Mrs. Robinson's father, Robert G. Houston, a lawyer and publisher of the *Sussex Republican* (later the *Sussex Countian*), put Kennan up at his Georgetown home while he researched the piece. Houston was a leading Addicks foe and ran for congress on the Regular Republican ticket in 1896. Years later he was elected to four terms in congress. I've taken a somewhat different view of Addicks than Kennan and Houston did, but then I was observing the fray from a distance of nearly a century.

PART FOUR: COMMERCE AND CONSTRUCTION

Early issues of the Wilmington *Morning News* were very informative about the early history of the Baltimore Trust Company as were Dorothy Pepper's notebooks. I found good biographical information on various Townsend partners of this period in Bevan's *History of Delaware, Past and Present*, volumes three and four. I also made my first use in this section of Louise S. Johnson's unpublished memoirs *A Narration of Many Memories, Several Detours and A Few Thoughts* (Newark, Delaware, 1975) which were of such importance in later chapters. At the time of my original research this work was in unedited typed manuscript form. Mrs. Johnson had originally written the book in longhand at a time when she was legally blind. A nicely edited edition complete with photographs has since been published by Johnson family friends Judith M. Pfeiffer and Robert C. Barnes.

The information about the Republican and Democratic state and national conventions of 1904 is drawn primarily from newspaper sources with some reliance on family recollections and other primary sources. Newspaper accounts and Dr. Hancock's Addicks study were also useful in the discussion of the last days of the Union Republican Party and the subsequent reshuffling of party factions.

T. Coleman du Pont wrote a wonderful article in a 1912 issue of *Scientific American* magazine detailing his ambitious plans for the Coleman du Pont Boulevard. Included in the article was an artist's sketch of the original boulevard concept, the original of which is now owned by the State of Delaware. Unfortunately, it is too large to be easily copied for reproduction in this book, but anyone wishing to see it should be advised that at this writing it is on display in the lobby of the Delaware Department of Transportation building in Dover. I obtained some choice personal accounts of Coleman du Pont's trips to Sussex from his nephew, Edmund H. Harvey, before his death in 1978. As a boy, Mr. Harvey accompanied du Pont on a few of his trips and obtained other tales from close relatives. du Pont, himself, told him about having an electric shocking device hooked up to his car. Neither Mr. Harvey nor I could understand why those on whom he used it weren't furious. Another useful source of information on the road was the article "Coleman du Pont and his Road" which appeared in *Delaware History* magazine several years ago.

PART FIVE: THE RACE FOR GOVERNOR

In this section concerning John G. Townsend's 1916 campaign for governor, newspapers were the most useful source of information. Specifically, I used files of the Wilmington *Morning News*, *Evening Journal* and *Sunday Star* for the period. Because of the very pronounced differences in journalistic and editorial slants of the various newspapers it is useful to study as many different ones as possible. Also of value in this section of the book were several secondary histories of the period including Samuel Eliot Morison's *Oxford History of the American People*, William Manchester's *The Glory and the Dream*, George H. Mayer's 1964 book, *The Republican Party, 1854-1964*, and *The Autobiography of William*

Allen White. Also useful here were Volume One of Reed's *Delaware–A History of the First State*, and William H. Carr's *The du Ponts of Delaware–A Fantastic Dynasty*.

PART SIX: THE TOWNSEND ADMINISTRATION

The Delaware Public Archives has a very extensive collection of the gubernatorial papers of John G. Townsend's administration. Happily, the staff of the archives had begun cataloguing them just at the time when I needed to begin working with them in the late 1970s. The papers include not only the usual assortment of official correspondence but also a wonderful selection of personal and business correspondence. While the manner in which Governor Townsend conducted private business in the governor's office and official business in his Selbyville business office might raise eyebrows in the present restrained age, it is wonderful for biographers because it means that a whole segment of his business papers that would otherwise have been destroyed have been preserved. Included are letters to and from his children, items about the strawberry and lumber and canning businesses, banking, land purchases and sales, and a wonderfully varied assortment of letters from various cranks and eccentrics. Another important repository of documents useful for this section of the book is the Eleutherian Mills Historical Library at Greenville, which has a fine assortment of documents relating to the "Great School Fight" of 1918-21, to the Coleman du Pont Road and to general political and business life in Delaware during the period of the Townsend administration, 1917 to 1921. Newspapers were of considerable value here, the *Morning News* and *Sunday Star* in particular. Also helpful Louise S. Johnson's memoirs covering the years when her husband, Everett, was serving as secretary of state. Also of great value were the first of the Townsend family scrapbooks which begin with his election as governor and extend through the rest of his career. Robert J. Taggart's "Pierre S. du Pont and the Great School Fight of 1919-1921" (*Delaware History*, XVII, Spring-Summer 1977) was a valuable source of information about that episode which was so central to the history of the Townsend administration. Also of interest was Anthony Higgins's *"Mary Wilson Thompson Memoir"* which appeared in four parts in *Delaware History* in 1978 and 1979.

PART SEVEN: THE TWENTIES

The Townsend family scrapbooks were very useful for this section of the book as were papers of T. Coleman du Pont and others in the collection of the Eleutherian Mills Historical Library. Also very helpful were interviews with Mrs. Edith Townsend Tubbs, Mrs. Lyla Townsend Savoy and Mr. Preston C. Townsend. A small but very useful book of great help here was Daniel O. Hastings's *Delaware Politics, 1904-1954*. Hastings was Townsend's contemporary in state Republican politics and a fellow U. S. senator. Though his book presents little more than an outline of the political events of the period, Hastings's account is important for having been written by a participant. Again I relied in this part of the book on Dorothy W. Pepper's notebooks and on Louise S. Johnson's memoirs. Also useful were general social histories of the nineteen twenties.

PART EIGHT: THE EARLY SENATE YEARS

By far the most useful sources here are the Townsend family scrapbooks which provide almost a day-by-day account (or at least a "newsworthy event-by-newsworthy event" account) of Senator Townsend's Washington years. Of value here also are interviews with family members and such friends as former Senator John J. Williams of Millsboro, and former Senator J. Caleb Boggs and Armel

Long, both of whom worked in and around Senator Townsend's office in Washington. I used some of the vast array of secondary source material on Roosevelt and the New Deal and histories of the Hoover Administration and early Depression years to place the newspaper accounts from the scrapbooks in perspective. Among the most useful works here were Arthur M. Schlesinger, Jr.'s *The Crisis of the Old Order, 1919–1933* from *The Age of Roosevelt* series, William Manchester's *The Glory and the Dream*, James MacGregor Burns's *Roosevelt–The Lion and the Fox*, Rexford Guy Tugwell's *The Brains Trust*, John Kenneth Galbraith's *The Great Crash, 1929* and *Jim Farley's Story: The Roosevelt Years* by James A. Farley.

PART NINE: THE POLITICAL LIFE

Many of the same sources cited for Part Eight were useful here as well, particularly the Townsend family scrapbooks. The section on the history of the Delmarva poultry industry was taken largely from my own 1976 book, *The History of Sussex County*. I should note, however, that since I conducted my research on the history of the poultry industry, Dr. William H. Williams has published an excellent new book that serious students of the subject may wish to consult, *Delmarva's Chicken Industry: 75 Years of Progress*.

PART TEN: THE ELDER STATESMAN

The real heart of this section of the book is the unpublished diary which Senator Townsend kept during his visit to England and Europe as an alternate delegate to the United Nations General Assembly in the winter of 1946. One of the most interesting aspects of the diary is the insight it affords into the way that Senator Townsend operated behind the scenes to get things done for what he considered to be the good of the nation. It reveals his completely bipartisan view of the proceedings and shows how he was able, through his friendships with leaders in both major parties, to serve as a mediator of their disputes. Helpful in filling out that source were *Eleanor: The Years Alone* by Joseph P. Lash, *Plain Speaking: An Oral Biography of Harry S Truman* by Merle Miller, *Dulles: A Biography of Eleanor, Allen, and John Foster Dulles and Their Family Network* by Leonard Mosley, *Paris Journal, 1944-1965* by Janet Flanner (Genet), *Present At The Creation* by Dean Acheson, and *The Diaries of Edward R. Stettinius, Jr., 1943–1946*, edited by Thomas M. Campbell and George C. Herring. Again the Townsend family scrapbooks were of great value in this section of the book, as were family interviews.

The conclusion of the book and its title were suggested to me by a discussion I had with the late Mrs. Edith Townsend Tubbs concerning her father's final illness. The idea of Senator Townsend's interest in clearing new ground, even during his last illness, seemed to me to be appropriately symbolic of his lifelong pursuit of new thoughts and ideas and improved ways of doing things. He looked always to the future.

INDEX

Caulk, L. D. Company, 144-145

Cedar Creek Hundred, Sussex Co., Del., 66, 103

Cedar Neck, Baltimore Hd., Del., 442

Centerville, *See* Roxana

Chambers, Whittaker, 557

Chandler, William Burton, Jr., 301

Charles I, King of England, 27

Chase Manhattan Bank, 406

Chase National Bank, 427

Chesapeake Bay, 5, 6, 9, 10, 26; ports on, 6, 36n, 54, 56; as alternate route of commerce, 166

Chestertown, Md., town of, 454

Chiang Kai-Shek, 550

Chicago, Northwestern & Union Pacific R.R., 311

chicken processing, 535

China, Japanese invasion of, 503

Chincoteague Bay, Md. & Va., 475

Chincoteague Inlet, 391

Chincoteague Island, Va., 28, 214, 306-308, 524; railroad links to, 36n, 89; J. G. Townsend, Jr., moves ice plant to, 185; economy of, 306

Chincoteague oysters, 112

Chipman, James, M.D., 101

Choptank River, 56

Christiana Hundred, New Castle Co., Del., 107

Christiana Securities, establishment of, 201

church, importance of in lives of Worcester Countians during 19th century, 30

Civilian Conservation Corps (C.C.C.), role in Delaware, 501

Civil War, 238

Claridge's Hotel, 558

Clarksville, Del., village of, 374

Clay, Gen. Lucius D., 572

Claymont, Del., town of, 70, 391

Clayton House Hotel, 97

Clayton, John M., 94, 173, 377

clerks of the peace, 80, 82

Cleveland Petroleum Corp., 449

Cleveland, Grover (U. S. president), 401

Coast Guard, U.S., 443

Cockran, Wilbur S. (Col.) and mosquito control projects, 501 n

cockerals (roosters) 443-444

Cold War, the, 555

Collins family of Worcester Co., Md., 10

Collins, Bertha *(sister of Mrs. J.G. Townsend, Jr.)*, baptism at Sound Camp, 33

Collins, Edward *(father of Mrs. J.G. Townsend, Jr.)*, 33

Collins, Edward & Mary family, attendance at Sound Camp, 33

Collins, Effie *(sister of Mrs. J. G. Townsend, Jr.)*, baptism at Sound Camp, 33

Collins James *(brother of Mrs. J. G. Townsend, Jr.)*, baptism at Sound Camp, 33

Collins, Jennetta, *(Mrs. John G. Townsend, Jr.) See* Townsend, Jennetta Collins "Jennie"

Collins, Mary *(mother of Mrs. J. G. Townsend, Jr.)*, 33

Columbus Hotel, 458

commission merchants, 51

Communist Party of U. S., presidential candidates of, 433

Congress of the United States, 56th, 77; and passage of Prohibition (18th) Amendment, 230; and declaration of war against Germany, 1917, 232

Congressional Record, the, 518

Connally, Thomas (U. S. sen., Texas), 552

Connecticut State College, 583

Connelly, William M., 120-121

Conrad, Henry C., 152

Constitution, Delaware State, of 1831, 76, 82; of 1897, 82-84, 124

Constitution, U.S., refusal of Del. Gen. Assembly to ratify 13th, 14th & 15th amendments to, 62-63; 17th amendment to, 68, 208; 18th (Prohibition)

N

O

Wood, Will R. (U.S. rep., Ind.), 419

Woodland Orchard Co., 189

Worcester County, Md., 5, 44, 48, 57, 97-99, 126; plantation economy of, 9; population of in 1870, 11; old plantation families of, 11; arrival of Townsend family in, 12; division from Somerset County in 1742, 12; large percentage of loyalists among population of during American Revolution, 13; farm life of, 29; religious camp meetings in, 30; out-migration of young men from, 41-42; and wage scales in 1890's, 42; effects of high freight rates on, 56; banking in, 133-134; John & Jennie Townsend's 1st home in, 141; Rev. Staton native of, 142; commerce in, 155; fruit growers in, 185; and canal links to Del. Bay, 186; Orlando Harrison moves to, 188; E. N. Vallandigham's family natives of, 214

Worcester County–Maryland's Arcadia by Millard G. Les Callette and Reginald V. Truitt (1976), cited 14, 21

Worker Party (communist), 390

Worker's Compensation Act, proposed by J.G. Townsend, Jr., 219; enacted, 231

World Court, 556

World War I, entry of U.S. into, 232-233, 363, 365, 418; referred as the Great War, 549

World War II, 411; 501; labor shortage during, 355 German invasion of Poland, 501; suspension of arms embargo, 506; effects on 1940 presidential election, 506-7; German blitzkreig into France and Denmark, 508; surrender of France, 508; 515; ended strawberry production in Delaware, 543; end of European hostilities, 547

Y

Yalta, Ukraine, 550

Yellowstone National Park, 313

York Imperial Orchard Co., 189

Yorktown Sesquicentennial Commission of 1931, 453

Yorktown, Va., 453

Z

Zwaanendael Museum, 454